THE SOCIAL IMPACT OF INFORMAL ECONOMIES
IN EASTERN EUROPE

Transition and Development

Series Editor: Professor Ken Morita
Faculty of Economics, Hiroshima University, Japan

The Transition and Development series aims to provide high quality research books that examine transition and development societies in a broad sense – including countries that have made a decisive break with central planning as well as those in which governments are introducing elements of a market approach to promote development. Books examining countries moving in the opposite direction will also be included. Titles in the series will encompass a range of social science disciplines. As a whole the series will add up to a truly global academic endeavour to grapple with the questions transition and development economies pose.

Also in the series:

Institutional Change in Transition Economies
Edited by Michael Cuddy and Ruvin Gekker
ISBN 0 7546 1977 X

Forthcoming titles:

Small Firms and Economic Development in Developed
and Transition Economies: A Reader
Edited by David A. Kirby and Anna Watson
ISBN 0 7546 3060 9

Enhanced Transition Through Outward Internationalization
Outward FDI by Slovenian Firms
Andreja Jaklič and Marjan Svetličič
ISBN 0 7546 3134 6

The Social Impact of Informal Economies in Eastern Europe

Edited by

RAINER NEEF

MANUELA STĂNCULESCU

ASHGATE

Published by
Ashgate Publishing Limited
Gower House
Croft Road
Aldershot
Hants GU11 3HR
England

Ashgate Publishing Company
Suite 420
101 Cherry Street
Burlington, VT 05401-4405 USA

Ashgate website: http://www.ashgate.com

British Library Cataloguing in Publication Data
The social impact of informal economies in Eastern Europe.
   - (Transition and development)
   1.Informal sector (Economics) - Social aspects - Europe,
   Eastern 2.Europe, Eastern - Social conditions - 1989-
   3.Europe, Eastern - Economic conditions - 1989-
   I.Neef, Rainer II.Stanculescu, Manuela
   306.3'0947

Library of Congress Cataloging-in-Publication Data
The social impact of informal economies in Eastern Europe / edited by Rainer Neef and Manuela Stanculescu.
       p.cm.-- (Transition and development)
   Includes bibliographical references.
   ISBN 0-7546-1950-8 (alk. paper)
   1. Informal sector (Economics)--Europe, Eastern. 2. Europe, Eastern--Social conditions--1989- I.Neef, Rainer. II. Stanculescu, Manuela. III. Series.

   HD2346.E852 S63 2002
   330--dc21

                                                      2002074452

ISBN 0 7546 1950 8

Printed and bound in Great Britain by Antony Rowe Ltd, Chippenham, Wiltshire

Contents

Foreword

Raymond Pahl

Despite two decades of scholarly debate, a clear consensus about what precisely is an 'informal' economy, whether it is appropriate to consider it as a separate economy and what the key issues relating to it may be has yet to emerge.

This book is a welcome addition to what has become a substantial literature. Some would still argue that there can be only one economy but there can be a variety of activities that escape being reflected in National Accounts, no matter how cleverly they are examined. According to this view, the national income of rich countries would decline every time a man married his housekeeper. Similarly, in stateless societies an informal economy would be a contradiction in terms. Admittedly, an outside observer could label certain 'productive' activities and exchanges as 'economic' and write about the substantive economy of such a society or tribe but that would be of more comparative or external interest than much revelation to the actors concerned.

In the case of the four countries considered in this book, it is perhaps relevant to ask whose interests a focus on the informal activities actually serve. It does not, of course, follow that policy makers are necessarily punitive: they may be anxious to facilitate informal work by removing cumbersome and unnecessary rules and regulations – or they may just want to know how on earth people manage to survive. Some will, inevitably, blame the victim believing, perhaps, that a modern economy with possible aspirations for joining the European Union, cannot have the embarrassment of informal survival strategies. This may be particularly difficult when, as Chavdarova shows for Bulgaria, the cultural and behavioural roots of reciprocity and informal redistribution are deeply embedded in Bulgarian history. Who is a patriot under these circumstances – one who encourages for the sake of tradition, or one who seeks to destroy for the sake of modernity?

The ethical dilemmas posed by the ethnography reported in this collection deserve more serious attention than they have received. There is much more about means than ends. Most of the studies focus on the poor and powerless. Those who read this book, apart from students interested in passing their examinations, will be more likely to be rich and powerful. The ethical issues need to be addressed. The line between academic researcher and informer to the powerful is a narrow one and some consideration of the issues involved would be helpful.

Ilie's admirable attempt to explore the polarizing effects on incomes in Romania is particularly relevant but does not go far enough. As is so often the case, it is the very rich who escape detailed scrutiny when they are likely to be biggest actors in the informal economy. This is embarrassingly the case in Russia. The fortunes of the illegal money-launderers is reputed to be colossal and various forms of piratical activity associated with privatization have been well reported and published. There is a curious convention that tends to keep separate the super-frauds of the rich and the pathetic, if not derisory, survival strategies of the poor.

Social scientists need to recognise how inadequate their studies of the very rich and powerful are. Investigative journalists seem to be prepared to live more dangerously. Maybe in the transitional world of post-Communist societies there are still stronger limits on what indigenous researchers can attempt. It would at least have been possible to recognise that in some contexts the fraudulent tax evasions of the very rich are so great that if researchers want to be sure to avoid seriously nasty accidents, they are wise to head for the rural outback.

Perhaps one of the most welcome aspects of this book is the commitment by most of the authors to discover what people actually do, irrespective of what politicians, armed with dubious statistics, might want to believe. The idea of a truly popular sociology, a sociology of the people, must inevitably be a little subversive. The danger then, as Alvin Gouldner noted many years ago, is that an alliance with the underdogs often leads to putting blame on the middle dogs and ignoring the top dogs.

I hope that this book is widely read and that it leads to a better-grounded understanding of the real living conditions in the countries concerned. The editors have gathered together an impressive team and have provided most useful introductory and concluding chapters. If the debate on the informal economy in the countries concerned is now better informed, I hope that will ensure that the situation of those who are struggling as best they can to survive under difficult conditions can be improved. They have given their responses and information in good faith.

May their trust be well justified.

Institute of Social and Economic Research, University of Essex
E-mail: raypahl@compuserve.com
February 2002.

Observations on the concept and forms of the informal economy in Eastern Europe

In the course of the transformation of society in Eastern Europe an unprecedented variety of economic activities has spread out. Customary forms of the 'secondary economy' from the days of state socialism have been transformed, while the opening of the frontiers and the withdrawal of the state from the direction of the economy have permitted the rise of new forms of informal economy similar to those of many western and developing countries. The size of this economy is without question very large and, at least in the countries of south-west Europe and the former Soviet Union, its importance has increased to such an extent[1] that it is not clear which economy is in fact the 'normal' one. Since its discovery by social science the informal economy has been held up as a resource enabling households to cope with poverty, unemployment or economic uncertainty and/or to develop a new material basis. This preface deals with the question in how far its modes of functioning help households to make ends meet – or in how far they prolong dependency. The following contributions than focus on the economic and social role informal economies play in eastern European transforming societies.

No satisfactory attempts have so far been made to explain the informal economy under the conditions of transformation. Before 1989 it was tabu in most countries and it is only in Poland and Hungary that it was examined with official support. Here we see the development of a partially legal 'secondary economy' beyond the reach of state control – encouraged by the state for subsistence purposes of households, partially opposed as small private service and trade enterprises, partially tolerated, accepted as a supply economy between large firms, opposed as embezzlement and theft of materials (Cassel et al. 1989; Gábor 1989; Grossmann 1989). The resulting

[*] Assistant professor, Soziologisches Seminar Universitaet Goettingen, Platz der Goettinger Sieben 3 D-37073 Goettingen. E-mail: rneef@gwdg.de.

attempts at explanation are partly linked to the function mechanisms of the today no longer existing 'economy of shortage' (Gabór, 1990), partly to an ordoliberal approach which discusses perhaps its economic significance, but not its social implications (Cassel et al. 1989, 40 ff. and 376 ff.) and for which there is in eastern Europe a more adequate subsequent concept: institutionalism (Feige, 1999, see below). As this last approach only relates to specific aspects and areas of informal household activities one has otherwise to fall back on insights from other parts of the world.

The significance of the informal economy was discovered by the social sciences and development politics in the early seventies in Africa. Studies on the question as to how the quickly expanding population – especially the migrants from rural areas – could survive in the big cities, produced a mass of activities yielding in the main only meagre rewards with which individuals or whole families had to try to make ends meet. Following the studies of Hart (1997/1971) and then of the ILO, common characteristics came to light: informal activities are small in scale and take place on unregulated easily accessible markets with strong competition; they stretch from diverse activities of a single person to small family businesses; they are characterized by high work intensity, a lack of capital and on the part of the employees inadequate qualifications acquired mainly on the job; most often local – mostly traditional – technologies and resources are applied. The informal economy operates in spheres removed from state regulation and can call on no formal institutions for the purposes of finance or pressing its own interests. It allows the cheap reproduction of labour and ensures the survival of populations struck by poverty. The absence of taxes and social contributions is paid for with high social risks. It is basically keyed to covering needs and consumption, while accumulation requirements are secondary (Charmes 1990; Heimburger 1990, 8 ff). On the level of empirical description and measurement these characteristics sum up well what since the seventies has been called the 'informal sector'. It does not however explain its economic functioning or the dynamics of its development.

Modes of functioning and development dynamics of the informal economy: three useful approaches

With the expansion of research there has been a growth of diversity in what has been called the informal economy – and an increasing difficulty of coming to a serviceable definition. The logic of the lowest common denominator provides little by way of explanation. Charmes (1990) mentions the most usual criterion in research as being the *non-registration by state instances* and he emphasises at the same time that this minimal concept does not do justice to the heterogenity of the informal economy. Castells/Portes (1989, 12) characterize its central feature as *unregulated by the institutions of society, in a legal and social environment in which similar activities are regulated.* 'Informal' in this sense would be the status of labour, working conditions or management. This formula does cover the big differences of state regulation in the various countries and societies. In the following commentaries however Castells/Portes treat merely the development background of informal economies in advanced capitalist societies and in Latin America, especially in the new start-up countries.

Feige (1999) deals with the *dynamics of development* of the informal economy, particularly in the social transformation of eastern Europe. Every economy, and especially the market economy, needs an institutional framework in order to operate – and the more efficient this framework, the lower are the transaction costs and the sooner can investment become productive. The weaker and less efficient the institutions, the more means must be pumped in by the economy for the protection of its regular functioning, the more will its productivity be affected and so much more will 'non-compliant behaviour' be found. The tradition of non-compliant behaviour in eastern Europe creates, together with the transformation and weakening of the state, uncertainty in economic development perspectives. The economy tends towards only short-term investment, mainly in the distributive or finance sectors, the informal economy expands. In order to protect economic returns there is a move towards organised criminal action – which by comparison with the state is certainly more expensive and dangerous but more efficient. In other words: parts of the economy are increasingly going underground.

This model is taken from the development of Russia – plausible, but not comprehensive. Feige is concerned with the new adjustment of the (former) state economy to private profit, starting problems and the insecurity of the small private entrepreneurs, and the persistence of misappropriation of materials, fraud and corruption in the economy and the state apparatus. He ignores the customary economy of exchange and self-provision, which as a rule needs no institutional protection. Moreover, informal small firms can exist without an institutional framework by falling back on the network of social connections. Feige makes the important observation of the tradition of disobedient behaviour as an economic development determinant in eastern Europe, and of an immanent tendency towards the criminalization of economic relations when institutional networks fail in their long-term operation.

Portes (1994) is concerned with the *functional logic* of the informal economy. Economic relations can only function on the basis of mutual trust between the participants (cf. Granovetter 1984). This basis of relationships is normally supported by state guarantees of property rights and by the power of sanction of official institutions. On these the informal economy cannot fall back. While the criminal economy functions through the threat of violence, the actual informal economy is, according to Portes, carried by strong normative social ties. The less the influence of the state, the more will informal trade depend on social networks and adapt to market mechanisms. The more the state intervenes in the economy, the stronger is the tendency of actors to fall back on informal practices. He bolsters his argument by citing informal family businesses in Latin America and immigrant ethnic traders in North America.

In eastern Europe communities of common origin play a role only in the case of disadvantaged ethnic groups such as the gypsies, and social networks are not restricted to the circle of relatives and neighbours. They cover – in the past more so than today – wide networks of acquaintances ('friends of friends') which are able to offer by means of their position material advantage or helpful services. These wide acquaintance networks had at the time of state socialism a value of their own beyond their concrete utility. They were based on a morale which placed one's own circle in the centre and for this reason postulated the principle of using the maximum of state resources for one's own ends (Ledeneva 1998). To this extent they were not determined by clear norms and social sanctions, they were no retreat for small firms and clients, but the consensual basis for various forms of the secondary economy. According to Dallago (1990, 8 ff.), only a part of the informal economy is dependent on relationship networks: the economy based on the household and the community – in western as well as in eastern countries. Individuals or firms of the 'irregular economy' on the other hand work with *individual* or *institutional* methods such as deceit, fraud, swindling or mafia-like practices. Dallago does not explain which of these procedures have a permanent character and what it is which affects their long-term functioning. But his objection points to a multitude of *autonomously* operating informal economic forms, for which connections play either no role or only a minor one. They are either marked by individual skill or opportunities (such as street trading, fraud with sales or goods). Or they are linked with control over capital or means of violence, through which fraud or blackmail can be permanently established (such as precarious employment under the pressure of chronic poverty, usury or protection rackets under the threats of violence). Portes' analysis does however explain the functioning of those important areas of the informal economy which are governed by the division of labour and production chains, such as locally based production and repair firms, the retail trade, or services for regular customers.

Neither author deals with what Evers (1987) calls *subsistence production*, i.e. the production of households for home use, mostly linked with exchange or the sale of surpluses in the framework of social networks. Empirically, this takes in the main the form of food production, as also the production and maintenance of housing. In poor areas there are also other forms of home production (e.g. clothing, fuel, etc.). Evers does however not distinguish between traditional subsistence production on the one hand, which functions in the framework and according to the norms and regulations of traditional communities and organizations, and on the other hand, modern subsistence production, which is basically autonomous. *Modern subsistence production* (in the following termed 'home production') is carried out by households, which have grown out of traditional bonds and are dependent on modern production and supply systems: i.e. town dwellers, labourers in rural areas, and re-migrants from urban areas. Evers goes on to explain that households try to optimize their livelihood by combining 'subsistence production', informal jobs, and formal employment (Piirainen, Stanculescu and Wallace in the following contributions term this as 'household strategies'). A drop in real wages and increasing poverty lead to a growth of the informal economy and home production. Home production does not however grow in proportion to the need – i.e. corresponding to the poverty of the people concerned – but to the income – i.e. to the domestic property[2] of the households. The efficiency of the home production depends basically on the number of employable members of the household, their availability concerning employment and health and the domestic property of the household (land owned, buildings, tools and machines, etc).

Evers et al. neglect a second important distinction – that relating to household routine work. We term as informal not all reproductive tasks in the household, but only production and services generating income in terms of money or in kind. Teichert (1993, 64 ff.) distinguishes between 'household economy' in the first sense and 'self-provision economy' in the second. Social connections evidently play only a minor role – they are necessary only for the exchange of surpluses and for coping with emergency situations. Institutional regulations also play here only a minor role.[3] Nevertheless, a minimal provision with technical and social infrastructure is necessary, which must as a rule be financed by the households.

Development characteristics of the informal economy in Eastern Europe

In the following, the customary forms of the (former) secondary economy in eastern Europe, as well as the characteristics and functional logics and the attitudes linked with the informal economy since 1989 will be shown. This will be explained with the example of Hungary, the most liberal, and Romania, the most restrictive state socialist economy.

The state socialism was an 'economy of shortage'. According to Kornai (1980), its mechanisms could only produce hoarding and therefore a shortage of resources, both on the part of the producers and on that of the consumers. The state economy tended to an economic 'running idle' and self-obstruction. *Liberal* reforms enriched the economy only with elements of private enterprise, without touching the fundamental mechanisms (Kornai 1980, 314,ff. and 562,ff.). The *non-liberal* solution was a closer grip by the state and thus a sharpening of these mechanisms, as for example in Romania (cf. UN, 1999, 70 ff.).

Following straight on from Kornai, Dallago (1990, 47 ff. and 131 ff.) and Gábor (1989) explain the development to the increased informalising in the economy of shortage in the seventies, which became more acute in all eastern European countries in the eighties. The supply networks of the state economy became less and less reliable. The large state firms strived as best they could to fill the gaps through direct deals with western companies and direct exchange between the firms. Private production and services on a small scale were tolerated by the state if this improved the supply situation of the state economy and improved the consumption possibilities of the households – though this occurred in a very different way from country to country. The households themselves concentrated more than ever before on home production, particularly in agriculture and in trade services as well as tapping resources in the firms (misappropriation of materials, absenteeism and the private use of firm equipment, which all served to undermine the efficiency of the state economy). Many of these informal household services were exchanged in extensive social networks – this form of 'organizing' was often extended over the whole country, involving not only relatives, friends and neighbours, but often remote acquaintances ('friends of friends'). Secret or open side activities became more and more common, both with normal employees and officials (in the case of Poland cf. Cassel et al. 1989, 405 ff. and 459 ff.). These involved also illegal activities such as corruption, fraud and embezzlement, smuggling and half or completely criminal businesses. Some of these, like currency trading and speculation in goods and bonds were only forbidden in state socialism (there is little solid information available, but there are many reports; cf. Ledeneva 1998).

The eastern European informal economy of households was therefore marked by two characteristics: it was, in the main, practised as a secondary source of income on the basis of a secure formal job for practically all employees which guaranteed a decent livelihood. A part of these were 'autonomous' (Sik 1994) with their own home production, side activity, private business or criminal activity. The zones of tolerance laid down by the state were sometimes small and hard to calculate, as in Romania, sometimes they grew in a reliable way, as in Hungary. The second characteristic: the second economy reached into the state economy, in which 'integrated' (Sik 1994) informal forms and practices had nested; these could hardly be prevented, as employees and firm managers profited from them. The boundaries between legality and illegality were in many areas blurred – not least for the reason that wide sections of the population were involved, with a tendency to 'non-compliance' towards institutional requirements (for a closer description of these, see Roth in this volume). The informal incomes served mostly *to improve* the standard of living, but sometimes they were used for an accumulating legal, non-legal or criminal business.

The transformation of society brought about completely new conditions and elements which had as a result, not the decline, but the growth of the secondary or informal economy. The following developments were relevant:

The entire *state institutional apparatus* is being reconstructed in eastern Europe – partially very quickly, as in Poland, partially with much hesitation, as in the Ukraine. The years between the rescission of the old and the ordinance of new adequate economic regulations and tax systems, between the complete loss of legitimation of the old authorities and the building up of recognized and efficient new executives have left plenty of scope for all kinds of informal 'businesses'. The longer the process of institutional transformation is drawn out, the more the traditions pointed out by Feige (1999) of 'non-compliant' behaviour and the tendency towards the establishment of private, parallel authorities with a criminal stamp come to the fore. This is most markedly the case where large economic transactions are involved. Small informal activities, down below do not have sufficient financial potency and must take recourse to the protection of social contacts and networks (cf. Portes 1994; Sik/Wallace 1999). The reconstruction of the state is linked with the reduction of state provision, not least for the reason that government spending has been drastically reduced in all countries (UN 1999, 79s.) The resulting gaps can more rapidly be filled by informal rather than formal services as they are much cheaper.

The *opening on the world market* allowed an uncontrolled flow of goods and workers to and from the eastern European countries. In the first few years the considerable differences in prices and exchange rates encouraged trade and smuggling in the adjacent countries and in this connection there was also a boom in the informal currency trade. This was accompanied by a rise in the number of blackleg workers from south-east Europe and the ex-Soviet countries in the central European countries and Turkey; central-eastern Europeans went moonlighting in the near-by west European countries (Sik 1994; Sik/Wallace 1999). This boom in international informal trade and blackleg labour was matched by a second effect of the opening of the frontiers: the rapidly growing imports also closed gaps in the provision of firms and households and made redundant parts of the customary secondary market which thrived on scarcity.

The *privatising of the economy* was achieved by the pressure of the world market competition. In all countries, shortage of capital impedes technological modernization. In most countries, agriculture, trade, commerce and private services were quickly privatised: here the pressure is less and here the employment potentials hoped for were able to soften the inevitable fall in employment in the area of state and industry (ILO 1997, 141 ff.). Informal employment has also clearly increased in most of these areas – although many legal obstacles to the formalising of private business have been removed. In industry, radical cuts in costs were necessary in view of the shortfalls in productivity. Large reductions in employment were unavoidable, which as political hot irons were often delayed. Tax evasion and the use of blackleg labour were often more obvious methods of lowering costs (Sik 1994). The founding of all kinds of private enterprises, the voucher privatization, and the using up of uneconomic state companies resulted in a mushrooming of fraud in the finance and stock-markets. Often there were large-scale transfers of goods and money abroad from the large state enterprises (Chavdarova 1997): new forms of economic crime. As far as the large state enterprises were reorganized and modernized, informal opportunities have been reduced. Since however in the 'recombinant' state enterprises (Stark 1996) old structures often survive, one can assume that part of the old 'integrated' secondary economy can continue to exist in their shadow.

Under the pressure of *dropping employment* and *decreasing social transfers*, in all countries real income has suffered a marked fall. In the central European countries they are *on average* approaching the level of 1989 (in Poland this has already been passed), but in the other countries the average standard of living continues to decline. In all countries, the inequality of income has increased considerably. The unemployed and many old-age pensioners have fallen into poverty on account of inadequate social provision, while many farmers can feed themselves but are struggling to survive economically. In the southeast European countries and the former Soviet Union the wages of ordinary workers and government employees have sunk to the edge of bare subsistence. So, an increasing number of social casualties is being forced to look for a source of informal supplementary income (cf. Haerpfer/Wallace and the reports on individual countries in this volume). It is precisely these who lack the capital. More than ever they depend on their own *potential*, on their qualifications, land property and working instruments, and these are poor for most of those concerned.

There is little empirical evidence on the new and old forms of the informal economy because it is only in few countries that direct studies have been made. The object of this volume is to give a survey. Some forms of the forbidden informal economy, such as private estate, finance and stock transactions, have become legal; though many have remained informal (Sik 1994). Many forms of small trade – such as home and casual work, day labourers – have to the present day been deprived of a legal status and so remained informal.[4] These casual workers have thus lost institutional protection and social security. Where there has been a sharp drop in the standard of living, as for example in Bulgaria, Russia or Romania, agricultural home production has increased noticeably (cf. Benovska, Fadeeva e.a. and Golibrzuch in this volume). Trade on the streets and open markets and border trade and smuggling saw a marked increase at the beginning of the transformation. In the meantime, they have become more difficult since the price differences and opportunities for profit have dropped and state controls have become more rigorous, thus raising the cost of bribing (Wallace 1999), but on the whole, the informal trade has stabilized at a considerable level. Numerous small operators continue to offer informal services to households, firms and crafts, as can be seen in Romania (Neef 1999). The extent to which their income represents only subsidiary earnings or allows the building up of an informal small business evidently depends on the economic situation in the various countries. Unregistered wage labour is certainly nothing new in eastern Europe – new however is the blackleg and in the main precarious employment of the unemployed and foreigners (Neef 1999; Sik 1994). Estimates of tax evasion have not developed beyond the early stages. There is no systematic information on misappropriation of materials and the private use of the firm's property and fraudulent practices against customers. Bribery and corruption have certainly increased at times and are by no means less prevalent than in the days of state socialism (Ékes 1994; Grødeland e. a. 1998). The extent of individual and organized crime can hardly be estimated owing to serious methodical problems, but there are reports of many new forms, especially in the field of gang and organized economic crime (Chavdarova 1997; Knabe 1998).

The difference between the possible development paths of the informal economy will be sketched here briefly in the case of two extremes.

Romania: In the eighties, an unbalanced emphasis on heavy industry, forced urbanization in rural areas, monstrous construction projects and general mismanagement led to economic stagnation from 1984 onwards. The promotion of export at the cost of inland consumption resulted in a drop in the standard of living and there were signs of impoverishment (Brezinski/Petersen 1990;

UN 1999, 225 ff.). The legal secondary economy remained in Romanian state socialism narrowly restricted to private farming (every family was allowed to cultivate 0,3 acres), making up a considerable part of agricultural production.[5] The building of private houses, particularly in rural areas, was permitted to a very small extent, as also private coaching and special small repair and service firms. Around these there was a mushrooming of illegal trade and repair workshops, currency speculation and misappropriation and theft of goods and services in state firms. The share of the legal secondary economy in the eighties is estimated at 10%, that of the illegal one at a further 10% (ibid.). The repressive control of economic life varied with periods of tolerance of forbidden economic activities as the government knew how important these were for the provision of the broad masses, not to mention the fact that many officials also drew a profit from them. So it was that a large section of the informal economy grew in the underground, corruption blossomed and there was a general spread of passivity and anti-collective attitudes.[6]

This provided two essential components for the rapid growth of the informal economy in Romania after the revolution of 1989: a needs-related system of small-scale production and private distribution which had developed essentially through social networks and corruption connections; and, after high hopes in the beginning, a widespread attitude of mistrust towards institutions after the experience of their continuing failure and of growing social inequalities. The serious transformation recession which has continued to the present day has presented the framework for the further development of the informal economy. Three factors have marked these:

The widespread *privatization of land and dwellings* in 1991/92 has turned almost half of the population into owners of small plots and 90% into owners of their dwellings. Agricultural self-production has increased considerably. The maintenance of housing is practically entirely in private hands. Building activity is divided into small, mainly informal businesses and a few large firms. The sluggish privatization covered in the main agriculture and parts of the trade and of the services for households and firms, while the state-run heavy industry and the government administration and social services remained almost untouched until the end of the nineties. Rapidly changing regulations, bureaucratic hurdles and corruption as well as the exorbitant company taxes levied until 1996/97 hindered the development of small private enterprises. They can often only survive if they are completely or partially operated informally (cf. Ciupagea in this volume).

The *industrial decline* resulted in the closing of firms particularly in rural areas, which in its turn produced gaps in the provision of consumer goods. Generally speaking, there was no serious restructuring but a policy of 'same procedure as before!' on the part of the state large firms with growing deficits (UN 1999, 71 ff.). It is highly probable that private tapping of resources in big state firms still continues on a fairly large scale.[7] The stagnating development of the formal economy has left many gaps in services, trade and the production of consumer goods. Imported consumer goods are readily available – but these are mostly expensive and only cover the needs of those with high incomes. This leaves ample scope for informal activities. In fact, a minimum of 30% of total trade goes through informal channels (farmers and street markets, sale through friends and neigbours – see Duchêne 1998, 50). But almost all informal actors suffer from a lack of capital and the sellers or producers of consumer goods and household services are struggling in the face of a sinking demand and register low profits.

Romania is since long a poor country. The *collapse of real incomes* after 1989 resulted in bitter poverty *en masse*. For the poor an informal basic income has become an existential necessity. Home production in agriculture has become the main source of survival of the poor. Since they lack as a rule not only capital but also marketable qualifications, they have at their disposal only a limited range of informal possibilities of drawing income (cf. Stănculescu in this volume).

Hungary: Alongside the state economy, which tended more and more towards stagnation, a blossoming secondary economy has grown up in the sixties in agricultural production, small trade and personal services as also within the state firms. With the object of providing a new impetus to the economy as a whole, the government inaugurated at the end of the sixties a system of giving incentives (bonuses for achievement, import of western consumer goods) and the encouragement of private initiative. Private sidelines in tourism, in academic professions as well as in trade on open markets have been officially tolerated since the seventies. Small-scale private agricultural production was so successfully legalized that at the beginning of the eighties half of all households were involved. Their surpluses made up almost a third of the agricultural product. Private building activity which was licensed at much the same time made up half the housing construction, and in rural areas four fifths. In 1981/82 small private businesses were licensed for repair work and other services, in trade and commercial production. From 1981 onwards machines and equipment of state firms were rented to so-called private 'intrapreneurs'; the intention was to increase the efficiency of the economy. These new branches soon became a sought-after side-line for employees and managers. As an attempt to swing the secondary economy onto legal paths this development programme was a ailure insofar. The secondary economy certainly took on 'new colour', but this was 'not bringing about any decrease in non-legalized activities' (Gábor 1990, 357). Side by side with the continuing informal services and small-scale production there still persisted moonlighting, fraud, currency trade, tax evasion and bribery. Ékes estimated (1994) that the non-legal part accounted for more than half of the turnover in secondary economy. A third of this were non-legalized activities in trade, services and repair workshops and two thirds illegal, i.e. activities sanctioned with prosecution. This multi-coloured picture inside 'the jolliest hut in the socialist world' was however purchased at the price of extremely long working hours, and it led to an ever-growing social inequality. In 1987 the official economy began to shrink, for the first time there was unemployment – and at the same time the legal and non-legal secondary economies grew at an astonishing rate[8] (cf Ékes 1995, and Gábor 1990).

The secondary economy evidently paved Hungary's road into the market economy.

The *moderate inflation* in the early years after 1989 shows that, unlike the congestion of purchasing-power in other countries which sparked off a super-inflation, the demand had largely been served throughout the eighties by the secondary economy. The informal economy has, after a first impetus at the beginning of the nineties and a minor recession following, become more or less stabilized (cf. Sik/Tóth in this volume).

Hungary took the 'gradualist' path of *privatization*. In the first years it was mainly a matter of small businesses; one can take it that this includes also the privatization of previously informal small forms. The state sector was only moderately reduced. Private business services have increased considerably. There is no information available concerning the informal economy in these spheres – it is unlikely that their extent has increased. Many other formal services have only shown a weak development – here the informal economy seems to have held its ground; that is certainly what one can gather from the development of informal household consumption and open markets (cf. Sik/Tóth in this volume). There is no information on informal, 'tapping' activities in the remaining or 'recombined' big state plants.

Hungarian industry and agriculture experienced a rapid and drastic *drop in employment* in the first years – until 1993 by 30%; it has since then remained constant. The informal economy which grew considerably at this period (Ékes 1995) has evidently soaked up a portion of this reserve. The other part retreated into non-activity altogether. The extent of poverty in Hungary has been for a long time similar to that found in the developed western countries. It is not as severe as that in most eastern European countries; the social security system and the family bonds keep the majority – with the exception of some minority groups – from existential poverty (Sik 1996). Most people are therefore relieved from the pressure to take up precarious informal jobs at starvation wages or engaging in subsistence farming – but there remains a strong incentive to keep up informal side activities.

Research on Hungary to date seems to show that the informal economy most nearly resembles the southern European type: a relatively extensive economic field between normal financial and economic criminality, non-legalized small businesses and a multitude of informal sources of subsidiary income, often very family-centred. For the households it represents partly a source of extra income, partly a productive independent 'business'. In Romania there are certainly similar forms of extra earnings or 'business', but in addition, under conditions of economic collapse and poverty, a form of the informal economy has developed which is dictated by the needs of survival.

The informal economy in eastern Europe – three forms and logics

There is certainly no region in the world with so many different forms of the informal economy as eastern Europe, which makes it all the more difficult to give a succinct explanation. At the outset one should recall the definition of Castells/Portes (1989):

- The informal economy creates new income in money or goods, which are available for consumption or investment. Thus, those parts of household work which serve only to contribute to the normal functioning of the household do not count towards the informal economy.[9]
- The informal economy is unregulated by the social institutions in those cases where it normally would be regulated. *Traditional* forms of agriculture and crafts which have been practised for centuries are framed by reglementation which is just as stable although not governmental – such as customary law, community norms or clan authorities. Traditional crafts and peasant farming therefore are *not* part of the informal economy. Subsistence agriculture and crafts conducted by (previous) wage labourers, especially after 1989, have to find their own rules and regulations, often depending on local social networks or new business relations. Therefore they *are* informal even when they take over traditional forms of production (cf. Benovska in this volume).

The most wide-reaching definition of the informal economy is that of the 'unrecorded economy' (Feige 1990). It explains very little because there is a mingling here of informal economic forms and parts of the formal economy. Studies in this direction aim basically at the identification of various forms of tax evasion or at the improvement of statistical reporting. Empirically, they lead to overestimates of the informal economy (cf. Adair/ Neef in this volume).

Attempts to distinguish by legality for the formal economy and illegality for the informal one (Sik 1994) prove of no value. In eastern Europe there remained for many years large gaps in legal regulation. The quick change of newly passed laws and the tradition of non-compliant behaviour make the divide between legality and illegality uncalculable for most of the actors and strategically irrelevant (cf. Wallace 1998).

More helpful so far as eastern Europe is concerned is the sorting out of the types of the informal economy according to the logic of their functioning. The criminal economy in principle makes part of the informal economy (cf. Adair/Neef in this volume). But on account of the blurred distinction between legality and illegality in eastern Europe and of the very specific research methods required, it is not dealt with in the following. In contrast with Piirainen (in this volume), we term as informal, alongside with the market oriented activities, also the economy based on networks and households. Exchange in social networks thus belongs just as much to the informal economy as the home production which has developed outside the spheres of traditional farmers and craftsmen.

In the following, the different types and forms of the informal economy shall be resumed.

Forms and types of the informal economy of households in Eastern Europe

Formal sphere	Formal economy	
(Criminal economy)	(criminal activities)	*Traditional sphere*
1. Informal business	– tax evasion	
	– informal production and services for customers	traditional crafts
2. Consumption improvement/ secondary job	– informal distribution from formal firm	
	– informal wage-labour	
3. Survival economy	– exchange in social networks	traditional agriculture
	– household production	
Household sphere	routine household work	

The informal economy by definition is separated from the formal sphere. The limits are blurred however: tax evasion as well as the tapping of firm's resources is integrated in the formal economy but is informal. It is separated from the traditional sphere because of its different kind of regulation (see above). The household sphere includes routine household work which is not an *economic production*, and the household production which makes part of the informal economy.

The situation in the three dimensions of the informal economy, as discussed in the first part (three approaches) can be seen as follows:

a) The transformation of the *institutional system* and the cutting-back of the state have left more scope for the informal economy (see above). Two further aspects are relevant for its manner of functioning: Firstly, the co-existence of old and new structures has often turned the bureaucracy into a non-transparent and, above all on account of corruption, costly obstacle to private economic activities. Secondly, the modernization of the state school and university system took place too slowly for the new demands of economic life, especially in the realm of modern services. The necessary qualifications were therefore by and large provided on a private basis: through private (expensive) training centres, which mushroomed up everywhere; or through personal – informal – further education for all those who could not afford such schools.

b) *Social networks* became, under the conditions of transformation, less reliable, closer and more specialized. They suffer from a generally experienced shortage of time, which is not least due to the increase in informal work, but from increased distrust, partially linked with a withdrawal into the family (cf. Chavdarova and Fadeeva e.a. in this volume). Extensive networks, characteristic for social relations under state socialism, spread over widely varying social positions; they are of particular value because offering a variety of options and resources. In the business world 'upstairs' there has been an 'economization of relationships' (Ledeneva 1998, 191). Expectations and the exchange of help are related to the provision of financial resources and the access to the possibilities of making profit. For the informally employed 'downstairs' the need for security in the turmoil of the transformation stands in the foreground. The withdrawal into the sphere of family and close relations, in which norms and obligations still apply, bring more 'predictability' – as does the clear situation of bribery and patronage protection through officials (Wallace et al. 1999, 766), compared to the extensive and unreliable links of traditional social networks.

c) The *household potentials* are governed by the lack of capital. *Capital in the form of money* is on account of the high inflation rates and the sinking real incomes available only to small minorities which have become rich suddenly, and to those who have access to credit by good contacts to officials. *Capital in the form of goods* was traditionally

acquired in the state firms, but on behalf of rationalization these opportunities have decreased. The majority of the (formally) non-employed
quickly loses the contacts in the firms. The privatization of land
ownership, or in other countries the tolerance towards private farming
on land owned by the state or collective has nevertheless provided for
many of the poor a subsistence basis. Because of the lack of capital in
the form of goods, the *human capital* available in the household is
decisive for informal economic performance (cf. for the following
Stănculescu in this volume and Neef e. a. 1998, 136 ff). Firstly, it is the
employment potential which is relevant: households with several
wage-earners combine more money potential, they have access to firm
resources, but their formal jobs restrict the time which can be used
informally. Households with many non-actives but employable members have more time, but less material resources. Those with the worst
cards informally are the 'dependent households' with many members
who are unemployable. Secondly, it is their professional experience
and qualifications which are relevant: the collapse of industry has
debased manual work, the unskilled, trainees and older skilled
workers have little market value. Persons with low qualifications have
access to informal niches in the retail trade and in household services
where earnings potentials are low. Those with qualifications in the
sphere of health and education can profit from the cutting-back of state
services. The best informal opportunities are to be found by workers
in modern services. Thirdly, it is age and orientations which count:
younger people are often more flexible, prepared to take a risk and oriented towards market opportunities and a quick high profit, they aim
at maximum consumption. Older people are often unflexible and traditionally minded, they prefer security to high profit (see also
Piirainen 1997, 160 ff.).

In the present economic situation these three dimensions which are relevant for the functioning of the informal economy combine to give – apart
from the criminal economy – three types:

1. *Informal business* functions in a manner analysed above all by Marx in his
'Capital' which need not be discussed further here. The 'ravenous hunger
for surplus value' drives the informal entrepreneur to exploit all human and
material potential for the greatest possible profit, which must be *accumulated*. Exploitation finds an inner limit only in the durability of the material
capital and in the limits of endurance of the human capital. Informal businesses do sail in the 'lee' of the formal economy, which has social security
contributions and usually also higher wages to bear; but the clear backward-

nesss of informal production usually sets this advantage to nought (Charmes 1990). What in addition drives up the costs is the necessity of paying bribes to government control personnel and/or protection money to informal 'forceful persuasion firms'.

The shortage of material capital is a major obstacle – especially where many industrial workers have become redundant and are looking for a new perspective in the informal production and repair trade. Services (of a work-intensive nature) go best with informal business, good profits however can only be made with modern services, as qualifications needed here are still in short supply. With other services and in informal trade competition puts pressure on the profits. The credit system is inadequate for small informal entrepreneurs. Access to cheap credits is at best available to large informal firms, which are in a position to make a generous return to the officials. Small informal entrepreneurs are cautious of taking advantage of connections: these give access to cheap resources and sales opportunities, but at the cost of reduced prices or profits as well as limited possibilities of expanding. So they tend to harness the resources of their own families – the formal incomes of family members and their possible contacts inside government firms (examples from Romania in Neef 1999).

For this reason, informal entrepreneurs can for the most part only increase their profit by *exploiting human capital*, especially through extending the working-hours (Marx 1966, 245 ff. and 531 ff.). For one-man firms, i.e. the self-employed, this means 'self-exploitation' (Sik 1994). In informal family businesses the limits are set down by the formal jobs of the family members and the family ethic: the cohesion and the future of the family must not be threatened. The limits of exploitation are not so severely drawn in the case of informal labourers, particularly in the light of the present conditions of growing unemployment and poverty. Often however the employees of small informal entrepreneurs are recruited from former fellow-workers, relatives and villagers, and it is moreover these who prove the surest market. In this way, many small informal entrepreneurs remain shut inside the limited range and socio-moral norms of social networks.

The functional type of informal business is therefore divided up into the upper sphere, in which a high economic potential and profitable contacts lead to good possibilities of expansion, and a lower sphere, which is economically and socially limited. Informal entrepreneurs shy away from legalizing because of bureaucatic difficulties, high taxes and charges and/or the cost of bribes. The formal institutional hurdles are certainly being gradually removed (cf. Ciupagea in this volume), whereby the rate of legalizing enterprises undoubtedly is rising – but the economic and social conditions of existence of the small entrepreneurs is by no means improved.

2. *The improving informal economy* – corresponds best in its way of functioning to the old 'secondary economy'. It rests on stable formal incomes,
which can at least cover the basic needs of the household members. It gives
those concerned the chance of *choosing* between informal earning possibilities. The options are however limited by formal working hours. On the
other hand they can use the firm's resources. Pensioner households have a
higher time budget, but are restricted in their efficiency for reasons of age.
The aim is optimising the welfare of the household – alongside the increase
in consumption also the safeguarding of the future, cultivation of social contacts and the care of relatives. Thus, the improving informal economy is particularly strongly tied to value orientations and norms. Backed by formal
incomes the product of this category can be offered relatively cheaply: this
is their great market advantage.

Qualification is a characteristic of the households with improving informal activities. It is only qualified formal jobs which are stable, it is only they
which result in acceptable pensions.[10] And it is only this basis which provides
flexibility in the optimising of informal activities. They take therefore typically the form of modern services and of crafts – whether as self-employed
or in wage labour. Informal farming is time-consuming and is therefore mainly conducted by the formally non-actives to raise the standard of living. The
involvement in social networks limits perhaps the formal profits, but reduces
the risks, provides informal work resources and gives security, as it provides
social exchange services (mainly non-monetary assistance).

The 'improving' informal economy of households has a favourable market position, can compensate for lack of capital through qualification, is
however, for the reason of a simultaneous formal job or reduced efficiency
in old age, not very dynamic (the majority of the 'improving' interviewees
in Romania had no wish to expand – cf. Neef 1999). They do not function
in accordance with the capitalist market logic, but with a logic of need on
the basis of a formally covered basic need – precisely for this reason they
have market advantages and will remain as a massive remnant of the old 'secondary economy' as long as the institutional infrastructure remains weakly
developed in the transformation countries.

3. *The survival economy:* The households concerned have no choice in the
question of their maintenance. Their formal income lies below the existence
minimum and they have no property which can be adequately implemented.
They are therefore forced to snap up any informal opportunity which presents itself. Typically these are households with many 'dependent' members,
at best with manual qualifications and with a low level of education. For this
reason the only openings for them are informal dead-end jobs with high

competition, low wages and a strenuous and depressing work situation (Neef 1999).

Subsistence farming is the rule. Since this produces only low monetary returns the result is a closed circuit and dependence on the natural economy, while the cost of transport which has risen everywhere ties them to the spot.[11] This does not prevent some of them from making good harvests and finding enough to keep body and soul together – but their lack of money and qualifications means that there is no escape from farming. Characteristic for the non-agricultural survival economy is otherwise the informal casual work of the unemployed. Their overall dependence can be exploited by employers, as far as is permitted by moral norms such as are to be found in village networks – in the towns their situation is more miserable. Other manual autonomous activities produce low earnings as a result of sinking demand and an inadequate infrastructure and instruments of work. The fluctuation of demand leaves no scope for the build-up of reserves. Network contacts prove of little value to those in the subsistence economy, as, even if they are not socially isolated, they have close contacts mostly with others in a similar position of poverty (cf. for Russia Fadeeva e.a., for Romania Golibrzuch and Stănculescu in this volume).

The various forms of the survival economy move therefore in a circle of dependence, in which resources and reserves are used up for pure survival and no qualifications can be built up. Common to them is the fact of no escape from living hand-to-mouth – even when, under conditions of subsistence farming, the hand may be filled with good food – there is a lack of all other goods.

Résumé: The informal economy of households in eastern Europe serves to a considerable extent the cheap provisioning of the poor sectors of the population. It offers a large number of them earnings outside the (often shrinking) formal employment openings and social transfers. In countries with a long-lasting transformation recession like Romania the demand in the lower social ranks is constantly dropping, and with it the earnings of a large part of the informal economy – while the number of the unemployed looking for work in the informal economy continues to rise. In countries such as these there is a drastic polarising tendency between the different informal entrepreneurs – between those better placed with good resources and the struggling small entrepreneurs and self-employed. The continuing downward path of the economy has aggravated the position of the landless lower classes as their sorry informal activities can barely enable them to survive. Finally, the sinking real incomes force more and more of the formally employed to take up informal side activities. In countries such as Hungary, where the level of (formal) employment has become stabilized and incomes are rising again, informal 'businesses' can increasingly be expanded into veritable small enterprises. Thus a new middle class can evolve, which certainly reacts against any further state involvement (cf. Piirainen in this volume). The transformation has also led to increased poverty in these countries – but this has not meant *deeper* poverty. So it is that the majority of the transformation victims do not have to fight for pure survival, but for a standard of living worthy of human beings – and this can only be achieved through informal work.

*

Most of the following contributions result from empirical projects. Eight texts stem from a conference[12] in June 2000 that brought together researchers from seven countries active in empirical projects. Some of the texts have been reworked significantly, and others have been added. We hope and trust that this collection can mark the starting point of more cooperation and gives inspiration for political action.

Haerpfer/Wallace give an overview of informal economies in eleven eastern European countries between 1991 and 1998 based on panel data. They adopt a pragmatic approach, including only those activities that can be grasped by standardised enquiry. Based on their data on the formal economy, household economy (mostly agrarian self-producing), social economy (informal exchange and voluntary work within social networks) and the black economy (non-regulated cash incomes), we can see that the informal economy has an inverse correlation with the formal one: high performing eastern economies have smaller informal economies in comparison with low performing ones (see also Ciupagea's calculations in this volume). While household economies can be found in nearly every country and people from every social strata are active in it, they are most important for poor households and countries. The black economy is most important in south-eastern Europe and some ex-Soviet countries, while more unemployed and young people with median qualifications, especially in big cities, participate in it. As Ilie's findings for Romania illustrate, both the rich and the poor profit from it. The limits of standardised surveys become apparent when we look at the insufficient information available on the development of social economies.

This volume is organised according to countries, with *Bulgaria* at the start. The three contributions dealing with Bulgaria, from Chavdarova, Roth and Benovska, are both historically and theoretically far-reaching. *Chavdarova's* understanding of the informal economy differs from the one introduced here and the notion used by Haerpfer and Wallace. Drawing on

Polanyi's theoretical foundation, she traces the cultural and behavioural roots of informal redistribution. She argues that informal redistribution is deeply imbedded in Bulgarian history and links this to the fact that native communities have always been confronted with regulation systems imposed or imported from other places. The tradition of reciprocity and informal redistribution within social networks complemented and helped to uphold the socialist economy. However, in the period before 1945 and after 1989, it also undermined the development of formal institutional behaviour necessary for a functioning market. Since informal behaviour patterns can be found in all segments of the Bulgarian economy, Chavdarova is very sceptical about the prospects for a rapid transformation to a market society.

Although *Roth* could not discern specific practices and strategies for getting by in socialist times, a specific *cluster* of newly developed and traditional practices did exist. His understanding of these practices differs from Stănculescu's, for example, in that he calls them *deliberate* actions and interactions that are marked by a separation between official and informal 'registers'. Further, using these registers is specific for socialism. He distinguishes between ten strategies, including (mostly opportunistic) co-operating adaptation and circumvention within the functioning system, self-help and informal exchange within social networks, the tapping of state resources, and obstruction. He also indicates how useful private conversations are for attaining goals and for emotional relief. He does not address, however, the question of what present-day strategies might be. See Fadeeva e.a. for a correlation between the strategies Roth identified for the Soviet times and a present-day account.

Benovska's text illustrates the forms in which rural households in Bulgaria and Serbia work, by comparing the situation before and after the social transformation of recent years. Bulgaria is reminiscent of the situation in south eastern Europe and the (ex-) Soviet Union in many respects, while the Serbian case shows western patterns of developing. This makes the many details in Benovska's text relevant and generally interesting. According to her thesis of *re-traditionalization* in Bulgaria, pre-modern work forms and old ways of reciprocity within the parentele have returned. This testifies to the perseverance of old customs and social configurations as well as to the difficulty of surviving by relying only on other strategies. The example of Serbia shows that re-traditionalization is not at all universal. Under the communist regime in Serbia, family farming did not disappear and is now developing into a capital-intense rationalised economy. As the Bulgarian case suggests, an informal economy based on private property *can* be related to a fall back into low-performing, pre-modern ways of producing and reproducing. At the same time, the Serbian example, with its alternative path to modern forms of informality, shows that other developments are possible.

The four articles from *Romania* contribute to both a country-specific and a methodological discussion. It becomes clear in these articles that both the informal economy in this country and a wide research approach are important. *Stănculescu* gives the most vivid and complex picture in relating data from a standardised survey and material from qualitative interviews. She explains that agrarian self-production (the 'household economy' in Haerpfer/Wallace's terms) is most important for large rural households and urban-rural 'household-networks'. Pensioners and some unemployed people rely on agrarian self-production as well. 'Cash informal' activities are very heterogeneous, important for the younger and middle generations, the unemployed or underemployed, households with low-wage earnings (especially those with children), and for formally well-established households. Those who rely primarily on the informal economy generally suffer from dependent or precarious situations in or near poverty. Those who informally complement their stable, formal income with earnings from the cash informal economy do so in order to improve or secure their relatively good social situation. On the whole, the household economy makes a second and the most important pillar of social security. At the same time, the cash informal economy leads to rather polarising effects.

Golibrzuch portrays the living situation of households in the countryside in detail. The picture she paints of subsistence agriculture is in many aspects reminiscent of what Benovska calls 're-traditionalization'. The respective families produce almost entirely for their own consumption and cannot afford modern farming technology. This self-production can improve the life situation of those who receive acceptable wages or pensions in addition. A strata of day labourers who fall into the category of traditional fringe groups and who struggle to survive from one week to another can be found at the bottom of the social hierarchy. Another group is made up of those in 'stable poverty'. They are still in poverty, but in a stable situation due to their stronger social imbeddedness and/or a more stable availability of work. Only a few rural households are in a good social situation thanks to their ability to develop modern entrepreneurial informal farming in the household as a supplement to their stable formal jobs. Golibrzuch ends with propositions for developing the capacities in self-help and diversifying activities.

A rare case of precise data on the topic, the text by *Ilie* carefully maps the different kinds of formal and informal incomes based on survey data and exposes the unequal social distribution of informal incomes. Whereas the largest amount of agrarian self-consumption can be found in the middle social strata, households in poverty – generally with few qualifications and many children – are disadvantaged both in formal employment and in agrarian self-production. In contrast, the rich, generally smaller households made up of the well-qualified profit most from formal and informal gainful activities. The informal economy in Romania thus simultaneously helps to balance income deficits and has socially polarising effects. Without diminishing gains from Ilie's precision, it is important to keep in mind the limited value of indications on informal cash incomes in standardised surveys.

The problem of obtaining reliable raw data is more relevant for *Ciupagea's* calculations. According to his thesis, inflation and institutional inefficiencies are the driving forces in informal economies. He tests this in using the most probable of a series of economic estimations of the informal economy in Romania. In addition to the level and growth rate of the GDP, also emphasised by Haerpfer/Wallace, he identifies the burden of social duties, the share of non-wage labour and, to some degree, the rate of long-term unemployment as main driving forces. According to his calculations, agriculture is mostly informal; trade and catering have a remarkably high proportion of informal activities; and informal transport has the highest dynamics in this respect. We should add that his data is based only on experts' estimations and official statistics. The latter are blurred precisely because of informal activities in numerous branches. Reliable indications exist only for agriculture.

The chapter on *Hungary* deals with a country praised for a good performance in the period of recent social transformation. We find some hints of this performance in the accounts of *Sik* and *Tóth*: They document an upsurge in the informal economy in the early nineties, similar to the development in all eastern European countries, and a decrease to a comparably low level since the mid-nineties. These authors illustrate that informal consumption and open markets are particularly common in large settlements, irrespective of the social position of the households. At the same time, informal labour markets are concentrated in large cities and tend to retreat into the hidden sphere of bars and social networks. Sik and Tóth argue that the signs of a decrease in these forms of informal economy in the late nineties are indicative of a normalization in economic development in Hungary. This data shows, however, a continuing and remarkably high level of informal activities at the same time.

Sik's report on an open informal labour market-place in Budapest touches upon the tip of an iceberg of informal labour in Hungary. It is a market of excess supply and of low demand. The demand for temporary, informal labourers, mainly in construction, is lower than expected. Unskilled labourers from Romania and some groups of unskilled Hungarian workers are at a disadvantage in this situation. The skilled Hungarians, on the other hand, enjoy a relatively better situation on the informal labour market. Contrary to expectations, ethnic aspects and discrimination are only of minor importance. While the article includes insight into the daily course of transactions based on non-participant observation, the author offers little information on the working and living conditions of the casual labourers concerned.

The lively account by *Fadeeva, Nikulin* and *Vinogradsky* shows two types of getting by in two different agricultural forms in *Russia*. The efficient, modernised type of large-scale farming is comprised of a cleavage between a few better-off 'in the centre', on the one side, and the majority of working families whose wages have fallen below minimum livelihood, on the other. In the second agricultural type, the kolchos is divided up. A lucky few gain control over the more productive units, while the majority of the population has access only to the left-overs. In both cases, family agrarian subsistence production has developed, complemented by informal channels of provision. This is embedded in 'business' and 'amorous' social relations, the latter binding especially parents and adult children. The interesting insight from these examples is that in the 'modern' type of farming, the informal economy is a permanent, but only supplementary part of the formal economy. In the crisis-ridden type of agricultural production, the informal economy permeates the whole (ex-) kolchos. The latter situation seems very far away from modern western market features and the direction in which it is likely to develop is not at all clear.

Unfortunately, it was not possible to include a text from *Piirainen* that would have contradicted these findings. He sees a clear development towards an accommodation to the requirements of a market economy in urban Russia. Based on his research in 1993-1996 (see Piirainen 1997) and 1998-2000, he deduces a social differentiation between different segments of society. Whereas the elite remain oriented towards the official market economy, 'the people' rely primarily upon their household economy and informal exchange, the market economy complementing only their basic livelihood. The underclass depends mainly on wages and transfers in the public sector while an emerging 'middle class' orient themselves (based on their professional qualifications) increasingly towards a market economy, while continuing to participate in informal household and exchange activities. This may well be a particularity of large cities like St. Petersburg – there is no evidence of such a middle class in, for example, the findings from Fadeeva e.a.

Adair and *Neef* round out this collection with an assessment of the advantages and deficits in the methods of researching informal economies. The dominant and quasi-official procedures, like the monetary method in economies or the standardised representative survey in the social sciences, are by no means more explanative, and sometimes even less adequate, for researching informal economies and activities. Adair/Neef further summarise the main forms of informal economy: moonlighting, social welfare contribution fraud, misappropriation of incomes and resources, and subsistence agriculture. In the end, they emphasise the heterogeneity of informal economies and point out the contradiction between the two dominant political strategies to cope with them. The answer to informal economies is either to increase state control and efficiency in collecting social welfare contributions or to tolerate informal activities as being inherent to any market. Their review does not do justice to the whole range of methods used in the projects presented in this volume. Documentary or ethnographic studies and time budget surveys are, for example, not discussed. The methodology in this volume reflects the situation of its subject matter: the large variety of informal economies and activities in eastern Europe demands just as many varieties and new combinations of research methods.

Notes

1 Macro-economic estimates were based to date, as pointed out by Ciupagea and Adair/Neef in this volume, on problematic indicators, such as electricity consumption or cash flow. According to these, the share of the 'non-official economy' in the eastern European countries from the eighties to the mid-nineties should have doubled or tripled to between 15 and 46% of the GNP (Müller 1998, 211; a critical survey by Adair/Neef in this volume).

2 Pahl/Wallace (1985) came to a similar conclusion in a comparison of the 'self-provisioning activities' of unemployed and single – and several – earner households in Great Britain.

3 Even *formal* property rights are helpful, but not necessary, as the extensive home-production on occupied land has shown from the Ukraine to Ghana and from Indonesia to Mexico.

4 Incisive here is in Romania the loss of a work-book including social security for day labourers (cf. Golibrzuch in this volume).

5 According to Brezinski/Petersen 1990, in 1980 this represented 42% of the entire agricultural production – in the light of theft and misappropriation of state goods, this is certainly an over-estimate.

6 'Not stealing from the socialist sector is seen as a sign of ignorance, while the misappropriation of private property is vehemently condemned.' Brezinski/Petersen, 1989, 77.

7 There is no serious research on the topic. Some hints from a qualitative enquiry in 1996 (Neef e.a. 1998) indicate that state employees tap firms' resources more often and more intensely than do private employees. Interviewees who in Romania (according to a qualitative study in 1996) reported on the intensive use of the firm's materials or infrastructure were nearly all employed in state firms.

8 According to Sik, the 'illegal' – meaning the private – money earnings grew from 15 to 25% from the beginning or middle of the eighties to 40% of the GNP in 1989, while Ékes held (1994) that the volume of the informal economy had in the period 1986-1992 grown almost fivefold to 25% of the GNP.

9 It is certainly difficult to mark this off empirically from productive household work. There is however little sense in examining the development of the 'household economy' overall

in eastern Europe, as was done in the new Democracies Barometer (cf. e.g. Rose/Haerpfer 1996) inspired by Rose. Household work is almost ubiquitous and the question as to its extent leads to 95% answers which explain precious little.

10 Young non-earning households only have a chance of developing lucrative informal activities if they combine high qualifications with extensive network contacts and the preparedness to take risks. The typical pattern here is that of young people with a middle- or upper-class background and a good basic education and relevant qualifications in the service sector (for Romania cf. Stanculescu in this volume, and Neef e. a. 1998, 137 ff.).

11 In Romania for example, the rise in bus fares in country areas resulted in many children from poor families no longer going to school, while adults found themselves as a result of the high transport costs tied to the miserable and one-sided offer of work in the immediate vicinity.

12 This conference took place from June 23 to 26, 2000 in Marburg, Germany. It was sponsored partly by the *Südosteuropa-Gesellschaft* and partly by a project on shadow economies in Romania financed by the *Stiftung Volkswagenwerk*.

References

Brezinski, H. and Petersen P. (1990), 'The Second Economy in Romania', in *The Second Economy in Marxist States*, ed. M. Los, London, Macmillan.

Cassel, D., e.a. (1989), *Inflation und Schattenwirtschaft im Sozialismus*, Hamburg, Steuer– und Wirtschaftsverlag.

Castells, M., Portes, A. (1989), 'World underneath: The Origins, Dynamics, and Effects of the Informal Economy', in *The informal economy: studies in advanced and less developed countries*, ed. M. Castells, A. Portes, L.A. Benton, Baltimore – London, Johns Hopkins.

Charmes J. (1990), 'A critical review of concepts, definitions and studies in the informal sector', in *The informal sector revisited*, ed. D. Turnham e.a. Paris, O.E.C.D.

Chavdarova, T. (1997), *From Hidden Privatization to Criminalization of Bulgarian Economy*, paper for the Conference 'Cities in Transition', Berlin, 19.-22.7.97.

Dallago, B. (1990), *The Irregular Economy. The 'Underground' Economy and the 'Black' Labour Market*, Aldershot, Dartmouth.

Ékes, I. (1994), 'The Hidden Economy and Income: the Hungarian Experience' in: *Economic Systems,* vol. 18, No. 4, pp. 309-334.

Evers, H.D. (1987), 'Schattenwirtschaft, Subsistenzproduktion und informeller Sektor' in: *Soziologie wirtschaftlichen Handelns*, ed. F. Neidhardt e.a. Opladen (KZfSS Sonderheft 28).

Feige, E. L. (1999), 'Underground Economies in Transition: Noncompliance and Institutional Change', in *Underground Economies in Transition*, ed. E.L. Feige and K. Ott, Ashgate Aldershot.

ILO (International Labour Office) ed. (1997), *Yearbook of Labour Statistics 1997*, Geneva.

Gábor, I. R. (1989) 'Second economy and socialism: the Hungarian experience', in *The underground economies*, ed. E. Feige, New York u.a., Cambridge University Press.

Granovetter, M. (1985), 'Economic Action and Social Structure: The Problem of Embeddedness', in *American Journal of Sociology,* vol 91, pp. 481-510.

Grødeland, A.B., Koshechkina, T.Y, Miller, W.L. (1998), 'Foolish to Give and Yet More Foolish Not to Take' – In-depth Interviews with Post-Communist Citizens on Their Everyday Use of Bribes and Contacts', in *Europe-Asia-Studies,* vol. 50, no. 4, pp. 651-677.

Grossman, G. (1989), 'Informal Personal Incomes and Outlays of the Soviet Urban Population', in *The Informal economy: studies in advanced and less developed countries*, ed. M. Castells, A. Portes, L.A. Benton, Baltimore – London, Johns Hopkins.

Hart, K. (1997), 'Informal income opportunities and urban employment in Ghana', in *Perspectives on Africa*, ed. R.R. Grinker, C. Steiner, Oxford/ Cambridge (Mass.), pp. 142-162 (1st publ. 1971).

Heimburger, C. (1990), *Die entwicklungspolitische Bedeutung des städtischen informellen Sektors*, Frankfurt/M. e.a., Lang.

Knabe, B. (1998), *Die System-Mafia als Faktor der sowjetisch-russischen Transformation. II: Die Instrumentalisierung des organisierten Verbrechens*, Köln, Bundesinstitut f. Ostwiss u. Internationale Studien.

Kornai, J. (1980), *Economics of Shortage*, Amsterdam e.a., North Holland.

Kornai, J. (1996), 'Transformationsrezession', in J. Kornai, *Unterwegs. Essays zur wirtschaftlichen Umgestaltung in Ungarn*, Marburg, Metropolis.

Ledeneva, A.V. (1998), *Russia's Economy of Favours*, Cambridge, Cambridge University Press.

Marx, K. (1966), *Das Kapital. Kritik der politischen Ökonomie*, 1, Bd. Berlin, Dietz Verlag.

Müller, K. (1998), 'Postsozialistische Krisen' in: *Postsozialistische Krisen. Theoretische Ansätze und empirische Befunde*, ed. K. Müller, Opladen, Leske & Budrich.

Neef, R., e.a. (1998), 'Working situations, incomes and social situations of households performing informal activities', in *The informal economy in Romania. Final report*, coord. G. Duchêne, Paris: ROSES/ Brussels: E.U.

Neef, R. (1999), 'Formen und soziale Lagen der Schattenwirtschaft in einem Transformationsland: Rumänien', in *Berliner Journal für Soziologie*, vol. 9, No. 3, pp. 397-414.

Pahl, R.E. and Wallace, C. (1985) 'Household work strategies in economic recession' in: *Beyond Employment. Household, Gender and Subsistence*, ed. N. Redclift/E. Mingione, Oxford: Blackwell.

Piirainen, T. (1997), *Towards a new social order in Russia*, Aldershot e.a., Dartmouth.

Portes, A. (1994), 'The Informal Economy and Its Paradoxes', in *The Handbook of Economic Sociology*, ed. N.J. Smelser, R. Swedberg, Princeton N.J., Princeton University Press.

Rose, R. and C. Haerpfer (1996) *Change and stability in the New Democracies Barometer*, Glasgow: Univ. of Strathclyde (Studies in Public Policy 270).

Sik, E. (1996), 'The Social Consequences of Unemployment in Hungary – A Household Perspective', in *Innovation*, vol. 9, No. 3, pp. 355-367.

Sik, E. (1994), 'From the Multicolored to the Black and White Economy: The Hungarian Second Economy and the Transformation', in *International Journal of Urban and Regional Research*, vol. 18, No. 1, pp. 46-70.

Sik, E. and Wallace C. (1999), 'The Development of Open-air Markets in East-Central Europe', in *International Journal of Urban and Regional Research*, vol. 23, No. 4, pp. 697-714.

Stark, D. (1996), 'Recombinant Property in East European Capitalism', in *American Journal of Sociology*, vol. 101, No. 4, pp. 993-1027.

Teichert, V. (1993), *Das informelle Wirtschaftssystem: Analyse und Perspektiven der wechselseitigen Entwicklung von Erwerbs – und Eigenarbeit*, Opladen, Westdeutscher Verlag

UN (United Nations, Secretary of the Economic Commission for Europe) ed., *Economic Survey of Europe in 1999*, no. 1, Geneva/New York, United Nations.

Patterns of participation in the informal economy in East-Central Europe, 1991-1998[1]

Claire Wallace* and Christian Haerpfer**

Acknowledgements: We would like to thank the sponsors of the New Democracies Barometer – the Austrian National Bank and the Austrian Ministry of Science and Research. We would also like to thank Manuela Stănculescu for her careful and perceptive editing.

The informal economy was an integral part of the former Communist economies and is now also an important part of the transition economies in Central and Eastern Europe (Sik, 1993). This paper will consider the relative size and dynamics of the informal economy in different countries during the course of transition and the forms of participation in the informal economy. In doing so, it draws upon a survey, the New Democracies Barometer (NDB) for the years 1992, 1994, 1996 and 1998. Here we consider the following countries: Poland, Czech Republic, Hungary, Slovakia, Slovenia, Croatia, FRY, Romania, Bulgaria, Belarus and Ukraine.

What is certainly clear is that rather than being a universal phenomenon, the informal economy is socially and economically embedded – that is, it can take different forms and have different importance in different contexts. The question we need to ask therefore is: what kinds of informal economic activities are important in Central and Eastern Europe and how are they embedded? In order to answer this question we consider the different kinds of participation in the informal and formal economies in different countries. We also consider how these have grown or declined.

* Visiting Professor at Glasgow Caledonian University and Head of the Sociology Department of Institute for Advanced Studies, Vienna. Stumpergasse 56, A-1060 Vienna, Austria. E-mail: wallace@ihs.ac.at.
** Visiting Professor at Glasgow Caledonian University and Senior Researcher at the Institute for Advanced Studies, Vienna. Stumpergasse 56, A-1060 Vienna, Austria. E-mail: haerpfer@ihs.ac.at.

Formalization and informalization of activities

In most industrial societies, the state sector has been cut back in favour of the formal market economy in the trend towards privatization in recent decades. The state, however, continues to regulate the formal market sector, ensuring rules of exchange, contracts, payments of social insurance and labour regulation as well as the collection of taxes for state revenue. The rules of economic activity are therefore transparent and legally regulated by national or even international law. In post-communist countries, the state sector has been drastically cut back and more activities have moved into the formal market economy. However, the formal market economy is often poorly regulated and the legislation underdeveloped or inappropriate. The institutions of civil society which could also help to control economic behaviour (professional associations, churches, Trades Unions) are likewise underdeveloped in Eastern and Central European countries. The formal economy is therefore struggling against the informal market economy, driven by profit, but governed by different rules and regulations. However, in the informal economies, the rules of exchange are not legally regulated and are therefore often not transparent. They are subject to various forms of private or informal understanding (Portes 1994, Wallace et al. 1999) or they are also subject to criminal control which can be brutal and violent, as when various so-called 'Mafia' interests take over.

In post-communist countries, the retreat of the state has taken place faster than legislation to control market activity could be passed and implemented. Such legislation is also subverted by the agents within the state who are interested in 'grabbing' state resources in their own interests or tunnelling out state institutions from the inside (Sik, 1994). This means that some of the transfer to the market has taken place informally. The absurdity and non-via-bility of some legislation in the transition period (such as taxes on profits of up to 100%, the necessity of applying for dozens of authorizations in order to legitimate business activity and so on) further encourages such transfer along with the tradition of rule-bending and corruption in communist states (Morawska 1998, Wedel 1992). In Central and Eastern Europe the house-hold sector has also grown as a result of the economic crisis there – many households are forced back on the resources of friends and relatives and upon growing their own vegetables to survive. In other words, it has regres-sive tendencies. Thus, in post-communist societies, it may be the case that the retreat of the state economy along with the inadequacy of the formal market economy has lead to a growth in the informal market economy and in the social and household economies.

However, we need to take into account the fact that different regions in the post-communist Europe have different paths of transition (Agh 1998,

Wallace and Haerpfer 1998). Whilst the informal economy may play an increasing role in some circumstances, it may play a declining role in other circumstances.

The consequences of informalization

The deleterious consequences of the failure of the formal market economy to take over from the retreat of the state economy have been described by Sik as well as Schneider and Enste. They can be summarized as follows:

A fiscal crisis of the state

The state in transition societies is losing revenue from the consequences of the transfer of property to the private sector, whilst, at the same time, the rise in poverty, unemployment and so on makes increasing demands on state resources. The failure to be able to collect taxes and other revenues as a result of economic activities going underground means that states lose still more money. They may respond by increasing the burden of regulation and taxation which may further push activities underground and create a disincentive for activities to be formalized. In the long run, this could mean the take over of parts of the economy by mafia-type organised interests and loss of control by the state where large areas of economic activity are not transparently regulated.

The undermining of economic indicators

Where large parts of the economy are unregistered, the government's ability to estimate GNP, inflation and employment is called into question. These indicators, crucial for measuring economic performance are rendered very inaccurate or even meaningless because they cover only part of the national economy.

The weakening of social policies

Where large parts of the economy disappear underground, the revenue necessary to pay for social policies such as health, housing, unemployment and pensions benefits are unavailable. The consequence is that these benefits are not paid, the public service staff are underpaid and demoralised, leading to an even greater tendency to circumvent the official system with unofficial payments and earnings. Furthermore, social policies can be entirely inaccurately targeted, when the informal economy disguises who is really poor and who is really well off.

The distortion of market forces

A large underground economy distorts the positions of profit and loss in different economic enterprises and ventures and changes their relative market positions. This is important in the context of privatization, when it is important to know the market position and value of different enterprises in order to privatise them successfully. The hidden economy, especially in the form of network relations has undermined much of the privatization process in Central and Eastern Europe whereby an apparently profitable company can have been 'tunnelled' out and undermined from the inside. In this way, privatization can actually contribute to the growth of the informal economy.

The undermining of public morality

The informal economy can lead to the reinforcement of the tendency to bend and break rules, including rising corruption and some examples of super-exploitation (for example, by not paying illegal workers) in situations where the rules of exchange are not transparent or governed by the rule of law. In transition countries, Schneider and Enste (2000) show that rising corruption is correlated with the informalization of large sectors of the economy. This can lead to either a vicious or a virtuous spiral of growth and reform. Thus, some of the wealthier OECD countries as well as countries in Eastern Europe find themselves in the virtuous spiral of good rule of law, more revenue and less tax evasion, and a shrinking or small informal economy, whilst other countries, especially in the former Soviet Union, find themselves in a vicious spiral of low tax revenue, weak rule of law, high corruption, high tax burden and an expanding informal economy. The decline of public morality, in turn undermines public confidence in the state and its institutions which are seen as more and more irrelevant for governing and regulating economic activity. This further increases the loss of control of the state over economic life.

The function of the informal economy in transition countries

As mentioned already, under some circumstances of transition, the informal (household and social) economies can represent the regression to an earlier form of subsistence peasant-style self sufficiency as a survival mechanism in post-communist transition societies. For many families this is the main way to survive situations where living standards have plummeted and many households are left with small or even no incomes. For these families there can be a downward spiral of greater dependence on the informal economy encouraging a further retreat from the formal economy, and no time to search for alternatives, as families spend all their time growing vegetables.

However, the informal economy can also be a seed bed for new enterprise as it represents new kinds of market type activity which can provide the capital for more formalised small businesses later on (Okolski 2001). It can be the place where entrepreneurial skills are practised and honed and where more 'middle class' aspirations encouraging further entrepreneurship are nurtured (Piirainen 1997). This leads us to ask: is the informal economy only part of a survival strategy or is it a source of new wealth?

The answer is that it can be both. Empirical studies indicate that some people use informal activities as a way of surviving, some as a way of supplementing incomes and some as a way of profiting (Duchene, Neef et al., 1998). People distribute their activities between the official state economy, the private market economy (both formal and informal parts of it) and the household economy. The extent that they depend upon one or other of these can determine their positions in the new emerging status hierarchy (Piirainen 1997). Richard Rose and Christian Haerpfer (1992) describe also argue for the idea of 'portfolios' of economies which include the formal, the social and the 'uncivil' or illegal.

However, these more detailed studies of household activities in the informal economy can inform us about the different role this plays in different countries, not about how this might have changed over time. The aim of our study therefore is to consider the role of households within different economies both comparatively and over time.

Methods of research

Our own typology is based upon questions which it is possible to ask in a survey.[2] Thus, we have rejected the legal/illegal distinction because it is not always possible to ask about this in a questionnaire and expect to get honest answers. Furthermore, because laws and regulations are changing constantly in the countries with which we are concerned, activities become legal and illegal in the process, in a manner that is impossible to build into our model. However, we have divided the formal economy according to sources of income, including those from the main job in either the private or public sector, from pensions or benefits and additional sources of income which we may term 'cash' economy. We should remember that main job is not necessarily the same as main source of income – it could be that people earn much more from their second job than from their main job. The dimension of monetized/non-monetized has been included and we have also included the extent to which economic activities are integrated into the main national economy or autonomous from it (Sik 1995).

Figure 1   Typology of formal and informal work in East-Central Europe

Level of integration	*Level of monetization*	*Economic sector*	*Activity*
Integrated	Monetized	Formal economy	Employment/ Pension/Benefit in formal sector
Semi-integrated	Monetized	Cash economy	Getting foreign money, earnings from second job, incidental earnings
Semi-autonomous	Non-monetized	Social economy	Obtained as favours, help from friends and relatives
Autonomous	Non-monetized	Household economy	Growing own food, repairing house

Thus, the continuum stretches from *integration* to *autonomy*. We assume that the formal sector is the most integrated, followed by the cash economy, which is a kind of 'shadow' of the formal sector. However, we assume that the household economy is the most *autonomous* – it can exist in almost any form of economic organization, whilst the social economy is also more or less autonomous and perhaps dependent more upon social cohesion in the society than upon economic organization. The success of household production, on the other hand, does depend upon access to a plot of land or allotment, which is in turn a product of the social and economic organization of the society.

In our study we rely mainly upon the direct measures of household economic activity as measured by surveys.[3] We can then compare this both with subjective indicators, such as attitudes, and with more objective indicators, such as income, age and education. We can also compare this with aggregate indicators such as GDP per capita and economic performance. The disadvantages of such data collection methods have been indicated already. The main questions we are using to construct a household typology of formal and informal activities are a series of questions asking about what is the main sources of income for their family – then giving a range of alternatives which span the formal economy, household production, social and cash economies (details are given in Figure 1). Respondents were then asked what was the second most important source of income for their households which enabled us to look at how households combined different economies. We then looked at the changes over time and at variations between countries as well as the social characteristics of households using different economies.

The information about the formal economic activity we would assume would elicit reasonably honest answers as there is no need to conceal this information and it can be corroborated with other questionnaire items. The question about household production is also unlikely to be concealed and we would assume that this was also reasonably accurate. The questions about the social economy however, are difficult to answer in a simple way, because the social economy is a good deal more complex than our questions imply. In addition, people may want to conceal the fact that they depend upon friends and relatives for help. The questions about the social economy are therefore likely to under-estimate the extent of activity in this economy and since the numbers were small, we have left them out of much of the analysis. The questions about the cash economy are likewise likely to be an under-estimate of this kind of activity. People are likely to want to conceal their activities in the cash economy from an interviewer and also the complexity of such activity is not covered in our questions. To sum up, we would assume that, whilst we have a reasonably good measure of the formal and household economies, we would be under-estimating the social and the cash economies in our analysis. Nevertheless, the data can give us some indication of activity in these sectors and the relative consistency of these data over time indicates that they are reliable. Hence, we can check on the reliability of data by using repeated measures over time.

Which economy is most important?

In each year of the NDB survey, a question was asked about which sources of income were most important and which were second most important for the survival of the family.[4] The responses were clustered according to whether they represented the *formal* economy (earnings from regular job, pension or benefit, benefits from place of work), the *household* economy (growing own food and repairing house), the *social* economy (getting favours or help from friends and relatives) and the *cash* economy (earnings from second job, incidental earnings, getting foreign money) (Rose and Haerpfer, 1992). The relative importance of each sector can be seen in Table 1. In each country, apart from Romania, the formal economy was the most important source of earnings: in each country it was the main source of income for more than 50% of families. The household economy was the next most important source and in general, the less reliance on the formal economy, the more the reliance on the household economy as source of income in each country. In Romania, the household economy was the most important source of income. The cash economy, however, did show some variations. Although low in all countries as a main source of income, in Croatia and FRY it was the highest, reaching more than 10% of households in those countries.

If we now look at how this has changed over time, we can see that in terms of the *formal economy* there are three main clusters of countries. In the Czech Republic, Hungary and Slovenia, it is high (more than 80% of households in 1998) and has generally been increasing in importance over time. In the second group of countries (Slovakia and Poland) it has fluctuated and even declined, standing at around 70% in 1998. In the third group of countries (Bulgaria, Belarus, Croatia, Ukraine, Romania) it is low and fluctuating. Although in some of these dependence on the formal economy has declined, in some risen, there is a less stable pattern in those countries. The reliance on the formal economy reflects very much the strength of the formal economy and the different paths of transition: those with the more successful transition trajectories are also those where more people depend on the formal economy (EBRD Transition Report 2000).

The *household economy* is very important in Romania, Ukraine, Belarus and Slovakia where its importance has generally *increased*. It is also important in Bulgaria and Poland. In the Czech Republic, Slovenia and Hungary, its importance has declined as the importance of the formal economy has grown. In Croatia and FRY, there is not much reliance on the household economy. Thus, we could say that the rise of the formal and decline of the household economy are successfully linked in some of the most successful transforming economies: Czech Republic, Slovenia and Hungary.

The importance of the *cash economy* has generally declined in most countries, but remains very important in the countries of the former Yugoslavia. In Belarus, Ukraine and Romania, the cash economy was more important in the early 90s than it is now. This would tend to indicate that increasing economic crisis (inability to live from the formal economy)

Table 1   Changes in different economies over time

Country		1992	1994	1996	1998
NDB mean	FORMAL ECONOMY	68	67	70	68
	HOUSEHOLD ECONOMY	22	22	21	22
	CASH ECONOMY	7	7	6	6
Czech Republic	FORMAL ECONOMY	80	82	88	85
	HOUSEHOLD ECONOMY	17	15	9	11
	CASH ECONOMY	7	2	2	2
Hungary	FORMAL ECONOMY	80	77	80	83
	HOUSEHOLD ECONOMY	16	19	15	14
	CASH ECONOMY	2	3	4	3
Slovenia	FORMAL ECONOMY	71	64	59	80
	HOUSEHOLD ECONOMY	25	33	37	11
	CASH ECONOMY	3	3	4	7
Slovakia	FORMAL ECONOMY	78	80	82	70
	HOUSEHOLD ECONOMY	20	15	14	25
	CASH ECONOMY	2	3	3	4
Poland	FORMAL ECONOMY	82	82	67	70
	HOUSEHOLD ECONOMY	13	12	21	21
	CASH ECONOMY	3	4	7	5
Bulgaria	FORMAL ECONOMY	67	67	63	69
	HOUSEHOLD ECONOMY	24	22	28	24
	CASH ECONOMY	7	9	5	4
Belarus	FORMAL ECONOMY	71	59	78	64
	HOUSEHOLD ECONOMY	14	26	12	26
	CASH ECONOMY	11	10	7	6
Ukraine	FORMAL ECONOMY	26	52	58	57
	HOUSEHOLD ECONOMY	59	30	30	33
	CASH ECONOMY	5	10	7	8
Romania	FORMAL ECONOMY	61	55	59	46
	HOUSEHOLD ECONOMY	26	29	33	47
	CASH ECONOMY	10	11	3	5
Croatia	FORMAL ECONOMY	69	66	71	69
	HOUSEHOLD ECONOMY	7	13	11	18
	CASH ECONOMY	21	17	14	10
FRY	FORMAL ECONOMY				68
	HOUSEHOLD ECONOMY				16
	CASH ECONOMY				14
	N=	10160	10709	10069	11296

pushes people more into the household economy, but only under some circumstances into the cash economy. The cash economy, by contrast is not a substitute for problems in the formal economy: it has declined in precisely those countries which have had the most problems.

We could say that there does indeed seem to be a 'vicious spiral' of reform in some countries where more and more people are dependent upon sources of income outside of the formal economy (Ukraine, Belarus, Romania) and a 'virtuous spiral' of reform in others where more and more people depend upon the formal economy. In the latter countries more aspects of economic activity have become institutionalised, in the former countries, they are becoming de-institutionalised (outside of the formal economy).

As we saw from the work of Piirainen (1997) and Rose and Haerpfer (1992), households tend to use a variety of economies in different combinations. How were these economies combined in our sample? For this purpose we combined the source of income which was said by the respondents to be the most important source with that which was the second most important source. The results are set out below:

Table 2 Combinations of formal and informal economies

Combinations	1992	1994	1996	1998
Household and Household	4	5	5	6
Household and Social	3	2	3	2
Household and Cash	3	3	3	4
Household and Formal	11	10	11	11
Social and Household	1	1	1	1
Social and Social	0.4	1	0.3	0.4
Social and Cash	1	1	1	1
Social and Formal	1	1	1	1
Cash and Household	2	2	1	2
Cash and Social	1	1	1	1
Cash and Cash	1	2	1	1
Cash and Formal	3	3	3	2
Formal and Household	36	33	36	32
Formal and Social	8	9	11	8
Formal and Cash	13	14	13	16
Formal and Formal	11	11	10	13
N=	10160	10709	10069	11296

We can see from this table that most households combine more than one economy. The numbers of households who are in the formal economy alone number about 10% (although this appears to be rising). The numbers only in the household or only in the social or cash economy are negligible. Large numbers (about one third of households) combine the formal with the household economy or the formal with the cash economy (about one in seven households). Around 10% also combine the household and the formal economy in reverse order. Thus, we can say that even where the formal economy is very important, it is usually supplemented by some other kind of economy. In Eastern and Central Europe, the portfolio of economies is the norm rather than the exception.

Another result from this table is that we can say that *around 90% of households* are active in informal economies as either the most important or second most important sources of income. Although this seems to be declining very slightly. In addition, we can conclude that around *one third* of households are *primarily* dependent upon the informal economy (either the household, social or cash forms) in Central and Eastern Europe. The stability of these scores over the period surveyed, gives us some confidence in the accuracy of this estimation using these sources and methods.

The social characteristics of households in different economies

Now let us consider the social characteristics of the households active in one or the other economy.

Table 3   Economic activity and different economies: 1998

	Formal	Household	Social	Cash
Economic Activity **Phi=.290 p<000**				
Employed full time	47	34	21	32
Employed part time	3	4	5	9
Self employed	5	5	3	5
Pensioner employed	2	3	1	4
Pensioner	24	25	13	5
Unemployed no benefit	3	9	15	20
Unemployed with benefit	3	5	7	7
Other benefit	4	4	6	3
Housewife/student	9	12	30	16
N=	7280	2449	268	672

Table 3 shows that there is a strong association between economic status (of the respondent) and activity in different economies (of the household). Unemployment is closely associated with increased participation in all informal economies, but especially in the cash economy. Further down the table, we can see that the important factor is being unemployed and without any benefits for participation in the cash economy. Being employed full time decreases participation in all alternative economies, although part time employment is associated with the cash economy. Pensioners are most likely found in the formal or the household economies. Housewives and students are most likely to participate in the social economy.

Table 4   Poverty and wealth and different economies: 1998

	Formal	Household	Social	Cash
Household Income Quartile				
Cramers V =.083 p<000				
First quartile	20	32	27	22
Second quartile	24	25	19	26
Third quartile	26	25	26	26
Fourth quartile	30	18	28	26
N=	4996	1968	202	499
Number of consumer goods				
Cramers V=.090 p<000				
None	14	23	19	12
1	29	35	28	27
2	25	23	27	26
3	24	16	20	26
All four	8	3	6	9
N=	6533	2359	252	655

Table 4 shows that the poorest people are those dependent upon the household economy, whilst the wealthiest sections of the population are found in the formal and cash economies. Wealthy people (fourth quartile) are not very likely to be active in the household economy – poor people are most often found there. A similar pattern is found if we look at the number of consumer goods possessed by the household. Those dependent upon the household economy have the least consumer goods, whilst those dependent upon the formal and the cash economy had the largest number of consumer goods – but here the cash economy overtook the formal economy in importance.

Table 5   Demographic characteristics and different economies: 1998

	Formal	Household	Social	Cash
Age				
Cramers V=.093 p<000				
18-19	5	5	16	8
20-29	19	17	32	32
30-39	18	17	19	23
40-49	20	19	10	18
50-59	16	16	6	13
60 plus	22	25	16	7
N=	7297	2454	268	675
Town Size				
Cramers V=.135 p<000				
<5000	33	59	29	32
<20000	14	10	10	16
<100000	20	13	21	18
>100 000	33	18	39	35
N=	6533	2359	252	655
Education				
Cramers V=.092 p<000				
Elementary	29	42	33	23
Vocational	25	25	19	22
Secondary	34	28	42	42
University	13	6	7	14
N=	7296	2453	268	675

Now let us look at demographic variables. Age does seem to be associated with participation in different economies. Young people are more active in the cash economy and the social economy, whilst older people are more active in the formal and the household economies. In this table we can see something very important about the social economy. It is comprised of young people. Parents and relatives are likely to be supporting young people, so this may be the reason why the social economy is more important for them and we also find that it is single young people who are most likely to be supported in this way. At the other age extreme, the household economy was most important for older people. Those in the cash economy are most likely to be aged between 20 and 40.

Those active in the household economy are most likely to live in rural areas, whilst those active in the other economies most likely to live in cities. This is perhaps obvious, because access to land is important for growing vegetables, breeding animals, keeping animals for food and general household subsistence of this kind.

Education also has an important effect on participation in the different economies. Those active in the household economy had low education, whilst those the highest educated people were polarised between the formal and the cash economy. There were many people with higher education to be found as active in both the cash and the formal economy. One factor could be the fact that higher educated people can sell their services both in the formal and the informal economy. Thus, teachers can give private lessons, doctors private consultations and so on. This implies that these two economies have some things in common.

Finally, we can see from table 6 that being active in the cash economy is associated with planning to go abroad. In Central and Eastern Europe, many people work abroad for short periods of time in order to support families at home (Wallace and Stola, 2001). Often this work is illegal. Working abroad was an important way in which household incomes could be supplemented.

Table 6   Working abroad and different economies: 1998

	Formal	Household	Social	Cash
Plans to go abroad				
plan to go abroad	39	41	58	63
not planning to go abroad	61	59	42	37
N=	7172	5056	1145	2123

Conclusions

Our results indicate that, when considering Central and Eastern Europe, it is important to distinguish between different kinds of informal economic activity. Merely looking at tax evasion or illegal work would miss some of the most important aspects of the informal economy and the role it plays in transforming societies. Hence, it is necessary to distinguish especially between household production, which is one of the most important aspects of the informal economy, and additional work as well as unpaid work. In fact, very different parts of the population are active in these different spheres.

Our survey results seem to indicate that the informal economy is rather extensive, but that it is mostly combined with other types of economic activity. Most people are active in the informal economy, although this is declining in the most successful transition countries. Almost 90% of all post-communist households are involved in different degrees in the informal sector, which is a sign that participation in some form of informal economy is a necessary condition for the economic survival of households in economic transition. However, it is seldom the case that households are found in only one economy. Rather, they have a portfolio of activities as is argued by both Piirainen (1997) and Rose and Haerpfer (1992).

In rural areas, the crucial form of household survival consists in the household economy because of the availability of land, which is a precondition of that type of household behaviour. The household economy is primarily a way of helping poor and elderly people to survive. We could say that it acts as a kind of social safety net in 'deinstitutionalising' countries where the official social safety net is not working properly. These are the most autonomous households, to a large extent outside of the money economy. In Romania, the household economy is of particular importance in this respect.

The cash economy and the formal economy are the most likely way to build up wealth at the household level. This is where the enterprising families are found. These are the most 'integrated' households (in Sik's typology) and so it seems that the cash economy is also a form of integration linked to the formal economy. The cash economy however, is particularly prevalent in particular countries, especially in Croatia and Serbia and in the CIS countries during the early transition period. This is perhaps an indication of the 'vicious spiral' of reform whereby entrepreneurial activity can gain little purchase in the formal economy (due to poor legislation and lack of institutionalization), and is therefore pushed into the cash economy. However, the unemployed, especially those without benefits, are also particularly active in the cash economy and so we could say that this is an alternative economic activity for those people. These are not necessarily the poorest people (Bedzir 2001). For poorer families it is the household economy that is most important. However, it does not seem to be such an important option for poorer families, which have high barriers to access the cash economy, much as they do in Western Europe (Pahl 1984).

The main participants in the social economy are young, single people living in cities and probably still family dependents. This does not seem to be an economy which can help most people. The cash economy, by contrast is mainly engaged in by more educated people, people in urban areas, those with larger households and those who are rather well off rather than the poor. The household economy, by contrast, operates perhaps as a safety net for the low income people in rural areas.

We can see that it is indeed the case that the more people there are in the formal economy, the less in the informal economies. However, it is the household economy that is most important in taking over, and under some circumstances, the cash economy. Some countries are evolving towards more and more integrated and formalized activities, other countries are going in the opposite direction.

There are also important differences between different countries. In the most successful transition countries, such as Czech Republic, Hungary, Slovenia, the informal economy, especially household production, seems to be declining and is gradually replaced by services provided in the formal economy. As these countries, evolve towards more 'normal' welfare capitalist societies, so they do less and less work for themselves and instead buy these services on the market. We could say that these are the 'reinstitutionalising' countries, because the economies and the welfare system are gearing themselves up to harmonize with the EU, incorporating more and more aspects of welfare and economic activity into the formal economy. However, in other countries where the transformation has rather changed things for the worse and where many households are plunged into steep poverty, unable to live from formal wages or benefits, the informal economy, especially in the form of the household economy, seems to increase its role. Such countries are Ukraine, Romania and Bulgaria. We could say that these are 'deinstitutionalising countries' because the institutional forms of welfare and economic activity are declining. Some have described this as the 'naturalization' of the economy with a retreat from formal, public life (Stănculescu 2001, Kovatcheva 2001). Thus, we could argue that in the former group of countries there is a virtuous spiral of higher state revenue, less regulatory burdens, and less informal economy, whilst in the latter group of countries there is a vicious spiral of lower state revenue, high regulatory burdens and taxation and an expanding informal economy.

Notes

1   An earlier version of this article appeared in the Österreichisches Zeitschrift für Soziologie and it forms part of a report to the European Bank for Reconstruction and Development.

2   The survey is based upon the questions designed by Richard Rose. However, in the above table, we have categorised them rather differently to him and also analysed them differently.

3   For the longitudinal survey component an analysis, of the New Democracies Barometer between 1992 and 1998 was carried out. This survey, organised by Christian Haerpfer and Richard Rose, involved face to face interviews with a random survey of 1000 people in each country in the years 1992, 1994, 1996, 1998. The regular New Democracies Barometer (NDB) surveys are undertaken by established national institutes regularly conducting nationwide representative surveys. All interviews are face-to-face. The basic sampling procedure in each country follows the ESOMAR principles of a multi-stage, random probability sample, in which the population is stratified regionally and with regions according to urban/rural divisions and town size. One hundred or more primary sampling points (PSU) are drawn. Within each PSU, individual respondents are chosen

on the basis of standard random procedures in the region (see Annex of Central and Eastern Eurobarometer Brussels, European Commission DGX No.9, March, 1996). Each national survey is checked for representativeness by gender, age, education, region and town size. Where appropriate, weights are introduced to match the sample to the census. In no case do weights produce major changes in the sample composition or responses. All the data reported here are for respondents aged 18 and upwards. In Croatia and FRY, the war zones are excluded from the sample.

4   Question wording: 'Which activity on this card is the most important for the standard of living of you and your family: Growing own food/ repairing house/ what we get as favours/ what we get with help of friends, relatives/ Getting foreign money/ Earnings of second job/incidental earnings/ earnings of regular job/ pension, unemployment benefit/ benefits at place of work/ don't know' The question was repeated for the second most important for the standard of living.

References

Agh, A. (1998), *The Politics of Central Europe*, ed. London, Thousand Oaks, New Delhi, Sage.

Bedzir, V. (2000), Migration from Ukraine to Central and Eastern Europe, in *Central Europe: New Migration Space*, edited by C. Wallace and D. Stola, London, Macmillans.

Duchene, G. and Neef, R. (coord.) (1998), *The Informal Economy in Romania. Final Report to the European Union*, ed. Paris, France, ROSES-CNRS, University of Paris 1.

Kovatcheva, S. (2001), *Households, Work and Flexibility in Bulgaria: literature review*, ed. Austria: www.hwf.at.

Mingione, E. (1994), 'Life strategies and social economies in the postfordist age', *International Journal of Urban and Regional Research*, 18, pp. 24-45.

Morawska, E. (1998), *The malleable homo sovieticus transnational entrepreneurs in post-communist East Europe*, Florence, European University Institute, EUI working papers of the Robert Schuman Centre.

Okolski, M. (2001), Incomplete migration: a new form of mobility in Central and Eastern Europe. The case of Polish and Ukrainian migrants, in *Patterns of Migration in Central Europe*, edited by C. Wallace and M. Stola, Basingstoke, Palgrave.

Pahl, R.E. (1984), *Divisions of Labour*, ed. Oxford, Blackwells.

Piirainen, T. (1997), *Towards a new social order in Russia. Transforming structures and everyday life*, ed. Aldershot, Sydney, Singapore, Dartmouth.

Rose, R. and Haerpfer, C.W. (1992), *New Democracies between State and Market*, University of Strathclyde, Centre for the Study of Public Policy.

Schneider, F. and Enste, D.H. (2000), 'Shadow Economies: size, causes, consequences' *Journal of Economic Literature*.

Sik, E. (1993), 'From the Second Economy to the Informal Economy', *Journal of Public Policy*, 12, pp. 153-175.

Sik, E. (1994), 'Network capital in capitalist, communist and post-communist societies' *International Contributions to Labour Studies*, 4, pp. 73-93.

Sik, E. (1995), Measuring the Unregistered Economy in Post-Communist Transformation. Vienna, Vienna Centre for European Welfare Research.

Stănculescu, M. (2001), *Households, Work and Flexibility in Romania: Literature Review*, ed. Austria: www.hwf.at.

Wallace, C. and Haerpfer, C.W. (1998), *Three Paths of Transition in Post-Communist Societies*, Institute of Advanced Studies, Vienna.

Wallace, C. and Haerpfer, C.W. (1999), 'Corruption and economic development in post-communist Central and Eastern Europe', *IHS Working Paper*.

Wallace, C., Shmulyar, O. and Bedzir, V. (1999), 'Investing in social capital: the case of small scale, cross-border traders in post-communist Central Europe', *International Journal of Urban and Regional Research,* 23, pp. 751-770.

Wallace, C. and Stola, D. (2001), *Patterns of Migration in Central Europe*, Basingstoke, Palgrave.

Wedel, J.R. (1992), *The Unplanned Society*, New York, Columbia University Press.

PART I
BULGARIA

Chapter 1

Bulgaria

Nikolay Nenovsky* and Darina Koleva**

The ten years of transition from planned to market economy in Bulgaria can be divided into two sub-periods. The boundary is the financial crisis of 1996-1997 that resulted in the introduction of a currency board (CB) in July 1997.[1] CB is not only a specific type of monetary regime, but also an institutional framework that imposed strong budget constraints on government, banks, firms and households.

1990-1996: stumbling reforms and accumulated imbalances

The Bulgarian economy's path was determined by two factors: first, the inherited initial economy's conditions during the end of the 80s (intensified CMEA integration, dependence on Soviet Union fuel deliveries and enormous external debt – 12 billion USD at the end of 1990) and second, the lack of vision for a comprehensive structural reform and permanent political hesitations. During the first years of transition, an institutional vacuum arose when new market institutions did not quickly offset the old institutional system break-up. A system of redistribution practices between different population groups was built in this vacuum framework. Liberalization, privatization and restructuring, the main tenets of transition, became the objects both of struggle between conflicting interests and the site of the struggle for economic power by various social groups (Olson, M. 1995). Although it is not correct to presume that the transition could be managed and deliberately

* University for National and World Economy, Department of Finance and Bulgarian National Bank, Research Department, Sofia. E-mail: Nenovsky.N@bnbank.org.
** University for National and World Economy, Department of Finance and Bulgarian National Bank, Research Department, Sofia. E-mail: Koleva.D@bnbank.org.

subordinated to a specific concept, all the same there was a room for comprehensive institutional policy.

The initial *price liberalization* took place in February 1991 and by the end of that year the inflation had reached 474%. This surge in prices was due, first of all, to the necessity of overcoming the artificially suppressed inflation and the so-called monetary overhang in order to bring the relative market prices into accordance to the economic relations. However, the subsequent administrative control over price-setting increased between 1992 and 1996 (especially the foods and essential commodities), resulting in market distortions (OECD 1999).[2]

Privatization was delayed. The land restitution launched in 1991 was very slow and in late 1996 only 18% of land properties were restored to their owners. In 1992, when the Law on Privatization was first passed and the Privatization Agency established, the share of the private sector in GDP was only 20% (agriculture not included). During the period of 1991 to 1997, only 20% of state assets were privatised (OECD 1999).[3] Small-scale privatization proceeded, particularly in trade, food processing and tourism, but no progress was made in privatizing large enterprises in heavy industry and manufacturing. The loss-making *state-owned enterprises* were subsidised directly by the banking system either through direct loans from the BNB or indirectly by issuing security bonds. The delay of privatization, the maintenance of inefficient productions and the transformation of loss into quasi-fiscal liability through money issuing mentioned above was in the interest of some groups of economic agents associated with the public sector and political authorities.[4] Though a full range of privatization methods was put into practice, as a whole the process of denationalization and creation of an efficient market were lagging behind.

The government was impeded by tax base contraction and low tax collection (tax revenues in % of the GDP declined from 50% in 1989 to 26.5% in 1996). This dynamics resulted in increased *external debt,* accounting to 243% of the GDP in late 1996.

The banking system and monetary policy were constitutionally implicated in this redistribution process. The loss-making state banks were totally dependent on conditions imposed by the government and state-owned enterprises. Newly created private banks issued non-performing loans as a result of the criminal lending and corruption practices and the lack of bank supervision. After all, the BNB was forced to save the banking system from collapse by refinancing, recapitalising and purchasing commercial banks.[5] There was no conscious monetary policy of the BNB, which, in the main tried to keep the interest rate level high. A run-off in foreign reserves resulted and foreign investment remained very low.[6]

Consequently, *the GDP* continued to decline until it reached the 1997 figure of 66,5% of its level in 1989, with the most severe drop between 1995 and 1997. This represents a fall of 17.1 percentage points (NSI 1999).[7] The *investments* slumped and in 1997 they made 13.9% of the GDP, which was only 55% of their level in 1991. Household consumption had been decreasing throughout, and savings declined from 60.3% of the GDP in 1990 to 19.2% in 1997.

Employment had decreased in 1997 to 72% of its level in 1989, and during the whole period registered unemployment made up 12-16% of the labour force (see data in the appendix). There are clear regional discrepancies[8] between both the capital and rest of the towns, on the one hand and between big towns and small towns/rural areas, on the other hand. Both can be understood as a consequence of the pre-1989 structure when small or middle towns depended on one or two industries. Meanwhile, the closure of large ineffective plants was the main factor behind the surge in unemployment in 1994, when it reached 16%. The process of impoverishment began and the small holdings and informal garage industries became the main source of household income.

The contraction of the *standard of living* in Bulgaria was accompanied by a rise in *income stratification*. According to IMF data[9], during the period 1989-1998, population impoverishment can be characterised as follows: among the employed, 44%; among pensioners, 54%; and in average for the whole population, 48% were living below the poverty line. In early 1997, about 36% of the population were living in poverty (World Bank, 1999). This means a serious rise in poverty in the years 1997 to 1998. For example, 63% of the people indicated that they could not afford to buy clothes and shoes. The *Gini coefficient,* measured by income per capita, rose from 23 in 1989 to 34 in 1993-1995 (Tanzi, V., G. Tsibouris 2000).[10] Growing income discrepancies could be considered as a normal consequence of market mechanisms, but the accumulation of wealth in a few hands and its appropriation for unproductive, respectively speculative stakes seems to be a Bulgarian particularity.

Putting the social assistance system into practice was one of the greatest challenges confronting the government. Until 1996, passive measures like unemployment benefits and social aid prevailed, whereas active ones like training courses, aimed at encouraging labour participation, have dominated since then. The accelerated social discontent resulted in large scaled strikes in the beginning of 1997, provoking new elections.

1997-2001: financial crisis, social problems and economic growth difficulties

The culminating point of this downward 'Bulgarian transition' was the financial crisis of late 1996 and early 1997.[11] The Bulgarian economy experienced a period of hyperinflation (prices rose 43% in January and soared 240% in February), depletion of foreign exchange reserves (to USD 440 million without monetary gold), closure of 14 banks that had held 25% of the consolidated balance sheet of the banking system and flight from the national currency (OECD 1999). Real output, which had grown in 1994 and 1995 for the first time since the start of reforms, contracted by more than 10% and foreign currency reserves declined to less than two months of imports (Gulde 1999).[12] There was a growing awareness of the need for *a new institutional framework* of the monetary regime and *a drastic change in monetary policy.*

After many *political uncertainties and discussions,* the socialist government was forced to accept a stabilization program – the 'CB' arrangement – in order to stop the vicious practice of continuously monetizing losses in the economy. The lev was fixed to the DM for *political considerations* in view of Bulgaria's long-term goal of joining the EU.

After functioning for almost four years after the CB was introduced, the Bulgarian economy underwent *definite structural changes* as a result of firm budget constraints imposed on the economic agents and particularly on the government. In late 2000, the share of private sector production in GDP was about 70%. The economic pattern of tendencies in recent years has changed: an obvious shrink in the share of agriculture sector can be observed, while the industry sector remains unaltered and the service sector experiences expansion (BNB 2000). The National Statistical Institute reported evident GDP growth during the last three years: 3.5% in 1998, 2.4% in 1999 and 5.8% in 2000 (NSI 1999).[13]

In recent years, the *state budget* has almost always been in balance, foreign debt was diminished, but the foreign debt burden remained heavy, making up approximately 84% of the GDP (at the end of 2000). Although some negative trends in *balance of payments* dynamics were observed recently, the foreign exchange reserves of Bulgaria have grown considerably – obvious evidence that Bulgaria is able to meet its current debt obligations.

The banking system is stable. Although the credit activity of the banks is slight, a process of a reorientation to the private sector, whose share in net domestic credit reached 67%, is taking place. Banks are liquid and well capitalised. The foreign capital inflow into the banking system is a source of additional stability and quality amelioration of banking activities. Financial markets development is lagging behind, but progress in this area can be expected with the development of investment intermediation, pension and health insurance funds, etc.

Two years of *low inflation* and months of deflation were followed by another rise in inflation in 2000 due to price level convergence with EU and outstripping price increases in services. Since 1997, *real income* increased (see the GDP per capita at PPP dynamics in the annex) as a result of price level and currency stabilization. The number of persons *employed* in the private sector increased from 779 thousands to 878 thousands in late 2000, but the *unemployment rate* reached a new maximum of 18% of the labour force as a direct consequence of the newly introduced monetary regime. After many amendments to the Labour Code, there is more room than before for legislative changes concerning labour market problems in general and real wages rigidity in particular. The inequality in personal income distribution rose sharply in 1999 and the Gini coefficient bounced from 25 to 43. The standard of living is one of the lowest in CEECs and there's still much to be done in the area of social policy.

The main challenge that the Bulgarian economy has faced since 1997 is the transition from a stage of financial stabilization to *sustainable growth*. Under circumstances of limited domestic financial resources, foreign investments are of crucial significance. Other important growth factors are bank-credits for business, high-technology production development as well as human capital investments.

The process of *EU integration* is also of significant importance for Bulgaria. Besides pre-accession funds, the EU can be viewed as an important stimulus for improving competitiveness and the restructuring of Bulgarian economy. And certainly the EU can 'import' a new institutional framework and new types of economic behaviour.

Notes

1   Technically a CB as a specific monetary system arrangement rejects all forms of monetary policy and relies on the automatic relationship between balance of payments dynamics and money supply. At a more disaggregated level this means that the domestic currency (levs) issuing is possible only if a corresponding foreign-exchange equivalent exists at the assets side of the CB's balance sheet.

2   The energy and most of the services prices were also held below their international standards level (Minassian, G., N. Nenovsky, 1998).

3   According to the results of an IMF study, the total index of Bulgarian economy restructuring during 1989-1994 is considerably lower than that of advanced CEECs. The total index for Hungary is 2.6, for Poland 2.4, and for Bulgaria only 1.4. In the next period

(1995-1997), the total index for Bulgaria increases to 4.1, while those for Hungary and Poland are 6.5 and 6.2 respectively (Fisher, S., R. Sahay, 2000).

4   See Koford, K., (2000) for a detailed survey of Bulgarian transition. He uses Mansur Olson's theoretical approach, which presents politicians and bureaucrats as different types of bandits. See also Frye, T., A. Shleifer (1996).

5   For more details concerning Bulgarian banking system see Caporale, G., and alii (2001).

6   During the period from 1989 until mid-2000, foreign direct investments were 162 USD per capita with 681 USD per capita in average for the CEECs in transition.

7   At the end of 1996, the GDP of Bulgaria was 25% of the average of OECD countries. At the same time, for example, the percentage of the GDP of the average level in OECD was 64% in the Czech Republic, 47% in Hungary and of 35% in Poland.

8   A detailed analysis of regional discrepancies is made in the Human Development Report by UNDP (2000), which presents for the first time the municipality index of human development with very low values in most of the regions.

9   It is worth mentioning that even today there are no consistent poverty statistics available, a sign of the lack of consistent national policy against poverty.

10 According to our own calculations (gross household income per capita approach) the Gini coefficients values are similar to the ones just mentioned. In the rest of the world in the same period the Gini coefficient developed as follows: it bounced from 24 to 48 in Russia, from 23 to 47 in Ukraine and increased smoothly from 21 to 23 in Hungary, from 23 to 28 in Poland and from 19 to 27 in Czech Republic.

11 A detailed and comprehensive description of this transition is provided by the Economic Commission for Europe (2000). For Bulgaria, see Gulde (1999), Nenovsky (1999), Mihov (1999), Miller (1999), Bristow (1996), etc.

12 Paradoxically, in the end of 1996 BNB extended a direct loan to the Ministry of Finance to the value of 18% of GDP in order to prevent eventual break in external debt service.

13 Gros and Mark (2000) in their empirical study of 'true' level of development of CEECs suggest that the 'potential' development level of Bulgaria and Baltic Countries 'should be quite substantially above what their low per capita GNP tells us'. This result can be regarded as an evidence for economy's hidden potential in 1996. While the statistical GNP per capita at PPP (USD) is a little bit more 4000 USD, the potential GNP per capita at PPP (USD) is quite more than 8000 USD.

References

BNB (2000), *Annual Report*, Bulgarian National Bank.

Bristow, J. (1996), *The Bulgarian Economy in Transition*, R.J. Hill (ed.), Edward Elgar, Cheltenham e.a.

Caporale, G., Miller, J., Hristov, K., Nenovsky, N. and Petrov, B. (2001), 'The Banking System in Bulgaria' in *Banking Reforms in South-East Europe*, Z. Sevic (ed.), Edward Elgar, Cheltenham.

Economic Commission for Europe (2000), *Economic Survey of Europe* vol. 3 (2/3), United Nations Publications, New York.

Fisher, S., R. Sahay (2000), The Transition Economies After Ten Years, *IMF Working Paper, WP/00/30.*

Frye, T., Shleifer, A. (1996), The Invisible Hand and the Grabbing Hand, *NBER Working Paper Series, WP 5856.*

Gros, D., Mark, S. (2000), *What is Special About Transition Economies?*, presented at EAST -WEST International Conference European Integration & Economies in Transition, organized by University of the Aegean and University of Crete, January 2000.

Gulde, A. (1999), The Role of the Currency Board in Bulgaria's Stabilization, *IMF Policy Discusion Paper, PDP/99/3.*

Koford, K., (2000), Citizen Restraints on 'Leviathan' government: Transition Politics in Bulgaria, *European Journal of Political Economy,* vol. 16, pp. 307-338.

Mihov, I. (1999), The Economic Transition in Bulgaria 1989-1999, forthcoming in *Transition: The First Decade,* M. Blejer and M. Skreb (editors), MIT Press, now available on http://faculty.insead.fr/mihov/Research.htm.

Miller, J. (1999), The Currency Board in Bulgaria: The First Two Years, *BNB Discussion Papers, DP/11/99.*

Minassian, G., Nenovsky, N. (1998), Curbing Inflation: The Case of Bulgaria, *Inflation and Unemployment in Economies in Transition, ACE-PHARE Project No. P95-2145-R.*

Nenovsky, N. (1999), Une économie en transition a-t-elle vraiment besoin d'une Banque centrale? La Caisse d'émission en Bulgarie, *Revue d'études comparatives Est-Ouest,* vol. 30, no. 4, pp. 65-96.

NSI (1999), *Bulgaria. Main Macroeconomic Indicators*, National Statistical Institute.

Olson, M. (1995), Why the Transition from Communism is so Difficult, *Eastern Economic Journal no. 21,* pp. 437-462.

OECD (1999), *Economic Survey of Bulgaria.*

Tanzi, V., G. Tsibouris (2000), Fiscal Reform over Ten Years of Transition, *IMF Working Paper, WP/00/113.*

The World Bank Staff (1999), *Bulgaria, Poverty During the Transition*, June 7, Report no 18411, http://www.worldbank.bg/data/poverty.phtml.

UNDP (2000), *Bulgaria 2000, Human Development Report. The Municipalities Mosaic.*

Chapter 2

The informal economy in Bulgaria: historical background and present situation

Tania Chavdarova[*]

The key to understanding the specificity of the informal economy in Bulgaria is the historically shaped contradiction between formal social relations and personal relations, between formal and informal institutions. In this paper I try to do the following: (1) elaborate theoretically the concept of the informal economy specific to the post-communist period using the example of Bulgaria; (2) trace historically the contradiction between the formal and informal economies; and (3) delineate the major directions in the development of the informal economy during the last ten years of social transformation in Bulgaria.

The concept of the informal economy

In elaborating the concept of the informal economy, the definition of institution proposed by Mary Douglas (1986) is taken as a starting point. She distinguishes between two levels that constitute the institution. The first one embraces the conventions or rules that establish the structure of order. People are not deeply bound to them, which demands considerable control over their observance. Norms and value attitudes regarding the right course of action and behaviour that are deeply rooted in the national cosmology constitute the second level. They attach to action a feeling of mutuality and weight, are followed by tradition and are passed down to new members (Douglas 1986). The definition of formal and informal institutions is derived

[*] Associate professor at the Department of Sociology, University of Sofia 'St. Kliment Ohridski', 125, Tzarigradsko Shosse Blvd., Bl. 4, 1114 Sofia, Bulgaria. E-mail: tania@sclg.uni-sofia.bg.z.

from this distinction. Conventions and rules embody not just the formal level of each institution, but more abstractly could be defined as the formal institution itself. Respectively, the norms and values that govern action represent the essence of informal institutions.

This conventions vs. values distinction, related to the economy as a separate sphere of social action, will lead to the conclusion that the formal economy embraces all economic activities that are governed by legislative rules and the economic policy's arrangements. Consequently, they are recorded by the formal measurement and accounting system in society. The informal economy consists of those economic activities that are governed by the shared norms and values in a given group or community and do not stick to the official economic conventions in society. Hence, the informal economy is one that is not registered. Equally unregistered are criminal economic activities, but, in contrast to the informal ones, they are performed explicitly against the accepted rules and conventions and their final product is forbidden (Castells and Portes 1989: 14).

Thus, alongside the official (regular) economy and the officially recognized illegal (criminal) economy, the informal economy is a third part of economic space. In defining it, I begin with the typology described by Stuart Henry (1981: 7) and try to adapt it to the current Bulgarian situation (see Table 2.1). Stuart Henry distinguishes between informal economies according to the degree to which they are *integral* or an *alternative* to official institutions and according to their *legal* vs. *illegal* status (ibid.: 6 ff).

There are two kinds of *legal* informal economies. The alternative informal economy, called the *social economy*, consists of domestic production (food, clothing, etc.). It also includes the social exchange of products and labour in personal networks. The integrated *non-official economy* would encompass all those activities that occur within official institutional settings, but that are not officially recognised as part of these institutions. Volunteer labour is one such instance. In the Bulgarian transformation period, these are primarily the unpaid family workers who work without social insurance.[1] Unofficial activities and practices that are *illegal* and integrated constitute a separate economy called the *hidden economy*. It is composed mainly of transactions and not of work activities. For the hidden economy in Bulgaria, the most widespread of these activities are hidden privatization, corruption and tax evasion (see Chavdarova 2001a).

A problem with distinguishing between hidden and *black economies* appears in the Bulgarian case and probably in all transformation countries. There are plenty of cases in which the conditions of the written labour contract do not correspond to the real working conditions, particularly to the payment terms and working time. Companies might declare official wages lower

Table 2.1   Legal and illegal informal activities

Legal

Official	Integrated	Alternative	
REGULAR	**NON-OFFICIAL**	**SOCIAL**	
(Formal)		**DOMESTIC**	**COMMUNAL**
	Unpaid family		
Regular, official	workers;	Domestic production	Social exchange of
employment	volunteer labour	for own consumption	products and labour

Illegal

Official	Integrated	Alternative	
	Transactions	Non-regulated work	
CRIMINAL	**HIDDEN**	**NON-REGULATED**	**BLACK (Underground)**
Mafia and	Hidden		
racketeering;	privatisation;	Employment on a	Employment and
criminalisation of	corruption; tax	non-labour or fake	self-employment
the economy	evasion	labour contract	without any contract

than the real ones. In this way, a part of the newly created income of the enterprises in not declared officially. A modification of the latter is hiring people to perform a particular job by a civil contract. Their work is at least partly non-regulated, which is different from black work. Black and non-regulated work are both – fully or partly – socially unprotected and not subject to social regulations. Non-regulated work differs from hidden transactions in that it is productive, and from black work by being integrated in the official institutional framework. Black work, in contrast, is an alternative activity.

A detailed view of the types of production and exchange that characterise the different informal economies shows other essential distinctions (see Table 2.2). In terms of production, informal economies are very heterogeneous. They vary from in kind economies to market economies. In terms of exchange, more features are held in common. They all rely – to different degrees – on networks where respect, loyalty and social position are exchanged or even traded. Despite the different types of production, reciprocity dominates as an exchange mode in all kinds of informal economies. This has to do with the fact that all informal institutions are governed by norms and values shared within a certain community.

Table 2.2 **Informal economies according to the type of production and exchange**

Economies	Production	Exchange		
		Exchange mode	Means	Network type
Non-official	Social	Reciprocal, social	Respect, authority	Loose network, common ideas
Social	In kind	Reciprocal, social	Respect, loyalty, barter	Family, relatives, friends, neighbours
Hidden	Market integrated but not productive	Redistributional, reciprocal	Social position, trust, money, barter	Chain of commercialised personal connections
Non-regulated Black	Market	Market, reciprocal	Money, barter, trust	Personal connections; family, relatives, friends

Reciprocity turns out to be the most essential feature of informal economic institutions. In the following section, I shall try to show that reciprocity as a mode of economic integration has deep roots in Bulgarian history, with the consequence that a contradiction between formal and informal institutions has been continuously reproduced. Hence, the informal economic institutions have played a decisive role in shaping the long-run path of Bulgarian socio-economic development. It is through path-dependency in the process of institutional change[2] that the sustained preferences for informal forms of associations and co-operation in the Bulgarian society can be explained.

The formality – informality contradiction in Bulgarian history

Theoretical framework

Mary Douglas' definition of institution implicitly assumes that there is no contradiction between its two levels, i.e. between conventions and rules vs. values and norms. This might hold true of the Western institutions as an ideal type. With respect to Bulgaria, this is questionable, even though – or perhaps exactly because of this – the Western models have been referential ones throughout Bulgarian history. In the Bulgarian case, there is a historically determined discrepancy between conventions and rules embodied in official institutions, usually imposed from the outside, on the one side and norms and values expressing the historically shaped Bulgarian traditional culture, on the other side. A distinct and important contradiction between formal and informal appeared. *Formal* presupposes abstract public rules linked with 'imported' modern institutions. Formal rules are perceived as alien to the traditional culture and *artificial,* in the sense that they are not organically engendered in society, and hence, they are not seen as trustworthy. *Informal,* in contrast, is perceived as *natural.* It consists of viable norms and values that govern face-to-face relationships.

Table 2.3   Theoretical framework

Integrative patterns	Dominant patterns of economic organisation	Dominant social structures	Dominant economic actors
Reciprocity	Interpersonal networks	Informal communities, clans	Community
Redistribution	Hierarchical formal organisations	Bureaucracy	The state, other central authorities
Market exchange	Freely established formal organisations	Associations of free individuals	Individuals

In terms of the economy, the dichotomy formal vs. informal could be expressed through the relationship between the different basic patterns of economic integration that allow a description of the fundamental characteristics of each economic system. Here I follow Polanyi's differentiation between *reciprocity, redistribution* and *market exchange* as such integration modes. According to Polanyi, *reciprocity* indicates the relationship between some symmetrical groups, in which the mechanisms of social obligation, loyalty and acknowledgement are in place. Reciprocity provides the basis of the social economy, which is embedded in certain traditions and social norms. Whereas reciprocity implies a pattern of symmetry, *redistribution* is bound to the pattern of centricity: the economic processes flow towards or from a certain centre (Polanyi 1965: 48-9). Here, the economic interaction is characterised by the dominance of a distinct authority. *Market exchange* ensures the dispersion of economic power among all participants in the transactions. Typically, they are profit maximisers and the exchange between them is governed by price-dominated bargaining.[3] Thus, reciprocity assumes a symmetric system of grouping, while redistribution implies some form of centricity, and free market exchange a system of market price formation.[4] All these economic modes have their place and can be found in every society. The socio-economic specifics come from the way they are combined and relate to each other in particular historical periods. The integration modes are also important determinants of the economic organizations and their historical change (see Table 2.3).

Reciprocity is the only integrative mode in which the rules and conventions (the formal side of each institution) and the norms, values and beliefs (the informal side) overlap. Each economic action, as linked to reciprocity, is dominated by the principle of adequate response and has validity within the community (family, neighbourhood, relatives, friends, colleagues, etc.). Redistribution and market exchange presuppose a specific process of formalization of economic organizations that gives conventions and values relative autonomy.

The discrepancy between formal and informal institutions in the Bulgarian case takes on the form of a specific constellation of reciprocity, redistribution and free market exchange throughout Bulgarian history. Reciprocity preserves its essential role by either subjugating or penetrating redistribution and the market.

Formality vs. informality in the periods of radical change in modern Bulgarian history

One of main explanations for the formal-informal discrepancy is related to the *incremental alienation from the state*. Bulgaria was subject to foreign rule for long periods of time since it came into being in 681: the Byzantine Empire (1014-1185), the Ottoman Empire (1396-1878) and Russian dominance during socialism (1944-1989). Even after liberation from the Ottoman Empire in 1878, a foreign king dynasty governed the nation-state until 1944. Bulgarians have been treated as 'second hand people' by foreign dominion (Paunov 1996: 203). As a result, they developed an unstable and ambivalent national self-consciousness. The self-underestimation has often lead to non-critical acceptance of foreign, especially Western, models of organization and behaviour. This goes hand in glove with the self-overestimation tendencies that counteract the vulnerable sense of national identity (Genchev 1987). Informality, networks of personal relations, turned out to be the shelter for personal salvation and self-confirmation.

The formal-informal clash also has a *religious background*. It has its roots in the influential dualistic heresy *Bogomilism*[5] that was widely spread in the 10th century and thereafter, remarkably at the time when the Bulgarian state covered the largest territory in its history and Bulgarian culture flourished. *Bogomilism* thought that there are two worlds in constant struggle: the lord of bad forces created the real visible world, and the lord of good forces created the invisible one. *Bogomilism* rejected the real visible world and, in particular, the need for church procedure, respect for icons, the church itself, wealth, power in all its forms, and all earthly rituals. This is one of the sources of the Bulgarian *disrespect of any kind of hierarchy, formal authority or power*[6] and of the efforts to outwit people in such positions. Further, Eastern Orthodox religion softened nihilism and engendered a kind of sceptical worldview.

The period of the Ottoman Empire (1396-1878)

As part of the Ottoman Empire, Bulgarian society was of a traditional peasant non-market type, marked above all by insecurity. As Polanyi points out, reciprocity and redistribution coexist in non-market societies. Reciprocity is the most powerful mode of integration when it dominates redistribution and the market (Polanyi 1992: 37). In the period under consideration, *reciprocity and redistribution coexisted without being subordinated to each other.*

The redistributive mode of economic integration was at the core of the Ottoman Empire. It manifested itself most clearly in the property and taxation systems. There was no private property in the Ottoman Empire. The Sultan was the owner of all land that he distributed on the basis of standardised holdings via the courts in each territorial commune. Later, in the 17th century, the Sultan started distributing plots of land to some members of the upper social strata *(asceri)*, which had no Bulgarian representatives, as a reward for special services rendered. Nonetheless, he retained the right to take them away whenever he wished. In order to preserve these as their private property, subjects took advantage of a specific Ottoman regulation.[7] As a result, a kind of *hidden private property system* was created in the 17th century. The lack of inheritance rights was a specific feature of the Ottoman Empire (the *prebend system*), which was the main source of hidden economic transactions and corruption in the Ottoman Empire (Inalcik and Quataert 1994).

The taxation system was organised on a basis of the number of plots of land distributed and not on the social unit (individual or family). Although the nuclear family and even the individual were responsible for paying taxes, factually all economic activities were shared within the framework of the extended family, which was patriarchally organised on a household basis. 'Norms of reciprocity' were socially institutionalised within extended families and between them in the frame of the neighbourhood and the peasant commune (Grosdanova 1979). The reciprocal exchange of labour was both an existential and an ethical imperative. Even poor peasants shared their resources with their neighbours and other communities, knowing that help from them would likely be needed at another time. There was 'little scope for the profit maximising calculus of neo-classical economics' (Scott 1976: 4).

There was a specific type of the extended family, existing not only in that period, but also earlier in medieval Bulgaria, the *zadruga*.[8] It was distinct by virtue of involving collective ownership, collective property disposal, collective work and consumption, and collective responsibility for all its members. Collectivism, solidarity and economic equality are its basic features, conveying the symmetry needed for reciprocity to operate. In contrast to the *zadruga*, family structure in other types of extended families was such that the leader was the sole owner of the household's property and his role in making economic decisions was much stronger than in the *zadruga*. Respectively, the strict hierarchy of personal relations reduces the scope of reciprocity.

Bulgarian economic life was deeply embedded in community structures and followed customary law. Ottoman legislation provided a formal economic framework, but everyday economic life was determined by the informal rules of Bulgarian habits. It seems that formal and informal rules did not coincide. They operated at different levels, those of command and of social economy, and reflected different integration forms, those of redistribution and of reciprocity.

Some market development had already taken place prior to liberation from the Ottoman Empire. Bulgarian producers had begun taking advantage of the huge market of the Ottoman Empire. The act of Liberation resulting from the Russian-Turkish war of 1878 and the establishment of a new nation state radically interrupted this smooth process of shaping market mechanisms and capital accumulation (Hadzhijski 1974). The nation state was established in the form of administrative-bureaucratic structures before the emergence of the nation itself. This is a typical feature of the historical development of nations in East Central Europe that contrasts with the development process in Western societies (Seligman and Füzer 1994: 197).

The first capitalist period (1878-1944)

The beginning of capitalism in Bulgaria was marked by a sharp renunciation of traditional values and by the detachment of the nuclear family as an economic community from the extended family. Given the scarcity of private capital in the context of economic backwardness and poverty of the country as a whole, private capital could rely only on state capital. Thus, at the very beginning of capitalist development in Bulgaria, the state occupied a strategic redistributive position in the economy. Conceiving of the state as something 'foreign', business strategy consisted of devising means for 'clandestinely improving the terms of exchange...while avoiding open confrontations' (Scott 1976: 231). The economic actors' personal dependence on the political factor shaped the new economic ethics of prosperity. It allowed, tolerated and even required informal contacts and connections with political figures in the form of patron-client relationships.[9]

The patron-client relationship was also a reaction to the absence of any conditions for replacing the personalised trust between contracting parties with *systemic trust* (Luhmann 1982) or *faceless commitments* (Giddens 1990). Given the unstable and, to a certain degree, contradictory nature of legislative reforms, some special measures to ensure a contract's execution and avoid fraud had to be taken. The lack of trust in the public domain was compensated for chiefly by creating personal networks in order to mediate both between the individuals and between them and formal institutions (see Chavdarova 2001c).

Economic behaviour was marked by this specific *network rationality*. It was different from that of Western rationality (see Münch 1993) because it presupposed that actors decline to enter into impersonal economic transactions. One of the consequences was that competition became group competition (Hirschleifer 1982). Community-like economic groupings developed that used social proximity and common cultural identity as social capital, with the purpose of providing personal knowledge about potential trade partners and thus guaranteeing their loyalty.

Economic transactions included whole networks, which lowered transaction costs. The kin-based networks were gradually enriched and complemented with friendship, neighbours and colleagues-based networks. In sum, all possible informal networks were mobilised as part of the strategy for profit seeking.

Informal networks were not only an economic resource like in the preceding historical period, but took on the functions of *capital*. In these groupings, trust is not just a characteristic of personal relations, but also a subclass of risk (see Luhmann 1988, Coleman 1990). In the case in which a network is built upon functional substitutes of trust, it is profit-oriented and return-sensitive. The very access to such networks is permitted based on the candidate's capability to contribute to the profit. These networks can also be treated as capital because they are subjects of reinvestment and accumulation.[10] Because informal networks became an organizational principle of social action, success was regarded as the result of the whole network rather than that of an individual's action. Because there was no functioning market, in which the private and public sphere would have become obvious, individualism did not develop[11] (see Bahrdt 1974: 59 ff). In Bulgaria after liberation from the Ottoman Empire, the market remained subordinate to the political sphere. This gave birth to another type of social integration. The economic actors in the market were not treated as equals and there was no dispersion of economic power. Protectionism and informal power relations dominated. That was why the domain of formal relations was hostile to the individual and why individuals developed a kind of self-defence *by playing tricks*.[12] What appeared as inconceivable to the Western mind (the mixture of the public and private) seemed quite natural to a Bulgarian. The historical constellations prevented the thorough development of individualism in a modern sense. Other individuals' well-being (material or otherwise) was assumed primarily to be the result of personal connections rather than the consequence of the *worthiness* of their own personality.

Even in the best periods for private capital, the state maintained its extraordinary role in the economy. The 70 years of capitalist development could not consolidate free market exchange as the dominant mode of economic integration. The infiltration of redistribution and reciprocity into market mechanisms did not permit this. The specific features of the first capitalist period are concentrated in *the overlapping processes of the official institutionalization of market exchange and the unofficial re-institutionalization of reciprocity and redistribution.*

Socialism (1944-1989)

Socialism has generally been seen as a period of breakdown. The focus has been primarily on its opposition to the advanced capitalist societies. In this paper, socialism is considered as a period of *historical mediation* between the first capitalist period in Bulgaria and its rebirth after 1989.

In the context of the broader historical process of change in the dominant integration mode (from reciprocity through redistribution towards free market exchange), state socialism represents a sort of turning back to redistribution. Here it is the intertwined state and communist party's institutions that built up the redistributive centre. The highly developed division of labour under state socialism naturally required complete dominance on the market. The destruction of the market via the totality of redistribution principles turned the former relatively sovereign economy into politicised territory.

Were market exchange principles really destroyed under socialism? It could be argued that within the framework of socialist structures, market mechanisms functioned as informal structures. The officially forbidden market shaped its own 'second economy', which was parallel to the official one and had multidimensional relations with it – 'driven out the door, they came in through the window'. While the informal economies in advanced capitalist states aimed at profit maximization, thus *complementing* the official economy, the second economy under socialism had *compensatory* functions. It oiled the wheels of an 'economy of shortage' (Kornai 1980).[13] These two economies needed each other to survive. Endless bureaucratic obstacles to the production processes made the second economy flourish even more. The greater the number of regulations, the greater the opportunity for the second economy.

The total elimination of civil society and the social atomization re-affirmed individuals' communal identities (in circles of family, relatives and friends). Given the lack of impersonal trust under socialism, the only way to keep society together was to strengthen personal ties.[14] Thus, reciprocity as a historically established way of confirming trust, loyalty and social recognition, preserved its significance in the socialist era. It created at least minimal certainty and provided a cognitive and expectational map that made social interaction beyond circles of kinship and friendship possible. As the second economy, governed by the market, reciprocity also took on the function of partially *compensating* for the deficits that the command economy constantly produced.

Market exchange principles that were not permitted, but that were, as already mentioned, required by the level of industrialization, infiltrated the area of reciprocity. Thus, social recognition and loyalty became mainly a subject of instrumental economic interest. The state's domination in the public sphere generated a market in the private sphere. *A market of personal connections* was developed (Chavdarova 2000). Personal ties were exchanged and accumulated as capital that produced profit. In this way, the informal network became more strongly commercialised than in previous periods.

The social integrity of economic man came from 'token' institutional behaviour: the norms of representation were preserved, but not necessarily accepted[15] (Bahrdt 1974). The leading feature of this token behaviour was evasion, the outwitting of the formal institutions as a prosperity strategy. The attitude of individuals to take from society without giving, morally justified by the illegitimacy of socialist institutions, extended into a disregard for others in person-to-person relationships and a game to outwit those who did not belong to a particular community-like circle. Thus, the idea of the morally autonomous person and the modern values of individual rights remained exterior and alien in Bulgaria's pre-transformation era. Such behaviour legitimised the informal network of human relations as a vehicle and a real regulator of social life.

In conclusion, the paths of history embedded strong communitarism and particularism in social relations. *Informality* appeared to be the key organizational principle of society along with the coinciding principles of *action in networks and rejection of authority*.

The informal economy during the transformation period

Reciprocity and redistribution as disintegrative mechanisms in economy

As the irrationality of socialist planning became increasingly obvious, some market developments were brought about in the 80s. A number of second economy activities were legalised.[16] At the same time, capital started to be exported in the legal form of joint-stock companies with foreign participation under the control of the secret services.[17] In 1989, the process of capital export gained legitimacy and was intensified.

From this standpoint, the events of 1989 did not interrupt the previous developments. Redistribution in harmony with reciprocity continued to play the predominant role. *Yet,* in another sense, a critical discontinuity took place: the socialist redistributive institutions disintegrated and an institutional gap was created. The political change in 1989 was not a result of any inherent processes of ripening; it was rather caused by external circumstances. The *lack of incremental institutional change* (North 1990) is expected to cause *incremental structural deformations.* The combination of reciprocity and redistribution does not contribute any more to economic integration but takes on *disintegrative forms.*

Reciprocity preserved its cohesive strength at a micro-level within the frame of particular groupings. The personal bonds and loyalties that had been passed on for generations led to a situation in which economic 'wars' between some clan-like groupings begun about control over the plundering of particular economic institutions. The former political and economic *nomenklatura* and its offspring, the secret service networks, those of 'newcomers' in the power elite, and certain criminal networks ('wrestlers') could be deemed the most vital reciprocal groupings. Besides, for the new political anti-communist elite which emerged as poor as everybody else, political power has become the only source of individual enrichment. Thus, it is in the interest not only of the old, but also of the new political elite that the state functions as a 'political capitalist'.

As in the first capitalist period, the absence of private capital and a proper credit policy for small businesses turned the decapitalization of the state into the only way of private capital accumulation. Patron-client relations reappear and influence private businesses from their inception. In the sphere of politics, this leads to a new power oligarchy. In the sphere of the economy, it stimulates hidden privatization: illegal transferring of income and capital from state enterprises to the private sector.[18] It functions as a vicious circle: the private sector is strengthened at the expense of the state, the state transfers its losses to the population, and the population at large does its best to minimise them. One small group of the population is getting richer at the expense of the majority of the people who are getting poorer,[19] provided the level of wealth in society remains relatively constant.

At present, reciprocity mainly serves this process of redistribution of national wealth that is causing the *disintegration of the economy* at large. Under the conditions of a weak civil society, it leads to the gradual *disintegration of citizenship*. One of the symptoms is the lack of a consistently implemented program for introducing market principles.[20] Another symptom is the extraordinarily high crime rate, especially among teenagers. The crimes mark a desire to share in the on-going hidden redistribution, and, in this sense, it is an important part of it. Another strong piece of evidence is the introduction of a currency board (see Koleva/Nenovsky, in this volume). Perhaps the most emblematic symptom is the deep moral disorientation.[21] Faced with the reality of crime, poverty, unemployment and social disorder, the initial enthusiasm of the early 90s was fully exhausted and turned into an anomic state, in which commonly shared conventions and norms that kept society together began to disappear. These structural and value changes illustrate the failure of market institutionalization so far. They appear to be a result of the special disintegrative link between reciprocity and redistribution.

The informal economy: a central aspect of the economic and social dynamics in Bulgaria

Mainstream economists argue that an institutional vacuum can be found in Eastern Europe today. Indeed, a workable institutional framework which could enforce the market mechanisms in Bulgaria is still missing. Because of this, informal institutions are filling up the formal institutional gap. The informal economy turned out to be a central aspect of economic and social dynamics; it is at the core of Bulgarian society today, as is typical in less-developed countries (Portes, Castells, and Benton 1989).

Whereas the official GDP decreased constantly to 66.5% (1996) of its niveau in 1989, the shadow economy in Bulgaria has increased. Estimations show wild discrepancies, but all of them mark peaks in the early nineties and in the mid-nineties, esp. in 1996.[22] The following results were presented by Kyle e.a. (2000), who studied the whole period: the absolute peaks were in 1990 with 32.2% and 1996 with 34.4%. After the introduction of the currency board on July 1, 1997, a macroeconomic stabilization and accompanying price and trade liberalization took place. Consequently, the shadow economy has shrunk since 1997-1998. According to Kyle e.a., the shadow economy decreased by one-third to 21.9% in 1998. Thus, the increases of the shadow economy and the GDP are negatively correlated.

The informal economy, however, does not shrink to an equal degree in all its parts. The *hidden economy*, composed in the Bulgarian case of corruption, hidden privatization and tax evasion, seems to have shrunk since 1997. Corruption is the main technique for avoiding taxation. Due to high taxes and duties, entrepreneurs often officially document lower costs.[23] The introduction of the currency board marked a steady rise in tax revenues to the GDP that resulted in a stable improvement of Bulgaria's placement in the *Corruption Perceptions Index (CPI)*: from 66th to 47th place in the period of 1998-2001[24] (Transparency International 2001). Yet, it seems that in case of Bulgaria, the CPI reflects not as much the real fall in corruptive practices, but more the process of macro-economic stabilization that made the socio-economic situation more accountable.

The falling tendency concerns the *social economy* development as well. The domestic[25] and communal economies have always been widespread in Bulgaria. During the transformation period, the in kind production increased on a breath-taking scale. Representative survey data from 1999 show that about 36% of the population do not go to the market for basic consumer goods (Rajchev et al. 1999). One-third of the population produces at least half of the food that it consumes.[26] In the period 1990-1996, the share of the in kind production in the total household income gradually increased from 14.4% to 27.6% (NSI 2000). Since then, the respective share declined (17.7% in 1999; ibid.; see also Wallace and Haerpfer in this volume).

The pattern of development of the *non-regulated and black activities* is difficult to estimate. The World Bank 1995 estimations show that 8.5% of the active population was employed in the black economy in 1995. According to the data gathered by a national survey in 1996, 6.8% of the respondents openly admitted that they work without any contract and social insurance (Hristoskov et al. 1996: 13). In 2001, according to the NSI, these responses still made up 6.1% (Chavdarova 2001b). According to another non-representative inquiry among small and medium-size businesses in Bulgaria, the number of the employed without contract made up only 2.2% in 1998, but had grown by one-fifth by 1999 (Kyle et al. 2000: 44). Working on a fake labour contract is a much more common and significant way to flourish in the informal sector of the economy. Its share is relatively high – 22% of all contracts, according to the 1996 national survey. In 1999, nearly two-thirds of the managers in a survey believed that it is a common practice for most firms.[27] Black work is mostly spread in agriculture and trade, in villages and small towns. It is to be found in the co-operatives and private firms only, not in state-owned firms. The cases of working on a fake labour contract are mostly typical for trade and construction and for regional centres and private firms (ibid.: 45-50).

The processes of macro-economic stabilization succeeded only partially in offsetting the informal economies, as the administrative and tax burdens, the legislative inconsistency and the burden of the permissions have remained incentives for informal business. The drastic impoverishment and the high unemployment still encourage people to work in domestic and black economies. Although the firms and individuals benefit from informal operations, on the macro level the total effect of the informal economy on the economic development of Bulgaria is rather negative. It weakens national competitiveness, slows down the economic growth, prevents the enforcement of economic policy and the proper functioning of market forces. In sum, the economic disintegration that took place before 1997 is still not overcome.

In regard to social dynamics, due to its heterogeneity, the informal economy plays various roles in shaping the new social inequality and the new institutional order. On the one hand, it has the potential to cope with poverty or to increase well-being on micro level, and on the macro level it can absorb unemployment and create its own social order. On the other hand, it contributes to increasing social inequalities. This is especially true for the illegal *hidden economy* as opposed to the black and social economies. On the micro level, the hidden economy turned to be the most successful profit – and rent-seeking strategy. Respectively, those involved in it – mainly entrepreneurs, politicians and state administrators – were able to rapidly change their socio-economic status. However, in Bulgaria there is no reliable data for determining the incomes and economic power of socio-economic groups participating in the hidden economy (for Romania see Ilie in this volume). On the macro level, the enormous pervasiveness of the hidden economy has blurred the border between the state and private economies, and the private sector has penetrated the state economy.

The role of the social, non-regulated and black economies appears to differ greatly from the hidden economy. They all represent a sort of a survival strategy for the individuals. For those people who rely exclusively on in kind production or non-cash economy for their existence, the market economy is an imaginary concept. The *domestic economy* – in Latin American style – has turned out to be a source of hidden wage labour, which is a spontaneous solution to the unemployment and poverty problem. However, the domestic economy cannot bring any dynamics into the economic development. On the contrary, it mirrors the reality of the enormous tightening of the market forces and the shift towards in kind economy, regardless of the claims that a transition to market economy is taking place.

The *non-regulated and black economies* form another part of 'marginal society'. First of all, the black or non-regularly employed workers have only *one job*, are as a rule underpaid and work without social protection. Thus, they form the labour market periphery. The moonlighters, who have a second (typically non-regulated) job, and, to some extent, the informal self-employed, receive as a rule higher incomes compared to the non-regularly employed, and their participation in the non-regulated economy is not a matter of survival, but of accumulation. The moonlighters are in the best position, being socially insured at their first job, whereas the informally self-employed are very vulnerable in this respect.

In the short run, the non-regulated employment can absorb the high unemployment, soften poverty and thus decrease social tensions in society. In the long run, however, it undermines the labour legislation and social policy measures and creates labour relations associated with the darkest side of the 'wild' capitalism.

During the last ten years, the old cultural codes of economic behaviour, discussed in the second part, have been reproduced in that patron-client relationships, and networks based on reciprocity play a dominant role. Non-individualistic rationality was reinforced. It was determined either by the subsistence ethics and its 'non-maximising' patterns of action (i.e. by the social economy) or by the profit – and rent seeking via networks (i.e. by the monetised types of informal economy). The entrepreneurs who operate in the latter could be defined by their ability to develop a perfect sense of detecting and using legislative imperfections. There are new actors on the economic scene, but no new economic rationality has been institutionalised. Thus, the rebirth of capitalism takes on a re-creation of modes of socio-economic action genetically imprinted in the Bulgarian economy.

In conclusion

The market economy in Bulgaria during the first capitalist period was specifically embedded in redistributive and reciprocity mechanisms. Redistribution, as the main integrative form in communist society, led to the complete intertwining of economy and politics. At present, under the circumstances of the deep economic crisis and social anomie during the last ten years, the officially introduced market framework still does not function properly. Redistribution and reciprocity preserve their role, even though they no longer function as integrative forces. Strengthening them has made particular social groups winners; but, on the other side, it has led to a 'negative' integration of the economic system and brought about an erosion of citizenship.

One of the most serious problems for Bulgarian development is the disembeddedness from the formal normative regulation. Historically, formal legislation never had a chance to develop from indigenous customary law.

The legal system has always been either borrowed or imposed. From this point of view, the informal economy indicates the incompatibility of rules and everyday practices. The multiple forms of illegal informality in particular operate in 'no man's land', between the official principles and rules of public behaviour on the one hand, and the practices of 'invisible' control over the resources of Bulgarian society, established by tradition or unspoken public agreement, on the other. This no man's land is where an illegitimate redistribution of power and wealth is taking place.

The state and civil society are mutually responsible for the establishment of fair and realistic rules of institutional behaviour. Yet, the informal economy in Bulgaria during the last ten years has produced social and institutional deformations that cannot be cured simply by direct social and economic policy measures. Reducing informality seems to be a long-lasting process, the core of which is the improvement of institutional performance. This would provide incentives to entrepreneurs and citizens after years of misery and despair.

Notes

1   The National Statistical Institute categorizes unpaid family workers as 'persons who work without pay in an enterprise or farm owned and operated by a related person living in the same household' (NSI 2000: 15). There is no legislative requirement for the unpaid family workers to be socially insured. Because this category is very small (1.2% of the active population in 1999-2000) and as volunteer labour is almost non-existent in Bulgaria (Chavdarova 2001b: 176), the non-official economy will not be considered in this paper.

2   The model of path-dependence is formulated by D. North as follows: 'Path-dependence means that history matters. We cannot understand today's choices without tracing the incremental evolution of institutions. If, however, the foregoing story sounds like an inevitable foreordained account, it should not. At every step along the way there were choices – political and economic – that provided real alternatives' (North 1990: 98).

3   'The market economy implies a self-regulating system of markets...capable of organizing the whole of economic life without outside help or interference' (Polanyi 1965).

4   Polanyi's emphasis is on the process of expropriation of material resources: whether it is carried out as a social exchange, as a disposition with the recourses by a particular centre, as their passing on by virtue of law and custom, or finally as transactions between equal actors (Polanyi 1992: 33).

5   After the name of the Bulgarian priest Bogomil.

6   The country's small size contributes to the high personification of formal relations.

7   According to this regulation, if the land given as a reward was donated to a religious or other kind of institution, these could claim property rights over it. The *asceri* thus rewarded donated the land under the condition that they would govern it on behalf of the institution, and that after their death, this right would pass to their offspring.

8 The *zadruga* or kin commune was a typical unit of Slavonic tribes. In Bulgaria, in the period under consideration, it was comparatively weaker and was concerned with stock-breeding.

9 Various techniques of patron-client relationships were implemented. (1) Some contradictory rules and norms for private business forced the private entrepreneurs continuously to rely on the good will of the civil servant. (2) In other cases, the rules were quite unacceptable to the businessmen, who as a result felt they had to transfer the business (or part of it) to the informal sector. This consequently made them even more vulnerable. (3) Some civil servants required a commission for permitting some activity or transaction that was essentially legal. Businessmen had to be familiar with the unwritten regulations if they wanted to keep doing business. Thus, a 'socio-political concubine' between politicians and/or civil servants and private businessmen came to exist. (4) Another even stronger form of merging the social figures of owner and ruler was abuse of political power for the benefit of promoting one's own business.

10 In a number of common enterprises, the informal network of one market player meets the money of another one on equal basis, i.e. under conditions for sharing the profit. Networks could be borrowed for particular transactions with profit purposes, too.

11 'The market's emancipation presupposes public and private as two autonomous spaces, but equally 'own' for the person who is equally integrated and equally distant from the roles performed' (Bahrdt 1974: 63).

12 Outwitting formal authorities is a traditional practice, which is broadly reflected in Bulgarian legends and stories; typically, the winner is positively evaluated.

13 On this issue, see Gaertner and Wenig (1985), Sampson (1987), and Los (1990).

14 Indeed, the question of what kept socialist society together is much more complicated: was it the reinforced reciprocity or the mutual fear between individual and party rulers as Seligman and Füzer suggest (1994: 203), or the development of a second society (Hankiss 1990) – second economy, publicity, social language, culture – covered by the official socialist reality?

15 The meaning of this behaviour shifted from 'redemption from sin' against the power authority to a demonstration of compliance with it and recognition of its merits (Bahrdt 1974: 79-83).

16 The DCM 35 of 1987 permitted for the first time part-time private activity for those employed in the state sector and full-time private businesses for the pensioners and housewives. DMC 17 of 1987 allowed leasing in the service sector.

17 According to data published in the mass media, capital exports amounted to USD 15 billion which is more than the foreign debt of the country.

18 There are many channels of this 'privatization of profits and nationalization of losses' (Stark 1990). One of the most important of them has been establishing parallel private firms to operate on the 'entrance' and/or the 'exit' of state enterprises. As a rule, they are managed by people who belong to the informal circles of the state managers. The state has allowed the managers to transfer the information and the established contacts with suppliers and other agents to private hands. For example, they take orders that have been made to the state firm and by subcontracting execute them in the private one. They can sell 'reassessed' enterprise shares, too, i.e. artificial lowering of the state's stock value so that in the long run the sellers indirectly become buyers. For more details, see Chavdarova 2001a.

19 The drastic impoverishment of the Bulgarian population is also related to the high unemployment rate of 18.8% of the active population in 2001, according to the governmental data. The trade unions estimate the unemployment rate at 25%.

20 This has to do with the traditional high political instability in the country: there were ten governments in power in a period of eleven years (1989-2001). The political statistics shows that, in the period after the Liberation from the Ottoman Empire in 1787 up to 1944, the average duration of each government was one year and three months and of each Parliament – one year and five months.

21 According to a representative 1996 national survey, 57.6% of the population consider the impossibility to distinguish among good and bad as the gravest problem in Bulgaria (Genov 1997: 65).

22 According to other estimations following different approaches, the shadow economy made between 24% (Johnson e.a. 1997) and 33% (Lácko 1999; Kyle e.a. 2000) in the early nineties. Whereas it had increased to 32.7% from 1989-90 to 1991-92 according to Lácko (electricity consumption approach), it had decreased to 10.8-21.3% according to Kyle (same approach). It made between 17.3-21.6% (Kyle e.a.) and 40% (National Statistical Institute) in the mid-nineties, 15.2% (Nenovsky and Hristov, monetary approach) resp. 18% (National Statistical Institute) to 28.2-34.4% (Kyle e.a.) in 1996-97 and made between 21% and 23% in 1998 and 1999 (National Statistical Institute; Kyle e.a.).

23 The common practice is to cut enough for it to be lucrative, but not enough that the controlling inspectors would have to pay attention. That means paying of 50-70% of what is due plus a bribe of about 10%. Remarkably, the tax inspectors are last in the table of salaries from all the state administration (TI, Bulgarian Branch 2001).

24 CPI is build each year by the Transparency International. Bulgaria and Croatia are the only two states among the selected Central and Eastern European countries that have shown a non-controversial improvement of CPI in this period (For details see Chavdarova 2001d).

25 In 1991, 94% of the households were domestic producers on various scale (Rose and Haerpfer 1992: 13).

26 The share of the population producing selected food for themselves is as follows: fresh fruits and vegetables (39.2%); potatoes (38.5%); beans (35.9%); eggs (35.2%); meat (without chicken) (31.7%); chicken meat (28.7%); cheese (15.9%) (My calculations based on information in Rajchev et al. 1999: 8-9).

27 One indirect piece of evidence in this respect is the fact that though the share of the private sector is 63.3% in the total number of employees for 1999, the revenues to the National Social Insurance Institute amount to much less than 50% (Kyle et al. 2000: 8).

References

Bahrdt, H.P. (1974), *Die Moderne Grossstadt. Soziologische Überlegungen zum Städtebau*, München, Nymphenburger Verlagshandlung.

Castells, M. and Portes, A. (1989), 'World Underneath: The Origins, Dynamics and Effects of the Informal Economy', in A. Portes, M. Castells and L. Benton (Eds.), *The Informal Economy*, The John Hopkins University Press, Baltimore.

Chavdarova, T. (2000), 'Changing Modes of Economic Integration in Bulgarian History', in K. McRobbie and K. Polanyi-Levitt (Eds.), *Karl Polanyi in Vienna. Contemporary Significance of the Great Transformation*, Montreal, Black Rose Press, pp. 146-159.

Chavdarova, T. (2001a), 'Fostering the Criminal Economy: the Bulgarian Case', in Dittrich, E. (Hrsg.) *Wandel, Wende, Wiederkehr. Transformation as Epochal Change in Central and Eastern Europe: Theoretical Concepts and Their Empirical Applicability*, Würzburg: Ergon, pp. 139-156.

Chavdarova, T. (2001b), *Neformalnata Ikonomika (Informal Economy)*, Sofia, Lik.

Chavdarova, T. (2001c), Market Developments in Bulgaria: the Problem of Trust, in Lang, R. (Hg.) *Wirtschaftsethik in Mittel – und Osteuropa*, Proceedings of IV. Ostforum – Chemnitz, 2-5 March 1999.

Chavdarova, T. (2001d), Corruption under the Bulgarian Post-Communist Transformation, *South-East Europe Review for Labour and Social Affairs*, in print.

Coleman, J. S. (1988), Social Capital in the Creation of Human Capital, *American Journal of Sociology*, 94.

Douglas, M. (1986), *How Institutions Think*, Syracuse, New York, Syracuse University Press.

Friedman, E., Johnson, S., Kaufmann, D. and Zoido-Lobaton, P. (1999), Dodging the Grabbing Hand: The Determinants of Unofficial Activity in 69 Countries, *World Bank Discussion Paper*.

Gaertner, W. and Wenig, A. (eds.) (1985), *Economics of the Shadow Economy*, New York, Springer Verlag.

Genchev, N. (1987), *Sozialno-psihologicheski Tipove v Bulgarskata Istorija (Socio-psychological Types in the Bulgarian History)*, Sofia, Septemvri.

Genov, N. (Ed.) (1997), Bulgaria, *Human Development Report*, Sofia, UNDP.

Giddens, A. (1990), *The Consequences of Modernity*, Cambridge, Polity Press.

Grosdanowa, E. (1979), *Bulgaskata Selska Obshtina Pres XV – XVIII Wek (The Bulgarian Rural Commune during XV – XVIII Century)*, Sofia, Bulgarian Academy of Sciences.

Hadgijski, I. (1974), *Bit I Dushewnost na Bulgarskija Narod (Mode of Life and Spirituality of Bulgarian People)*, vol. 2, Sofia, Bulgarski Pisatel.

Hankiss, E. (1990), *Eastern European Alternatives: Are There Any?*, Oxford, Oxford University Press.

Henry, S. (1981), 'Introduction', in Henry, S. (Ed.), 1981, *Informal Institutions. Alternative Networks in the Corporative State*, New York, St. Martin's Press.

Hirschleifer, J. (1982), 'Evolutionary Models in Economics and Law: Cooperation versus Conflict Strategies', *Research in Law and Economics*, 4, pp. 1-60.

Hristoskov, J., Shopov, G. and Beleva, I. (1996), *Neistituzionalisiranata Saetost i Samonaetost. (Non-institutionalised Employment and Self-employment)*, Sofia, Institute for Market Economics.

Inalcik, H. and Quataert, D. (1994), 'General Introduction', in H. Inalcik and D. Quataert (eds.), *An Economic and Social History of the Ottoman Empire, 1300-1914*, Cambridge: Cambridge University Press.

Johnson, S., Kaufmann, D. and Shleifer, A. (1997), The Unofficial Economy in Transition, *Brookings Papers Eco. Act.*, 0: 2, pp. 159-221.

Kornai, J. (1980), *Economics of Shortage*, Amsterdam, North Holland.

Kyle, S. et al. (2000), *The Shadow Economy in Bulgaria*, Sofia, Harvard University, Agency for Economic Analysis and Forecasting, Institute for Market Economics, unpublished paper.

Los, M. (ed.) (1990), *The Second Economy in Marxist States*, Collier Macmillan.

Luhmann, N. (1982), *The Differentiation of Society*, Columbia University Press.

Luhmann, N. (1988), 'Familiarity, Confidence, Trust: Problems and Alternatives', in Gambetta, D. (Ed.), 1988, *Trust: Making and Breaking Cooperative Relations*, Oxford, Basil Blackwell, pp. 94-107.

Münch, R. (1993) [first 1986], *Die Kultur der Moderne*, Frankfurt, Suhrkamp.

National Statistical Institute (1999), *Bjudgeti na domakinstwata w Republika Bulgaria (Households Budgets in Republic of Bulgaria)*, Sofia, NSI.

National Statistical Institute (2000), *Saetost i Besrabotiza. (Employment and Unemployment)*, No. 1, Sofia, NSI.

National Statistical Institute (2000), *Statisticheski sprawochnik (Statistical Yearbook)*, Sofia, NSI.

Nenovsky, N. and Hristov, K. (2000), *Issledwane na parite w obrastenie sled wuwezhdaneto na parichnija suwet w Bulgaria (A Study of the Money in Transaction after Establishing the Currency Board in Bulgaria)*, Disscusion Paper, Sofia, Bulgarian National Bank.

North, D.C. (1990), *Institutions, Institutional Change and Economic Performance*, Cambridge, University Press.

Paunov, M. (1996), *Organisazionnata Kultura. (Organizational Culture)*, Sofia, Dino-In.

Polanyi, K. (1965) [1944], *The Great Transformation: the Political and Economic Origins of our Time*, Boston, Beacon Press.

Polanyi, K. (1992) [1957], 'The Economy as Instituted Process', Inc. from K. Polanyi, C. Arensberg, and H. Pearson (Eds.), *Trade and Market in the Early Empires*, The Free Press, in: M. Granovetter and R. Swedberg (Eds.), *The Sociology of Economic Life*, pp. 29-51, Oxford, Westview Press.

Portes, A., Castells, M. and Benton, L. (Eds.) (1989), *Informal Economy. Studies in Advanced and Less Developed Countries*, Baltimore and London, The Johns Hopkins University Press.

Rajchev, A., Kolev, K., Bundgulov, A. and Dimova, L. (1999), *Sozialnata Stratifikazija v Bulgaria sled 1989: Prichini, Faktori, Tendenzii. (Social Stratification in Bulgaria after 1989: Causes, Factors, Tendencies)*, Paper of the Sociodemocratic Institute, Sofia.

Rose, R. and Haerpfer, C. (1992), *New Democracies Between State and Market. A Baseline Report of Public Opinion*, Glasgow: CSPP – University of Strathclyde Press.

Sampson, S. (1987), 'The Second Economy of the Soviet Union and Eastern Europe', in L. Ferman, S. Henry and M. Hoyman (Eds.) 1987, *The Informal Economy*, The Annals of the American Academy of Political and Social Science, September. SAGE.

Schneider, F. and Enste, D. (2000), Shadow Economies: Size, Causes, and Consequences, *Journal of Economic Literature*, March, vol. XXXVIII, pp. 77–114.

Scott, J. (1976), *The Moral Economy of the Peasant. Rebellion and Subsistence in Southeast Asia*, New Haven and London, Yale University Press.

Seligmen, A. and Füzer, K. (1994), 'The Problem of Trust and the Transition from State Socialism', *Comparative Social Research*, vol. 14, pp. 193-221.

Stark, D. (1990), Privatization in Hungary: from Plan to Market or from Plan to Clan, *East European Politics and Societies*, 4, pp. 351-392.

Transparency International, Bulgarian Branch (2001), *Corruption in Bulgaria*, Sofia, non-published paper.

Transparency International (2001), http://www.transparency.org.

Chapter 3

Practices and strategies of managing everyday life in a village in socialist Bulgaria

Klaus Roth*

'Of all the State secrets in the keeping of communist régimes, one of the closest guarded was undoubtedly the nature of everyday life, its practical contexts, its ground rules and its long-term effects' (Bertaux/Malysheva 1994, p. 238).

Culture, to use a broad definition of the word, is a set of shared meanings and orientations, beliefs and knowledge, values and norms, behaviors and artefacts which enable man to make sense of, and to act sensibly in, his natural and socio-cultural environment. For the management of everyday life, man uses as a resource a number of behaviours, strategies, and institutions that have – over time – proven to be effective. Changes in the conditions of the environment, be they caused by nature or technology, by the economy or by politics, must eventually result in the adaptation of these behaviours and institutions to the new conditions, because otherwise life cannot be managed adequately. Rapid changes in the environment usually lead to more or less radical socio-cultural changes.

On the other hand, behaviours and everyday knowledge, once they have become part of the socio-cultural system, of language, and of the collective memory, by their very nature often tend to be tenacious and to persist even if they are no longer functional. It is this complex mixture of adaptation and perseverance, of culture change and continuity that is particularly characteristic of everyday culture.

The *sociology of knowledge* considers culture as a system of shared meanings and common-sense knowledge enabling the individual to organize his daily experiences and to manage everyday life. By doing this, it provides a good approach to the study of everyday culture at the micro-level of concrete individual or collective behaviours. The related school of *ethnometho-*

---

* Prof. Dr., Full professor, Institut für Volkskunde/European Ethnology Munich University, Ludwigstr. 25 D-80539, Munich, e-mail: k.roth@lrz.uni-muenchen.de.

dology, on the other hand, adds the focus on the recurrent 'patterns of stable action', the basic elements of those practices that are used in the same manner in varying everyday situations. These recurrent practices or *methods* are employed by the individuals of a given social group (*ethnos*) in a regular way, they are supra-individual, and they are deeply ingrained as they are mostly learned in the process of socialization. As 'natural' and taken-for-granted resources, they are fundamental to everyday thinking and acting (Patzelt 1987: 10 f). Attention turns to them only if, for some reason, they are no longer available or if their 'naturality' is put in question.

Alfred Schütz has observed, that the *life-world* of man consists of multiple realities, among whom the reality of everyday life functions as the paramount reality. It 'presents itself as normal and self-evident, ordered and objective, and taken-for-granted as such' (Wuthnow 1984: 32). It is overarched by the realities of, in Berger's and Luckmann's terms (1966), the 'symbolic universes' of mythology, philosophy, religion or ideology, all of them powerful systems of affirmation providing legitimacy to the social world. *Ideology*, in particular, as a set of ideas, is used to legitimate the vested interests of parts of the society, but at the same time it also interprets and directs the order of society and of everyday reality.

The social life and the everyday culture under the conditions of the *communist ideology* are a good case in point. The socialist state founded on this ideology legitimates itself through its 'historic task' of striving for the Utopian goal of lasting economic and political equality and justice for everyone. In order to achieve this humanitarian ideal, socialist ideology demands the construction of a new classless society, a new 'socialist personality', and a new 'socialist way of life', in other words: the transformation of most of the basic conditions of the existing life-worlds. Indeed, the political and economic changes brought about by the system implemented in the countries under Soviet rule were so fundamental that one can say that there has probably never before existed an ideology that has affected the everyday life of so many people with such a totality and ruthlessness. Only now, years after the end of the socialist system, the consequences of these changes on the everyday culture of the socialist countries are becoming clearer; and they turn out to be far deeper and more lasting than anybody anticipated in the wake of the events of 1989.

So far, a few ethnologists and sociologists have studied aspects of everyday culture under 'real socialism',[1] but its relevance has not yet been generally acknowledged (cf. Bertaux 1994: 197). Péter Niedermüller has pointed out (1996: 144 f.) that socialism has produced a cultural world, a life-world of its own. 'Er hat Regeln einer kulturellen Welt aufgestellt, hat die Bühnen des gesellschaftlichen Lebens geschaffen, hat die Dramaturgie … und die verschiedenen Verhaltensrepertoires ausgearbeitet.' Niedermüller insists that for ordinary people there was no other choice but to accept this world and its rules, and that living in any such life-world means its appropriation by the individual, regardless of his political convictions. The fact is that no one can live in a society and permanently ignore its socio-cultural order. This means that the life-world and the social rules of socialism, the entire order of everyday life became an integral part of the lives and life-histories of millions of individuals.

The focus of this paper will not be on this social order and the rules set by the socialist life-world, but rather on the everyday practices and strategies which people employed to manage their lives. The following analysis departs from data gained through research in the village of Raduil,[2] located some 80 kms south-east of Sofia, where we gathered large quantities of archive materials and made some 90 life-history interviews. The present analysis is thus a case study, but observations in other Bulgarian villages, my personal experiences in Bulgaria since 1964, research data gained in the Thuringian village of Merxleben in the former GDR, as well as the extant research litera-ture[3] indicate that the following practices and strategies were common beyond this village and beyond Bulgaria in most socialist countries.

On the other hand, some limitations have to be acknowledged. Some important differentiations had to be left aside, such as differences in the socialist everyday-life depending on gender, age group, social class, Party membership or the position in the hierarchical structures; there is no doubt that the members of the *nomenklatura*, the powerful and the privileged of the system, also had their own practices and strategies of managing their every-day-life. As a consequence, the findings of this study are of a more general nature, and concern mostly the 'ordinary people'.

The focus is on the daily *practices* and *strategies* as they emerge from the sources. I use the term '*strategy*' quite deliberately, as it denotes a set of practices, procedures or courses of action that are taken to achieve a certain goal; but unlike 'practice' or 'habit', it implies a degree of rational planning and strategic thinking. The sources indicate that, mostly in the initial phase of socialist rule, 'strategy' is indeed the adequate term to describe the every-day actions and interactions people chose quite deliberately in order to react to and counter the new practices and strategies of the socialist Party and the state authorities. As is normal for innovation processes, the strategies were more and more internalized over the years and became unquestioned prac-tices that were mostly applied automatically. After a period of familiariza-tion they became habitual and 'normal' behaviors, and, particularly among the younger generations, the only available resource. It is precisely their high degree of internalization and habitualization that makes these everyday behaviours a burdensome legacy of socialism.

The socialist system of rule and economy is fairly well known, at least at the macro-level. The original 'ideal socialism' with all its promises was soon discredited because of the coercive measures of the state, the malfunctioning of the economy, and the harsh realities of everyday life. As early as in the 1950s, 'ideal socialism' had turned into totalitarian 'real socialism' which shaped an everyday culture that was characterized by an ever growing tension between ideal and reality, between plan and accomplishment, between propaganda and the visible life-world. The discrepancy between the two, the permanent deception and double-talk of all official communication produced a kind of 'everyday schizophrenia' (Wnuk-Lipiski 1982) that permeated virtually all spheres of life and forced people to develop a 'socialist habitus'.

But is it, we must ask critically, correct to speak of a 'socialist habitus'? Are the practices and strategies which will be described below 'typically socialist'? None of them is in any way new or specific, each of them is known from other (political) systems, countries or periods. What entitles us to speak, nevertheless, of a 'socialist habitus', is the very specific *cluster* of such reactive behaviours which resulted from the specific nature and the duration of the socialist system. It appears that there were three fundamental conditions that had the strongest impact on everyday life, namely (1) the *totalitarian system* of rule and control, of social care-taking and tutelage, that entailed the permanent encroachment of the Party or the state bureaucracy into the lives of the people, (2) the *deficit economy* resulting from the blatant malfunctioning of the economic system and the ideologically motivated policies such as the collectivization of agriculture, the liquidation of private property, and the forced industrialization, and (3) the simultaneous process of *socialist modernization* (cf. Srubar 1991) which reached the agrarian countries of East and Southeast Europe in its socialist variety. The specific character of socialist everyday life and of the 'socialist habitus' is probably a result of the unique combination and interplay of these exclusively exogenous factors.

Within a period of only a few years around 1950, many behaviours, practices and attitudes that had weathered decades or even centuries became inadequate and were no longer accepted. They had to be given up or adapted to the changed environment if one wanted to avoid unfavorable living conditions, disadvantages at the workplace or at school, expropriation, displacement, or even imprisonment. Other practices, however, proved useful or had even to be revived from the repertoire of traditional behaviors. Altogether, in this process of societal learning one can note three different courses of adaptation of the people to the new political and economic environment, namely:

a. the adoption of behaviours and strategies that were *new* to the people,
b. the continuation of *traditional* practices and strategies, and
c. the adaptation and even enforcement of *traditional* behaviours and attitudes. The latter course appears to have been the most frequent one which, in turn, led to the traditionalization or even 'archaization' of some sectors of the society or economy described by Benovska-Sabkova (1995) and by other scholars.

In the following, I want to differentiate between three aspects and want to ask questions on three levels: (1) What did ordinary people have to *know* to cope with socialist everyday life? What were the origins and the structures of their knowledge? (2) What were their everyday practices, their typical behaviours and strategies to cope with the impact of totalitarianism, permanent deficit economy and modernization? (3) Did people talk about these practices and strategies and what was their *awareness* of everyday life then, and what is it now in their recollections? How did they talk about it, and what functions did talking about it serve?

Repertoires of knowledge

Let us first look at the *stock of common-sense knowledge* ordinary people had to have to cope with socialist everyday life. What sets of knowledge, what intellectual skills, what orientations were required to manage life in the socialist political, social, and economic system? What knowledge became obsolete and what remained useful and was to be kept, and what knowledge was to be talked about openly and to whom? The data show that people in the socialist village had to acquire a great deal of new knowledge, particularly in the Stalinist era and during the process of collectivization in the 1950s. The villagers had both to learn new, and to unlearn old attitudes and patterns of knowledge, but they soon found out that, in order to survive, they really needed *two* sets of knowledge – and on top of that they needed to know when to apply what set of knowledge. In other words: they needed two *registers* (cf. Trümpy 1991: 216 f.) and in addition to that, a meta-knowledge of when and where and how to use what register.

The one register consisted of the legitimate and *official* knowledge and skills desired and instilled by the Party and the state; this officially acquired knowledge was a predominantly *formal* knowledge transported through the channels of official education and communication. The other register included the *unofficial* knowledge and skills, the 'strategies of the second order' (Bourdieu 1987: 198-203); they were acquired unofficially and were an exclusively *informal* knowledge passed on by means of oral communication through everyday narrating, gossip, rumors and jokes in small circles of families and kin, of trusted neighbors and colleagues.

Each individual normally has at his disposal several registers or stocks of knowledge and behaviour and usually knows when to apply them. The specificity of the 'socialist habitus' lies in the fact that the duplicity (and rivalry) of two such incongruous registers was so all-embracing and ubiquitous that it permeated and structured the entire thinking, feeling, and acting in everyday life. It concerned not only the cognitive, but also the affective sphere and, very importantly, also the value orientations, the everyday morality. A pervasive double morality guided the actions not only of the Party and the state, but more importantly, of all individuals. They all made a clear distinction between the private sector, respectively private property and the public sector, respectively state property or, as Wnuk-Lipiski (1982: 81-85) said with regard to the Polish society, they had 'two different circulation systems of ... values'. Tzvetan Todorov has characterized this attitude in his book *On Human Diversity: Nationalism, Racism, and Exotism in French Thought* (Cambridge, Mass. 1993, p. vii): 'I was never a direct victim of the regime, since my reaction ... was not to protest or challenge it, but to take on two distinct personalities: one public and submissive, the other private and independent.' For both sectors there existed different 'laws' and norms of behaviour which were followed alternatively. 'Doing things the second way (*po vtorija nain*)' is a recurrent phrase in the interviews denoting the practices that were common in the public 'socialist sector'.

The traditional knowledge of the villagers was thus complemented or replaced by a lot of new knowledge: on the one hand, the officially propagated 'progressive' 'socialist' knowledge, and on the other hand, the unofficial knowledge that reached them mostly indirectly through clandestine and oral channels. Compared to what they knew and had to know until around 1950, the structure of their knowledge became more complex and the life-world became more complicated than ever before – and it carried many new risks.

Practices and strategies of socialist everyday life

In order to accommodate to the obvious discrepancies of 'real socialism' and to lead a life that offered at least some degree of security and comfort, the villagers developed new practices and strategies in the 1950s which soon became everyday routines. Which one of the registers of value orientations and behaviours was applied depended mostly on the actual situation, on the actors involved, and on the convictions or interests of the individual. The data show that the behaviours of individuals were by no means consistent: in the case of conflicting interests and loyalties, and in a given situation, a member of the Communist Party could very well resort to unofficial or even illegal practices, and vice versa, an ordinary villager could willingly act in accordance with official norms. At certain occasions, as for example at 'socialist life-cycle festivals', the villagers could – in a syncretistic manner – even act in accordance with two conflicting sets of norms consecutively or at the same time, playing out two different registers (cf. Roth 1990: 117, Petrov 1998).

The analysis of the interviews and of the protocols of the village council and the agricultural cooperative (TKZS) indicates a number of behaviours and strategies that were very common in the village. It is certainly no coincidence that the same or very similar behaviors also emerge in the sources from the East German village. This set of adaptive behaviors seems to have formed the backbone of the 'socialist habitus' and to have become so deeply engrained that it survived the system that produced it. It goes without saying that all these behaviors and strategies are interrelated and are usually combined with each other in real situations. They are discussed separately here, for analytical purposes.

Cooperation

The active and enthusiastic cooperation was always limited to relatively small numbers of people. They were either true idealists or they were, mostly, members of the Communist Party and/or held high positions in the village. It was far more common, however, for villagers to cooperate for opportunistic reasons, particularly among those who wanted to make their careers in or through the system, or to be a fellow-traveler. The large majority of the villagers made their peace with the system, with the powerful, and the Party hierarchy, and (partly) accommodated to the system. In many cases, cooperation was enforced through direct or indirect, soft or hard pressure: people did 'voluntary work' in the construction of the 'House of Culture' (*italište*) or cleaned the village streets as 'voluntary Saturday labor' (*sbotnik*), in order to avoid disadvantages – or to gain privileges. The same holds true for cooperation with the Communist Party, so that in the 1950s the BKP in Raduil had to be 'cleansed' of opportunistic fellow-travelers. Nevertheless, there was a general adaptation to the system. It occurred mostly through 'structural amnesia', i.e., because the socialist life-world became the 'natural' life-world and people were unaware of their adaptation to it. Very few villagers were able to make other experiences, e.g. through travels abroad.

Opposition

Open opposition or resistance against the socialist regime was a rare exception; it was only in the early 1950s that six villagers were arrested and five
of them sentenced and sent to the concentration camp of Belene (on the
Danube) and other camps for several years (MVR: investigation file
3983/d.115/1952). Covered and indirect opposition was far more typical.
The sources show that most frequently it found expression in passive
disobedience and obstinacy, in evasion and dodging. At the workplace it was
reflected in indifference, laziness, and absenteeism; these behaviors actually developed into the most serious problem for the economy and the entire
socialist system.

> *In February 1984, the protocol (no. 3) of the village council meeting complains
> that 'the shopkeepers have not fulfilled their plans, namely Marija K. who fell
> short of her plan by 5800 leva. Although she was put in another place, it showed
> again that she does not at all want to work. She does not order products
> regularly. She is absent from work whenever she wants, and from where she gets
> her sick-leave certificates we don't know. She does not serve her customers in a
> civilized manner' (Village archive: mayor's office Raduil).*

The villagers displayed a lot of cunning and creativity to oppose the
measures of the authorities. When, for example, the authorities (on account
of the state's atheist policy) forbade the *public* blessing of the lambs before
Easter or other days of offering by the local priest, the farmers opposed this
regulation by moving the blessing to their *private* courtyards or folds and
inviting the priest there.

Circumvention

A very common behavior was, as the sources show, to circumvent or to disregard official laws, orders, and regulations. In most cases, this happened
clandestinely and indirectly, but often it was done quite openly. Inflicting
damage to the authorities, the Party or the economy was often done quite
provocatively and cunningly, as is demonstrated by farmers who cut wood
and either bribed the local policeman or paid the fine with a laugh, or who
bought up scarce goods and sold them illegally:

> *In its 1954 annual report, the village council complains that 'in the shop of the
> village cooperative, 17 tons of artificial fertilizer were bought up and used by
> the farmers. The basic mistake we made in the distribution of the fertilizer was
> that we did not anticipate that it would be sold out so fast and that part of the*

*farmers would get no fertilizer while some other irresponsible farmers sold it
outside the village for grapes, etc.' (SGODA f. 240, f. 1, ae. 31, l. 2). The shop
of the local cooperative illegally sold cigarettes to pupils in order to fulfill its
sales plan (village archive: protocol of the village council of July 21, 1986).*

'Organizing'

One of the most frequent stratagems was to do one's work in the cooperative
farm (TKZS), in the state forestry (DGS) or in the shops in such a way that
part of the yield went into one's own pocket. The 'branching off' of resources at the workplace was common practice (cf. Srubar 1991: 420 f.) and
was legitimated with phrases such as 'We take from the state because the
state is us'.

*The 'Report on the State and Observance of Socialist Laws' in the village of
March 21, 1960, mentions penalties for illegal cutting of wood and reports the
theft and illegal sale of construction materials, and other instances of breaking
socialist laws (SGODA: f. 892, op. 2, ae. 2, l. 139-156).*

The illegal or half-legal procuring of deficit goods and services, as well
as getting privileges without being entitled to them or paying for them adequately were very common practices. The informants repeatedly insisted
that 'doing things the second way' was normal and in many cases was the
only possible alternative.

*Ivan B. insists in the interview that almost everybody in the village went out by
night to cut trees in the forest; some neighbors went to prison for that, but this
was the only way to get wood for construction purposes. The women working in
the agricultural brigade regularly stole potatoes or other produce, taking it
home in bags or even under their skirts. Truck drivers stole cement and sold it
to the farmers. Already in 1954 the management of the TKZS (protocol of Oct.
8) complained that the members used the cattle for their private plots, and the
protocol of the village council of May 25, 1985 still reports that the saw-mill is
used illegally on weekends to cut wood for private purposes.*

The socialist deficit economy and the common practice of bartering
goods and services made it indispensable for every villager to maintain tight
networks of social relations and connections (*vrzki*) which could in case of
need (and based on the principle 'do ut des') always be activated and utilized
(cf. Srubar 1991: 421).

In 1962, the village council complains in a report that 'we must not close our eyes to the fact that there are still salespersons who, after receiving deficit goods store away these goods in secret places and distribute them exclusively to their own kin. This is not adequate for a contemporary socialist salesperson' (SGODA f. 892, op. 2, ae. 17). In an interview (April 28, 1996), a village woman reports that her family had no problems procuring furniture, because the person in charge of the warehouse was a class-mate of hers.

Managing scarcity

The shortage economy necessitated a permanent coping with scarcity and thus produced a 'culture of scarcity management' in all socialist countries (cf. Smollett 1989, Benovska 1995, Schier 1997, Lutz 2000, Dzigiel 1998, Srubar 1991). Accordingly, deficit goods (*deficitni stoki*) are a frequent topic in the interviews and protocols, but also in the media and in literature. The economic situation forced people to maintain and even extend a very intensive and all-encompassing barter economy, an economy in kind based on the everyday exchange of goods and services, and it necessitated various forms of subsistence economy, an 'economy of jars' in the private sector (Smollett 1989).

Ivan B., brigadeer of the TKZS, and his wife give several instances of payment in kind in their interview: the construction workers who built his house were paid in wheat. Jordan D., the president of the cooperative, remembers that transportation services of the TKZS were paid in wheat or cement, that wood from Raduil was exchanged for potatoes from plains villages, and that the workers of the TKZS and the MTS (Machine-Tractor-Station) often received their wages in kind.

For their everyday management of shortage, people developed a great amount of inventiveness and improvization. The gift of combination and the ability to improvise and to react flexibly to changing conditions is certainly one of the behaviours which, as Benovska-Sabkova (1997) and Lutz (2000) have demonstrated, help the people in the post-socialist countries to survive.

'Help yourself and help your kin'

In traditional rural Bulgaria, there existed a complex system of mutual aid. The Party tried to instrumentalize this system for its collectivization campaign, but with little success. It was much more important that for the management of socialist everyday life the traditional system was utilized or even expanded by the villagers for the safeguarding of self-help through mutual assistance. The deficit economy, financial need, and the lack of craftsmen forced them to do many things themselves or with the help of their family, their kin, their neighbors, friends, or colleagues. The high value placed on the little private plots (of c. 1 ha) and the high significance of the subsistence economy on it has often been stated (cf. Höpken 1985: 624-628, Grosser 1988, Roth 1989). But working for one's own needs went beyond agricultural products. The above mentioned Ivan B. recalled that people produced bricks for private houses and TKZS buildings with their own hands, because construction materials were too costly and very hard to get.

The system of mutual aid, self-help and subsistence made everybody – in a reciprocal relationship – dependent on the help of members of his group and, in turn, made them dependent on his cooperation.

A brigadier reported that for the construction of his private house the women of his work brigade came over to help, and neighbors supplied transportation services. Other informants told us that the workers in the saw-mill worked for a colleague so that he could bring in the harvest from his private plot.

These behaviours and close social ties perpetuated the traditionally strong dependence on, and trust in, intimate social groups, and gave further relevance to familism.

'Grease the system'

Even more destructive for the entire system was the ubiquitous corruption, bribery and nepotism ('*vrzkarstvo*'), a system of connections (*vrzki*), which was based on, and further strengthened, informal personal relationships.

Most informants agree, that bribery and corruption were extremely common. Officials, shopkeepers, presidents of cooperatives, everybody in control of scarce or deficit goods had to be greased, usually with alcohol, money, services or other 'presents'.

Adaptation and exploitation

As I have pointed out before, the villagers adapted themselves to the socialist system to a fairly large extent. But the reverse was also true. It was an important practice of them to make the system fit their own needs, to adapt and to change it in a manipulative manner, and to change its functions in accordance with their own goals. They attempted (and often achieved) the tacit 'correction' of the ideals and goals of the Party and the authorities, mostly through obstinacy, indifference or cleverness. A great amount of energy went into the active utilization (and steady expansion) of margins and leeway, e.g. with the socialist life-cycle rituals.

> *The rituals of the official 'system of socialist holidays and rituals' were gradually adapted by the villagers to their own ideas and needs in such a way that their ideological content was gradually removed (cf. Roth 1990, Petrov 1998).*

Looking for one's own advantage consisted very much in the exploitation of the social security system and the rights and benefits it granted. Sick-leave certificates were issued almost at will, and benefits were often received without legal basis. In this 'adaptation' and appropriation of the resources of the system, the villagers again displayed a high degree of inventiveness.

'Pretend to work'

The common practice of sham cooperation undermined the economic or political system in a similar way. To fake, to pretend activity, to fulfill the official norms only superficially or formally or, in Bourdieu's words (1987: 200), 'to abide by the official rules only seemingly and thereby to satisfy one's own interests' – all these were strategies that were very common and highly effective. They were applied not only by the villagers vis-à-vis the local elites and authorities, but also by the local functionaries vis-à-vis their superiors in the capital. One of the most popular slurs in Bulgaria was 'The state pretends to pay us, we pretend to work'. Through the strict or exaggerated observance of official orders people often proved the system (or the Party) ridiculous or absurd.

Withdrawal

Resignation and putting up with the system was a wide-spread attitude in Raduil, in Bulgaria and in the other socialist countries. The sources indicate that as early as in the 1950s the rate of alcoholism and absenteeism was notoriously high.

> *The workers were permanently drunk and the brigadier or the superiors of the cooperatives could not do anything about it, Jordan D. reported. The TKZS protocols of April 1954 complain that the workers do not work their minimal working hours, and the protocol of the village council of Sept. 16, 1959 states that cooperative workers till their private plots while the sheaves of the coopera-*

tive rot in the fields. The management of the TKZS reacted either with promises or the distribution of bread or flour, or it denied them their regular bread rations, according to an interview.

In most sectors of the society there was to be observed an escapism and withdrawal that took on many different forms. It was:

- a retreat into social and everyday life *niches* with sharp boundaries drawn between the in-group and the out-group[4]; in Raduil, this found its expression, among others, in the distance between the villagers and the local '*viladii*', the owners of summer cottages, most of whom were members of the Party elite from Sofia (cf. Wolf 1997: 187f.);
- a retreat into the *private* sector, i.e. the family and relatives, the private plot of land and the garden, the cottage in the countryside. In Raduil, a very large amount of energy and money was invested into the private house or plot, usually at the expense of the public sector;
- a retreat into *inner spaces* of (spiritual) freedom, like religion, mythology or the belief in extra-sensual phenomena. The pronounced religiosity of the villagers (Petrov 1998) can be viewed as such a withdrawal; or finally
- a retreat into a '*golden past*'. Characteristic of Bulgaria was the strong folklorization of traditional folk culture (which was partly supported and instrumentalized by the Party) and the nostalgia for the 'unforgotten past' of the 19th century 'National Revival' or for the culture of the pre-war urban bourgeoisie.

As a result, most people lived two very different and separate lives, a public and a private one. This tendency was stronger in the cities than in the villages, though, mainly because of the greater intimacy of social relations in the villages. The 'everyday schizophrenia' thus became an almost constitutive element of socialist everyday reality.

Narrative practices and strategies

Everyday oral communication played a tremendous role in socialist Bulgaria (cf. Roth 1992). Due to the fact that Bulgaria already had a strong oral tradition and that unofficial knowledge could only be transmitted in direct oral communication, intimate face-to-face communication with trusted persons acquired a relevance and meaning that has no parallel in modern Western societies. As all the mass media, from book printing, newspapers, journals, and film to radio and television, were controlled by the Party and the state, everyday narrating became virtually the only uncontrolled means of individual and societal communication. Narrating became an essential part of socialist everyday life in two important ways: talking as *part* of everyday life and talking *about* socialist everyday life. Both aspects are, of course, related to each other in real life.

Narration as part of socialist everyday life

Everyday narration was an important practice to cope with the complexities of the socialist life-world and with the hardships of everyday 'real social-ism'. However, particularly in the early years of socialist rule, talking too frankly could be dangerous; being overheard by an informer or even by ill-wishing colleague or neighbor could have very negative consequences. Thus, official or public communication was often quite formulaic and well-guarded in order to avoid disagreement, as one never knew when the other person could be helpful in case of need or in providing useful information (cf. Srubar 1991: 422). The benefits of talking outweighed its dangers, as the spoken word was the only means to give expression to the experiences of socialist life. Nights after nights, families and relatives, friends and neigh-bors, but also colleagues and class-mates would sit together (usually in the kitchen) and comment on political or other events, discuss their daily expe-riences, and exchange information: on the lack or availability of goods, on access to deficit goods and services, on measures of the Party or the autho-rities; they would tell rumors, gossips, and jokes, and they would discuss on end what to do to get this permit or to avoid that penalty, whom to bribe to get construction materials or whom to invite to get access to a much desired color TV set.[5] To a large extent, this was 'strategic communication', often quite emotional, but mostly in the form of rational discussions to work out plans and to determine the course of action to be taken to achieve a certain goal. An important prerequisite for success was a sound knowledge of the inner workings of the socialist system.

Narrating about the socialist everyday life

Narrating *about* the manifold problems of everyday life, about the con-tradictions and failures of the socialist system, on the other hand, satisfied important emotional and intellectual needs. By telling stories and jokes, daily experiences and impressions, by complaining about politicians and func-tionaries, people gained a lot of emotional relief and reflected about their life under the socialist system. Everyday narrating was thus a means of daily sur-vival (Banc/Dundes 1986: 13). Today, years after the collapse of the system, narrating has become a means of coming to terms with that important part of one's own life-history, as Dobreva[6] has observed in the same village.

Some results

A comprehensive history of everyday life under the socialist system, of 'its ground rules and its long-term effects' (Bertaux 1994: 238) has not yet been written. What I have tentatively tried to do was to outline some of the 'ground rules' at the micro-level, to throw light on the reservoirs of knowledge people had to acquire and to internalize to master their lives in a new system, what practices and strategies they developed and how they talked and reflected about all this. As they could not escape the normative life-world of 'real socialism', the villagers of Raduil – and with them millions of people in the socialist countries – developed a reservoir of behaviours as part of their 'socialist habitus' to counter the overpowering influence of the totalitarian state.

Almost all of these strategies were, to be sure, defensive strategies of the powerless. But as it turned out, these counter-strategies were very effective in eroding the system from the inside and in contributing to its collapse. Today, the problem is that many of them continue to persist after they have accomplished their goal. Some of them have even deteriorated into outright criminality. It is these inconspicuous everyday behaviours and strategies that today can be a resource (cf. Lutz 2000, Benovska-Sbkova 1997), but more likely they constitute a threat to the development of democracy and a civil society in Bulgaria and in other post-socialist countries.

Notes

1   cf. Smollett 1989, Roth 1989, 1990, 1992; Srubar 1991, 1998; Bertaux 1994, Benovska 1995, Verdery 1996, Dzigiel 1998.
2   The research project was financed by the Deutsche Forschungsgemeinschaft, Bonn, and lasted from 1993 to 1999. Apart from myself, Doroteja Dobreva and Petar Petrov (from the Institute of Folklore at the Bulgarian Academy of Sciences, Sofia) and Gabriele Wolf and Barbara Schier (from the Institut für Deutsche und vergleichende Volkskunde at Munich University) worked in this project; the research in Raduil was carried out by D. Dobreva, P. Petrov, and G. Wolf, while B. Schier studied the Thuringian village of Merxleben.
3   The findings are corroborated particularly by those of Ilya Srubar (1991, 1998), which are based on materials from several socialist countries.
4   The society of the GDR has often been labeled a 'niche society', but this can certainly be said also of the societies of the other socialist countries.

5   Eleanor Smollett has described these situations in her article (1989) and I myself have witnessed them many times.
6   see her contribution in this volume, and Dobreva 1997.

References

Banc, E., Dundes, A (1986), *First Prize: Fifteen Years! An Annotated Collection of Romanian Political Jokes*, London, Toronto, Associated University Presses.

Benovska-Subkova, M. (1995), Archaic Cultural Models and Totalitarianism, in idem (ed.), *Ethnologia Balkanica*, Sofia, pp. 162-178.

Benovska-Sabkova, M. (1997), Tradition as a Means of Survival Under the Conditions of Economic Crisis in Bulgaria, in *Ethnologia Balkanica* 1, pp. 113-123.

Berger, P.L., Luckmann, L. (1966), *The Social Construction of Reality*, Garden City, NY, Doubleday.

Bertaux, D., Malysheva, M. (1994), Le modèle culturel des classes populaires russes face au passage à l'économie de marché, in *Revue d'études comparatives Est-Ouest*, 25, pp. 197-228.

Bourdieu, P. (1987), Sozialer Sinn. Kritik der theoretischen Vernunft, Frankfurt/M, Suhrkamp (Le sens pratique, Paris, 1980).

Dobreva, D. (1997), Razkazi za socialistieskoto selo. Km slovesnoto ovladjavane na minaloto i nastojaštoto [Narratives about the Socialist Village. Coping with the past and the present through narratives], in *Balgarski folklor* 23, 5-6, pp. 4-27.

Dobreva, D. (2000), Zeitrhythmen und Umgang mit Zeit im Arbeitsalltag des sozialistischen Dorfes. Das Beispiel eines Gebirgsdorfes in Bulgarien, in *Ethnologia Balkanica*, 4, pp. 67-89.

Dzigiel, L. (1998), *Paradise in a Concrete Cage. Daily Life in Communist Poland. An Ethnologists's View*, Krakow, Arcana.

Grimm, F.-D., Roth, K. (eds.) (1997), *Das Dorf in Südosteuropa zwischen Tradition und Umbruch*, Munich, SOG.

Grosser, I. (1988), *Private Landwirtschaft in Bulgarien*, Berlin, Duncker & Humblot.

Gumpel, W. (ed.) (1984), *Das Leben in den kommunistischen Staaten – Zum alltäglichen Sozialismus*, Köln, Bachem.

Höpken, W. (1985), Bulgariens Landwirtschaft vor Problemen, in *Südosteuropa* 34, pp. 611-628.

Kaschuba, W., Mohrmann, U. (eds.) (1992), *Blick-Wechsel Ost-West: Beobachtungen zur Alltagskultur in Ost– und Westdeutschland*, Tübingen, Ludwig-Uhland-Institut.

Lutz, R. (2000), *Knappheitsmanagement*, Über den subjektiven Umgang mit Arbeitslosigkeit, in idem (ed.), Knappheitsmanagement, Münster, Lit.

Mullins, N.C. (1981), Ethnomethodologie: Das Spezialgebiet, das aus der Kälte kam, in Wolf Lepenies (ed.), *Geschichte der Soziologie*, Frankfurt/M, Suhrkamp, pp. 97-136.

Niedermüller, P. (1996), Interkulturelle Kommunikation im Post-Sozialismus, in Klaus Roth (ed.), *Mit der Differenz leben*. Münster, Munich, Waxmann, pp. 143-151.

Patzelt, W.J. (1987), *Grundlagen der Ethnomethodologie. Theorie, Empirie und politikwissenschaftlicher Nutzen einer Soziologie des Alltags*, Munich, Fink.

Petrov, Petar (1998), Conquering the Feast. The Socialist Transformation of a Religious Feast in a Bulgarian Village, in *Ethnologia Balkanica,* 2, pp. 123-132.

Roth, K. (1992), Narrating in Socialist Everyday Life. Observations on Strategies of Life Management in Southeast Europe, in Simon Bronner (ed.), *Creativity and Tradition in Folklore,* New Directions, Logan, Utah State UP, pp. 127-139.

Roth, K., Roth, J. (1989), Das Erbe der bäuerlichen Kultur und die jüngsten Reformen der bulgarischen Landwirtschaft, in *Südosteuropa,* 38, pp. 344-362.

Roth, K., Roth, J. (1990), The System of Socialist Holidays and Rituals, in *Ethnologia Europaea,* 20, pp. 107-120.

Roth, K., Roth, J. (1999), One Country – Two Cultures? Germany After Unification, in Å. Daun, S. Jansson (eds.), *Europeans. Essays on Culture and Identity,* Lund, Nordic Academic Press, 1999, pp. 159-180.

Schier, B. (1997), *Alltagsleben im 'sozialistischen Dorf': Zum Wandel eines thüringischen Dorfes während der Jahre 1945-1990 vor dem Hintergrund der SED-Agrarpolitik. Eine Fallstudie,* PhD thesis, Munich.

Schier, B, (1997), Alltagsleben und Agrarpolitik im 'sozialistischen Dorf', in *Aus Politik und Zeitgeschichte. Beilage zur Wochenzeitung Das Parlament,* B 38 (12 Sept. 1997) pp. 38-47.

Smollett, E. (1989), The Economy of Jars. Kindred Relationships in Bulgaria – An Exploration, in *Ethnologia Europaea,* 19, pp. 125-140.

Srubar, I. (1991), War der reale Sozialismus modern?, in *Kölner Zeitschrift für Soziologie und Sozialpsychologie,* 43, pp. 415-432.

Srubar, I. (1998), Lebenswelt und Transformation. Zur phänomenologischen Analyse gegenwärtiger Gesellschaftsprozesse, in K. Müller (ed.), *Postsozialistische Krisen. Theoretische Ansätze und empirische Befunde,* Opladen, Leske & Budrich, pp. 68-88.

Trümpy, H. (1991) [1970], Sphären des Verhaltens. Beiträge zu einer Grammatik der Bräuche, in Martin Scharfe (ed.), *Brauchforschung,* Darmstadt, WBG, pp. 216-224.

Verdery, K. (1996), *What Was Socialism, and What Comes Next?,* Princeton, NJ, Princeton UP.

Wieschiolek, H. (1997), *'... und ich dachte immer, von den Wessis lernen heißt siegen lernen!' Kulturelle Modelle von Arbeit und Identität in einem mecklenburgischen Betrieb,* PhD thesis, Hamburg University.

Wnuk-Lipiski, E. (1982), Dimorphism of Values and Social Schizophrenia. A tentative description, in *Sisyphus. Sociological Studies,* 3, pp. 81-89.

Wolf, G. (1997), Der gebaute sozialistische Raum. Die räumlich-funktionale Umgestaltung eines bulgarischen Dorfes seit den 50er Jahren, in F.-D. Grimm, K. Roth (eds.), *Das Dorf in Südosteuropa zwischen Tradition und Umbruch,* Munich, SOG, pp. 165-195.

Wolf, G. (2000), 'Mangelwaren', Konsumentenerwartungen und 'Beziehungen'. Einkaufen in der sozialistischen Konsumgenossenschaft, in *Ethnologia Balkanica,* 4, pp. 90-116.

Wuthrow, R., Hunter, J.D., Bergesen, A., Kurzweil, E. (1984), *Cultural Analysis. The Work of Peter L. Berger, Mary Douglas, Michel Foucault and Jürgen Habermas,* London, Boston, Routledge.

Abbreviations

BKP = Blgarska komunistieska partija (Bulgarian Communist Party)
DGS = Dravno gorsko stopanstvo (State Forestry)
MVR = Ministerstvo za vtrešni raboti (Ministry of the Interior, Archive of the Secret Service) in Sofia
SGODA = Sofijski gradski i okren draven arhiv (State Archive of the City and District of Sofia) in Sofia
TKZS = Trudovo-kooperativno zemedelsko stopanstvo (Labor-Cooperative Farm)

Chapter 4

Informal farm work in North Western Bulgaria and Eastern Serbia[1]

Milena Benovska-Sabkova*

Bulgaria is a small country where distances are short. This determines the migration on Saturdays and Sundays from the big city to the village where the urban inhabitant has either a Sunday house with a vegetable garden and fruit trees, or takes part in the farming activities of his parents and relatives (cf. also Stamenova 1995: 103). Departing from the big city, the cars are overcrowded with people, empty bottles and jars, instruments and all kinds of things. Coming back, the cars are 'sprawling' under the weight of a variety of foods, taken from the village. Similar sights can be seen of trains and buses on Saturday and Sunday. This picture is typical both for the socialist and for the 'transition' period. This is part of the specific dimension of *rurbanization* (cf. Prosici-Dvornici 1992), brought about not only by the operation of cultural and historical factors, but also under the impact of economic coercion.

Subject to attention in this article are different forms of agricultural activity in North Western Bulgaria and Eastern Serbia during the socialist and the 'transition' period. This work is based on field research: in North Western Bulgaria, the Vratsa District (1997, 2000) – in the villages of Zverino and Ignatica, located in the Western part of the Balkan Mountains Range; and in Eastern Serbia, 1998, in the town of Svrljig (30 km away from Nish) and the nearby villages of Beloinje, Crnoljevica, Izvor, Merdželat, Niševac. The Serbian centres of population have been affected by depopulation. Since the census of 1953, the population of the municipality of Svrljig has declined by one-third and now numbers about 20,000. There

* Senior Research Fellow at the Ethnographic Institute, Moskovska 6-A Str. Sofia-1000, Bulgaria. E-mail: milena@tusk.icn.bg.

are in 39 centres of population, 6000 people living in the town of Svrljig (Golubovich 1992: 173). The largest of the Serbian villages studied, Crnoljevica, had a population of 248 in 1998. The Bulgarian villages are more populous: Zverino has 2300 inhabitants and Ignatica – 900.

In the problematic years of 'transition' in Bulgaria, the informal economy has turned into a means of physical survival for an entire social strata in the country (cf. the definition of poverty in Sanders 1977: 58). My thesis is that there has been a return to a way of life, to a livelihood using techniques bequeathed by tradition as a means of survival. A typical arena for the unfolding of this process is the village and the small town (population under 15 000), despite of the fact that the big cities have been considerably influenced by it, too (cf. Stamenova 1995: 106).

Under socialism, informal activities were a strategy of coping with the chronic shortages of goods (cf. also Creed 1998), while today, during the problematic 'transition', they are a strategy for dealing with the crisis. These phenomena are likewise geographically determined. Following the restitution of the land (after 1992), in the plain regions, where prior to collectivization there had been large-scale farm ownership (mostly in the Dobrudja), specific forms of large-scale market-oriented farming are also gaining grounds today (cf. Giordano & Kostova 1997a). In the mountainous and hilly regions, where the arable land is little and petty ownership predominates, the situation is different.

North Western Bulgaria

Throughout the entire socialist period, the population in the villages and in the small towns supplemented their incomes by producing (above all, to meet their personal needs, and in most of the cases, without farming being the basic occupation) fruit and vegetables and raising farm stock (Smollett 1986 [1989]; Stamenova 1995: 102-105; Benovska-Sabkova 1997; Creed 1998: 191-192), confined to the courtyard or small 'private' plots of land (most often 0.1-0.2 ha), granted by the local authorities. These were usually plots of land where families cultivated a small market garden and/or a vineyard. According to an extensive sociological survey, conducted in 1977 and published in 1987, 61.6% of all the Bulgarian families maintained vegetable gardens or orchards, 51.3% raised fowl, and 41.5% – farm animals. About 16% of the animal produce thus obtained was meant for the market, 84% for their own family and network partners (Kjuranov 1987: 145-146).

But this 'informal economy', characteristic of the socialist period in Bulgaria, has roots in the more distant past. During field research in North Western Bulgaria[2] I established that the original form of that kind of 'informal economy' originated as far back as the early decades of the 20th century. Contrary to the traditional conceptions of ethnography regarding the division of labour by sex and by age, women between the 1910s to the 1950s were largely occupied with ploughing, which was also an activity considered a concern of the men (Marinov 1914: 154). Women had almost entirely taken over the obligations associated with farming, whereas men oriented themselves more often to non-farming trades and professions. In 1931, the existence of ten craftsmen was registered in Zverino: tailors, a blacksmith, an iron master, coopers, a stone worker, carpenters (Jubileen sbornik 1931). Data from the interviews show that the railwaymen, the builders, the petty merchants, teachers, inn-keepers, butchers, and so on had also been well represented in Zverino and Ignatica, but not registered. A similar phenomenon was common during the same period in other parts of Bulgaria (the regions of Tran or in the Pirin mountain), where seasonal labour migration by men ('gurbet') was widespread. However, in the region of Vratsa the men tended to engage in non-farming trades without leaving the centre of population and without giving up entirely farm work. Almost identical was the picture in other mountain regions – the regions of Lovech and Samokov – in the early 20th century. The men were primarily occupied with some trade (building, pottery, dying and painting, carpentry and the like) and helped with the field work in periods when they were not engaged with their craft (Wolf 1997: 42; Grebenarova 1999: 323). The growth of the craft occupation in the 1930s was also discussed as an aspect of modernization. In 1936, 'the craftsmen's workshops in the villages were more numerous than those in the towns' (Popova 1999: 277-278).

Therefore, farming as 'informal economy' was common even prior to the socialist period, but under socialism that trend intensified parallel to the processes of social diversification in the village. 'The partial involvement in farm work is essential for the socialist system' (Creed 1995: 847). Socialism seems to have further developed some cultural strategies preserved from the past, lending to them a new meaning and a new rhythm includig formal labour activity within a framework of fixed working hours.

Under socialism, the development of farms as extra-vocational or extra-professional activity was formally encouraged by state and party decrees in the 70s concerning 'self-sufficiency of the population'.[3] In 1978, some 53 800 ha of arable land were distributed for *personal usage* and some 5254 *auxiliary farms* were set up (Zlatev, Mateev, Migev 1981: 229). The auxiliary farms were a non-family form of farm production – agricultural units (pig farms, market gardens, and so on) set up alongside the industrial enterprises.

It seems obvious that the issuing of party and state decisions on 'self-sufficiency' was an attempt to counteract the advanced (but not officially recognised) crisis in agriculture after the 70s. The agricultural land that was distributed 'for personal usage' was cultivated because this coincided with the attitudes of broad strata of the population in the villages and in the small towns. This was also an expression of the double standards typical for socialism. On the one hand, programmes were vociferously advertised (on the idea of Todor Zhivkov's daughter Ljudmila Zhivkova) supporting the formation of 'a personality of all-round development'. In practice, however, a lack of spirituality existed due to an overwhelming pre-occupation with physical survival (about the rapidly declining cultural standards in the village cf. Creed 1998: 4).

An investigation, carried out in the 70s and 80s in the ethnically mixed region of the Eastern Rhodope Mountains (the region of Kardjali), gives a good idea of the personal farm and of the preparation of food preserves. A considerable number of the urban population was covered by the investigation and it was discovered that two-thirds of the households in the district had their own personal farm. There they grew vegetables, pulse, fruit, potatoes, and grapes. Farm animals were raised in 59% of the households of the Kardjali region; fowl – in 65% (Stamenova 1995: 102-103). Labour in the time off work is burdening (Creed 1998: 4) turning a five-day working week into a six- or seven-day week (Stamenova 1995: 104). Gerald W. Creed points with respect to the village of Zamfirovo (North Western Bulgaria) that:

> *In nearly all collectivized agricultural systems, the cooperative or state farm provided workers a small plot of land to cultivate for household consumption. This sustained the economic viability of disadvantaged agricultural workers in the socialist economy and allowed the state to continue exploiting them. In 1987 the Zamfirovo farm allowed villagers 5 decares of land for such use, including the yard around their house [...]. Typically, villagers used 3 decares of this land for corn and wheat production. The remaining 2 decares were divided equally between a vineyard and a vegetable garden. [...] Typically they (villagers – M.B.) had one goat, several sheep, a pig and several chickens (Creed 1998, pp. 95-96, 97).*

Naturally, household production does not mean the absence of a market and of trade in farm produce; they not only provide for the subsistence of the farm workers, but also service that part of the population which has not been involved in 'subsistence' farming. Vegetables were kept processed and/or preserved (cf. Kepov 1942: 43-44; Vakarelski 1974: 212-226). The making of preserves and the processing of vegetables and meats has been operating without any interruption to this day, along with the more recent technology (probably originating in the towns) of making stewed fruit preserves and jams. In the 70s and 80s, in the region of Kardjali 94.8 % of the population annually made stewed fruit preserves, fruit juices, canned vegetables and fruit, marinated vegetables. Some 65.8%, respectively, made meat preserves and home-made sausages each year or more seldom (Stamenova 1995: 98).

The model of petty farming has been common in North Western Bulgaria and has been aimed at securing food. The following combinations could be pointed out, as a rule: a vegetable garden and fruit trees in the courtyard, a vineyard and a second, separate vegetable garden. The need for two vegetable gardens – one in the courtyard, and another one elsewhere – was determined by: a) the small size of the courtyards in mountainous conditions; b) the presence/absence of water supply. Outside the courtyard, vegetables are planted close to a brook or a river, where the traditional ways of irrigation are possible (Bogdanova 1997: 16). In the plain part of the region, the vegetable gardens are combined with a melon field because of the suitable conditions for growing melons and water melons, whereas the courtyards also contained (because of their greater size – 0.2-0.3 ha) vineyards.

Engagement with stock breeding greatly varies depending on individual capacities and wishes of each family. In the investigated mountain villages, there is a general practice of raising a dozen or so hens and a pig. Cows are a rarity. As has been pointed out, in the conditions of a complex family, the elders are mostly engaged in stock breeding. Most often, a family's sheep and goats herd consists of about ten animals or less. Where the animals remain in the village (and are not taken to graze in the mountain), in the warm seasons they are brought together in a common neighbourhood herd, which is grazed 'na zareda', i.e. for each day the families appoint one member who goes shepherding (cf. Vakarelski 1974: 544).

Whereas in socialist practice people relied mostly on shops to get milk and dairy products (cf. also Stamenova 1995: 100), since the social transformation after 1990 this has changed: nearly half of the families in the villages investigated produce now dairy products in the household. Unlike the variability in the forms of stock breeding, petty farming (most of all market-gardening and vine-growing) was during socialism and is now exercised practically by everybody – not only people in retirement, but also working people, young families included. Unlike the region of Kardjali during socialism, here there have been no exceptions to the practice of keeping a petty private farm. What draws the attention is the fact that vegetable gardens are grown in the courtyards of families who, far from being in financial dire straights, may be considered fairly well-to-do, in terms of Bulgarian scales and standards. In other words, informal farming occupations are not only and always the result of economic coercion; obviously, this is a matter of enduring attitudes in terms of values. Whether the market garden is well or poorly kept is also an element of an individual's personal prestige in terms of village public opinion.

The process of restitution of the land proceeded differently and yielded different results in the mountainous and in the plain parts of North Western Bulgaria, respectively. For instance, in the plain area of the Vratsa and Montana regions new agricultural cooperatives have been operating since 1990, representing a compromise between the restitution of small plots and the real need of large-scale farming (concerning the cooperatives cf. Kaneff 1995, 1996). They offer possibilities for combined forms of cultivation of the land. In successfully functioning cooperatives in the plain villages of the region, the owners – members of the agricultural cooperatives have the right to a choice. Part of the invested land is managed by the board of the cooperatives. On another part of the land the owners decide for themselves what crops are to be grown. These are usually small plots (from 0.1-0.2 to 1 ha), planted with fodder crops – maize, barley, and wheat – in order to secure animal feed. Against certain payment, the cooperative performs the mechanised operations of ploughing and sowing.

In the mountainous region where I worked, these mechanisms do not operate; there are no conditions for the mechanised cultivation of maize and other fodder crops. Involvement in the kinship network of mutual assistance compensates this to some extent. The mountaineers till the land, which was entered into the agricultural cooperative by their relatives living in villages in the plain. In such cases, all able-bodied members of the families get organised and travel to the village in the plain, where they are occupied with digging for a day or two on the land 'borrowed' by the relatives.

For the first time in decades there are families who do not buy bread, but bake it at home using their own flour. Somewhat forgotten technologies are being restored on a wide scale in the villages and in the smaller towns: cooking with lard rather than vegetable oil; use of home-made soap from sow's fat; traditional sweeteners are being prepared in home conditions (using sugar beet or pumpkins) – rachel, pestil, madjun. The extensive preparing of 'zimnina' (preserves to last during the winter) has not changed since socialist time. This is characteristic for almost the entire country, including the capital, where part of the preserves are made using vegetables and fruit bought in the market.

Primitive techniques are being applied in the re-traditionalization of farming. The main implement is the hoe. Sometimes one can observe how elderly men are ploughing with a wooden or iron plough, in which they have harnessed to a donkey or themselves. In fact, this type of farming 'for one's own usage' is more primitive than private farming prior to the Second World War, because people now have neither any farm implements, nor the 'live power' of the draught animals. As is well known, farm implements and the draught animals, together with the land, had been handed over to the cooperative farms in the process of collectivization of the land in 1948-1958 (cf. Migev 1995: 295-297; Dobreva 1997: 72-86). Bulgaria is known as the country where collectivization of the land was carried out most thoroughly, almost 100%.

Obviously, informal farming activities (both under socialism and during the post-socialist period) have been taking place within the family. This fact raises the question regarding the economic functions of the family under socialism. In other words, 'subsistence' farming has obviously run counter to the familiar cliché many times repeated regarding the family's economic functions reducing during socialism. That contradiction has been detected in the sociological survey 'The Present-day Bulgarian Family' (Kjuranov 1987: 293). Indeed, the economic functions of the Bulgarian family were reduced under socialism insofar as there was *de facto* no private ownership of the means of production. At the same time, however, private farms were a kind of informal economic activity which made up, to a certain extent, for that reduction.

Informality is a principle equally valid for the two sexes and of various age groups, no matter whether what is considered is a nuclear, or a complex family. In the socialist and mostly also in the post-socialist period, men and women alike have been active in non-farming employment and in private farming. Owing to the massive employment of women outside the framework of the family household, like the men, they also work on private farms in their 'leisure time'. This has been valid for the socialist and – largely – for the post-socialist period, as well.

As far as the sex and age division of labour goes, petty subsistence farming differs from traditional/pre-modern farming. The change is most clear-cut with respect to children. They were involved in working on personal farms in only 6% of families, which had such farms in the 70s (Kjuranov 1987: 152). This does not imply, however, an even labour loading between representatives of the two sexes within the framework of the family. If for the men, farming occupations in their time off work were a double labour burden, for the women this was a triple employment, because they also did most of the household work (Kjuranov 1987: 151; Creed 1998: 4).

The activation of traditional mutual assistance should also be pointed out as part of the process of re-traditionalization, mostly within and via the kinship networks. Mutual assistance has undergone reduction and considerable modifications in different historical periods, but has never ceased to exist. Its forms are extremely varied. However, it is indisputable that a strong, ramified and well-organised family network is in a position to produce tangible economic and social effects.

We are now witnessing the revival of the old forms of reciprocity. Material assistance is, for the first time, being directed to parents from their children as well. A great number of working sons and daughters help their parents on pensions with cash. This observation can be illustrated by a specific case, observed in the village of Zverino. The oldest woman in the complex family, 'great grandmother' Stefanka, aged 84, looks after (with the help of her son and daughter-in-law) a cow, a few sheep and several pigs. But the family does not sell the milk; it makes fetta and yellow cheese out of it, which, along with the milk, is sent out twice a week to 'the children' living in Sofia. Despite the seemingly 'descendant' orientation of the distribution of the material values, the positive social effect extends to the 'great grandmother', too. Without the support of younger family members she would not have been able to provide food for the animals. This makes an undisputed advantage with regard to her lonely coevals: a friend of hers is living in scarcity and under worse living and sanitation conditions. In another case (in the village of Ignatica), widow Petra gives her arable land to her sister and brother-in-law; in return they supply her with milk and dairy products.

The re-traditionalization as a means of survival is, of course, relative. There is no complete or mechanical reproduction of the traditional life. Modernization proceeds with re-traditionalization (Roth 1996: 245-260), and most of all, with its most outstanding manifestation, i.e. technological progress. Insofar as technological progress is a global process, Bulgaria cannot remain isolated from it, despite the acute crisis. It is not a matter of telecommunications or computers alone here, but most of the household equipment, whether acknowledged or not, symbolises the Bulgarians' modernized quality and standard of living. It is precisely during the period of transition that the video recorder and the freezer have become widespread, while access to satellite or cable television is not an exception in the villages. The paradoxical combination of crisis and poverty with the purchasing of expensive objects can be explained by the value system of the Bulgarians, who tend to endure privations, while investing their money in durable objects, assessed as a sign of prestige and prosperity. A short digression: it is precisely the identification of modernization, which began in the wake of the Second World War (actually as a global process), with the socialist period that is one of the explanations (though not the only one, cf. Creed 1995: 845) for the nostalgia for socialism expressed mostly by elderly people.

Obviously, these are regressive socio-economic trends. On the one hand, the re-traditionalization helps the physical survival of quite a few social strata and on the other hand, runs counter to economic progress. It is impossible to predict how lasting these trends will be, whether they are just a temporary phenomenon, a response to the critical situation. The return to certain forms of tradition may also be seen as mobilising the internal reserves of a system; evidence of mechanisms whereby the latter counteracts its own destruction.

Eastern Serbia

The comparison between agricultural employment in Bulgaria, on the one hand, and Eastern Serbia, on the other, provides material for deliberation, which goes beyond the confines of the subject of the informal economy. The manifestations of the informal economy most clearly bring out the differences in the present-day functioning of everyday cultures in the two regions. As in Bulgaria (cf. Smollett 1986; Creed 1998: 186; Roth 1999), the complementary dependence between formal and informal employment in Eastern Serbia unfolds on the territory of the family, the household and the kinship circle. But the differences are more numerous than the similarities.

The role of the complex family as the social environment for carrying out agricultural activities as a combination of formal and informal type of employment is illustrated by several examples, which outline a pattern economically based on private farming. Its specificity is the supplementation of farming as a basic and informal occupation, with non-farming trades and professions (bringing in either a salary, or some other steady income). Individual variations in the structure and composition of individual families notwithstanding, the principle remains one and the same. The men of three generations have *dual employment*: a certain non-farming trade or profession and the farming activities traditionally considered 'male'. *As a basic occupation, farming is a characteristic feature of the older generation of women,* born prior to the end of the Second World War. Young women (born after) have the same dual employment as men: paid work outside the house and informal agricultural employment, traditionally defined as 'women's' (cf. Filipovic 1982). The youngest in the family – the great grandchildren – help their parents and their grandparents.

The family household in Crnoljevica village is made up of four generations. Presented in age from the oldest to the youngest members it takes the following appearance: 'the great grandmother' Dobrica – the mother of Vinko (1914); the first family couple – 'granddad' Vinko (1941) and 'grandma' Negosava (1939); a second family couple comprising their son and daughter-in-law, and their children – grandchildren of Vinko and great-grandchildren of the great grandmother. The family has about 15 ha of land, some of it covered by meadows. Negosava (like her mother-in-law Dobrica) has never worked outside her house, but it is her obligation to tend the nine cows and calves, seven pigs, a dozen or so sheep, rabbits, and poultry; to perform a great number of other farming operations considered lighter; and, of course, to do the house-keeping. In Yugoslavia, working hours officially start and end early – from 7 a.m. to 3 p.m. Following the rules of absente-eism, men leave work earlier (around 2 or 2.30 p.m.); they get home and they are engaged in farming activities until the evening. Bearing in mind that Vinko has held prestigious jobs, including the position of director of a textile mill, enables us to explore the power of the principle of mutual supple-mentation between farming and professional and vocational employment.

In this family they mostly rely on their son Miodrag (born 1957). When asked how they manage to cultivate so much land, Negosava answers: "We have a son. The son, and myself and the daughter-in-law. Well, now, the grandchildren have grown up and lend a hand. The granny cannot, she stays home." 'The son' and 'the daughter-in-law' keep a shop. They combine trade with farming – in the remaining time. As evident from the quotation, the grandchildren (teenagers) also lend a hand in the farm work. Only the old 'great grandmother' remains outside the organization. Farming and stock breeding are the main occupation of Negosava. For the rest of the family members, these are informal activities.

Similar is the case of the family of Vidinka from Beloinje. And the third family – that of Slavko from the village of Beloinje – also incorporates four generations: this time three family couples, two great grandchildren aged up to four, and a lateral extension – the widowed mother of a wife from the intermediary generation. The head of the household is the oldest man Slavko (1919) who weaves baskets. His son is working as a driver in the town of Svrljig. The 'son' has engaged a carpenter's workshop and does carpentry in his time off work. The grandson also has a permanent non-agricultural job. The workshop is a material embodiment of the principle of combination and supplementation of different activities. Stored in it also are the tractor and other farm equipment, as well as an old traditional vessel for the distillation of rakija (brandy). Running across the courtyard (about 0.5 ha) is a brook, from which water is collected in a small fishery (about 100 sq m) for fish-breeding. The old small flour mill is no longer in operation, but it is used to smoke meat.

Obviously, the family in Eastern Serbia has preserved its economic func-tions to a greater extent than in Bulgaria. Distribution of production func-tions according to the sex principle should be discussed in parallel. The pattern discussed depends on the full employment of the older generation of women in household farm production. The coordination and control over various production activities is exercised by them. Male roles in the labour activities have been significantly adapted to the modern way of life. The activities requiring mechanised labour are controlled by men who, with the help of machines, take charge in the traditionally male activities of ploughing, sowing and the like. In this way, mechanization fits in, without any conflicts, with the traditional division of labour obligations according to sex. What is more, the specific combination between tradition and modernization is a beneficial factor for the economic functions of the family.

The outlined pattern is not applicable to households of lonely people, which are numerous in these villages. They are also included in networks of solidarity and mutual assistance, along channels of which material resources, though much more limited, are also moving. Networks of lonely people are not organized on the family, neighbourhood and relationship principle. As in the case of widow Petra from the Bulgarian village of Ignatica, widow Rada from the village of Crnoljevica looks after the empty houses of five families, living in the nearby towns. She takes care lest some breakdown occurs in the absence of the owners. She looks after the four pigs of a family, who live in the town of Pirot and return to the village on Saturday and Sunday. In the same way as in Bulgaria, the lonely people help their relatives and friends. In return, they receive support, as well as recompense in kind.

Discussion

In the same way as in Bulgaria, the overlap between formal and informal activities secures self-sufficiency in foodstuffs ('subsistence'), in a much more extended form in the region of Svrljig. The ambition is the same: to buy as little as possible from the shops. This principle is much more consistently implemented in the region of Svrljig. If in Bulgaria in the present time of crisis some village families (by far not all) have returned to the making of bread at home, a tradition abandoned under socialism, in the villages of Eastern Serbia this is today mass practice, continuing without interruption. They are all kneading bread here out of the flour they have produced themselves. No bread is sold in the village shops either. Exemplary is the answer, given by an elderly Serb from the village of Izvor to the question whether they are making bread at home or they buy it: 'Some people, working in the town have the privilege of buying it; as for ourselves, we bake it here at home.' The question 'What do you buy from the shops' gets a fairly uniform answer practically everywhere: 'We buy olive oil, sugar, rice, vermicelli, beer...'. In other words, they only buy what they cannot produce at home. Almost the entire range of foodstuffs is covered by home production. An important supplementary item is game hunting: in Svrljig there are about 1000 hunters.

Here, too, like in Bulgaria, the household food industry has its original form in the traditional accumulation of foods, called in North Western Bulgaria 'zimnina', and in Eastern Serbia – 'zimnica'. Owing to the larger scale of household production in Serbia, that accumulation of preserves is more extensive and has kept more of its traditional features. The technology of food preservation here is closer to its 'traditional' variant: the vegetable preserves are kept in wooden casks, and bottles and jars are used less often than in Bulgaria. Indicative of the scope of preserve making is the information that, in Noviica's six-member complex family from the village of Merdjelat, 300 litres of rakija (brandy) are distilled annually.

Unlike the strategy of production in order to meet the family needs ('subsistence'), predominant in Bulgaria, there is considerable excess production here with market orientation, which supplements the cash revenues. Due to the presence of larger land property at a marketable scale, even in the conditions of the political trials and tribulations, crises, embargo and wars, there can hardly be a real production crisis in these Eastern Serbian villages. This implies a greater independence of the family from the influences of society at large. What is more, in the same way as in Bulgaria, in Serbia, too, the relatives in town receive a considerable share of what has been produced in the village. Asked what he delivers to 'the children' in town (the children being middle-aged), an elderly Serb from the village of Izvor answered: 'Everything – from onions to meat'.

There is a conception that, under socialism in Bulgaria, the informal economy contributed to preserving the role of the family and of kinship (Creed 1998: 186). The same, obviously, holds good for Eastern Serbia. No less truthful, however, is the opposite: i.e. that family and kinship have provided the basis for the functioning of the informal economy. The principle of mutual cooperation between the formal and informal sources of income is similar in Bulgaria and in Serbia. There are, however, substantial differences between the Serbian and the Bulgarian application of this model.

In the first place are the different natural and geographical factors. The villages in North Western Bulgaria are typically mountainous and the low-fertility soil is a setback for agriculture. It is not accidental that today, after the re-privatization of the land (1992), there is no agricultural cooperative in the village of Zverino, unlike some other big villages in the plain, where there are as many as three. The villages in the region of Svrljig are, on the other hand, located in a hilly valley offering fine conditions for farming. In addition, the closeness of several small mountains is rather beneficial, because it makes possible the use of mountain pastures. Obviously, there is no true disengagement from farming here; there is not even a tiny spot of uncultivated land.

The difference in the size of landed ownership is also great. As in the pre-socialist past, today after the re-privatization of the land, Bulgaria has become a country of mostly petty owners (cf. Giordano & Kostova 1997: 133) and the average size of landed ownership today (after restitution) is 5 ha. In the investigated region of North Western Bulgaria, the landed ownership is even more fragmented (rarely exceeding 1-2 ha). In the region of Svrljg, the average size of landed property is about 10 ha (from among the 14 families questioned, only one owned less than10 ha). The land was not collectivised, although certain (unsuccessful) attempts were made along this line. In the early years of Tito's socialism there had been certain restrictions regarding the size of ownership (not to exceed 10 ha), which today are no longer valid.

The state has had hardly any restrictive political impact on the development of private agriculture, and therefore in the Eastern Serbia villages investigated, 'the traditional culture' continued its development during the socialist period.

Negative factors have also had their impact on the villages in Eastern Serbia. Here modernization has followed other rates. The successful continuity of traditional private farming went along with belated modernization of collective services. It was only in the 70s that the villages of Beloinje and Crnoljevica were supplied with electricity (as a comparison, the Bulgarian villages of Zverino and Ignatica were linked to the power lines in 1948).

Notwithstanding set backs of migration and the decreasing population since 1953, those who have remained in the village have a relatively high living standard – higher than that of the Bulgarian villages investigated. This has largely been due to the flexible combination of informal and formal economic activity.

Of great importance is also the difference in the means of production. In the Serbian villages investigated there is practically no household without a tractor. Some families have complete parks of farming machines with large sums of money invested. This drastic difference in the rate of mechanization between North Western Bulgaria and Eastern Serbia is a result of socio-historical and societal factors.

In Serbia, mechanization has been accomplished thanks to the upsurge and liberalization of the Yugoslav economy since the early 1960s (Manchev 1999, p. 314). In the 70s, the government gave profitable loans to the farmers, and during that period most of them bought tractors on a repayment scheme. Gastarbeiters also played a role in this process as they helped in the purchasing of family tractors. But their share in this should not be overesti-mated. Mechanization considerably increases productivity of farm labour and enables the cultivation of greater areas by fewer people. As has been mentioned, during the collectivization of the arable land in Bulgaria (1948-1958) not only the land, but the draught animals and farm tools were also expropriated and replaced by central pools of big machinery unusable today. This is why villagers now rarely have anything else other than hoes.

Finally, the following conclusions can be formulated. Farming as an informal activity develops mostly in terms of the family and kinship net-works: and conversely, the latter succeed in preserving their social role via the mechanisms of informal employment. The private and larger ownership of land (including during socialism), the more favourable geographic fac-tors, the extensive use of agricultural machinery and the flexible family organization of labour has guaranteed the successful functioning of the Eastern Serbian agriculture. This enables a market orientation, as well as securing a fairly good level of meeting the producers' own needs. This secures relatively good living standards for the people and further develop-ment of the traditional cultural technologies, there is gradual transformation of the 'tradition'. The combination of the traditional family organization and the modernization of the means of production (farming machinery) is a model of fruitful coexistence of tradition and modernization. The informal farming in Bulgaria today, in the period of 'transition', is almost exclusively oriented to the family's own survival (on the edge of poverty) and largely proceeds as re-traditionalization.

More general conclusions could also be drawn here regarding the impact of the socialist heritage on the 'transition'. The course of the 'transition' depends also on the features of the socialism preceding it (Creed 1998: 25, 11). The 'soft' and 'opportunistic' socialism of Tito has left a heritage enabling everyday culture in Eastern Serbia to continue its evolution today without any sharp shocks, even when the society at large provides an acute-ly conflicting framework through the dramatic disintegration of 'great Yugoslavia'. On the other hand: 'the peaceful transition' in Bulgaria has not spared the Bulgarians either the hunger crises, or the daily stress in the lives of millions of people, because so far their efforts have proved insufficient to overcome the social and economic disproportion inherited from orthodox socialism. Ten years after the fall of the Berlin Wall, the everyday culture in two neighbouring Balkan regions continues to bear the imprint left on it by 'big' history.

Notes

1   This work has been sponsored by the Research Support Scheme Program, project No. 714/1998.

2   Data according to the Municipality Archive, village of Zverino (1997). Both villages belong to the Zverino municipality. Actually, in the archive exists a card-file of inhabitants; besides, the archive safeguards the local data from the National Census (1992).

3   These were: the 61st decree of the Council of Ministers, 1973; Decision of the Politburo of the Central Committee of the Bulgarian Communist Party of March 1977 on the year-round provision of fruit and vegetables for the population and on the self-sufficiency of the districts; October 1977 Decree on the self sufficiency of the population in fruit and vegetables, meat, milk, eggs and fish.

References

Bogdanova, S. (1977), *Vodosnabdjavaneto u balgarite. Etnologièni aspekti* [Water Supply Systems of the Bulgarians. Ethnological Aspects], Sofia.

Creed, G.W. (1995), The Politics of Agriculture: Identity and Socialist Sentiment in Bulgaria, in *Slavic Review*, 54, pp. 843-868.

Creed, G.W. (1998), *Domesticating Revolution. From Socialist Reform to Ambivalent Transition in a Bulgarian Village*, University Park, Penn., Pennsylvania State University Press.

Dobreva, D. (1997), Arbeiten im Kollektiv. Offizielle Norm und tatsächliches Verhalten in einem bulgarischen Gebirgsdorf in den 1950er Jahren [Working in the Collective. Official Norm and Actual Behaviour in a Bulgarian Mountain Village in the 1950s], in Fr. Grimm, K. Roth (eds.), *Das Dorf in Südosteuropa zwischen Tradition und Umbruch. Munich*, SOG, pp. 196-223, summary p. 274.

Drobnjakovici, B. (1960), *Etnologija naroda Jugoslavije*, part one, Belgrade, Nauèna knjiga.

Filipovici, M. (1982), Among the People, Ann Arbor, University of Michigan (*Papers in Slavic Philology 3*).

Giordano, C. (1994), The Informal Economy in Central and Eastern Europe. A Culturally Adequate Strategy for Development in the Post-Communist Transformation?, in *Anthropological Journal of European Cultures* 3, 1, pp. 95-196.

Giordano, C., Kostova, D. (1997), Bulgarian Land Re-privatization without Peasants, in *Ethnologia Balkanica*, 1, pp. 135-149.

Golubovici, P. (1992), Stanovništvo i naselja, in S. Petroviæ (ed.), *Kulturna istorija Svrljiga*, 2, Jezik, kultura i civilizacija, Niš, Svrljig.

Grebenarova, S. (1999), Semejstvo i rod [Family and Kinship], in *Loveški kraj, Materialna i duhovna kultura* [Lovech Region. Material and Spiritual Culture], Sofia, pp. 321-348.

Jubileen sbornik (1931), *Balgarskoto selo* [Jubilee Collection 1931: Bulgarian Village], Sofia.

Just, R. (1991), The Limits of Kinship, in P. Loizos, E. Papataxiarchis (eds.), *Contested Identities. Gender and Kinship in Modern Greece*, Princeton, NJ, Princeton UP, pp. 114-132.

Kaneff, D. (1995), Developing Rural Bulgaria, in *Cambridge Anthropology*, 18, 2, pp. 23-34.

Kaneff, D. (1996), Responses to 'Democratic' Land Reforms in a Bulgarian Village, in R. Abrahams (ed.), *After Socialism: Land Reform and Social Change in Eastern Europe*, Oxford, Berghahn Books, pp. 85-114.

Kepov, I. (1936), 'Narodopisni, životopisni i ezikovi materiali ot s. Boboševo, Dupniško' [Materials from the Village of Boboševo, Dupnica region], in *Sbornik za narodni umotvorenija*, vol. 42.

Manèev, K. (1999), *Nacionalnijat vapros na Balkanite* [The National Question in the Balkans], Sofia.

Marinov, D. (1914), Narodna vjara i religiozni narodni obièai [Folk Religion and Religious Folk Customs], in *Sbornik za narodni umotvorenija*, vol. 28, Sofia.

Migev, V. (1995), *Kolektivizacijata na balgarskoto selo* (1948-1959) [The Collectivization of the Bulgarian Village (1948-1959)], Sofia.

Popova, K. (1999), Bog li gi beše sazdal takiva? Mãjete ot dvadeseti nabor v selo Tešovo [Has the Lord Created Them Such? The Men Born in 1920 in the Village of Teshovo], in P. Vodeni_arov, K. Popova, A. Pašova, *Moeto dosie, pardon, biografija. Balgarskite modernizacii (30-te i 60-te godini) – ideologii i identiènosti* [My File, excuse Me, my CV. The Bulgarian Modernizations (1930s and 1960s) – Ideologies and Identities], Blagoevgrad, pp. 274-292.

Prošici-Dvornici, M. (1992), The Rurbanization of Belgrade after the Second World War, in K. Roth (ed.), *Southeast European Folk Culture in the Modern Era*, Munich, SOG, pp. 75-102 (=Südosteuropa-Jahrbuch 22).

Roth, K. (1992), Die Volkskultur Sudosteuropas in der Moderne, in idem (ed.), *Southeast European Folk Culture in the Modern Era*, Munich: SOG, pp. 11-28 (=Südosteuropa-Jahrbuch 22).

Roth, K. (1995), Bürgertum und bürgerliche Kultur in Südosteuropa. Ein Beitrag zur Modernisierungsdiskussion, in Ueli Gyr (ed.), *Soll und Haben. Alltag und Lebensformen bürgerlicher Kultur*, Zürich, Offizin, pp. 245-260. Engl.: Bourgeois Culture and Civil Society in Southeast Europe. A Contribution to the Debate on Modernization. Turku: Nordic Institute of Folklore 1997 (=NIF Papers 5).

Roth, K. (1999), Praktiken und Strategien der Bewältigung des Alltagslebens in einem Dorf im sozialistischen Bulgarien, in *Zeitschrift für Balkanologie* 35 (1999) pp. 63-77. Bulgar.: Praktiki i strategii za ovladjavane na vsekidnevieto v edno selo na socialistièeska Balgarija, in *Sociologièeski problemi* 30, 3-4 (1998), pp. 224-237.

Sanders, I. (1977), *Rural Society*, Englewood Cliffs, NJ, Prentice Hall.

Smollett, E. (1989), 'The Economy of Jars. Kindred Relationships in Bulgaria – An Exploration', in *Ethnologia Europaea* 19, pp. 125-140.

Stamenova, Z. (1995), *Etnosocialni aspekti na bita v Iztoènite Rodopi prez 70-te i 80-te godini* [Ethno-Social Aspects of Lifestyle in the Eastern Rhodopes in the '70s and '80s], Pernik, Krakra.

Vakarelski, H. (1969), Bulgarische Volkskunde, Berlin. Bulg.: *Etnografija na Balgaria* [Ethnography of Bulgaria], Sofia, 1974.

Windebank, J. (1993), 'Perspectivism as Interdisciplinary Methodology', A Case Study of its Application to Research into the Formal Economy in France, in *Journal of Area Studies* 3, pp. 6-19.

Wolf, G. (1997), *Der gebaute sozialistische Raum. Die räumlich-funktionale Umgestaltung eines bulgarischen Dorfes seit den 1950er Jahren* [The Built Socialist Space. Spatial and Functional Restructuring of a Bulgarian Village since the 1950s], in Fr. Grimm, K. Roth (eds.), *Das Dorf in Südosteuropa zwischen Tradition und Umbruch*, Munich, SOG, pp. 165-195, summary p. 273.

Zlatev, Z., Mateev, B., Migev, V. (1981), *Balgarija v epohata na socializma* [Bulgaria in the Socialist Period], Sofia.

PART II
ROMANIA

Chapter 5

Romania

Constantin Ciupagea*

The first years of transition in all transition countries were accompanied by a large-scale decline in the Gross Domestic Product (GDP). External factors bringing about a drop in the GDP included the global economic crisis at the beginning of the nineties, which hit developing countries particularly hard and led to a decrease in demand and consumption globally. An additional and more transforming factor was the destruction of the former COMECON system. Domestic factors are connected to the dissolution of the socialist central planning system, which was replaced by a weakly structured economy attempting to imitate features of a market economy in an environment characterised by an old-style mentality and behaviour. In Romania, the decline of GDP was not much different from the figures registered by the other CEEC (Central Eastern European Countries) during the same period. However, while other forerunners restructured their systems and changed their institutional framework during the early period of turmoil, Romania chose a policy of 'smooth transition' which allowed administrative structures to continue their behaviour, maintain confusion in the area of ownership and privatization, and supposedly attempt to preserve the social standards of workers. Consequently, after a short period of recovery which was not sustained through consistent economic policies (1993-1996), Romania entered a second cycle of economic decline in the late nineties. With this brief period of recovery, some structural and institutional changes were realised. The new wave of recession, however, eroded public support for reforms, the integrity of policymakers, and potentials for future transformation and growth. Until the year 2000, Romanian economic policy can be characterised as a 'stop-and-go' process, which further destroyed the government's credibility and the international image of the country's reform efforts. By the end of 2000, the real GDP of Romania was 77.4% of its 1989 level.

* Research Professor, Institute for World Economy, Calea 13 Septembrie nr. 13, 76117, Bucharest, Romania. E-mail: ciupagea@rnc.ro.

The structural heritage

The socialist form of economy was characterised by a particularly high level of concentration of firms in each economic sector (even in domestic trade activities). In the first few years of transition, sluggish reform and the uneven sectoral process of privatization led to major differences in the degree of market development between the sectors. In agriculture, the Land Reform Law in 1990 destroyed the former quasi-monopolistic presence of the state and induced the establishment of millions of very small household farms. Most of these farms began to produce within an informal market framework since, as a result of fiscal exemptions, there was no specific requirement to register their output. In industry, the degree of concentration remained extremely high for the most part, as a result of the markedly slow pace of the privatization process. In manufacturing, nearly 6.2% of all firms produced 80% of the total output from 1996 to 1998. Greater openness and competition could be found in the textile and clothing industry, leather and wood processing industries, and in the food industry. However, these sub-sectors do not belong to the group of engine-driving industries which serve to foster demand throughout the economy. With the massive decline in the industrial labour force, there was no compensation in the form of new jobs which are most likely to be created through an inflow of foreign investment (such investment remained very low throughout the decade). Numerous business firms entered the marketplace in the areas of retail trade, construction, banking and insurance, tourism, and catering. These sectors increased their share of the value added in the overall economy, nonetheless, the employment level remained low.

Another legacy is the low mobility of the working force. The former socialist system developed barriers to control and reduce the mobility of labour force by offering inexpensive, state-subsidised housing and/or other in-kind benefits in close proximity to the workplace. Further, the mentality inherited from the socialist system, which causing most Romanians to still consider a job to be a lifetime endeavour and professional retraining to be of no value, reduced career mobility.

Economic distortions and policies in the nineties

In the beginning of this period of transition, decreases in investment and the reversal from export excesses to increasing import excesses denoted the main macroeconomic aspects of the recession. In 1990, the decline in the real GDP was lower than in other CEEC as a result of an increase in the actual private consumption. This feature is specific to Romania and can be explained as a consequence of a pressure release on the side of consumption accumulated over the final twelve to thirteen years of communism. Lenient policy in the area of public consumption created huge budget deficits in the following years. This led to sharp increases in the consumption component of the aggregate demand, while investment and total capital formation severely dropped (in 1991, the real gross fixed capital formation was only 45% of its level registered in 1989 and, except for 1997, never again exceeded two-thirds of its 1989 level). Since economic recovery was not sustained by a high inflow of foreign resources after 1994, there was little potential for growth in Romania.

The structural and sectoral distribution of investments have suffered massive adjustments over the latest decade. The usual substitution of publicly financed (state) investment by private investment accounted for the decline registered in agriculture (in places privatization was not able to attract new investment resources) and in industry (especially in extraction and energy, which traditionally had been fuelled through governmental investment decisions). The same circumstances explain the growth in the share of investment for a number of sectors which developed at a faster rate in a market economy, especially in the areas of banking, communications, and trade.

Inflation is a fundamental feature of economic decline. Annual inflation rates varied between 256% in 1993 and 33% in 1995. Romania is the only country among the candidates for EU-integration which was never able to reduce its annual inflation rate to the level of a single digit.

The high inflation rate also upset the labour market for several reasons. First of all, ineffective stabilization policies led to a wage-inflation spiral, which brought further anxiety and insecurity into process of wage negotiations (in the official sector, during the negotiation of wages in the newly established social tripartite framework, because of the high inflation rates, labour providers had difficulty demanding adequate nominal increases). Second, inflation restrained investment by inducing unstable business prospects for investors and creditors. Third, high inflation allowed for larger gaps between a) self-producing households which, for the most part, suffered impoverishment despite being partially immune to the effects of inflation and b) households mainly dependent upon a monetary income which were exposed to inflation. Fourth, additional rising inequalities in income resulted from the uneven development between the various sectors and regions of Romania. The ratio between the highest and the lowest regional GDP among the eight Romanian Euro-regions increased from 1.6 in 1992 to more than 2 in 1999. The average unemployment rate ranged from 5.8% to 14.9% within the same regions.

Decreasing income and growing employment problems

The real wages evolution – presented in the Statistical Appendix – shows a huge deterioration of purchasing power since 1989, while regional income data confirms an expansion in the income gaps. Among the CEEC, Romania illustrates an extreme case of poverty with an upsurge of its poverty rate from 1993-1999. The uneven evolution of various economic sectors, as well as the high inflation rates led to increasing differences in the nominal wages between sectors amid widening gaps that induced social discontent and uprisings. Consequently, this motivated Romanian policy-makers to accept lax income policies and/or to prolong the subsidization of inefficient state-owned firms. The ratio between the highest and lowest average net wage related to economic sectors increased steadily from 1.8 in 1990 to 4.2 in 1998. Simultaneously, the number of wage-earning employees decreased from 8.1 million in 1989 to 4.5 million in 2000. Since social contributions were usually paid in correlation with wages, the basis of the social contribution budget revenues severely contracted during the transition period. In order to ensure social welfare protection for an increasing number of people in need, policy-makers were motivated to increase the tax rates accordingly. With this restructuring process and world-wide economic decline, the number of pensioners and the number of unemployed individuals increased more or less continuously. This, together with the number of people living below the poverty line as well as the 10% living below the subsistence line, led Romania to have the highest social contribution tax rate of all the EU-candidate countries by the end of 1999.

Within the larger context of a deteriorating macroeconomic framework, the growth of the informal economy's share in Romania was induced, among others, by the following phenomena:

First, the transformation of the economic sectors left enough room for the development of informal economic activities, especially in agriculture, in trade, of small artisans, and of some households as well as in business services, despite unstable financial and fiscal regulation and excessive changes in the legal framework of income taxation and distribution or corporate taxation.

Second, the unemployment phenomenon together with the unstable social protection system were important factors for fomenting public discontent and a decline in the standard of living in Romania. Rising unemployment, combined with the lack of mobility of the labour force motivated more and more people to shift from official to informal activities. From 1992 to 1996, an impressive number of new small businesses quickly emerged, most of which were run by self-employed individuals. This development, however, did not compensate for the increase in unemployment figures whatsoever (see Appendix). Only after 1998 did governments begin to develop active labour policies. This fostered greater labour force immobility throughout the 90s.

Until 1999, the general standard of living of the Romanian population deteriorated and large imbalances appeared in the performances of various groups of economic actors. The fiscal policy occasionally exhibited features characteristic of an underdeveloped economy, including very low shares of consolidated budget revenues and expenditures in GDP, a weak financial discipline and high deficits, and increasing tax rates in an escalating number of taxation categories. *The reduction in real government expenditures, in equipment, and in human capital led to further social pressures.*

The financial and banking system was not able to develop in such a manner able to support economic development, and thus, Romania was barely able to avoid a financial crisis following similar crises in various regions of the world. The recognised inability of Romania to cope with competitive pressures and to develop a market-style economy reduced the availability of financial resources to cover the lending requirements. Consequently, the country's rating on international markets was reduced several times over the period from 1997 to 1999. The slow pace of privatization – especially in the public utilities sector and in energy-intensive industries – diminished opportunities for restructuring and for embarking on a path of sustainable growth. By the end of 1999, the Romanian economy lagged behind all other EU-candidates, and there was a tremendous need to establish a consistent set of economic and social policies that would reverse the negative trends in the development of the economy and the standard of living.

Prospects for a consistent transformation after 1999

The slow process of social and economic reforms began to bear fruit by mid-1999, after the country was able to avoid entering a financial crisis despite external prognoses, and to curtail its long period of recession. With the change of government in December 1999, Romania witnessed a more consistent set of economic policies for the first time in the history of its transition. Interrupted by a short delay as a result of the election period in late 2000, the new line of reform policy designed to align Romania with European standards brought the country in 2001 onto the path of more rapid economic growth.

The process of fiscal consolidation and development of a sounder monetary policy accompanied by the acceleration of privatization in the banking sector led to improvements in Romania's international image and economic rating. These factors increased the credibility of the policy-makers and opportunities for economic recovery. Until now, budget deficits have been kept under control through a low inflationary pressure, a decline in financial arrears, and finally, through the beginning of the process to privatise public utilities and large state-owned firms in metallurgy, oil processing, and the machine equipment industry. Altogether, this gives some cause for optimism. Nonetheless, the inherited negative social problems listed below still need to be solved.

By the end of 2001, the share of agricultural employment in the total labour force was still near the 40% figure. There exists a mentality gap and behavioural gap between the rural and urban populations in Romania, in terms of perceptions over new reforms and market economics. In addition, strongly focused policies aimed at raising productivity in the agricultural sector are needed. At the same time, the Romanian economy needs a long period of rapid growth in the labour demand – especially in emerging dynamic industries – in order to reduce the share of 'rural' employment and to induce re-migration from rural to newly developed urban areas.

In spite of pressures from the high demand for social expenditures, the fiscal burden needs to be reduced and restructured, in order to fuel economic recovery and long-lasting growth. The low income tax base and rather high income tax rates in Romania as well as the overall fiscal system do not offer incentives for dynamic foreign or domestic investment. Without immediate changes in this area there will be continuous pressures on firms and on the labour force to engage in or to continue in informal market activities.

Of late, there is a growing trend toward income inequality which will probably remain high over the following years. The poverty rate is very high in Romania and varies greatly between regions and communities. A reform of the social security system is underway, but remains weak, inefficient, and lacking in financial and managerial resources.

Chapter 6

Romanian households between state, market and informal economies[1]

Manuela Stănculescu*

In the Romanian transition economy, the marketization process is accompanied by significant non-market activity. The transition should thus be understood as a transition not to capitalism, but to a plural economy, consisting of capitalist/market activities, state activities, and an autonomous household economy. Marketization swings between regulating and de-regulating processes and the absence of norms and market institutions has favoured a fast expansion of the informal economy (see Ciupagea in this volume). The collapse of the communist regime left a 'vacuum' in which households have been able to achieve (newly) autonomous actions that may have little to do with, either by way of response or resistance to, the specific goals of state policy and that may have unexpected impacts on emerging structures (Burawoy and Verdery 1999). Thus, household economic behaviour cannot be viewed solely as a response to the transitional environment, but also as an innovative adaptation to continuously changing circumstances.

Which households in Romania are more likely to operate in the informal economy? What are the goals of the informal economic activities performed by the Romanian household? Is informality in Romania synonymous with poverty (ILO) or with popular entrepreneurial dynamism (K. Hart, 1997), or with both (R. Neef 1999; T. Piirainen 1997)? To answer these questions, we use a national representative survey (RIQL, October 1998) and in-depth interviews (105) within households operating in the informal sector (carried out in different regions of the country in June-August, 1999).

* Senior Researcher, Research Institute for Quality of Life, str. 13 Septembrie, nr. 13, 76117, Bucharest, Romania. E-mail: manuela@iccv.ro.

Household behaviour in a plural economy

A given 'social conjuncture' (P. Bourdieu), provided by *habitus* and a specific set of social and economic conditions and a given position on the market, define the field of goals (more or less socially accepted) and alternative means (legal versus illegal, formal versus informal, public versus hidden) within which households, as collective actors, make choices and take actions.

Figure 6.1   Determinants of the economic practices and strategies of the households

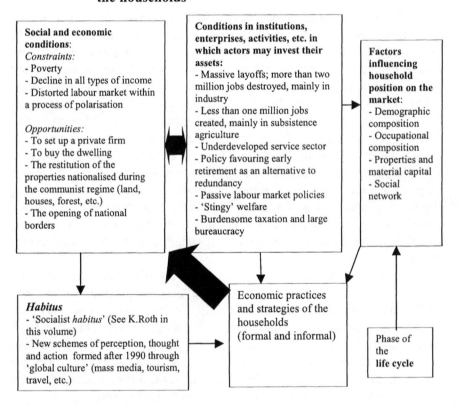

The Romanian economy had reached a structural crisis by the early 80s, and started to decline by the few years preceding 1989. In the first year of the transition (1990), a reparative-type of social policy was promoted. Thus, despite the decline of the economy, the population was kept out poverty. Since then, the economic decline has been accompanied by a 'stingy' social policy, which has entailed a continuous reduction of social protection transfers. For instance, in 1998 (the year of our survey), the net average wage represented 61.5% of its level in 1989. In the same year, 1998, the average pension (state social insurance) represented 37.2% of the net average wage and 122.5% of the minimum wage. The state child allowance represented only 6.2% of the net average wage, while the unemployment benefit was 31.4%, unemployment allowance (which replaced the unemployment benefit after 270 days and lasts for eighteen months) was 14.7%, and social aid (offered to families in severe poverty) was 13.2% (C. Zamfir et al. 2001). As a result, the poverty rate[2] has grown continuously; e.g. from 25.3% of the country's population (1995) to 44% (2000) (Teşliuc, Pop, Teşliuc 2001).

After 1989, opportunities for developing new economic activities emerged as well. The properties confiscated by the communist state were returned to their previous owner and people were offered the opportunity to purchase the dwellings in which they lived at low prices. Since 1989, people are also able to travel abroad freely. As a result, smuggling to and from neighbouring countries and working temporarily abroad has become a part of the economic strategy of a continuously large number of households (Sandu 2001, Stănculescu and Ilie 2001). These changes define the space of opportunities and constraints in which the Romanian households operate (see also 'Romania' in this volume).

Referring to household economic strategies does not necessarily 'imply that a deliberate strategy is used in which the jobs and consumption of the different members are mutually agreed upon ... but that membership permits patterns of economic activity that would not otherwise be possible' (B.R. Roberts 1991, p. 52). The economic strategy of the household, defined as 'the concrete pattern of asset placements that the households have chosen to build' (T. Piirainen 1997, p. 42), is identified in the *concrete combination of income sources of the household* (R. Rose's 'portfolio' 1996) that aim at economic accumulation, making a better living or simply surviving.

The 'social conjuncture' and the position on the market shape the household economic strategies and practices. Based on our survey data, we started our analysis by identifying the main types of households with respect to the demographic composition and the occupational composition corresponding to the different phases of the life cycle.

Table 6.1   Demographic and occupational composition of households

		Total sample	Employed all	Employed more	Non-employed more	Non-employed all	Pensioner + employed more	Pensioner + non-employed more	Pensioners all
Number of cases		1132	222	188	86	105	221	163	147
School years attended by the household	Mean	9.5	11.7	10.5	8.9	8.3	9.8	7.8	7.2
members of 15 years and over	Std. Dev.	3.0	2.4	2.0	2.4	2.4	2.4	2.6	3.6
Age of the household members	Mean	43.2	35.9	34.2	33.2	35.6	45.5	49.2	66.7
of 15 years and over	Std. Dev.	13.4	7.1	6.3	5.1	9.8	7.8	11.9	7.4
Number of members in the household	Mean	3.6	3.2	3.8	4.4	4.1	4.4	4.0	1.7
	Std. Dev.	1.6	1.1	1.2	1.2	2.1	1.6	1.8	0.6
out of which (%) are:									
children 0 - 14	Mean	8.7	19	21	14	25	10	10.1	0
children 15 and over, pupil/student	Mean	4.6	5.5	7.0	10.9	2.1	3.8	3.9	0
non-employed members over 15	Mean	22.2	0	27.1	43.3	70.4	9.5	41.5	0
formally employed members	Mean	31.9	72.5	43.5	25.9	0	40.0	4.8	0
pensioners	Mean	25.5	0	0	0	0	35.9	38.2	100

Data: Social Problems, Living Standard and Informal Economy, IQL, Romania, 1998.

The occupational composition of the households was determined by taking into account the formal occupational status.
The children 0-14 years and persons of 15 years and over attending school are grouped in (children). People of 15 years and over that do not attend school and who are not retired are either formally employed (registered employed or employer) or non-employed. The pensioners irrespective of their age are grouped in (pensioners). Combining these groups of status we obtain seven theoretical types of occupational composition:
1. employed all + (children);
2. (employed $\geq$ non- employed) + (children) = (employed more) - households with or without children, in which, among members of 15 years and over, the number of formally employed exceeds or equals the number of non- employed;
3. (non- employed > employed) + (children) = (non- employed more);
4. non- employed all + (children);
5. pensioner(s) + (employed $\geq$ non- employed) + (children) = pensioner + employed more - households with or without children in which, among members of 15 years and over, there is at least one pensioner and the number of formally employed is larger or equal the number of non- employed;
6. pensioner(s) + (non- employed > employed) + (children) = pensioner + non- employed more;
7. pensioners all (single or couple).

Household occupational composition and the life cycles

The work and professional trajectory of millions of people changed dramatically after 1989. Demographic factors combined with the economic transformations have intensified the increase of the non-employed population started 25 years ago. Starting in 1990, both the fertility rate and the number and percentage of the population in school age (younger than 15 years) have declined. Among the young, the share of the unskilled with extremely low chances to enter the labour market has risen due to the decrease in the enrolment rate in secondary education (high school and vocational school) from 91% in 1990 to 68% in 1998 (National Human Development Report, Romania 1999, UNDP, p. 88). The massive layoffs and the lack of newly created jobs led to an increase in the number of unemployed people of working age (15-59 years). After 1990, the policy encouraging early retirement has resulted in a significant increase in the number of pensioners. Between 1989 and 1998, the number of retired persons grew by 2.7 million[3] people; since 1997, the number of retired persons has exceeded the number of employees by 400,000 people.

Household composition can be broken down as follows: in 1998, 5% of the respondents to our survey lived in one-person households, 17% were married couples without children, 27% were married couples with dependent children (those under 15 years and those attending school), 28% were married couples (with or without dependent children) living together either with their adult offspring or with parents/other relatives, and 23% were unmarried, divorced, or widow living together with relatives.

Five typical combinations result when these forms of households are combined with data on occupational status (see Table 6.1), qualifications, and life cycle phases. As a rule, the higher the education level/qualifications within the households, the higher their occupational rate. Those households with poorly educated members tend to include significantly more non-employed, but also pensioned members.

1. Young adults (up to 24 years) mostly live with their parents until they marry (and most Romanians continue to marry early),[4] especially when they cannot find a stable job. Nearly all young couples without children who succeed setting up their own households are double income families.

2. Couples in parenthood make up 27% of all households (three-quarters in the age group 25-44). This group includes double income households (40%, mostly with good education and more urban than rural), single income families (29%, mostly vocational school level), and families entire-ly non-employed or with very insufficient employment (one-quarter, mostly low skilled households who live mostly in the countryside or in small towns). It is worthwhile to mention that half of the young couples with chil-dren (up to 24 years) are non-employed.

3. A fifth of the adult population is in the life phase of *working life after children have grown up*: parents (mostly 35-54 years old) living with adult children of 17-24 years and sometimes with younger children and/or grand-children. In about 40% of this group, all or most of the household members are out of work, low skilled or unskilled, mostly living in rural areas. Thus, this type of cohabitation is largely a household strategy to cope with unemployment and poverty. The rest of the population in this category belongs to the group of well-employed households headed by skilled workers living in cities. We shall see below that this is also expres-sion of an economic strategy.

4. Twenty-seven percent of the population live in *two or three generation households* either of pensioners and formally employed (64% of this group) or pensioners and non-employed. Most of these households are made up of a couple, 50 years or older, with adult children (40% also have grand-chil-dren). This type, characteristic not only for Romania, but also for southern, south-eastern and eastern Europe, follows a 'minimal' economic strategy in that the two family nuclei share only a part of their income, expenditure and time. The head couple owns the dwelling, has pensions that cover most of the household costs, and takes care of the grandchildren in the parents' absence. The younger couple works or is unemployed and mainly provides for their children.

5. Most of the households in the last life-cycle phase are those in *pensioned age after the adult children have left*. They include 16% of the population and are the almost universal type of pensioned couples (about three quarters of this group, including also pensioned men with housewives below pension age). One-quarter is single (mostly widows), to be found in the city and country, in the East as well as in the West. In the country, women generally receive only the low farmers' pensions since they used to work in the former Agricultural Co-operatives, whereas men used to work in industry and thus are entitled to receive the better social insurance pension.

Nearly half of the Romanian households master the turbulence of social and economic transformations either by adopting a deliberate strategy of cohabitation or by taking up traditional forms of living together. The others simply follow normal patterns of living. Only some of the household combinations can be understood as strategies, whereas all households follow economic strategies in adjusting their assets (property, qualifications, working experience) to market conditions. This shall be explained in the following.

Making up a household portfolio by combining economies

Along the theoretical line presented above, we can distinguish between three economies: the state economy, the emerging market economy, and the informal economy (T. Piirainen 1997). The first two economies make up the official economy.

The *informal economy* refers to all income-earning activities 'unregulated by the institutions of society, in a legal and social environment in which similar activities are regulated' (Castells and Portes 1991, p.12). Regarding Romania in 1998,[5] we can distinguish between the household economy and the cash informal economy:

* The *household economy* includes autonomous activities such as subsistence agriculture, gardening, animal-breeding, and food products received through social networks (family and friends). Consequently, the household economy is rather autonomous and non-monetised.
* The *cash informal economy* encompasses black work, casual work, self-employment, day labour, trade with agricultural products, small trade, and work 'on the side'. These activities are partly informal and partly on the border of the informal economy with both state and market economy. Therefore, the cash informal economy is semi-integrated and monetised (See also Wallace and Haerpfer in this volume).

Wages from official jobs, profit from official businesses, and various social transfers are all formal incomes, while non-monetary incomes resulting from the household economy and monetary incomes from the cash informal economy are counted as informal incomes (see also Ilie in this volume). The household portfolio is determined by the combination of all sources of income. The formal incomes are divided in two groups, namely those (wages/profit) corresponding to the formally employed people, and those (pensions) corresponding to retired people. Combining these groups of income sources results in seven theoretical types of portfolio: 1. I + (low level social transfers) – non-monetary and/or monetary informal incomes combined with child allowance(s) and/or unemployment benefit or social aid; 2. (wages/profit); 3. (pensions); 4. (wages + pensions); 5. (I + wages); 6. (I + pensions); and 7. (I + wages + pensions).

To illustrate the specific ways in which, in Romania, households build portfolios by combining formal and informal activities/sources of income, we have selected three typical cases: households with persons in their fifties with different demographic and occupational compositions. The generation of those in their fifties has witnessed all social and economic transforma-tions and all political regimes that have ruled in Romania after World War Two. The majority had parents who lived in the country; in 1948, the urban network included 33 cities, inhabited by only 22% of the population (Cen-sus data). Their early working adulthood coincided with the period of urba-nization, industrialization, and co-operativization of agriculture; thus, most moved to the newly created urban areas (in 1989, the urban population rep-resented 54% of the total population). Most of them acquired industrial qual-ifications and, before 1989, worked in a workplace in which, in fact, they expected to continue to work until retirement. A regular job, a dwelling, one spouse for their entire lives, and two or three children represented the norm.

The life course changed dramatically for most people after 1989 and life projects needed to be drastically redefined. The employment rate of this age group decreased dramatically, from 70% to 44% for the age group 46-55 and from 22% to 5% for 56-65 year-olds, while the share of retired people increased for these age categories to 26%, respectively to 83% (D. Dăianu et al. 2001). Thus, due to the policy of early retirement, most people over 55 were entitled to pensions and retired. One-third of the 46-55 year-olds (par-ticularly women) lost their jobs from the planned economy and has not found another; they were thus literally forced into engaging in informal activities as a 'waiting retirement' strategy. In addition, education, occupa-tion, and housing for their children have all become problems to be faced and tackled by these parents, given that children's well-being comes first in parents' hierarchy of responsibilities in Romania, particularly in the de-re-gulated institutional context of the transition.

Household 1: (Roma ethnicity – 'Gypsy, but, from the settled ones, who have nothing to do with bad business («şuşanale») or jail'), Bucharest	*(pensioner + non-employed more) (I +wages + pensions)*
1. *man 59, primary school+ woman 55, primary school*	– *sick retirement + housewife*
2. *son 37, gymnasium, industrial qualification + spouse 35, primary school + nephew 19, general secondary education, no qualification + nephew 16, gymnasium*	– *unemployed + housewife + registered unemployed + unregistered unemployed*
3. *son 33, primary school + spouse 33, primary school + niece 8, pupil + nephew 7, pupil*	– *driver + cleaning person*
4. *nephew 14, gymnasium*	– *unregistered unemployed*

I: After 1990, I could take back grandfather's silver appropriated in the 'Sole maker's' (Ceausescu's nickname) time and I started to work. My older boy started travelling abroad. From time to time he bought a car, sold it and left again. My younger boy was off to the Russians; he even reached Baku by selling our own products (a ring, an earring) or other stuff made in Romania. My daughters-in-law, with their fortune telling, succeed to pinch a hen, a cloth and other small things.
O: What is your family's most important source of income?
I: I would say it's mine, because it is a pension and plus that, there is no month without selling something I produce. If I think of my son's and my daughter-in-law's wage from the City Cleaning Company, I don't know if they are important because I don't know if they will be permanent. With this unemployment and with these cuts (layoffs) done in all departments, nothing is sure anymore. You can get sacked anytime, or you do not get the money. You know how it is: the bank has no money, the enterprise has no money, and bankruptcy is on the way. Consequently, my pension plus money from a ring, an earring, and other stuff I produce represent the main source of income for us all. I will always find a business to get some money out of it.

Household 2: Bucharest	(employed more) (I + wages)
1. woman 47, vocational school + man 56, vocational school, industrial qualification	– non-employed + seller

I: I used to work as a hairdresser in a state beauty shop. When this was closed, I didn't find any place to work because I graduated only eight classes and a vocational course (for hairdressers). That's why I went on several trips to Russia and to Hungary together with a neighbour and I brought two hairdressing helmets, scissors, hair curlers, hair drier and I started working at home. My husband worked until 1993 at a state enterprise. His department was closed and he was kicked out and due to this he got an ulcer. Only in 1996 did he find a part-time job selling newspapers.
O: What is your family's most important source of income?
I: Most important is what I earn, because the amount is higher and it is relatively regular. For the rest, our parents and godparents help us, in turn we give to our children, and these compensate.
O: Do you intend to change something in your (informal) activity? Do you intend to develop it?
I: I would like to increase the number of clients, but not to register the activity. To be honest, paying taxes does not suit me. In 10-15 years from now I will be eligible for retirement. I have sworn that after that I would never again touch these (chemical) solutions or smell them for five minutes.

Household 3: village	(pensioner + employed more) (I +wages + pensions)
1. woman 51, University + man 53, University	– pensioner + agricultural inspector
2. son 24, high school + daughter 23, high school + daughter 21, high school	– non- employed + temporary teacher + non- employed

I: Until 1991, when the Agricultural Ministry was restructured, my husband and I, we worked as agricultural engineers. After that, my husband was lucky to find a new job. I didn't find one and I was temporary employee at the village school until this year (1998). (...) This year I was able to retire and in addition I have found a job without contract as a seller in the village shop. Our son was enrolled in the Technical University for three years. After that he dropped out of school and worked in Bucharest as doorkeeper, night watchman and other such jobs. Now he is in-between jobs. The second daughter has not succeeded in entering the university and she has already worked for three years as temporary teacher in the village. The other daughter left for Bucharest and worked without contract in a small shop. She is also trying to get into the university. (...) Our two hectares of agricultural land is leased out to some villagers who give us a part of the production in return. With these products we raise few pigs and hens. We also have a small garden.
O: Do the wages provide for safety?
I: No way. Except for my pension, all the incomes are insecure. Nonetheless, the situation is a little better now (with three wages and a pension), but until the children find official jobs, regular and well-paid, they depend on us. Therefore, we need more money. In this respect, we play Bingo regularly, the children plan to emigrate, and my husband waits to retire.

The examples above illustrate three different situations. *Household 1* represents a model of traditional cohabitation. The lack of formal education is partially compensated by a marketable qualification the father acquired traditionally and his inherited properties recovered from the socialist state, doubled by the sons' risk-taking attitude, enabling them to search for money-making opportunities within the country as well as abroad. In their words, '*(after 1990) we were no longer kept on a leash. We were free, we did what we wanted and what we could to make money. Everybody used the occasion, which suited. If your brain runs, you can get rich in these days, whereas in former times [of Ceausescu], the minute you moved on something, the next moment the police knocked to your door.*'

In contrast, the people in *household 2 and 3* perceive transition as a 'danger'. It is not new freedom to be cherished, but the economic security to be regretted. The industrial qualification of the man in household 2 as well as the high qualification of the woman in household 3 both lost value in the new context. Therefore, in waiting for retirement, both accepted jobs much below their qualifications. The hairdresser's experience gained in the former state beauty shop in developing and concealing an activity on her own account proved profitable in the new context too. The initial material capital came from the investment in smuggling abroad. The grown up children left, which made available room within the apartment for developing the informal beauty shop, whereas the extended social network provided the clients. In household 3, the man succeeded in gaining a good job, thanks to the powerful position he held in the former state agricultural co-operative, and the young members develop informal activities until they achieve either higher education and/or a 'better life' by emigrating. In the meantime, they turn to illusory opportunities such as pyramidal games or Bingo.[6] Both households (2 and 3) compensate for the insufficiency of their income by taking advantage of the agricultural assets they or their rural relatives own.

In 1998, just 26% of all Romanian households made a living only from the formal economies (state and market), 9% made a living from informal economic activities combined, at best, with low-level social transfers, while the rest of the households (65%) pooled income sources from various economies (see Table 6.2). In one hundred households operating in the informal economy, 64 produce food within the household or get it from relatives and friends, 11 perform casual activities, work on their own account or 'on the side', and the other 25 combine the two types of informal economic activities.

Making more money versus cutting expenditures

Comparing households with different occupational compositions (Table 6.2) and in different life cycle phases, we see that the (employed all) households have the lowest rate of overall involvement in the two economies considered informal. Nonetheless, 55.5% of these households does participate in the informal economy. The households with working-age members, with both formally employed and non-employed adult members, are the most active in the cash informal economy, combining all sorts of activities performed either by the adult members, by the older children who have not succeeded in entering the official labour market, or by both. Thus, if only 13-20% of the households (employed all), (pensioners all) or (pensioner + employed more) operate in the informal cash economy, the proportion increases to a quarter for (pensioner + non-employed more), a third among (employed more) or (non-employed more), and reaches 61% of the households (non-employed all).

Table 6.2   Occupational composition of households and portfolio of income sources

		Number of cases	% of the household type	FORMAL INCOME Poverty rate	% of households have incomes from household economy	% of households have incomes from cash informal** economy	TOTAL INCOME Poverty rate
Employed all	Wages, profit	94	44.5	10	0	0	10
	I + wages	117	55.5	13	86	23	6
Employed more	Wages, profit	55	30	39	0	0	39
	I + wages	128	70	49	87.5	41	20
Non-employed more	Wages, profit	22	27	43	0	0	43
	I + wages	60	73	83	87	52	41
Non- employed all	I+ low social transfers*	101	100	99	68	61	58
Pensioner +	Wages + pensions	59	30	29	0	0	29
employed more	I + wages + pensions	138	70	41	91	28	13
Pensioner +	Pensions	16	11	79	0	0	79
non- employed more	I + pensions	103	67	92	90	27	49
	I + wages + pensions	34	22	80	88	35	16
Pensioners all	Pensions	32	22	10	0	0	10
	I + pensions	112	78	61	92	21	15
TOTAL SAMPLE (%)		1071		55	64	27	28

Data: Social Problems, Living Standard and Informal Economy, IQL, Romania, 1998.

Poverty was assessed following the methodology established by the NIS based on the HIS (UNDP 1999).

Poor household = total income per person is lower than the 60% of the average national expenditures per person, updated for October 1998 (about 40 USD);

Formal income includes all types of officially registered incomes: wages from formal jobs, profit from formal private businesses, state social insurance pensions, pensions for farmers, scholarships for pupils and students, state child allowance, unemployment benefit and social aid.

* Low social transfers include state child allowance, unemployment benefit and social aid;

** The cash informal income refers to incomes from: work on own account / on the side, casual work, and selling agricultural products.

While cash informal activities increase monetary income, growing one's own food and breeding animals guarantee the food supply, thus diminishing the household's monetary expenditures. The involvement in the household economy varies significantly depending on the household occupational composition. The share of the households (employed all) operating in the household economy is 47%; rises to 61-64% for households (employed more), (non- employed more), and (pensioner + employed more); and reaches 68-80% for the households (non-employed all), (pensioners all), and (pensioner + non-employed more). Taking into consideration that, at the national level, the share[7] of the food expenditure represents about 65% of household's total consumption expenditures, we can better understand the importance of self-provisioning for the household's well-being.

> *Now, if we were to live on wages only, this would mean that we could not pay for the apartment maintenance fees, not buy clothes, that is to give up many things. Generally, my incomes covers the needs of the family and this is because we do not have to pay for most of the food. Without the income [products] from agriculture, I don't think we could manage.*

As the data in Table 6.2 clearly shows, the majority of Romanian households develop informal activities to decrease monetary expenditures rather than to make more money. At the macro-structure level, this contributes to the de-monetarization of the economy.

More than half of the households depending on the informal economy have no formal incomes or only extremely low social transfers (state child allowance, unemployment benefits, and social aid). At the same time, their informal activities and especially their informal gain are so low-rewarding that they have no choice but to cut back their consumption to the survival level.

> *O: How do you manage in winter?*
> *I: We slaughter the pigs and we sell brooms, some 30-40 a month. It is very hard. I am thankful for the hens and pigs, otherwise I don't know what we would do. Now and then, our neighbour gives us one or two litres of milk, we make a polenta and this is how we manage. (...) We walk to our places of work; we work here in the village. The people we work for give us food (three meals per workday). We buy bread, cigarettes, oil, and stuff like this from Mrs. D. and we pay when we have money. We heat our houses with wood taken without paying from the forest on the hill. Clothing and shoes we rarely buy and when we do, it is from the «handicapped» (second hand shop). We buy shoes in autumn to have over winter, because in summer we walk mostly barefoot. (Couple in their 30s with three adult children, all day workers, village).*

The cities have a larger and more diverse offering of informal jobs, but most of these require particular qualifications. Consequently, unskilled and uneducated people have great difficulties in finding a job in both the formal and informal economies. Agricultural day work remains a possibility only for those located in small/middle cities linked to nearby villages. Casual jobs like loading/unloading and unskilled jobs in construction represent opportunities mainly for men, while unskilled women might find work only in housekeeping. Since the returns of these informal activities do not include meals, the small cash informal income they earn is almost entirely spent on food, while the non-food consumption is completely cut-off. The worst situation is when their kinship network does not include a rural nucleus provider of food products to help them reduce monetary expenditures.

The household economy

Involvement in the household economy is strongly determined by rural location, ownership of agricultural assets, a vulnerable occupational household composition, and belonging to a supportive network with a rural nucleus. The more of the above conditions are fulfilled, the higher the probability that people invest their assets in the household economy, irrespective of their age, education, and formal incomes (see the regression model 1, Annex). The location in the rural area is the strongest explanatory factor of the involvement in the household economy; nearly all rural people produce their own food, whereas the share decreases to 43% in urban areas.

As part of the 1991 economic reforms, land that had been collectivised between 1948 and 1962 was returned to its previous owners or their descendants (up to ten hectares). As a result, about 90% of the people 55 years and over own land in rural areas and 65% own land in urban areas. More than four-fifths of these households of pensioners are active in the household economy.

In rural areas, particularly women receive only very small farmers' pensions,[8] thus many households are pushed to compensate for the insufficiency of the formal income by producing their own food. The elder urban dwellers were returned land in a village situated somewhere in the country, sometimes hundreds of kilometres away from their present homes. Some of them lease out the land to a newly created agricultural association or to villagers, receiving in exchange an annual quota of products and/or money. Another part, particularly those living in smaller cities, is involved in the household economy either for a strategic economic purpose or guided by their *habitus*.

I: My husband and I, we graduated high school in the 40s. In 1983, we retired, and after 1990 we got back the land. In the last ten years we worked in agriculture even though it wasn't worth it – a lot of work and more money spent than benefits received. We work for nothing, but land should be worked. We sell what we can and we manage from one month to another.
O: Do you mean that monthly you have to give up things?
I: We didn't give up anything. Every week we can buy a kilo of meat and everything else we need. It is just our life, working our land and reading or watching TV the rest of the time. (Couple in their 70s, pensioners, village).

The elderly in rural areas divide their property among their descendants based in the village. Thus, most of the households with members in working age located in rural areas own (or use) some agricultural assets. The involvement of these rural households in the household economy is not explained by the insufficiency of the formal income per se, but by the pressure put on them by economically dependent children (minors or not): the higher the share of children in the household, the higher the involvement in the household economy. The formal income of these households does not cover the costs related to the children's education (especially when they attend school in a nearby city), even when most of the household adults are formally employed. Agricultural self-production significantly reduces the monetary expenditures and selling a part of the products provides some monetary incomes. In fact, among all rural households, these younger ones are the most active in selling agricultural products and the most market-oriented ones.

In urban areas, households with members of working age, particularly those well-employed, are more involved if embedded in a network of households. As a rule, the elderly parents and the grown-up children who have not left the village form the rural nucleus, while their adult children who left the village make up the urban part of the network. The rural nucleus provides the urban relatives with food products and, in return, the urban children offer other products or services, such as help in case of illness, accommodation in the city, help in work on the weekends or, rarely, monetary help. This explains the low share of pensioner households that sell their agriculture products.

I: My father has a social insurance pension and a farmers' pension. My mother has a pension for farmers because she worked in the Agricultural Co-operative. In the winter, the pensions are the household income sources, while the summer is better because my brother and I earn money too, twice as much as the pensions sometimes. I work with a cousin in construction, nothing registered. My brother used to do carpentry, but the wages offered by the employer were so low that he changed to agriculture, particularly after dad got sick. (...) We have two hectares of land, a vegetable garden, a cow, three pigs and poultry. Since we got back the land, we have worked it, but we have not sold the products, not even when we have had more than we need. We give them to my brothers who left for the city. (...) When we need money, my brothers have always helped. They have never refused. One lives in Gaesti (city, 18 km), the other in Odorheiul Secuiesc (city, 300 km) and both are workers in industry. When my father was ill, they sent medicines and the one from Gaesti took him to the hospital. They also help us with work in agriculture (on the weekends and holidays). The far away one comes less. Even so, we share with them what we obtain, irrespective of how much they have helped us in work. (Couple in their 60s, pensioners, and two non-employed sons, village and two sons left for the city).

A particular group of households involved in the household economy has moved from cities to the countryside. This group is made up primarily of retired people with low pensions who moved back to their native villages and became involved in the household economy in order to reduce monetary expenditures. Further, the younger people who move to the country are often inheritors of agricultural assets who lost their city jobs and failed to find new ones. Within the context of agricultural restitution and massive industrial layoffs, the national migration pattern has reversed. The urban-rural flow has continuously increased, from 3.5% of the total migration in 1990 to 33.8% in 2000; starting in 1997, it has become the dominant migration flow.

I: I have always been engaged in agricultural activities, but the job came first. When I was laid off, I tried to find work in Botosani (mid-sized city), but I did not succeed. Since I got back this land (2 hectares), I moved here to work it. I started breeding animals (sheep, pigs, horses), less in the beginning, then more. From a little, I gradually made a household here. (...) Agriculture represents the main household source of income, providing 90% of the family food. We make a little money selling the surplus at various agricultural fairs. My wife's income is not secure, it depends too much on the market demand. She is a self-employed tailor and sells her products on the open market. Now that I have been found eligible for a pension, the situation will improve a little. (Couple of non-employed and registered self-employed in their fifties and non-employed son, village).

Self-provisioning is not an innovative adaptation that has emerged during transition, but rather is either part of the traditional way of life of rural households or a development of kinship networks as a response to the state socialist 'economy of shortage' (J. Kornai). Nevertheless, for households with members who have lost their jobs, the retreat into the household economy niche represents an innovative adaptation. In conclusion, the household economy includes two-thirds of the Romanian population and is thus a rather homogeneous and permanent pillar of the Romanian household portfolio.

The cash informal economy

The cash informal economy is more heterogeneous, including all sorts of economic activities: legal, illegal, or not regulated by law; from unskilled to highly specialised; performed mostly irregularly (*'when we find'*). Consequently, a large variety of household types operate in the cash informal economy driven either by opportunities or by constraints.

Informal cash economies by opportunity

The *first type* is comprised of people in formal occupations who strive to improve their standard of living by investing their household assets (productive equipment and tools, work room, second dwellings, qualifications, and time) in the cash informal economy, e.g. *household 10*. The *second type* are informal entrepreneurs, households that develop an informal business, their cash informal economy representing the transitory phase to the market economy. The informal entrepreneurs who develop modern market-oriented farms make up this type in the agriculture sector (see Golibrzuch in this volume). The following household was representative of the first type for seven years and is now changing to the second type:

Household 4: large city	*(pensioner + employed more);* *(I + wages + pensions)*
1. *man 32, first stage of secondary education, no qualifications + woman 30, vocational school + son 5*	– *non-employed +* *employed*
2. *father in law 68, vocational school + mother in law 64, vocational school*	– *pensioner + pensioner*

I: We used to work in a state enterprise in which we were exasperated by the job insecurity and the small salary. This is why I went to Turkey in 1992 for the first time during my holidays and illness leaves [in the job of locksmith in a big state plant]. I worked mainly as an unskilled worker in construction. Since then I have continued to work in Turkey for six-eight weeks every year. Four months ago I left the enterprise for good and went to Turkey again. When I'm there I send home money and various clothes, which are sold here by my wife. This has proved to be a profitable business. Therefore, my wife did all papers to set up a firm. Soon she is going to resign her job, as painter and she will take over the kiosk I am building now in our garden. After I finish the construction and everything is set, I will return to Turkey to work and to supply the shop.

Informal cash economy by constraints

The *first type* includes households with low formal incomes, more generally without any kind of assets, for whom the new transition context presents no choice but to operate in the cash informal economy (for situations of day workers in rural regions see Golibrzuch in this volume).

Household 5: Bucharest	(non-employed all); (I)

1.   *man 48, uncompleted gymnasium +*
     woman 48, gymnasium
	– *casual worker +*
	    housekeeper for the owner
	    of the house they live in

I: After I was kicked out I ended up in this situation. I have searched for a new job a lot but black work is all I have found, now at a warehouse as loading/unloading worker. Nobody hires me because I am old and uneducated. (...) My biggest hope is to find an employer to hire me with a contract. I would accept any work, it doesn't matter what, if in this way I would complete the work-years required for a pension.

The other two types by constraints refer to households performing cash informal activities only in certain phases of the life cycle. The *second type* is made up of households based in cities in the parenthood life phase who are under pressure to provide for their children and who need to supplement their formal income, particularly when they do not belong to a supportive network with a rural nucleus.

Household 6: large city	(employed all);(I + wages)

1.   *man 43, vocational school, industrial*
     qualification + woman 43, vocational school +
2.   *son 23, student + daughter 21, student +*
     daughter 13, pupil
	– *employed + employed*

I: We have no land and our parents are needy peasants who own just a small piece of land. Thus they cannot help more than sending a bag with dried beans now and then. (...) Without an additional income it would be impossible for the children to continue school due to the fees, transport, accommodation, and all the other costs. The boy tries to help by performing casual activities to earn some pocket money, but we have to provide for the rest. Therefore, we both work additionally. I work overtime for the firm and on the side for various persons (metallic confections) and my wife paints apartments for less money, mainly for relatives and friends. When we badly need money we work wherever we can find something, even as day workers in agriculture. (...) I would like to develop my activity, but only until my children graduate and find a job, then I'll rest.

The *third type* by constraints consists of students and young people performing informal activities only until they complete their education. In a more vulnerable situation are those with no parental economic support or with other people depending on them. The following example represents also a strategy of household cohabitation.

Household 7: Bucharest	*(pensioner + non-employed more) (I + wages + pensions)*
1. *man 25, high school +*	– *non- employed +*
2. *father 64, post secondary school + mother 54, vocational*	– *pensioner + housewife*
3. *sister 29, high school + baby*	– *employed*

I: In the last ten years our sources of income changed a lot. My father has retired so he brings less money into the household. My mother got sick so she has earned less and less. My sister graduated from the university, but she married and moved to her own house. The other sister, on the other hand, divorced and came back to live with us together with her child. She earns a salary but must cover the costs related to the baby so she's not helpful for the rest of us. Consequently, I had interrupted my university studies several times. After a while I dropped it altogether because I have had to earn more money. (...) In '90-91 I bound newspapers, sold newspapers, and for few months I worked in a greenhouse. In '92 I was a day worker in a warehouse and then I worked in a plumbers' team. In '93 I was waiter in various restaurants. In the same year I was accepted at the university but during summer holiday I worked again as seller in a small shop. Then I combined working in restaurants and attending classes until '96 when I dropped the study of constructions and started with graphics. Now, I have just obtained a legal authorization for self-employment in advertising and I plan to enter to the Architecture University.

The regression model (see regression model 2, Annex) indicates the more relevant properties owned and the higher the share of dependent children, the higher the probability that households are involved in the cash informal economy, irrespective of age, education, and formal income. The lack of formal income and assets pushes households (non-employed all) to operate in the cash informal economy. In contrast, in the case of households (employed more), the level of the formal income does not play a significant role.[9] The households (pensioners all) and (employed more), particularly those based in rural areas, engage in cash informal activities aimed at improving their standard of living up to a 'good life'. The latter tend to operate in the cash informal economy during the parenthood phase, while ownership of properties significantly increases the chances of households (non-employed more) and (pensioner + employed more) to perform within the cash informal.

The involvement in the cash informal economy is more difficult to be statistically modelled or to be typified within the qualitative interviews due to the high diversity of the encompassed activities. Many of these are non-regular or limited to certain life phases or social situations. Therefore, the cash informal income does not represent a pillar, but rather a heterogeneous and impermanent contributor to the portfolio of a third of all households in Romania.

Developments of the household economic situation

How successful are the households in reaching well-being by developing a large palette of informal activities? In order to understand the developments of the household economic situation, we have designed a typology that considers the formal income as the starting point and the total[10] income (formal + informal) the ending point of the household economic trajectory.

Figure 6.2   Developments of the household economic situation

	Poor[11] total income	Medium total income	Rich total income
Poor formal income	**Dependency 24%**	**Precarious 23%**	**Improving 7%**
Medium formal income		**Fortified 33%**	
Rich formal income			**Stable 13%**

Data: Social Problems, Living Standard and Informal Economy, IQL, Romania, 1998 (N = 1070).

The households in a *dependency* situation do not manage to escape poverty, but rather live at the margins of survival. The households (non-employed all), (pensioner + non-employed) and (non-employed more) are over-represented among the households in the dependency situation, making up 58% of these overall. Nearly all these households include an informal source of income in their portfolio. Given that most of them have no agricultural property and poor qualifications, the household economy niche is blocked for them and the main means of livelihood is casual work. Many of the children of these families dropped out of school before achieving qualifications. Consequently, the dependency situation is associated with extremely low life chances and tends to be transmitted from one generation to another.

Household 8: small city	*(non-employed all); (I)*
1. woman 24, gymnasium + man 26, gymnasium + daughter 3	– day workers

I: I finished only eight classes, so finding a job is very difficult. We are day workers wherever we find. I go to the block of flats and ask if someone needs a cleaning woman or has some work for me or I go in the nearby villages and find work to some farms. My husband works in construction; he mainly paints apartments together with a team of people. We earn money just enough to eat. (...) We have no one to help, except my mother, who takes care of our three-year old daughter from time to time. We have no land and no rural relatives. (Therefore) we have big debts; we haven't paid the apartment maintenance fees for quite a while.
O: What do you intend to change in your activity?
I: We want to sell this (costly) apartment and to move to the country. At least to have bread daily on the table would be something.

The cases of *households* 8 and 5 represent typical examples of people found in different phases of the life cycle who all live in a dependency situation. The older ones used to hold marginal positions in the state-socialist economy too. Because of their lack of assets, they could not take advantage of the life chances created by transition. The younger ones, lacking minimal qualifications and thus without access to the official labour market, are being pushed into insecure and low paid jobs in the informal cash economy. Consequently, their earnings are just enough to survive. They repeatedly encountered uncontrollable downturns in the first years of transition. Subsequently, they reacted with helplessness to the new events, according to the motto '*we manage how we can*', either without plans for the future or with a pessimistic outlook on how things will develop. Thus, these people learn helplessness (M. Inglehart 1991), entrapped in a dependency spiral through a series of repeated failures.

The households in a *precarious* economic situation pool various sources of income, each of which being insufficient in itself. The informal incomes add to the poor formal incomes, which provides a certain equilibrium compared to the dependency situation. However, the risk to fall into poverty is very high. Most of these people just get along with a total income near the poverty line. About a half (54%) of them rely only on the informal income combined either with low-level social transfers or with farmers' pension from the communist agricultural co-operatives. On the other hand, around a third of the households struck by unemployment and/or low pensions – (non-employed all) and (pensioners all), (pensioner + non-employed more) – are in a precarious situation. Most of them (79%) are based in villages and the household economy helps them to ensure a medium consumption with poor monetary incomes. The rest live in cities and are couples over 45 years old (some whom have non-employed children over 15 in the household) in the 'waiting retirement' situation.

Household 9: Bucharest	*(pensioner + non-employed more);*
	(1 + pensions)
1. *man 49, gymnasium + woman 49,*	– *non-employed + pensioner +*
gymnasium + son 21, vocational school	*non-employed*
+ daughter 17, pupil	

I: My wife and me, we worked until 1992 in the wagon-sorting unit from Bucharest railway station, as wagon janitors. We got unemployed, they sacked us, and in 1993 my wife retired due to sickness. I worked where I found. Between 1992-1993, I was janitor for a church, then I worked in constructions and now I am loading/unloading at Scânteia pavilion. Because I don't have education, I am old (they all tell me this), and I am not trained, I had to do black work where I could find it, because otherwise we would have starved. However, black work means no taxes, no labour book, no contribution for pension, no work seniority, and no health insurance. In other words, you have no way of arguing with the boss or with the bailiff if they cheat you because you did not sign anything with them. They rub you for 12 hours and pay you scratch; you have no more time to give a party, to make visits. If you ask for more, they send you away because there are another hundred people like you waiting for a job. So you can only shut up, swallow your words and work for nothing. (...) I keep looking for a job; maybe I can get somewhere, learn something new, and earn more money. This work just helps us to mend things.
(...) Our son (21) was a pupil until 1995, then he found no place to work; he worked for a vulcanization shop for some two years and then he was drafted. Now, he works as a security agent for a private company. He is in the trial period, no contract, no nothing. When the boss cheats on him, he can do nothing because he has nothing on him.

The other half of the households in a precarious economic situation combines the informal source of income with wages or wages and pension (as in examples of *households 1* and *7*). The majority of these wages is equal to or near the minimum[12] wage, mainly coming from an unskilled activity. The pensions are small too. Consequently, only in a third of these households does the formal income represent the most important source of income. The other two-thirds of these households are located in the rural areas and have agrarian self-provisioning as the main pillar of their portfolio of income sources.

In contrast, the portfolios of the households in a *fortified* economic situation are built around a wage near the medium national wage and/or a pension of a similar level, which make a rather solid base of livelihood. Thanks to their medium to rich formal incomes, these households do not need to operate in the informal economy in order to escape poverty. However, half of them fortify their portfolio with informal sources of income, thus improving their standard of living. Qualified people living in cities form 80% of the households in the fortified economic situation. (For other illustrations in different phase of the life cycle and residential areas see *households 2, 3, 6, 10*).

Household 10: small city	*(employed all); (I + wages)*
1. *man 39, high school + woman 35, high school +* *son, pupil + daughter, pupil*	*– locksmith + seller*

I: I am locksmith at the city municipality and my wife is a seller in a private sweet shop. After we married and had children, we could no longer manage with the wages alone. This is how I started working as plumber and tile maker for various private persons. I had the qualification acquired from my former work place. One mate initiated me. I started with friends and the clients network gradually extended. (...) The most important source of income is my wage, which is good and safe enough. The additional money is not regular, thus you can't always rely on it. (...) In case we are in need, we have good relatives from whom we can take food and money and support. (...) When a client calls me I leave my place of work because my mates cover me in front of the boss so that I am not afraid. The only disadvantage is that I have not time enough to spend with my kids. (...) Our budget is reasonable; we have no changing plans.

A small group of households (7%) is in an *improving* economic situation. They achieve relatively high consumption through informal incomes, with low to medium formal incomes. Eighty percent of these are households of modern informal farmers located in the rural areas. Most of them either breed a large number of animals or work large surfaces of land partly leased in from other villagers with their own modern equipment. Most of their products are sold for profit and the entire activity is permanently shaped according to the demand on the market (see also Golibrzuch in this volume). In the urban areas, small informal entrepreneurs who invest their assets (productive equipment, small workshops, qualification and time) in the cash informal economy are, for the most part, in an improving situation, as illustrated by *household 4*.

The households in a *stable* situation have the highest formal income and total income, so that these households have at least a decent standard of living even without their informal income. The highest share (54%) is made up of those with all adult members formally employed (with or without children and pensioners). The households (employed more) reach a stable situation only with the supplement of informal sources of income. More than three-quarters of the latter are located in cities and are made up of highly qualified household members. Overall, among the households in a stable economic situation, 70% perform an informal activity, partly for non-economic purposes like working the land, motivated by *habitus*, pleasure, personal development, or hobby (like in the *households 11* and *12* presented below). Especially those who establish a firm begin their activities in the informal economy in order to gain experience and to accumulate capital. Owners of registered firms develop an informal buffer, like tax and social contributions evasion, as part of their formal business in order to attenuate the unpredictable changes of the legal and business environment.

Household 11: (Saxon), village	*(pensioners all); (I + pensions)*
1. man 70, gymnasium + woman 67, gymnasium	*– pensioner + pensioner*

I: After 1990, chance was on our side. We got back the land. I am 70 and my wife is 67. We both worked and retired right after 1989, we didn't want to stay (employees) anymore. Our sons are all grown up. Two of them left[13] for Germany and the youngest son has his own household here in the village. I'm absolutely positive that if we asked, my boys would help us with anything we need. Only in case of illness would it be more difficult. (...) For hard working people, it was good before 1989 too. In Ceausescu's time we succeeded in buying two houses, one for each of our older sons and we endowed them with a bathroom, parquet, tiles, and such. (...) When I got the land, I sold the three cows and the horse and I bought a tractor. My wife owns 6,7 hectares that are leased out to the Saxon's agricultural association. I own 4 hectares that I work on my own with the tractor. I sell the products on the peasant market and the money I get is deposited at the National Saving House.

Household 12: Bucharest	*(employed all); (I + wages)*
1. woman 27, University + man 27, University	*– teacher + software engineer*

I: In 1995, I graduated from the university. I worked for one year on a temporary contract and subsequently I became full time high school teacher (...) with a very small, but very safe wage. My husband got a degree in mathematics, but left teaching in 1997 due to the small salary and was hired as a software engineer in a private firm. This improved our (economic) situation a lot. We became able to buy a car, a new TV set, and we spent a holiday abroad. His wage brings safety to our situation and we look positively towards the future. (...) My additional activity is teaching in private. I started this right after I graduated. Although after 1997 I could have stopped, I didn't because I have too much free time compared to my husband and additional money does not upset anyone. By doing this we save about 200 USD per month so that we can leave[14] Romania for always.

The respondents' assessments of the relationship between their current household income and needs are consensual with our findings. The dominant opinion shared by the respondents living in households in dependency or precarious economic situations was *'we can't satisfy even the basics'*. At the other extreme, people from households in fortified or stable economic situation mostly assessed their current income as *'enough for a decent living or even better'*.

Is your current income covering your needs?

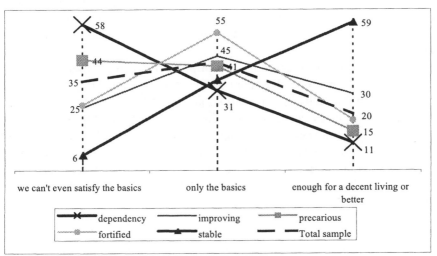

Data: Social Problems, Living Standard and Informal Economy, IQL, Romania, 1998 (N=1070).

* * *

In the transition Romanian context, in most households, irrespective of the occupational composition, people develop a portfolio of income sources, most frequently combining formal incomes from the state economy with non-monetary incomes from the household economy. The household economy represents a permanent pillar of the Romanian households, the primary function of which is the maintenance of the consumption and the reduction of the monetary expenditures. In contrast, only a minority is active in the cash informal economy. The latter is highly heterogeneous in activities and, depending on the economic situation of the performer household, covers a large span of functions – from enabling the survival of households in dependency to fortifying very moderate social situations to stabilising businesses for the enrichment of households. Thus, it is an irregular and transitory contributor to the household portfolios in Romania.

In the transformation conditions of continuing insecurity, the informal activities make up a necessary pillar of livelihood for half of all Romanian households. In this case, informality is rather synonymous with poverty, buffering the social costs of transformation by compensating for continuously falling wages and low social transfers (for many below the subsistence level). For households in the dependency economic situation, involvement in the cash informal economy is a must, because it enables households to survive. Taking into consideration the development of the labour market in the last ten years, we would say that it tends to become the permanent and unique pillar of their portfolio. For the households in a precarious situation, the informal activities are still necessary for survival, but tend to be limited in time, bridging the gap until a secure pension or a qualified job can be attained.

For a third of the households, the informal activities provide improvements that the underdevelopment of the market cannot produce. Thus, households in fortified economic situations increase their monetary incomes and consolidate an insecure portfolio through informal activities.

In Romania, informality is similar to entrepreneurial dynamism for less than a fifth of the households, namely those in a stable or improving situation. Only within households in a stable economic situation do people perform informal activities for pleasure and as part of personal development projects.

Annex

The regression model 1:

0.33 * HE = + 0.41 * Rural + 0.19 * Agricultural Assets + 0.13 * Rate of economic dependency + 0.10 * Supportive social network

HE = involvement in the household economy = monetary counter-value of the products obtained within the household and/or received from relatives, friends.

Notes: The values represent R square, respectively Beta coefficients (p<0.5). Durbin Watson coefficient = 1.8. The other predictors were insignificant.

The regression model 2:

0.07 * CIE = + 0.17 * Assets convertible in the cash informal economy + 0.11 * Rural + 0.11 * Rate of economic dependency + 0.07 * Income deprivation

CIE = involvement in the cash informal economy = amount of money earned in cash informal activities by all members of the household.

Notes: The values represent R square, respectively Beta coefficients (p<0.5). Durbin Watson coefficient = 1.9. The other predictors were insignificant.

Both regression models used the same predictors:
– Rural = dichotomic variable, 1 = located in the rural areas.
– Agricultural assets = dichotomic variable, 1 = own land, vegetable garden and/or cattle.
– Assets convertible in the cash informal economy = continuous variable (0 to 4) counting the following: tools and equipment, second dwelling, workshops, small shops.
– Rate of economic dependency = share of the children and non-employed members within the total number of members.
– Formal income = sum of all officially registered incomes of the household per capita (see Notes below Table 6.2).
– Income deprivation = the gap between the amount of money subjectively declared as enough for a 'good life for a family like yours' and the formal income of the household.
– Age stock = average age of the households members 15 years and over.
– Education stock = average number of attended classes of household members 15 years and over.
– Supportive social network is the SSN index presented below.
    The set of potential kinds of help considered in our questionnaire includes the following: 1. help with money; 2. help to take care of the children; 3. help when someone in the family is ill; 4. help in work; 5. help with domestic services; 6. help with relations, knowing someone who knows someone...; 7. help in difficult situations.
    The set of potential alteri includes: 1. relatives; 2. friends; 3. neighbours; 4. work colleagues.

We computed the likelihood of getting help of kind i (Snijders T. 1999)

$$
s_i = \begin{cases} 1 & \text{if two or more alters are willing to help of kindf i} \\ 0.7 & \text{if exactly one alter is willing to help of kindf i} \\ 0 & \text{if no alter is willing to help of kindf i} \end{cases}
$$

The reliability of the social network was determined as follow:

$$
R = \begin{cases} 1 & \text{if 'I get help anytime I need'} \\ 0.5 & \text{if 'I get help only sometimes or I have to manage on my own'} \\ 0.2 & \text{if he/she gets help but 'does not need it'} \\ 0 & \text{if 'there is no one to help me'} \end{cases}
$$

The importance of the help provided by the social network for the household well-being determined:

$$
I = \begin{cases} 1 & \text{if 'it is very important, without it we would not manage'} \\ 0.7 & \text{if the help is 'important'} \\ 0.5 & \text{if 'it is useful, but we can manage without it'} \\ & \text{if he/she gets help but 'does not need it'} \\ & \text{if 'there is no one to help me'} \end{cases}
$$

The supportiveness of the social network: $SSN = I \times R \times \Sigma s_{ii}$

$$i = 1 \text{ to } 7$$

The SSN index estimates the 'quantity' of various kind of help the household gets, weighted with how important this is for the household's well-being and the reliability of its social network.

Notes

1   The research project 'The Development Potential of the Informal Economy in Romania' (1998-2001) has been coordinated by Rainer Neef (University of Goettingen, Germany) and was financed by the Volkswagen Foundation. The research has three components: 1. the Research Institute for Quality of Life carried out the survey 'Social Problems, Living Standard and Informal Economy, Romania, October 1998'; 2. a qualitative household-level inquiry (105 in-depths interviews in June-August 1999; 3. 10 interviews with local authorities from different regions of the country, 2000.

2   Expenditures per adult equivalent below 60% of the national average, methodology elaborated by the National Institute for Statistics (NIS) based on Household Integrated Survey (HIS) (UNDP 1999).

3   Between 1989 and 1998 the number of pensioners increased from 2.3 million to 4 million (social insurance pensioners), 0.2 million to 0.5 million (disability pensioners) and from 1 million to 1.68 million (farmers' pensioners), Romanian Statistical Yearbook 1995 and 2000, NIS.

4   In 1998, the mean age at first marriage was 26.4 years for men and 23.2 years for women, Romanian Statistical Yearbook 1995 and 2000, NIS.

5   Our data refers to 1998. In 2001 the General Income Tax was introduced.

6   After 1990, many pyramidal games were highly popular despite the public exposure of their failure. Bingo is one of the most popular gambling games in recent years. 55% of the adult population declared that at least one member of their household played Bingo in April 2000, a share that decreased to 25% in October.

7   According to our survey, the peasants supply from their own resources, in average, more than 53% of the total household income, the pensioners and unemployed 31%, while in the case of the firm owners the proportion drops to 4%. Our results are very close to those reported by the NIS on the basis of HIS: 55% for peasants, about 40% for pensioners and unemployed, and 10% for employers. A one-dimensional variance analysis showed that the differences between these values are significant.

8   In 1998, the average farmers' pension represented 25% of the average social insurance pension, 10% of the net average wage and a third of the minimum wage.

9   The higher the gap between their formal income and the income subjectively defined as being enough for a 'good life', the higher the probability of involvement within the cash informal economy.

10 Total income is determined as the sum of the total monetary income and the monetary counter-value of the products obtained within the household. According to the methodology of the budget calculation (used also to assess poverty), the products obtained within the household (non-monetary income) are converted in an amount of virtual money (see Ilie in this volume), which is summed up with the real money. On this imaginary scale, the households are ranked irrespective of the type of their concrete income and sorted into poor and non-poor.

11 Poverty was assessed following the methodology established by the National Institute for Statistics based on the Household Integrated Survey (UNDP 1999). Poor formal (total) income means that the formal (total) income of the household per person is lower than the 60% of the average national expenditures per person updated for October 1998 (about 40 USD). 'Rich' refers to the 20% of the households, which compared to all the others, have the highest formal (total) income.

12 In 1998, 5.1% of the total number of employees earned a minimum wage (NIS and UNDP, National Human Development Report, Romania 1999).

13 In 2000, 7% of the population over 18 years declared that at least one member of the household left (formal or informal) temporarily abroad. (Public Opinion Barometer, Open Society Foundation 2000).

14 In 1999, a third of the people with a university degree declared that they would be willing to leave the country temporarily or permanently. (Political Barometer 1999).

References

Burawoy, M. and Verdery, K. (1999), *Uncertain Transition*, Boulder, Rowman and Littlefield.
Castells, M. and Portes, A. (1991), 'World Underneath: The Origins, Dynamics and Effects of the Informal Economy', in A. Portes, M. Castells and L.A. Benton (eds.), *The Informal Economy*, The John Hopkins University Press, Baltimore.

Dăianu, D. (coord.) (2001), *Winners and Losers in the Process of European Integration. A Look at Romania*, Romanian Center for Economic Policies / WP no. 31 / Bucharest, http://www.cerope.ro.

Hart, K. (1997), 'Informal Income Opportunities and Urban Employment in Ghana', in R.R. Grinker and C. Steiner (eds), *Perspectives on Africa*, Blackwell, Oxford/Cambridge (Mass.).

Inglehart, Marita R. (1991), *Reactions to Critical Life Events. A Psychological Analysis*, PRAEGER, New York.

Kornai, J. (2000), *Drumul nepietruit al transformarii*, Ed. Kriterion, Bucuresti - Cluj

Neef, R. (1999) 'Formen und Soziale Lagen der Schattenwirtschaft in einem Transformatiosland: Rumanien', *Berliner Journal fur Soziologie*, vol. 9(3), pp. 397-414.

Neef, R. (2002), 'Forms of the Informal Economy in a Transforming Country', *International Journal of Urban and Regional Research*, vol. 26.

Piirainen, T. (1997), *Towards a New Social Order in Russia. Transforming Structures in Everyday Life*, Aldershot, Sydney, Singapore: Darthmouth.

Roberts, B.R. (1991), 'Employment Structure, Life Cycle, and Life Chances: Formal and Informal Sectors in Guadalajara', in A. Portes, M. Castells and L.A. Benton (eds.), *The Informal economy*, The John Hopkins University Press, Baltimore.

Rose, R. (1996), 'Who needs social protection in East Europe? A constrained empirical analysis of Romania', in *Societies in Transition. East-Central Europe Today*, AVEBURY, England.

Sandu, D. (2001), 'Migratia ciculatorie ca strategie de viata' (Circulatory Migration as Life Strategy), *Sociologie Romaneasca (Romanian Sociology)*, 2/2000, Bucharest.

Snijders, T. (1999), 'Prologue to the Measurment of Social Capital', *The Tocqueville Review*, vol. XX, no. 1.

Stănculescu, M. and Ilie, S. (2001), *Informal Sector in Romania*, UNDP and RIQL, Bucharest, http://www.undp.ro/news.htm.

Teşliuc, C.M., Pop, L. and Teşliuc, E.D. (2001), *Saracia si sistemul de protectie sociala (Poverty and Social Protection System)*, Polirom, Bucharest.

UNDP (1999), Stănculescu M. (ed.) *Saracia in Romania 1995-1998 (Poverty in Romania 1995 – 1998)*, Vol. I. Coordonate, dimensiuni si factori (Coordinates, Dimensions and Factors), Bucharest.

Zamfir, C. (coord.) (2001), *Poverty in Romania*, RIQL and UNDP, Bucharest, http://www.undp.ro/news.htm.

Chapter 7

Informal activities in rural areas: family situations in farming and day labouring

Esther Golibrzuch[*]

Acknowledgements: We would like to thank Dr. Rainer Neef for various stimuli and criticisms that have influenced this text.

The economic development of rural areas before and after 1989

The economic conditions and the potential for development in the villages of Romania have until today been characterised, as in other east European countries, by changes in rural areas prior to the 1989 revolution. The industrialization imposed by Ceausescu progressively destroyed the system of individual farms specialising in different production sectors. All private property was entirely or partially expropriated and transformed into state-owned large farms (IAS = Intreprindere agricola de stat) or co-operatives (CAP = Cooperativa agricola de productie). These types of farms developed at village outskirts or between villages in those areas which were particularly favourable to agriculture, like for example, Transylvania or the Banat plane. On the other hand, in those regions with poor soil and in the mountains, where agriculture was least developed, the collectivization was less rigorously carried out, especially in the mountain areas where much private property was maintained. To every farmer in the co-operative a piece of land (approx. 0.15 – 0.5 ha, cf. Stewart 1998; Rieser 1997) was assigned by the administration, to run it privately. Because the state and collective farms could not fulfil their production norms, a program for the promotion of the private initiative was presented at the beginning of the 80s. Not only could these much more productive private farmers cover most of their personal requirements (subsistence farming) by working on the side, they were also able to generate 42% (in 1980) of the agricultural gross production of the

---

*Dipl.-Ing. (city-planning/urbanism), Flachsland 16, 22083 Hamburg. E-mail: e.golibrzuch@onlinehome.de.

country. In spite of smaller available land area and a deficiency of technical infrastructure, this high profitability could be attained thanks to an increase in the working hours in the private sector at the expense of work in collective farms and the illegal use of machines, fertilisers, pesticides, etc. taken from the state and collective farms (cf. Groß 1995).

The concept of large scale agricultural production and the aim of bringing urban and country living conditions closer together destroyed a large part of the diversified village infrastructure. Some villages became important centres. Shopping centres, schools and kindergartens were established next to the administrative offices of the state and the collective farms, and they were easy to reach with local public transport services. Other villages became subordinate to those with the function of centres and became small residential units. Many people in working age, especially those who had to come from villages without shuttle services to the large farms or to the closer industrial centres, moved to major villages and towns (cf. Knappe 1997).

The farms undertook much of the development work, including construction, transport development and repair work, etc., which did not pertain to agriculture, and in this way avoided, or at least contained, the development of other economic entities (ex., private businesses).

After the collapse of the communist system in 1989, the re-privatization of the land was carried out fast, under pressure from the population: 70% of cultivable land and 80% of the arable land was already privatised by 1992 (cf. Länderbericht RO 1995: 57, in: Rieser 1997: 94).

Due to the dependence on the state and collective farms, the whole village economy, that is all economic sectors linked to the village, broke down as a rule after their dissolution after 1989.[1] The whole agricultural distribution system broke down and until today has remained lacunary, and the sales and development potential of agricultural products is cut off from many city markets. At the same time, new businesses importing food products, with which the small farmers can barely compete, have begun to occupy the markets.

The privatization of the agricultural system hit the old state-owned farms and the CAPs prematurely, before they were turned into PLCs (independent new State farms) or associations. Every household received on average two hectares of arable land, for the most part divided into several small plots. The foreseen maximum of 10 hectares was rarely realised, due to disproportion between the land to be distributed and the number of people claiming return, especially since collective workers without entitlements sometimes also received some land. This gave rise to a lot of small private farmers working on the side, who now provide for their personal supply and mostly are not competitive. Due to the lack of capital and too small incomes these farms normally cannot extend or take on any new personnel. Many of the new landowners take up their tradition of farming as a second occupation, while others find themselves dealing with it for the first time. The farms in mountain regions which had remained private before 1989 can fall back upon their agricultural qualifications and potentials, which also developed over the years after 1989.

In the first two years, when the disorganization of the whole agricultural system was accompanied by insecurity concerning property rights and the dissipation of the land, the production in agriculture decreased by one third; in 1992 there was also a particularly bad harvest (cf. Rieser 1997: 94) and in the following, fluctuated around the 1989 level (Lukas 2000). The mechanization of agriculture had been put into reverse by the destruction of state and co-operative property. The machines which remained were too big to work the small private plots. The number of those employed in the agricultural sector rose from 27.9 % in 1989 to 38.0 % in 1998 (NCS, 1999). This is because many former commuters who had lost their jobs in the cities[2] looked for jobs in the newly reorganised farm co-operatives, or they tried to extend their agricultural activities to an own small farm.

Starting from 1993 began the conversion of a part of the former state-owned farms into PLCs who are state property but produce autonomously. From than on, the production started to pick up again. The more capital and labour-intensive mass production, supported by modern machinery, may have contributed to this rise. Moreover, voluntary production-co-operatives have been established, which could not stop the dissipation of the land, but have some importance only in the southern plains where they cover at most 1/5 of the area. The co-operatives are especially popular with retired people or city dwellers, who cannot work the land they were awarded. Depending on the region (in Banat 30-40%, cf. Rieser 1997: 96) they receive different shares of production, paid out in money in successful years – in others in kind. The co-operatives and a few large and often informal farms have a quasi-monopoly on credits. In addition, the old machine stations transformed into private societies and the large farms, respectively co-operatives dispose of most of the machinery.[3] The prices for machine renting and for seeds and fertilizers increased drastically. So the poverty in capital on the one hand, the quasi-monopoly of the co-operatives and modern farms keeps most small farms off the possibilities of developing (Bădescu 1999).

The majority of the employees of the new state farms (PLCs) and associations work as day labourers. Before 1989, farms used to take on day labourers who were mainly recruited from village and ethnic fringe groups. They had then a workbook, and therefore, regular legal status and social insurance.[4] From 1990 on, the workbook for day labourers has been abolished.

Today, agriculture is the gathering place for the many unemployed who suffer the consequences of the industrial crisis, especially in regions with high employment rates in industry (for ex., Resita). For this reason, many people moved in the past years from the cities in the surrounding country-side. The part of town-country-migration increased from 3.5% (1990) to 28.4% (1998) of overall migration (cf. Stănculescu 2000). Except wages and pensions, farming in the form of subsistence 'weekend agriculture' (Pop 1997: 127) makes an insurance for one's own existence – especially since those who own two hectares or more of land (in the mountains, four) are not entitled to unemployment and social benefits. For others, only agriculture allows a decent livelihood, since most of the unemployment benefits do not suffice. Subsistence agriculture has become in the main a survival-economy. In '1996, 51% of all individual farmers did not bring any products to the markets, which means that production is used for personal needs – a subsis-tence economy' (Tomasi 1998: 227). The small household farms will how-ever be of significance, as long as they are needed for purporting the basic needs of those whose income and pensions are too low – and real incomes have continued to drop (see Stănculescu, in this volume).

The political strategies for the development of the rural areas still focus in the main on the agricultural sector (although, not very effectively). Due to European competition, increased efficiency in the agricultural production, the developing of non-agrarian economies, and their combination shall become more and more important in the rural areas. 'Better services and information networks will be needed, including agricultural expertise, which could be made available at the small town level and ensure better co-ordi-nation of private and state farm activity, for the latter have an important role as agents of modernization' (Turnock 1998: 104). Establishing businesses such as mills and bakeries, for example, would be plausible, as well as the combination of agriculture and stock breeding, and the development of new marketing networks. Many associations would be glad to move in this direc-tion. More regular members of staff could be employed with the same work load (in order to avoid strong seasonal fluctuation) and subsequent improve-ments in product quality would increase profit (cf. Rieser 1997: 102).

This development concerning job prospects in the rural areas is also revealed by our survey. In the rural areas almost all households run their own subsistence farming and the percentage of day labourers is high. Other infor-mal activities occur almost only in combination with day labour and/or sub-sistence farming. By and large we can distinguish three groups informally active: a) informal farming; b) day labourers; c) other informal activities d) would be households without informal activities, not included in our enquiry). We focus mainly on groups a) – informal farming and b) – day labourers, which will be treated separately in concerning the market and the employment conditions in a household perspective. Group c) – other informal activities – is very diversified, and therefore, will only be dealt with marginally. The evaluation is supported by 33 qualitative household-interviews in the rural areas[5] and will be completed by the results of the quantitative household-surveys carried out in 1998 ('Social problems and working situation').

The market and job situation from the households' point of view

Agriculture

The households, for different reasons, consider the developments in agriculture since 1990 and the current market situation rather negatively.

It has barely improved. So many people have taken the land and don't exploit it. I had little of it and made great efforts. But there are some fields where just weeds grow. People had no money for treatment. It would have been better if they had left the land as it was (woman aged 57, 6-person household).

Apart from problems associated with lacking investment potential (low incomes and no access to credits), the land fragmentation following the re-privatization process is also described as an impediment to development.

The disadvantages in agriculture stem from the fact that the land was divided into many small fields, with which no high-quality agriculture can be undertaken' (woman aged 51, 5-person household).

Farms can hardly fall back upon machinery, because they cannot afford to invest and those of the associations are too expensive to work on small fields. In the mountain regions, the problem is exasperated by lower soil productivity.

Only a minority of the people consider the by-and-large uneconomic development of agriculture since the beginning of the 90s to be connected with the poor condition of the economy as a whole, with corruption and the lack of subsidies.

The collapse of the communist system – undesirable, dishonest. We almost became the world's rubbish pit. We are obliged to eat poultry from America, meat from Hungary, eggs from Turkey brought in with forged papers without paying custom duties. Production is low. Development would be possible, if only taxes were honestly paid (Man aged 41, 3-person household).

The relative prices for those industrial products required for agricultural production (machinery, fuel, fertilisers, etc.) have increased above average in the last few years. Conversely, agricultural product prices fell behind, especially for meat and dairy products. Labour-intense farming leads to comparably (with EU) high production costs with low productivity. The consequences are low profit margins, the worsening of the farmers' financial situation and declining investments. In addition, the market is flooded by imported goods (cf. Davis 1999).

Since 1997, the price of agricultural produce has declined. The main reason for this is the lowering of custom duties. In Hungary pigs, are raised continuously, using highly mechanised agriculture. The Romanian market has been flooded with imported goods. We could not achieve the same level of productivity as on a farm, for that, one needs a tractor, and a combine harvester. Our agriculture remains primitive (Man aged 47, 4-person household).

The number of those farms which sell products has increased, in spite of declining prices, although these are for the most part subsistence farms, which do not generally produce in large quantities, produce first and foremost for their personal use, do not regularly sell their products, and don't line up their range of products with the market trends. In many cases, the farm structure remains unaltered, in order to remain faithful to tradition, even if productivity is low. In other cases, production is oriented to what the farmers think are the best market opportunities and prices.

I think market gardening is a good field. If I were to raise cattle I would not make any money. Pigs and cows are very cheap at the moment. It's better to buy them than to raise them (Man aged 47, 4-person household).

Agricultural product prices and sales potential differ at local and regional level, and therefore, do not allow for a generally valid statement of the economic potential of every single product or line of production.

In subsistence farming, labour and return in agriculture are unrelated. Providing a basis of food products is the main priority, even when it is time-consuming and requires high labour inputs. Price fixing in the case of sporadic selling is usually based upon current market price and financial input, while the labour hours are not taken into account. In the market-oriented agriculture, a balanced relation between labour and returns is the priority. Only through a balanced cost-use relation can long-term financial returns be generated, which in turn allow investments (ex., for time – and energy-saving technologies and machinery).

Day labour in agriculture and informal labour in transport and construction

In previous years it has become more and more difficult in the field of agriculture to find employment as a day labourer.

The labour market has suffered a great deal since 1991, with the closure of the CAP's, which were the major employers for day labourers, and with the establishment of private (for the most part, subsistence) family farms on between 0.5 and 6 hectares of land. Due to the small size and the lack of financial resources, private land owners do usually not require day labourers. Those who had done so in the past (e.g., those elderly people who were no longer able to cultivate their land) can no longer afford them. *However, offer of employment has **increased** as a result of high unemployment and a population shift from the cities to the country.* Those concerned (they mostly are long term unemployed, have few qualifications, and receive insufficient transfers) combine a variety of informal activities in order to achieve a minimal living income, which is the only way out to stay at the subsistence level. However, monetary incomes, including state transfers, are still way below this level. Daily wages in the agricultural sector in the summer of 1999 were between 35.000 and 50.000 Lei (2 to 3US $), including two to three meals. In many cases, part of the salary is paid in kind. In addition, only a minority of the day labourers in the household survey 1998 had a small plot (mostly below ½ ha.) for food production – most depended on their meager monetary incomes.

In larger farms, modernization has reduced the need for day labourers, and the same applies to the associations.

One could more easily find a job, when there wasn't so much mechanization. Now even corn and other types of vegetables are treated with weed control, so that there is no more need to cut back weeds (Woman, 30 years, 5-person household).

In one case, gypsies coming from nearby villages are considered as competitors. They allegedly work for lower salaries and therefore seem to take away from village inhabitants already scarce jobs. The by-and-large decreasing job prospects leads to increasing competition among the day labourers.

The situation concerning transport is different, according to local conditions. However, on the whole it has worsened over the past years. A large number of people have purchased a horse wagon of their own, in order to work the land and hope to gain some money as self employed by transporting for others. Only one of the interviewees working in this field stated that he had a surplus of work in the high season.

The situation of day labourers working for cooperatives and associations is more regular, as is the situation of shepherds. Their wages are calculated on the basis of the days worked, but they work on informal contracts on monthly payment with the cooperatives, respectively with the cattle owners in one or several villages. In both fields competition is increasing. Concerning the shepherds, the number of cattle in the village is also increasing, so that in the end there is work for everybody.

Informal wage labour in construction is also more reliable, because working periods are rather on medium term. Wages are a little higher (50-60.000 Lei, i.e. 3 to 3.5US $ per day), but meals are generally not included. In the long term, demand in rural construction is sporadic and unforeseeable, and informal construction work remains basically precarious.

Besides day or casual wage labouring, other usually less lucrative activities are carried out, such as broom making, tin making, etc. Only for forest fruit picking were increasing prices and sales potential reported.

On the whole, the situation of these informal day and occasional labourers is more regular compared to those working for private farms. But all (except the shepherds) suffer decreasing demand and increasing competition, all work and live in a fundamentally precarious situation, and throughout, their payment barely allows for a subsistence level living.

Households' economic and social situation

Informal economy has the character of a survival economy in a stronger way than assumed. Household potential is only used systematically for the establishment and development of a lucrative informal activity by a small number of households. In most cases, household members just take on different types of job opportunities in order to reach a subsistence level.[6] The prospects are worse in the countryside than in the city, due to a lack of infrastructure and a reduced number of customers. On the other hand, it is exactly this lacking infrastructure which provides opportunities to fill in the 'gaps in the market' with a variety of informal activities.

The economic and social features characterising every household can be grouped according to different household strategies. According to Neef (1999) and Wallace (1998), there are three main strategies:

Survival logic – Fluctuating economy, dictated by bare necessities. Generally, that of underclass households with low qualifications and material shortages.

Improvement logic – Households with better qualification levels and more regular employment. Through informal activities, they strive for an improvement of their living standards.

Accumulation logic – Generally, households with high education levels and regular employment. Informal activities and resources are for the most part turned into a 'business', which the household strives to develop; reaching a higher living standard is only a secondary motive.

The typifications carried out in the following are based on the most important informal activities for the households. Two groups of day labourers, the 'traditional village fringe group' and the 'stable poor day labourers' are distinguished. In addition, there are the informal 'subsistence farmers', one third of whom lives in poverty; and the modern 'market-oriented farmers'.

In the Romanian countryside, most households (nearly 80% of the rural population, 83% of the households interviewed – Household Survey 1998) use subsistence farming in order to cover part of their basic needs and to reduce expenditures. The basic needs in food and clothing can mostly be met by self-production, but the lack of money reduces additional provisions for most households to the necessities. Few public services (education, health provision and transport) are available, not to speak of the bad quality of the rural retailing system.

The living and working situation of two groups is determined by the *survival* logic: The day-working 'traditional village fringe group' are socially characterised by lacking qualifications, material shortages and few social contacts. And the poor 'subsistence farmers' whose household is too large in relation to the land they dispose of, or most members being too old. There were few poor subsistence farmers in the qualitative sample. In the household survey, the social characteristics of poor farmers do not differ significantly from the non-poor, except in household size (4 persons compared to 3.3 per household with the non-poor) and, naturally, for poor incomes and small land surfaces. Poor *and* non-poor subsistence farmers are resumed in one type we explain below. Contrary to the day labourers they mostly have sufficient food, but otherwise live like the first ones, in deprivation which they cannot escape. Both mostly receive some additional formal incomes, mostly state transfers,[7] which are insufficient for improving the livelihood but essential for vital monetary expenditures.

Two groups are able to *improve* their living situation by informal activity, although as a rule only slightly: the improving 'subsistence farming' households own larger plots and better working instruments than the poor ones, but their social characteristics do not differ very much, neither in qualifications nor in number of children; their households are somewhat smaller and they have better market incomes. The 'stable poor day labourers' on the other hand have different social features, f.e., better qualifications and more regular employment conditions than the 'fringe group day labourers' – they make a type in their own. Both 'improving' groups more often combine with non-agrarian formal or informal work, mostly low qualified and often casual labour, especially in construction and transport (mostly with horse wagons).

The third group are modern informal entrepreneurial farmers, who own relatively large surfaces (in our cases, between 4 and 97 ha) and good working instruments as well as good social and marketing relations. They follow the *accumulation* strategy.

So, it is mostly by combining subsistence farming with income from formal jobs and social transfers[8] that most households gain a greater security and can satisfy their basic needs. Households depending on subsistence farming gain a certain autonomy, but are at the same time largely disclosed from the market economy.

Day labourers

Twenty out of the thirty-three rural households interviewed were working as day labourers, most of them in agriculture, some in construction or as domestic help. Most households were large, and received, besides wages, both pensions and child benefits, while unemployment benefits had long since expired, if ever members were entitled to them. Transfer benefits are modest and make one quarter of the household income.[9] However, they are particularly important, given the fact that they are often the only reliable source of income, as twelve of the interviewees reported.

> *Child benefit: 'It is really very important. We wait for it like for God' (Woman aged 69, 6-person household).*

Some interviewees received at times social benefit, other times they applied for it without success. Other benefits in kind, such as food or material support, are rare and were only claimed by few households. Either they were considered as public expression of one's poverty, and therefore undesired, or the possibility of receiving was unknown.

The households' conditions are particularly precarious in the winter time, due to the heavy seasonal fluctuations in the demand for day labour (between November and March there is barely any work). Many, therefore rely exclusively upon transfers, only one quarter of the households can also count on low returns (in our cases, between 18 and 40US $) coming from a formal job like tractor driver, street cleaner or worker in a private company. Low informal returns from the selling of handmade pullovers and socks as well as cleaning services and snow shovelling are barely profitable and they do not guarantee any regular income.

In the months with a lot of work in the fields it is better, in the winter it is more difficult. Fortunately the lad (son) works and also receives food vouchers (woman aged 47, 2-person household)

Home property is widespread in Romania, which offers a certain security – indeed, only a few households live in rented accommodation.[10] Some cannot regularly pay council tax and have difficulties in dealing with the debts resulting. However, given the fact that accumulation of these debts rarely has consequences, it is also possible to run these up and spend the money on other expenses, such as additional housing costs, especially energy. Some others avoid debt by turning off the electricity supply as a precaution and using gas lamps and wood-burning ovens. An important strategy in dealing with (insufficient) household income ('domestic management') is buying on credit. Over a half of the interviewees stated that food products, especially, are bought this way and only paid once the household receives transfers.

What do you normally buy on tick? – Bread, oil, sugar, rice – food.– And when do you pay? – When we get the children's allowance (woman aged 36, 7-person household).

The regular paying-off establishes a mutual trust between debtor and creditor and debts are not accumulated. Creditors are generally members of the household, neighbours and village shops. In few cases, these debts are paid off in work stints. For most households it is impossible to save money, given the modest incomes. Three of them maintained they could save some money and only two households were able to put away some money for the winter expenses (Household Survey 1998: about one third of the day labourers can save occasional small amounts of money, nobody regularly).

In the day labourers' group we differentiate between the 'traditional village fringe group' (14 households) and the 'stable or regular poor day labourers' (6 households).

Traditional village fringe group

Most of them worked as day labourers in the CAPs, many of them had done so since their childhood or teenage. They had for the most part minor positions as un- or semi-skilled workers, while only a few had been employed as skilled workers, such as tractor drivers. However, they all worked with a work book until the collapse of the communist system, and therefore had the right to time off work, medical insurance and a pension. Since the closure of the CAPs, they have become socially marginalised. They barely have any qualifications, their education level amounts in most cases 8 school years, and they lack any vocational training. Only a few attended a professional school or an upper school; men at most have a 'tractor driver'[11] degree. Due to their long lasting activity as day labourers in different places, the entitlements for state transfers are modest. Moreover, most of them have only worked a few years with a work book and the low wages they got affect on the calculation of the transfers. Many elderly people retired after the breakdown of the CAPs, most of the younger became unemployed.

Most household members now work for the better-off village inhabitants, if these require them. They do not have any regular employer and take on pretty much every job they are offered.

I go when there's chopping to be done, when I'm called for, or for other work. It's not good really, without a job where you know that you're working for a month and getting wages (woman aged 47, 2-person household).

Therefore, they suffer even greater insecurity than the 'stable poor day labourers' who have more regular customers. Households, as much as household members, combine a variety of different activities (for example, day labour in the agricultural or construction sector, transport services with horse and cart, forest fruit picking and broom making), which however do not result in any reliable or sufficient income, due to their modest wages and irregularity. In rare cases, a member of the household, often one of the older children, contributes to the household income. This brings about regularity, although these are in most cases low wage jobs (tractor driver or road sweeper) which do not bring about an essential improvement of the material conditions. The bad social and financial situation of the interviewees often goes hand in hand with a state of alcoholism or illness/handicap of single household members. Most live in big households of 5-6 members. The prospects in the village are usually few. No or very few reliable network connections are established with people. When there are network partners, these usually find themselves in the same hopeless situation, and therefore can barely have a stabilising effect on the social situation. Some households run a little garden or orchard,[12] and keep a pig or poultry, which allows them to cover a small part of their food requirements and eventually to sell some when they are in urgent need of money. Two of the interviewed households own land, but do not exploit it. In general, they live day by day waiting for regular state benefits, if they receive some, and cannot or can only just cover their basic needs.

They rotate in a circle which can be characterised as 'learned helplessness'. Through their fringe position in society and lack of qualifications they have few alternatives in finding jobs. Some have tried to break out of the vicious circle and change something, but failure has led them to slip back into pessimism and inactivity. Others have never tried to change their situation and have not the slightest idea as to how they could change their standard of living. Their reaction to any outside change is one of helplessness, they have difficulty in adapting to new situations and take no initiative in tackling problems and new tasks. The children tend to be drawn into this vicious circle, since money for school and training is hard to come by and they have to make a contribution to the household income as early as possible and tend to take on the helplessness of their parents. Only outside help can break this circle.

Regular poor day labourers

Also in the group of the 'regular poor day labourers' the former main employer was the CAP. As opposed to traditional fringe groups however, they more often have a diploma and were frequently employed as skilled workers like electricians, carpenters, plumbers or mechanics. These qualifications constitute possible development potentials for the households, because there is still demand for them nowadays.

Most households combine two different informal activities (ex., agricultural day labour with tin producing and selling or with day labour in construction) and subsistence farming. For their work as day labourers, they usually have regular customers or work in one of the new associations, which gives them a more reliable basis (*monthly* wages). All of them own and run a garden and, except for one of the households, cultivate between one and four hectares of land and keep some animals. This way they are able to cover between 50 and 80% of their food requirements. Sometimes, surpluses are sold or exchanged with other products. The network connections consist in the main of a few people, but they are reliable. 'Regular poor day labourers' households tend to be smaller (2 to 4 people) and the combination of a secure market for their work as day labourers with sufficient subsistence farming and state benefits as a financial basis convey to them more security and stability. They are able to satisfy their basic needs, also when they are short of cash, which happens especially in the winter time. The household incomes stay also below or at poverty line level, and any widening of one of their activities is impossible, due to a lack of investment potential.

Subsistence farming

The households that we consider here (9 out of 33) deal first and foremost with subsistence farming, while only three of them carry out also other activities (transport by horse cart, kiosk saleswoman, welder). The great majority of the household members have a vocational school diploma or an upper school or university degree. Two generations live in the same household (the household size is on average 4 people), with only two exceptions. The members of the older generation are generally retired, while the younger ones have formal jobs. Only a few of them are unemployed. They work (or worked) in many fields – as mechanic, carpenter, welder, cook, non-commissioned officer, nurse or teacher. Their network connections are limited to a small number of people, first and foremost family members, but they are reliable. Only one household has a wider network consisting of friends, neighbours and colleagues. The household income mainly consists of formal incomes and state benefits, in some cases, incomes from informal jobs, as well as subsistence farming returns. Most households work less than a hectare of land, while a minority have two to six hectares of land.[13] Only one household does not keep animals. Almost all of them sell surpluses sporadically, some on a routine basis. In some cases, products are exchanged in kind. On average, they are able to cover two thirds of their food requirements (minimum 20%, maximum 90%) with their own products. In combining their incomes with the product of farming, all of them, except for one, can cover their basic needs, although they still have financial difficulties, and therefore, have to limit themselves to the bare necessities

> *We live modestly. As for food, we don't lack anything, but we can't afford anything else (man aged 52, 3-person household).*

Farming covers part of the survival of the households (survival logic), while in the case of the others, it contributes over and above to the improvement of the standard of living.

> *Without a [formal] job it is impossible to live. Working on the fields has improved our conditions. With our salary we can hardly pay the maintenance costs [for the house/apartment] and all the rest (woman aged 43, 3-person household).*

Some had also operated subsistence farming before 1989. However, most of them got their land back at the beginning of the 90s. Beside their main occupation, some worked their land at weekends and in the evening ('weekend-agriculture'), although with retirement this work was neglected. The wish to expand the farm and to carry out investment is expressed mainly by the households with an improved standard of living. Anyway, due to lack of money, they could not expand nor invest in agriculture. Others have no interest in change, or are too old to think about it.

Between 1993 and 1999 three of the households moved from the city to their home villages in the countryside when they started to receive their pension or when they got unemployed. There they have less expenses, and with the subsistence farming, they can live a somewhat better life.

I live somewhat better, but not in luxury (man aged 47, 4-person household).

Market-oriented agriculture

We deal here with those who combine marketing aiming at sale with subsistence production. All of them have regular customers: either private ones or factories (ex., sugar factory, oil press) which sell on the market. Sometimes, there is also exchange of goods (ex. potatoes with oil, spirits, fish). For all of the four households, agriculture and the selling of goods produce the most important income, state benefits are smaller, and some have small additional incomes (leasing land or renting an apartment). Most household members have a high school degree and were or still are employed in a good position (ex., superintendent in the city hall, vice-president of the CAP, mayor, bookkeeper). In all cases, the household members work on the farm. Their network connections, a circle of family and friends, are large and reliable.

They started or expanded their activity in the agricultural sector at the beginning of the 90s when the land was restituted. Like the subsistence-orientated households, they inherited the know-how from their parents (traditional agricultural knowledge). They chose this type of activity themselves, which allowed them to cover most of their food needs and, on the other hand to have returns from selling their products. They are able to cover without any problem all of their basic needs, they can invest and generate savings for their children.

There is nothing we would like and can't afford. We save because we can't spend all our money (man aged 70, 2-person household).

The size of three farms is four to nine hectares, one has 97 hectares, but also the smaller ones have expanded by buying or renting land. Market trends determine the focuses in cultivation and animal breeding. So, for example, the smaller farms focus mainly on milk production, because cattle breeding is more productive and milk prices are higher than those of cereals, sugar, etc. Beside productivity, they look for quality.

> *Sugar-beets are sweeter when no chemicals are used. We only employ farmyard manure. An engineer stated that a piece of land fertilised with farmyard manure could produce 22 kg of sugar for every 100 kg, as opposed to 17 kg where chemicals were used (man aged 59, 4-person household).*

In the long term, they want to expand and to invest in the purchase of cattle, land, machinery, etc., except those being too old for extending.

Development potential and prospects

The previously depicted economic and social situation of the households shows clearly the different household resources (education, financial opportunities, social networks, contacts abroad, material resources, etc.). In the following, I give some personal ideas on development possibilities in connection with the market and job conditions, with the potentials, wishes and prospects of the different households.

The resource levels of day labourers' households belonging to village fringe groups are very low, due to their low level of education and extreme financial and material deprivation. Their sole wish for change is, in most cases, basically to find regular employment with a work book again (f.e., in an association, or as housekeeper). But many have no idea how to change their situation and to improve their living standards. The 'regular poor day labourers' don't consider their professional jobs (carpenter, plumber, electrician, etc.) as having development potential. Their main wish is also to find regular employment with a work book.

Against that, most of the households running subsistence farming have concrete wishes and ideas. They want to expand their farm and buy the necessary equipment and machinery, they want to build a greenhouse, etc. However, they lack the money and don't receive support from the state. If they could receive credits with low payments at reasonable interest rates, many would consider to invest in the expansion of their farms. Others would prefer to invest in the setting up of a work shop (garage, welding work shop, or a bakery), but also mostly lack the financial resources. Those who were able to invest small sums of capital feared too low returns, given the bad market prospects. Subsistence farmers can cover at least their food needs, even if the proceeds from selling are at times low, and therefore carry out second informal activities, such as welding, only occasionally.[14]

Households working in marked-oriented farming had the chance to invest and to take up credits thanks to their better financial situation, or they managed to make greater profits through good investments, f.e. in pig raising, which at present gives quick returns. These have been used for longer term investments, like a tractor.

Many households in subsistence and in market-oriented farming considered the setting up of a firm, that is, the legalization of their informal activities. However, the bureaucratic costs and the high taxes kept them from taking this step. Only one household in our sample had founded a farming company in the starting years of the early 90s, because they received good credits and have been exempted from paying taxes for one year. After few years, they officially quit their firm because the credits had run out and the taxes increased, and continued informally.

The modernizing of agriculture in Romania requests good consultation for financial and material support as well as for the promotion of new businesses, in the field of farming and of services (e.g. mills, bakeries, garages), including support in marketing and management. Besides professional support, this could be also arranged in reciprocal help between experienced households. The same applies for the mutual exchange in technical knowledge in farming.

Well-directed transfer of knowledge and corresponding financial and material support can help for the developing of ecological agriculture, which in Romania at present has good marketing and export prospects. This applies especially in subsistence farming, where no or little fertilisers are used and where knowledge of traditional and alternative agricultural methods is wide spread.

Efficient support for day labourers remains a difficult question. The qualifying for second jobs could be promoted by government or private agencies. Marketing promotion in the field of less lucrative activities like forest fruit picking or broom making can help to expand these activities. In view of the deficient infrastructure in many rural districts, communal help for the co-operative starting of facilities like bakeries or of cheap transport services to city markets seems viable. The main problem with these initiatives seems to be how to break up the resignation and passivity of the 'fringe group' day labourers; this requests targeted activation.

Through the setting up and linking of different projects (ex., agricultural production and processing firms) new jobs can be created in rural areas, and in the long run, independent regional structures built up. In this way, firms and services can emerge producing, processing and marketing a variety of products with a local and regional character. This means that in addition to the strengthening of local markets with regional and national home products, the national market will be in a better position to hold its own against the run-of-the-mill import-articles. There are some successful examples of respective activities of National Government regional programs and of Non-Government Organizations' projects well suited to the particularities of local situations, which could be extended. But these need better targeting to the situations and activity potentials of the households concerned: if the household become a relevant unit of politics and planning, self-organization and social networks can be turned into decisive development variables (cf. Friedmann 1992).

Notes

1   The state sector still provides 2/3 of the jobs in urban areas, while in rural areas the fi-gure is only 1/4 (Stănculescu, 2000).
2   14% of those employed in private farming commuted to the next city before 1989 (Survey CURS – SA 1997 apud Stănculescu, 2000).
3   Following an enquête in four regions (Davis/Gaburici, 1999) only one fifth of the private farms disposes of own tractors, ploughs or cultivators.
4   The right to take time off, health insurance, pension; before 1989 there was no official unemployment, therefore unemployment benefits and period of notice were irrelevant.
5   The interviews were carried out in the summer of 1999 in the following (administrative councils) regions: Vrancea, Brasov, Alba, Hunedoara, Dambovita, Prahova, Telorman and Botosani. Village size was between 369 and 6735 inhabitants – on average 2305. The distance to the nearest middle or big city was on average 16,8 km (minimum 4 km, maximum 55 km). In the 33 households 179 people lived with an average household size of 4,5 people (minimum 2, maximum 9 people).
6   The minimum living income in October 1998 was 245.262 Lei (ca. 21US $) per person (indications of the NCS).
7   *Pension*: the pension amount depends on the last income and the number of years of work as stated in the work book. The retirement age is 57 for women and 60 for men. With 27 working years one can however already retire and in fact many subjects went into early retirement from the age of 50 on). In order to reduce unemployment, in accordance with the general restructuring and mass dismissal, a new possibility was introduced for combining unemployment benefits with early retirements.
    Child benefits: 65.000 Lei (ca. 4US $) were paid in the summer of 1999 per child. The paying of these benefits depends on school attendance starting from school age.
    Unemployment benefits are first paid for the first 9 months (the amount depends on the former income), a prolongation of 18 months is possible (here the payment is low and does not depend on the salary). If there are reasons for the dismissal, such as abuse of alcohol, there is no right to unemployment benefits. Land owners (from 2 ha., on the mountains from 4 ha.) do not receive these benefits (cf. Rieser 1997). Pension, Child and Unemployment benefits are centrally administrated and therefore regularly paid.
    Social benefit is paid by the local authorities. When this is not possible, allocations come from the central administration, and this money can be disposed of according to the local

administration's preferences, eg. for the local infrastructure. For this reason social benefit is no reliable resource for those entitled to it.

8   According to the Household Survey 1998 only 3% of the households practising the subsistence economy sell products regularly on the market.

9   On average 25.7 % of the total household income, which includes old age pension, CAP pension (much lower compared to regular old age pensions), child benefits and other transfers such as earnings-related benefits (Household survey 1998).

10 93% of the households in the Household Survey 1998 own the house or flat in which they live. Of the 34 qualitative interviews in rural areas only two – day labourer's – households live in rented accomodation.

11 Being tractor driver was already regarded as a bad job before 1989 and today does not offer any useful qualifications. Most of the farmers work with horse and cart, because the fields are too small to use a tractor.

12 Household survey 1998: of all day labourers' households 52.1% have less than 0.5 ha land. 39.1% have between 0.5 and 2.5 ha.

13 Household survey 1998: of all rural households working in agriculture 16.6% have less than 0.5 ha, 55.5% have between 0.5 and 2.5 ha land.

14 There was only one household in our sample in poor conditions who was very inventive and enterprising. In using waste material from the formal workplace, they built a mill on their own. The only fix costs were those for power. Owing to the fact that the next mill is about 20 km away, they had enough customers. Payments could be made either in cash (eg. with the pension) or in kind, which also allowed households in poor financial conditions to use the mill, whereas in usual agrarian enterprises payments must be made directly and in cash. The biggest returns from the mill were generated from autumn until spring. A chainsaw with the engine taken from an old tractor was built as an additional source of income for the summer. Except for the puchasing price of the old tractor, the only costs were those for fuel.

References

Bădescu, I. (1999), 'Structura sociala si clasa intermediarilor in mediul rural. Dictatura oligarhiei financiare si agricultura de subzistenta familiala', *Sociologie Romaneasca,* vol. I, pp. 53-60.

Davis, J. R., Gaburici, A. (1999), 'Rural Finance and Private Farming in Romania', *Europe-Asia Studies,* vol. 51, No. 5, pp. 843-869.

Economic Survey of Europe, Ed. UN-Secretary of the ECE,. Geneva/New York, 1996/97, and 1999 no. 1 and 2.

Friedmann, J. (1992), *Empowerment. The Politics of Alternative Development.* Cambridge/Mass.

Golibrzuch, E. (1998), *Wolfsberg: Traditionales Dorf, Ruine und/oder postmoderner Erholungsraum? Endogene Entwicklungspotentiale in einem deutschen Dorf in Rumänien,.* Diplomarbeit, Technische Universität Hamburg-Harburg, FB Städtebau/Stadtplanung.

Gross, P., e.a. (1995*), Reise in die Zwischenzeit – Begegnung mit Rumänien 1995.* Studienarbeit Gh Kassel, Fachbereich Architektur, Stadt– und Landschaftsplanung.

Heller, W. (1998), Experiences and assessments of the transformation from private households' point of view, in W. Heller (ed.), *Romania: Migration, Socio-economic*

Transformation and Perspectives of Regional Development, München, Südosteuropa-Gesellschaft (Südosteuropa-Studien, Bd. 62).

Knappe, E. (1997), Ländliche Siedlung und Landwirtschaft unter den Bedingungen des Transformationsprozesses in Südosteuropa, in F.-D. Grimm, K. Roth (eds.), *Das Dorf in Südosteuropa zwischen Tradition und Umbruch.* München: Südosteuropa-Gesellschaft (Südosteuropa Aktuell 25).

Lukas, Z. (2000), 'Die Landwirtschaft der Oststaaten 1999', in *Osteuropa-Wirtschaft* no. 2, pp. 98-119.

Neef, R. (1999), 'Formen und soziale Lagen der Schattenwirtschaft in einem Transformationsland: Rumänien', in *Berliner Journal für Soziologie,* vol. 9, no. 3, pp. 397-414.

Pop, G.P., Benedek, J. (1997), 'Die Verteilung und Entwicklung der kleinen Dörfer in Rumänien', in F.-D. Grimm, K. Roth (eds.), *Das Dorf in Südosteuropa zwischen Tradition und Umbruch,* München, Südosteuropa-Gesellschaft (Südosteuropa Aktuell 25).

Rieser, H.-H. (1997), 'Regionale Differenzierung der Transformationsprozesse in der Landwirtschaft – dargestellt am Beispiel der beiden Banater Kreise Karasch-Severin und Temesch,' in F.-D. Grimm, K. Roth (eds.), *Das Dorf in Südosteuropa zwischen Tradition und Umbruch.* München: Südosteuropa-Gesellschaft (Südosteuropa Aktuell 25).

Stănculescu, M.S. (2000), 'Romanian Households between State, Market and Informal Economies'. Paper for the Working Conference *'Shadow Economy and Social Resources in Eastern and South Eastern Europe',* Universität Göttingen/Südosteuropa–Gesellschaft, Marburg 24./25.6.2000.

Stewart, M. (1998), 'We should build a statue to Ceausescu here' The trauma of de-collectivization in two Romanian villages, in S. Bridger, (ed.) *Surviving post-socialism: local strategies and regional responses in Eastern Europe and the former Soviet Union,* London, Routledge.

Technologie-Netzwerk Berlin (Hg.) (1990), *Lokale Ökonomie: Exploration und Evaluierung lokaler Strategien in Krisenregionen,* Bd. 1, Zusammenfassung der Forschungsergebnisse (1988-1990), Berlin.

Tomasi, E. (1998), 'The development of Romanian agriculture since the land reform in 1991', in W. Heller (ed), *Romania: Migration, Socio-economic Transformation and Perspectives of Regional Development,* München, Südosteuropa-Gesellschaft (Südosteuropa-Studien, Bd. 62).

Turnock, D. (1998), 'Human resources for regional development in the Romanian Carpathians', in W. Heller, (ed), *Romania: Migration, Socio-economic Transformation and Perspectives of Regional Developmen,* München, Südosteuropa-Gesellschaft (Südosteuropa-Studien, Bd. 62).

Wallace, C. (1998), *Household Work Strategies Revisited,* Conference Paper, Institute for Advanced Studies, Vienna.

Household Survey 1998: 1177 standardized household interviews on 'Social Problems and the Working Situation' carried out in October 1998 (nationally representative sample).

Qualitative Household Interviews: carried out in July to November 1999. Total 105, 33 of these in rural areas.

Chapter 8

Formal and informal incomes of the Romanian households[1]

Simona Ilie[*]

General framework

Since 1989 several factors have forced people in Romania to look for something to replace their lost income in order to get along: the decrease in real earnings, the continuous deterioration of the labour market, and the difficulty in finding any job, not to mention a better paid one. In many cases, the solution was found outside of the formal or officially registered economy. However, even this path has not always guaranteed that the earnings are enough to provide for a decent living standard.

The data from a 1998/1999 study on the development potential of the informal economy in Romania reveal that because of their households' economic insecurity, many Romanians consider the last ten years worse than Ceausescu's time.

We had money [in Ceausescu's time] and everything we needed. There is not too much to say [about the last ten years]. At the beginning, we were happy to escape from queuing, quotas, fear of 'Securitate', and other such things. Then it became more and more difficult with prices that rise by the hour, the lack of money, the scarcity of jobs, and money that no longer has any value. We thought that the change would be our chance, but it has proved to be more chaos and uncertainty (woman, 57, primary school).

The disillusionment can be found among those who have experienced an acceptable economic development after 1990, as well. The new opportunities that arose were shadowed by economic insecurity and the general economic and social decline.

---

[*] Senior researcher, Research Institute for Quality of Life, Calea 13 Septembrie no. 13, 76117 Bucharest. E-mail: simona@iccv.ro.

At the beginning, I thought it was a fantastic chance, but suddenly it changed into disillusionment. After that, I put some order into what I was doing and things started to get better and better. Everything seemed nice at the beginning: we had the feeling that we were free, that we might do everything we could and wanted, but after a while I realised that doing what we want is very difficult, the costs are huge, and sometimes it isn't worthwhile (man, 27, university).

At the same time, there are people for whom the last ten years have been an opportunity and a successful period. Most of these profit from very specific situations or qualifications.

... it has been a successful period because I have had the chance to do everything I wanted to. It has been a good period from all points of view. I think that each of us had a chance in 1989, when the regime changed, but many people did not have the courage to risk at the right moment (woman, 48, high school).

This paper focuses on the relative importance of different formal and informal incomes of households in determining decreasing or ascending life situations. The first point to be discussed is the source and composition of incomes.

Income sources

The sources of households' incomes can be grouped as follows:

1. from work:
   a. work for firms or for private persons:
      – wages (on the basis of an indefinite or fix period contract);
      – occasional payment for work done.
   b. work on one's own account - owner, self-employed, freelancer:
      – incomes from profit;
      – earning as self employed person or freelancer.
2. from transfers:
   a. social benefits from the state: pensions, unemployment benefits, child allowances, social support for students, social welfare, other social benefits;
   b. intrahousehold help:
      – help from persons outside the household.
3. from assets:
      – from working the land (self-production and selling products);
      – from rented spaces or financial assets.
4. from illegal activities

As long as the incomes are officially registered and, when necessary, the subject of taxation, they are considered *formal incomes*. Otherwise, we are talking about *informal incomes,* a far from homogenous category. Some kinds of informal incomes are by nature unrecorded, like intrahousehold transfers (in kind or in money). In many cases, incomes are supposed to be formal, but different forms of tax evasion move them to the informal area. These are the so-called unreported incomes. Incomes from illegal activities, not declared by definition, make up the third category.[2] These are not subject of this paper.

Formal vs. informal

The non-compliant behaviour (Feige 1999) that nourishes the informal sector turns all 'cracks' in the legal framework into opportunities for personal benefit. In addition, certain activities sometimes appear as formal, sometimes as informal, making up the so-called *grey economy* (ILO 1999). This is the case with self-production (see below), especially in subsistence agriculture, the activity of the self-employed and paid domestic services.

The border between formal and informal incomes is permeable and as such allows for movement from one category to another. The 'X' in the table below indicates the main categorization of the income. The arrows point out the direction of sliding.

Table 8.1   **Income sources**

		formal	informal
1	Wage earning	X ⟶	
2	Occasional payment for work done	⟵	X
3	Incomes from profit	X ⟶	
4	Earning as a freelancer	X ⟶	
5	Social benefits (social transfers)	X	
6	Intrahousehold help (transfers)		X
7	Self-production	⟵	X
8	Incomes from rented spaces, shares	X ⟶	

Such sliding appears in particular circumstances. In the following, I offer some examples of how this movement takes place and point out what about them is specific to the Romanian situation.

1. Wage earnings are usually considered formal. A 1991 law allows that one's wages can be supplemented by a formal *second job*, providing the legal framework for hiring people who already have a formal job and regulating their social entitlements. It also made it possible for pensioners to work on a part-time basis while continuing to receive pension benefits. Due to the economic recession after 1996, regulated second jobs have become a more seldom way to supplement regular wage earnings.

Another form of earning an official income is the so-called *civil contract*. This is a way of hiring people for temporary work. When this arrangement was introduced, there were no social welfare contributions to be paid, except the tax on income. This allowed people to be legally 'hired', sometimes for long periods of time. However, in response to such practices, rather restrictive regulations were introduced in 2000, in order to protect employees: firms are no longer able to hire people on this basis for activities that are similar to the main activity of the firm. In addition, paid health insurance was added as a mandatory part of the contract. The legal framework is still considered inadequate concerning the day workers.

Grey/informal wage labour is not as rare as one might think. There are several different reasons for its prevalence:

- many people found themselves outside of the labour market due to the restructuring process in the 90s. This, combined with the slow privatization process and the depreciation of real earnings, forced many to accept any paid job they could find, even if it meant accepting temporary work and/or employment not based on a contract. The risks associated with precarious employment, with limited or no job security, pales in comparison to the alternative lack of financial resources.
- the tax system has been considered a too heavy burden by entrepreneurs, so employers often hire people without declaring for tax (so-called moonlighters or 'black workers'). A particular hidden form of non-declared work is popular especially among small private firms: both employer and employee agree to a trial period of few months in which the employee 'enjoys' less legal protection and earns less money, after which the employer refuses to extend the contract and instead hires someone else for another trial period according to the associated less expensive and more precarious conditions.
- the under-declared wage is another practice of diminishing taxes, consisting of declaring tax on only part of one's wages, the other part being a form of 'black work'.

Informal wages as described above are earned by people in all segments of the labour force, regardless of age, gender, qualification or education.

2. Occasional payment for work/services done is commonly part of the informal economy. This is the case with self-employment (see below, point 4), but also includes all kinds of occasional work that theoretically would have to be declared at the financial administration. Such reporting is in fact very rare.

The day workers are the most common cases in this category. They are frequently to be found in agriculture, construction, harbours, market centres and warehouses, where there is always something to do. It is well known that people move with their families, sometimes seasonally, to areas with a high demand for labour. Another example of this type of income is earning from housekeeping services, performed mainly by individuals. Small private firms providing such services have appeared on the market in the last years, but only in big cities.

3. Although *income from profit* has usually been seen as formal, this may not always be the case, especially if we examine the situation in small enterprises. The employers justify their evasion of taxes and social welfare contributions with the uncertain economic environment.

> *During the month when I write the bill, I have to pay the taxes on that value, although I see no money ... I would have rather worked on the black market because there are cases when we do not have what to pay [...] we have seen no money, but I have to pay the taxes. I did pay once the VAT 22000000 Lei. It is true that I took back the money, but after 6 months [eroded by inflation]: it was only then the beneficiaries had the money to pay us back (man, 27, university).*

Government incentives offered to new private firms have also been exploited, the example of tax exemption on new firms' profits being the most well-known of such practices.[3]

4. Earnings from self-employment was common for lawyers and artists in the time of communism. In 1991, a law reacting to the new conditions was passed to regulate self-employment. Because freelancers are, by definition, a mix form of employer and employee, the way in which taxes are evaded is also a mixture of not declaring incomes and the use of exemption facilities offered to small private economic agents. Once someone registers as self-employed, they have to record their activities in their financial papers. Many unemployed workers or young people who have never been employed, but who have the skills to act independently, enter the labour market every time the opportunity arises. They often delay official declaration for a long time, cancel their registration while continuing to work or don't declare at all. It is difficult to determine the degree to which these are formal or informal incomes. In the following, they are considered informal ones. We have assumed that their incomes are earned informally because most of them have no degree, and they do not share the profession of those who commonly act as freelancers. The activity of self-employed trade workers is also likely not to be officially registered. Another reason in this respect is offered by a social worker from a small town who identifies people's strategy of avoiding the official registration as a way of surviving.

> *Someone willing to set up a firm has to pay for authorizations, for renting space, tax for I don't know what else and adding all these together, there remains nothing. Consequently, he cancels the authorization and works underground. There are so many family associations and freelancers who worked formally for a while, after which they cancelled the authorization. ... At least a part of them should still be active, because otherwise... (social worker, small town).*

5. *Social transfers* are formal incomes given to those entitled that provide stability to the beneficiaries. Due to their certainty, even a small social transfer becomes more important than a larger uncertain earning that members of the family might receive.

6. *Intrahousehold help* is an informal transfer. This can consist of monetary transfers from relatives or neighbours or in kind help, most often childcare. It can also consist of small services in special cases like illness or family events. Taking care of grandchildren is a common custom in Romanian households, ranging from full-time care to filling in the gaps after kindergarten or the primary school program. Neighbours and acquaintances offer such help in exchange for money, products or services. Private firms in this field exist only in big towns. Food and clothing given to poor families are included in this category as well. The most common form of intrahousehold help in rural areas is assistance offered to close relatives and sometimes to acquaintances for working the land or for repairing the house. In the analysis that follows, we excluded in kind help or the services in return and included only financial help between families.

In our survey, between half and two-thirds of Romanian households could count on relatives, friends, neighbours and colleagues for this type of intrahousehold help. Half of the families interviewed would or have accepted child care, household and/or domestic help, while two-thirds would rely on help in special situations like illness. Only approximately 1% of them would call for institutional help.

7. Self-production: the value of goods produced on one's own is estimated on the basis of produced and consumed quantities and the price per unit. Here the *estimation is based on data* from our quantitative survey.[4]

The main relevant question is whether it *is correct to add self-production to the monetary households income in order to determine the household's income level.* From my point of view, this is the case with food production, most necessary for survival, which can be replaced with regular expenditure: it increases the standard of life.

Another problem may arise when two households with the same level of income are compared, whereby the income of one household is earned in money and the other household's income is comprised of self-production. If the first household can choose how to spend its money and the second household is only able to cover its food needs, are they really equal? I assumed yes, because, after all, it is a problem of choice: even if both households have incomes at a subsistence level, they can still choose to spend their money differently.

The last, but not least, debatable point is related to the nature of this source of income. The official statistics include it in the households' income budget and there is also a procedure that tries to integrate these incomes into National Accounts and GDP. All these estimations drag self-production into the formal sphere, but the general characteristics of the Romanian agriculture, primarily made up of self-production in the transition period, suggest that it may be more appropriate to count self-production to the informal sphere (Zamfir 1995).[5]

8. Most *earnings from rented space, shares, interests* come from renting flats, which does not function in a controlled framework in Romania.

Despite legal regulation that states that each person who rents a house has to declare it with both the financial administration and the police, this habit is rare: renting a flat is most often based on a non-written agreement between the two parties. Formal incomes from shares and interests remain only an occasional source of income, and are still quite rare. In 1998, there was no regulation concerning dividends. Regarding interest, it is important to mention the visible, though infrequent, behaviour among pensioners to supplement their current state pensions by interest from (generally small) bank deposits.

Concerning the nature of different income sources, only some can be convincingly specified by nature. With regard to the discussion above, the incomes are grouped as follows:

- *Formal incomes* – wages, wages from second jobs, income from profit, and social transfers.

- *Informal incomes* – freelance earnings, occasional payments for work done, self-production, income from selling agricultural products, intrahouseholds help, and income from rented spaces or shares.
- *Self production*, due to its specificity, is presented separately.

The following section explains the procedure in researching and verifying informal incomes, the incidence of their different forms and their importance in household budgets. Further, I will comment on the relationship between formal and informal income and poverty and discuss income inequalities and social backgrounds, with particular emphasis on the very poor and the rich.

The incidence of informal incomes

In the quantitative survey, 46% of the households declared to perform different *activities that help them to live better*. We consider these activities as informal ones. There were several cases whose declaration in this respect rather indicated overtime work or a regular second job, but the big majority was clearly informal. According to our computation on the bases of income declaration for the last month and their nature defined above, the share of those performing informal activities (without self-production) is 26.8%. By adding declared agrarian self-production this share rises to 72%.

However, should self-production be added to the informal activities or not? Among the additional activities declared, three-quarters of the respondents listed agriculture first. In addition, three-quarters of those who listed a second and third additional activity named agriculture again. On the other hand, almost one-third of the households with land that obtain products from it do not consider this as 'an activity which helps them to live better'. For many people, especially in rural areas, working the land is not something 'supplementary'; this makes part of their everyday life and work and is what they have been doing ever since they were born, even when members of their households have earned wages in other branches. All this supports the contention that self-production should be put into the informal sphere. Let us further note that adding self-production just to urban households makes the same share of 46% of households assumed informally active.[6] Among those admitting supplementary activities, 78% obtain *products* as output of their activity, 46% receive *money* and almost 5% get *services in return*.

Forty-two percent of those obtaining products meet less than half of their consumption needs from products obtained. Another 25% meet their household need almost entirely in this way. The surplus of products obtained (sometime just one sort) is either sold (25%), given to others (16%), or exchanged for other goods (14%).

In an attempt to put together all the information we have on this topic, we also used the data from the qualitative inquiry. The subjects of the qualitative inquiry were asked to specify how much they would need to spend per month in order to buy or pay for all items they produce in the household or receive from friends and relatives. I compared this with the data on self-production estimated in the quantitative survey. The results, presented in the table 8.2, have to be interpreted carefully, bearing in mind that the qualitative survey has no claim of being representative. The differences can also be explained by the fact that the question in the qualitative inquiry covers more than food products.

Table 8.2   Products got informally out of households' total income (%)

Percentage of household income	>=75%	(75, 50]	[25, 50)	<25%	**NA**
Self-production estimation in the *quantitative* survey	4.4	12.8	22.0	60.2	0.5
Subjects' estimation in the *qualitative* inquiry	12.4	10.5	3.8	67.6	5.7

Source: Social Problems, Living Standard and Informal Economy, IQL, Romania, 1998 (N=1177) and qualitative inquiry, 1999, 105 in depth interviews.

Those obtaining incomes from their informal activity (in the quantitative survey) were asked to estimate the money earned as a percentage of their household's total income. I compared this answer to the share of informal monetary incomes in the total households' monetary income as declared broken down according to sources of income. I included here the earnings from freelancing, occasional payment for work done, income from selling agricultural products, and from renting and shares. The two distributions are presented in table 8.3.

Table 8.3   Informal monetary income % of the total monetary income

Informal monetary incomes %	0	(0-20]	(20-40]	(40-60]	(60-80]	>80	NA
Declared by subjects % of households	0	27.3	20	17.9	6.0	9.8	19.1
Identified by sources % of households	52.2	11.0	10	6.2	7.8	13.1	2.6

Source: Social Problems, Living Standard and Informal Economy, IQL, Romania, 1998 (N=235).

The large discrepancies in estimating high and low shares of the informal income can be explained, putting some methodological problems[7] aside, by the tendency of subjects to under-declare informal incomes, especially in standardized procedure. Bearing in mind these under-declarations, in the following we use the data of the quantitative survey because it is more representative.

Incomes level

Due to the expected weakness of income declaration, the quantitative survey registered simultaneously the *incomes* gained by the households' members in the last month, in total and broken down by income sources, as well as the *expenditures* people declared for the same month. The two variables are significantly correlated at the 0.01 level.

Along with comparisons between incomes and expenditures, different income indicators have been computed using different equivalence scales. The income per capita registers an average value of 666 276 Lei, which represents around 70 USD, respectively approximately 30% of the national average net wage at that time. The incomes **tend to decrease with the increase in the household's size** (Table 8.4). When we use the OECD scale, the average value of income per person rises to 850 084 Lei. When we use the modified scale,[8] the income per person rises to the value of 1 028 243 Lei. The differences between groups of households are still visible, even when the decrease of income with increasing household size is not so obvious. The explanation can be found in the households' composition (different mixtures of those active and inactive in the labour force, adults and children).

Table 8.4   Level of incomes and expenditures by size of the households

	1 pers.	2 pers.	3 pers.	4 pers.	5 pers.	6 pers.	7 pers.	8 pers.	9 pers.
Incomes per ... (thou. Lei)									
Capita	*853.7*	*811.3*	*693.5*	*586.4*	*515.0*	*487.7*	*475.8*	*633.0*	*452.0*
Equiv. Pers – OECD	Same	889.3	956.1	860.3	710.3	673.0	636.9	628.3	542.4
Equiv. Pers – OECD modified	Same	1008.1	1155.9	1079.4	912.0	881.3	842.1	840.6	744.4
Expenditures per ... (thou. Lei)									
Capita	*866.8*	*754.4*	*739.2*	*638.3*	*515.4*	*476.0*	*449.4*	*436.7*	*360.6*
Equiv. Pers – OECD modified	Same	1084.0	1086.1	996.0	918.9	904.5	897.9	1212.4	929.1

Source: Social Problems, Living Standard and Informal Economy, IQL, Romania, 1998 (N=1177).

The expenditures register a similar tendency as for incomes. There are no significant differences between incomes and expenditures by size of households or by residence area. *The diminishing resources with the increase of households' size points out an increased poverty risk for those living in large families.*

The following analyses are based on *income per capita,* as an indicator of the households' living standard and its decile household classification.

In general, the expenditures tend to be greater than incomes, but a significant difference is statistically confirmed only for the first two deciles (the poorest households having higher expenditures than incomes) and the last one (the richest having higher incomes). Since we do not expect the poor to be more likely to conceal incomes, the difference between income and expenditure is, rather, understood as an expression of a poverty trap: the insufficient earnings push the households into a position of permanent money-borrowing, a habit identified in the qualitative inquiry, in order to satisfy their needs at least to a minimum. The expenditures cannot fall below the minimum need. *In fact, the average expenditure of the second decile equalizes the poverty threshold.*[9] Concerning the richest groups of households, the difference between income and expenditure is an indicator of their well-being: the incomes cover the monthly expenditure and allow people to build savings. *The average income per person at the disposal of those included in the top decile equalizes the value of the average national net wage.*

The distribution of resources is another topic to discuss. The incomes are more widely spread: the incomes of the richest households are almost twelve times greater than those of the poorest ones, while the expenditures ratio is just 4.5. The difference is confirmed by the Gini coefficient, which is greater when computed on the basis of income: 32.5, respectively 30.2 for expenditures.[10] The explanation can be found in the fact that the expenditures coincide with people's (minimum) needs better than incomes.

Households' budget structure

Let's remember the groups of income defined by their nature. We emphasized pensions, children allowances and unemployment benefits as the main social support among social transfers. Accordingly, table 8.5 presents the incomes structure by their level. Due to the structural similarity of the middle groups, we resumed these to quintiles, while the difference between the extreme groups is the basis for the decile presentation.

To what extent does each type of income contribute to the total incomes of the households?

- the share of *incomes from formal work increases with the increase of incomes,* from one fifth in the poorest 10% of households to half in the richest 20%.
- the share of *social transfers decreases with the increase of incomes,* the greatest part of them consisting of pension rights. Child allowances and unemployment benefits are important incomes for the poorest: the increased importance comes out from the low level of other types of incomes.
- *self-production* reaches its *largest contribution on to total income in the segment of middle incomes,* varying between one fifth and one-quarter of the total income of the households. The exception is the richest group, where self-production contributes with only 14% to the households' total income.
- *informal monetary incomes* reach the minimum on the middle of the distribution. They have a significant contribution to the incomes of the poorest and the wealthiest.
- *informal transfers* are even less significant, with a share smaller than 3%, and an average of 1.4% for the entire population.
- the *not-declared income* declared by source arises from the methodo-logy[11] and to a small degree, from computation.

Table 8.5   Incomes structure by level of income

Incomes from	D1	D2	Q2	Q3	Q4	D9	D10	total
Formal work	19.3	33.2	34.5	44.8	43.9	52.6	55.2	40.7
Formal transfers	43.2	30.8	29.5	27.2	22.8	16.2	8.3	25.9
Pension rights	19.2	21.8	23.8	23.1	20.4	14.2	6.6	20.0
Child allowances	15.1	4.9	3.2	1.9	1.3	0.7	0.6	3.4
Unemployment benefits	6.4	3.2	1.7	1.4	0.7	0.9	0.6	1.9
Informal work	11.8	7.6	7.3	3.3	6.2	5.5	19.9	7.9
Informal transfers	2.7	0.9	0.8	0.5	1.7	1.7	2.4	1.4
Self-production	20.7	24.8	26.6	22.6	24.8	23.2	14.1	23.1
Total	97.7	97.3	98.7	98.5	99.4	99.2	99.9	99.0
Not declared by source	*2.3*	*2.6*	*1.3*	*1.5*	*0.5*	*0.8*	*0.1*	*1.0*

Source: Social Problems, Living Standard and Informal Economy, IQL, Romania, 1998 (N=1177).

Informal monetary income seems of low importance for the households' budget. Despite this, 62% of those declaring that members of their households perform informal activities said that without those activities they wouldn't 'get along', and another 23% of subjects declared that these incomes 'are necessary to ensure the every day life'. Most probably they refered to in kind products they obtain from working the land.

Seeming contradictory, the qualitative inquiry showed that most people interviewed asked to specify the most important source of income for their household choose the formal income and not the informal one, even when the formal income in the household was lower. In fact, because formal income is more certain than informal income, it is perceived as being more important.

Informal incomes and poverty

Let us now turn to the question of informal income and poverty: Is poverty the reason that people perform informal activities? To what extent do informal incomes help people to escape poverty? The table below presents the poverty rates with and without informal incomes.

Table 8.6   Poverty rate[12] (share of households)

Average income per capita	40%	60%
Formal incomes	32.7	50.7
Formal incomes + self-production	15.3	29.8
Total formal and informal incomes	10.9	24.2

Source: Social Problems, Living Standard and Informal Economy, IQL, Romania, 1998 (N=1177).

Only half of the population would live above the poverty threshold if they would depend only on their formal incomes from work and social transfers. One-third would live in extreme poverty. Thanks to self-production, half of those who would otherwise live in extreme poverty are able to escape from it. Another 5% owe their escape from extreme poverty to monetary informal incomes.

As it can be seen in the 'non-poor' column of the table 8.7, 27.0% of households escaped poverty due to informal incomes (including self-production). Informal activities helped 6.4% of the households to escape extreme poverty, but still left them in poverty.

One-third of those escaping poverty thanks to informal activities are moved only marginally over the threshold, into the second quintile, and have to live very modestly. There is also the segment of 13% of those persons (which makes up 3.5% of the total) for whom informal activities have proved to be the key for well-being, allowing them to move directly into the fifth quintile.

Table 8.7   Effects of informal incomes (%)

State of poverty		Total incomes	
calculated with …		Poor	Non-Poor
Formal	Extreme Poor	6.4	15.4
Incomes	Poor	-	11.6

Source: Social Problems, Living Standard and Informal Economy, IQL, Romania, 1998
(N=1177).

A cross correlation between the size of the households and poverty incidence confirms that large size households are more affected by poverty than
others. Whereas one of four persons is poor, when considering the entire
population, at least 40% of those living in households with at least 6 members are affected by poverty.

Size and distribution of informal incomes[13]

The analysis of the income distribution broken down by source and a look
at the total income level, which increases almost twelve times from the poorest to the richest households as share of each source in total amount, put the
inequality problem in a new light. (Table 8.8)

**Table 8.8   Distribution of incomes by sources by level of total
income (% of the total amount of the source)**

Incomes from …	D1	D2	Q2	Q3	Q4	D9	D10
Formal work	1.5	4.0	10.9	18.8	22.4	16.1	26.1
Formal transfers	6.5	7.8	20.0	20.36	22.0	10.3	13.1
Informal work	4.2	3.3	9.2	6.5	16.2	7.8	52.7
Informal transfers	6.0	3.9	7.2	7.2	19.2	18.0	38.6
Self-production	3.5	5.7	17.9	17.4	26.8	14.6	13.9
Incomes – thou. Lei/capita	154.3	286.5	415.0	554.7	738.4	984.7	1823.6
Expenditures – Lei/capita	300.8	367.7	488.3	590.7	735.4	940.8	1345.3

Source: Social Problems, Living Standard and Informal Economy, IQL, Romania, 1998
(N=1177).

- *Income from formal work*, as it is expected from the budget structure, is concentrated among the rich households – one-quarter of this total income is at the disposal of the richest 10% of the population. The lowest deciles participate only marginally in formal work.
- The most equally spread are the incomes from *formal transfers*, but even in this case the higher groups dispose of an amount double that of the poorest groups. This is due to the fact that the top decile receives pensions that are more frequent and consistent, while the poor benefit more from child allowances and unemployment benefits.
- The *informal incomes from work* are the most unequally distributed. Half of the total income from informal work is earned by the richest 10% of households. Informal gain is also more common among the poorest, but its share in the total informal income is quite small. Leaving out the poorest group, the share of informal gain increases with the increase of the total income. Really rewarding informal business can be found only among the rich. The same applies to informal transfers.
- *Self-production* registers a relatively equal distribution, but is more unequal than social transfers. These incomes depend on different factors which are not common for the poor. They have a low potential for participating in self-production because these activities are mostly related to land and domestic property, of which most poor do not dispose. Among the middle and higher strata, income from self-production is more evenly distributed.

Although informal income is important in the budget of the poor, the informal income earned by the poor makes up only a very small part of total informal incomes. A look at the socio-economic characteristics of the households by incomes can provide some clues to why this may be:

Table 8.9   Demographic and economic characteristics of the households

	D1	D2	Q2	Q3	Q4	D9	D10
% of the total number							
Persons	12.8	11.0	20.6	19.4	18.5	8.6	8.2
Children	18.8	13.9	23.0	16.9	16.6	5.5	4.6
Pensioners	7.8	10.1	21.6	25.6	21.1	8.4	4.9
Average values of the groups							
Dependency rate	23.5	19.4	16.5	13.5	12.9	9.5	7.9
Education (years of school)	8	9	8.8	9.1	9.9	11	12
Persons/room	1.7	1.4	1.3	1.2	1.1	1.1	1

Source: Social Problems, Living Standard and Informal Economy, IQL, Romania, 1998 (N=1177).

As it can be noted, the demographic characteristics are distributed in a reverse order than the incomes.

- The poorest groups have larger households, as already mentioned, and they generally have more children. One-third of all Romanian children lives in a poor family and nearly one-fifth lives in extreme poverty. One of four, respectively one of five persons living in the poorest households, is a dependent person of working age who is unemployed, a housewife or a person declared 'without a job'. In the rich households, less than one in ten persons is dependent. Whereas there are more pensioners among the middle groups, very few can be found in rich households. The very poor are usually families with many children and include relatively few pensioners.
- Another difference between the poor and the rich is the number of persons sharing a room: among the poor, more people share one room than among the rich. This is the only one of our indicators that includes accumulated resources (assets).
- Income rises with the level of education. The very poor, and especially many agrarian workers, over-represented in the first two quintiles, have, on the average, only primary school education. The highly educated, regardless of whether they are employees or run their own business, are to be found for the most part among the rich. In the middle of the distribution range, we find educated people in medium qualified jobs.

The poor vs. the rich

The very poor and the rich households have very specific profiles; the following analysis is focused on these.

The richest households are not just of smaller size, but also have a smaller family dependency rate and a larger proportion of wage earners. We would thus expect a larger proportion of those informally active to be found in the poorest segment. The data, however, does not confirm this hypothesis. Informal income is concentrated in the richest segment and real support for the poor households is marginal. The poor households' disposable income is less than half of what they subjectively define as the minimum needed for an acceptable standard of living and almost three times less that what rich households consider the minimum income for an acceptable standard of living to be. This is related to significantly different attitudes.

Table 8.10   Characteristics of the poor and of the rich

Indicators	The poorest	The richest
Education level	Basic education	High school
Main resource in the budget	Social transfers	Wages
Informal monetary incomes	12% of the budget, representing 4% of the total monetary informal incomes	20% of the budget representing 53% of the total monetary informal incomes
Average household size	4.6	2.9
Wage earners	1 out of 10 persons	≈ 1 out of 2 persons
Informally active (incl. Self-production)	61% of the households	80% of the households
Average income considered *acceptable* minimum (Lei /capita)	384.9 thousands Lei , or 250% of their actual income per capita	1074.1 thousands Lei, 58.9% of their actual income per capita

Source: Social Problems, Living Standard and Informal Economy, IQL, Romania, 1998 (N=1177).

The *poor households* call for more state involvement to assure individuals' welfare, consider that state property should be extended and are ready to fight for state support. On the other hand, they refrain from risk-taking and think that only luck and social relations help to assure a better life.

At the bottom of the income distribution, we generally find poorly educated people who have lost their jobs and could not find another stable one. The work they could find helps them just to survive. Is not surprising that the state financial support is a key element in their budget and that they ask for it. They are not able to control their economic life and to withstand the frequent market changes, so they feel at the mercy of chance. Remembering the period before 1990, they see an organized economic life in which they played a role.

The *rich households* think that private property should be extended and that the individual is responsible for his or her own welfare. They also hold that risk-taking is the key to success and that work rather than luck or connections is responsible for a better life. They further claim that regardless of how poor they might become, they would not ask for state support.

At the top of the distribution there are highly educated people, having a well paid job and many working as freelancers. In their opinion, risk-taking and work are keys for individual success when one is looking for a better life.

The informal sector is hardly an alternative for those who have no skills to act on the official market. The bundle of attributes that help people to control their economic life on the official market are the same keys to success on the informal one. Their absence not only expels people from the official labour market, but also bans them directly to the margin of the informal sector.

Notes

1   The analysis of the present paper is based on the data provided by the research project 'Development Potential of the Informal Economy in Romania' (financed by Volkswagen Stiftung – coordinator R. Neef) carried out by the RIQL in 1998 and 1999. The project consisted of a quantitative survey on a national representative sample of 1177 cases and a qualitative one, consisting of 105 in depth interviews on households performing informal activities. The quantitative part was developed in cooperation with University of Bucharest.

2   The numbers in square brackets refer to the characterization above.

3   Such incentives were intended as a support to new firms and at the same time the entire private sector. However, a close look reveals that many of the new firms stopped their activity at the end of the exemption period.

4   Our quantitative survey provided data on goods produced and consumed in the last month, by 8 categories of products: cereals, vegetables, fruits, potatoes, milk, meat, eggs, wine. I compared the results with the official data of NISES. The major difficulty was to group the item of NISES publications in the same way it was asked in the questionnaires. To do this I used the equivalence coefficient, as they are known from practice (e.g. different sorts of cheese expressed in quantities of milk). The weakest point in this methodology is the price, which does not correspond to the month we analyzed, but to the year's average. The official statistical data do not provide detailed data for each group of products for every month. Because of this we needed another approximation at this point and there was no guarantee of a more precise estimation. The estimation produced data close to the official ones presented by NISES in the 1998 annual report.

5   Unfortunately, this category can not be split. The data were registered together due to the low contribution of the source in the households' budget.

6   Even between these two variables there is a strong association coefficient, 40% of the households do not fit the proper cells: 19.9% admit an additional activity, but do not declare side incomes, while 20.7% declare side incomes, without admitting additional activities.

7   Again, there were 15.9% households not declaring incomes as output of their informal activities, but declaring informal incomes in the last month (while 52.2% declared income as output but not incomes in the last month). This incongruity can be explained by the fact that 1) the question does not explicitly refer to the month in discussion. So, the answers can refer to what they generally gain informally as part of their total monetary incomes, or to the last amount of money gained this way and 2) the informal incomes have been overestimated by including incomes considered formal.

8   The common analyses on poverty in Romania are based on expenditures and a modified OECD scale, because of the greater probability of these being more precisely declared than incomes. We considered that the modified scale fits the Romanian reality better in regards to the distribution of expenditures among the households' members. This scale is: 1 - 0.5 (for other adult) - 0.3 (for children). We agree with this judgment in principle, but in the circumstances under which the research was made (at one moment in a month rather than with daily records during a month), we think that the risk of a wrong estimation is at least the same: it is more difficult for the subjects to remember exactly the daily expenditures one makes during a month than the income one receives 1-2 times a month.

9   60% of average expenditure per equivalent adult, using the modified OECD scale.

10 Gini value based on expenditures fits the official measure: according to computation based on Annual Household Integrated Survey, Gini coefficient value is 30.0 (Teşliuc et al. 2000).

11 The basis of our income computation was incomes declared by sources. For those households for which the computation was not possible, due to the non-answers, we checked with the income globally declared. If the last indicator had a valid answer, meaning there was specified one of the 13 options, we replaced the missing value of the computed income with the middle of the specified option. Otherwise, the income keeps the missing value. In the process of dividing the total income by sources, these households stayed outside the computations, so their income was not split by any source. Presumably, these incomes are informal ones and omitted in the declaration by sources, since they appear in the segment of the poor households who have a higher share of informal gain.

12 The poverty thresholds considered here are those defined by NISES for 1995, updated to the time of the survey by using the price index. These are defined as 40% (for extreme poverty), respectively 60% of the average expenditures per equivalent adult.

13 In the following, informal incomes are considered those resulting from data computation by sources.

References

Feige, E. (1999), 'Underground Economies in Transition: Noncompliance and Institutional Change', in Feige, E.L., Ott, K. *Underground economies in transition: unrecorded activity tax evasion, corruption and organized crime*, Ashgate Publishing Company, Vermont.

ILO (1999), *Key Indicators of the Labour Market*, Geneva.

Milanovic, B. (1998), *Income, Inequality, and Poverty during the Transition from Planned to Market Economy*, World Bank, Regional and Sectoral Studies.

Stănculescu, M., (ed.) (1999), *Saracia in Romania 1995-1998*, vol. 1, UNDP, Bucharest.

Teşliuc, C.M., Pop, L., Teşliuc, E.D. (2000), *Saracia si sistemul de protectie sociala,* Polirom, Iasi.

Zamfir, C. (1995), *Dimensions of poverty. Romania 1994*, Expert, Bucharest.

Chapter 9

Economic functions of informal activities in Romania

Constantin Ciupagea

Introduction

As one can discern from the results of new empirical studies, the informal economy grew at a rapid pace in transition countries during the 90s. They were challenged to build up a new system to replace the old one as quickly as possible, creating an arena for market forces and establishing the reign of economic and social equilibrium. As many authors have already pointed out (e.g. Blanchard 1997), the old system broke down at the beginning of transition more quickly than the new market economies with their accompanying institutions were built. A very high rate of growth of the informal economy can be found especially in newer economies with weak structures (see Dobrescu 1999). Romania was not an exception, and is perhaps an extreme case.

The size of the shadow economy in Romania

According to different reviews (Adair/Neef in this volume; Feige/Ott 1999; Schneider/Enste 2000), there are three large groups of methods for estimating the size or share of the shadow economy:
* direct approaches, which imply the use of surveys and samples;
* indirect approaches, which use discrepancies between various macroeconomic indicators;
* model approaches like multiple-causes models (Weck 1983) or labour supply-based macroeconomic models (Dăianu & Albu 1997).

Due to a relatively quick transformation within the statistical system, data in Romania have been available since earlier stages of transition. Several studies can be found that attempt to estimate the size of the Romanian shadow economy during the past decade. Their approaches are briefly outlined below.

Direct approaches

All the direct estimations based on various surveys are somehow related to the data provided by the former National Commission for Statistics, currently the National Institute for Statistics (INS). The surveys include household and labour force surveys (AMIGO, AIG), enterprise annual surveys and the population census (for a discussion of the methodology, see Clementina Ivan Ungureanu 1997/1998). These calculations were done for the first time in 1995 and have been published annually since then. They present two major advantages: a) they desegregate the results to the level of main economic branches, thus showing estimates of the share of industry, construction sector or various services in total informal and total underground economy; b) they offer separate figures for the size of the underground economy without the proportion of agrarian and household self-production and additional figures for the size of the informal economy with the share of agrarian and household self-production. The results for the computed (estimated) sizes of the informal and underground economies in total Romanian economy are presented in Table 9.1.

The INS figures for the underground economy (excluding the agriculture and household sector) also present an estimation of each sector's contribution to it. In 2000, 41% of the total underground economy took place in industry, 8.1% in construction and 50.9% in the service sector. There is a large probability of under-valuation due to, among other things, the downgrading of the declared income by the self-employed, family associations and farmers as well as the under-evaluation of the official wage-paid labour force. Estimations regarding the informal sector seem to coincide with other empirical calculations performed in recent years by various researchers. These results are presented below. As far as the household economy and the agricultural sector is concerned, the share of the underground vs. official economy was estimated at 22.4% of the informal sector in 2000.

Indirect approaches

From among a number of calculations based on indirect methods, two deal specifically with the Romanian economy. The first method to estimate the size of the underground economy in Romania (French et al. 1999) is based on the currency demand approach (originally introduced by Cagan 1958), which uses econometric techniques to calculate the ratio of demand for money in circulation to total deposits within the Romanian economy, assuming constant velocity in both formal and informal economies. The second study can be found among other methodological details offered by the author of the first Romanian transition economy's macroeconomic model (Dobrescu 1999, 2000) and is based on a double indirect approach. The share of the accounted GDP in the total Romanian GDP is evaluated using a monetary method for the pre-transition period and a combination of the monetary approach with the energy consumption approach afterwards.

There are several reasons for choosing such a mixed approach. During the 'communist' era, the entire price system was heavily controlled, reducing monetary volatility. Thus, money velocity could have been considered almost constant in the Romanian economy before 1989. After 1990, this nominal stability was severely disrupted, thereby reducing the reliability of any monetary method. Consumption remains the most stable macrovariable within the transition economy. It seemed natural to use a consumption based approach (in this case, energy consumption) in order to evaluate the share of the informal economy in relation to the economy as a whole.

The results for the two indirect methods described above are also presented in Table 9.1.[1]

Model approach

A global model based on the labour supply method was used by Albu et al. (1998) in order to estimate the size of the Romanian informal economy. Three versions are taken into account, differentiated by various assumptions about the productive national potential or about the people's preferences regarding their use of their leisure time. The period of time covered by these estimations is 1989-1995, and the results for the most reliable version are presented in Table 9.1.

The results of the various surveys (especially the direct methods) indicate a concentration of the informal economy in the following economic sectors: retail trade (commerce), transportation, construction, repair and maintenance activities (households, motor vehicles), agriculture, tourism, catering, health, and education (Ivan-Ungureanu 1997). These findings are supported by the official data within the framework of national accounting, where there are large operating surpluses for these sectors. On the other hand, the results of the surveys we conducted (Neef e.a. 1998, Stănculescu/Ilie 2001) do not support evidence of a large share of informal sector in the public services sector, except in public administration. They also point out increasing informal activity in sectors such as the textiles industry and both foreign and domestic retail sales.[2]

Table 9.1   **Estimated size of the informal economy in the total GDP in Romania**

Year	1995	1996	1997	1998	1999	2000
Share of informal economy in total GDP (%)	33.6	33.7	39.5	33.2	40.2	38.3
Share of underground economy in total GDP (%)	16.6	18.4	18.6	23.3	21.1	21.1

Source: INS, 2001.

Table 9.2   **Size of the non-accounted economy or underground economy in the total Romanian GDP (%)**

Year	1990	1991	1992	1993	1994	1995	1996	1997	1998	1999	2000
Dobrescu model	21.3	25.0	31.0	31.8	30.8	28.5	27.1	32.2	35.8	37.8	37.2
French approach	n.a.	n.a.	n.a.	9.0	12.0	15.0	16.0	20.0	33.0	n.a.	n.a.

Source: Dobrescu, 1998 and the 2000 version of the Dobrescu model; French et al., 1999, Paper for the Romanian Ministry of Finance.

Table 9.3   **Size of the informal economy in Romania (%) – model approach**

Version\Year	1989	1990	1991	1992	1993	1994	1995
Albu - Version II	19.9	25.0	29.4	32.1	33.1	32.8	31.7

Source: Albu et al., 1998.

The economic inter-relationship between the informal economy and the social-economic situation in Romania

There is increasing concern about the growth of the informal economy in the transitional Romanian economy. Informal activities may help to reduce the increasing income gaps among different population groups, but, at the same time, they slow down the long-term growth potential of the country.

The effects – negative or positive – of a large share of informal activities in the economy and society as a whole can be seen in several areas:

1. The economy's global development
    – transactions' speed is generally faster in informal sector;
    – the informal sector is sometimes de-coupled from the formal economy, thus establishing barriers to the development of an integrated system;
    – foreign trade is affected by tax avoidance and lack of standardization, and openness is delayed as an on-going process;
    – the channels through which competition and know-how may spread within the entire economic system are distorted.

2. The volume and the redistribution of income within society
    – there is a higher real income for the population, as informal incomes are distributed through household networks. This translates into higher consumption, thus inducing growth via the increase in domestic demand;
    – the budget's revenues are distorted and diminished, while the state's capacity to provide enough support for social assistance is reduced;
    – informal activities usually help to bring together already existing economic opportunities and agents; they seldom appear on bare ground. Consequently, the regional disparities are usually enlarged by the informal sector's relative growth.

3. The potential for durable/sustainable growth of the nation (the long-run growth)
    – by reducing the budget revenues, the possibility of financing the human factor quality (health, education and research) is diminished;
    – the actors in the informal sector have no interest in issues not directly related to them. A higher probability of inducing a non-ecological type of growth results in those areas in which the informal economy flourishes.

The extensive impact of the informal sector demands detailed analysis and research, in order to develop recommendations and policy suggestions.

In this next section, an analysis of the general causes for the growth in size of informal economies in all countries, regardless of their level of economic development or their social-political system (see Schneider and Enste 2000), will be related. Further, details about the more consistent factors in the particular case of Romania, draw from the interviews we conducted about the Romanian labour market, will be presented. Quantitative (econometric) support for the following theses will also be introduced based on time series for the impact variables.

The influence of economic growth and inflation. The estimations of the size of the informal economy in Romania allow us to establish a clear negative correlation between the rates of growth of the formal GDP and of the informal GDP during the decade of transition.

The GDP annual growth figures (see Appendix) and those presented in the previous section of this paper show that there is a possible delay of one year in transmitting signals of growth from the formal economy into the informal one. This means that within one year, the informal economy adjusts to the new formal environment. However, this global result hides contradictory inter-relationships between the two types of economies that use various channels of transmission.Figure 9.1 shows the evolution in the last decade of both the real formal GDP growth rates and the growth in the proportion of the informal economy in comparison. Official INS estimates are available starting in 1995. We used the shares calculated on the basis of Dobrescu's model for the period 1990-1994, both because these are closer to the official statistics than all other attempts presented (for 1995-2000), and they offer data for each year of the decade.[3]

Figure 9.1

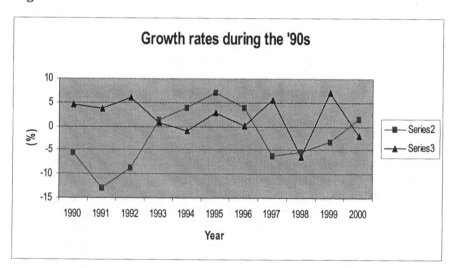

Series 2 – The real formal GDP growth rate.
Series 3 – The growth rate of the informal economy's share in the total GDP (Dobrescu model estimates for 1990-1994 and official INSSE estimates for 1995-2000).

Inflation is the most important factor leading to the proportional growth in the informal economy in Romania. Romania has not been able to reduce inflation to a level below a 33% annual figure between 1991-2000. On the other hand, inflation volatility was extremely high during the 90s. The channels through which inflation affects the normal development of the formal economy are diverse and numerous. Two of them are presented below, and I will make references to other impacts of inflation in other places, if necessary.

Inflation deteriorates the budget balance, increasing real costs (expenditures) and reducing the real revenues, especially when fiscal discipline and administrative capacity for the control and gathering of the budget revenues is low.

Inflation allows higher price distortions within the system and allows for deliberate discriminatory administrative decisions. The government allows delayed payments for the big indebted state-owned enterprises or public monopolies (public utilities), which reduces their real tax burden.

The higher the unemployment rate, the stronger the incentive to engage in informal activity. The explosion in unemployment and its permanence within the Romanian society make the issue an important one. Those people who remain unemployed over a long period of time are likely to turn to the informal sector, in order to escape from low income sooner or later. In estimating the impact of unemployment on the proportional size of the informal sector, we either can analyse the overall unemployment rate or refer only to long-term unemployment. Unfortunately, there is no data about exits from and entrances to the labour market in Romania for all the sectors, which would have made a positive contribution to the empirical analysis.

Higher social transfers and smaller real wages increase the incentive to work in the informal sector. In the case of the Romanian economy, the early years of transition brought a very 'soft' unemployment benefit system, with long periods of payments. The relatively high level of unemployment benefits compared to the minimum wage (higher than 100% during 1997-1999), and the lack of active employment policies, induced sluggish behaviour on the official labour market. Unemployed people had time to approach the underground economy, especially in sectors like agriculture or trade. A similar development can be observed in the special case of workers who became unemployed following restructuring and closure of enterprises. They received lump-sum payments equivalent to several months' wages, leading primarily to a disappearance of incentive to search for a new job. The proportional decrease and the very low actual level of the average wage in Romania was another factor for people to move towards the informal market. Even though the income in the informal sector is well below the official net wage, when added to unemployment or pension payment, it ensures an income that often enables people to step over the standard poverty line.

Especially in times of economic decline, when few new jobs are generated, a main driving force for informal activity would be related to the gap between net wage and total labour cost. Unfortunately, data for all the years considered is not available.

In the context of a generalised long-term decline, *the welfare-state effect* leads to a further deterioration in real wages, both in gross and in net terms. The total number of official wage-paid workers decreased tremendously in the transition years, reducing the wage taxation base and driving authorities to enforce higher taxes on total labour costs. Faced with higher real labour costs, employers felt the incentive to at least partially enter the informal sector (some of their employees work informally or some of the wages paid to their employees are not officially recorded). This development can be seen in the data provided in Table 9.4. The most affected sectors in terms of real net wage decrease were education, health and social assistance, hotels and catering, and construction, particularly in recent years.

Table 9.4   **The evolution of real net wages in Romania (percentage levels compared to 100 in year 1990; the CPI was used as a deflator for nominal wages)**

Industry\Year	1991	1992	1993	1994	1995
Total	81.7	71.0	59.1	59.3	66.8
Industry	83.3	73.3	62.7	62.4	73.0
Construction	78.8	68.2	57.3	62.2	64.1
Trade	86.4	73.4	60.1	59.7	61.5
Hotels, catering	76.5	61.9	47.6	45.4	51.3
Public administr.	80.1	66.0	55.3	55.9	63.7
Education	84.1	68.5	44.0	41.4	40.6
Health	90.6	72.2	43.6	45.3	46.6
	1996	1997	1998	1999	
Total	73.2	56.5	60.4	59.9	
Industry	80.9	62.9	64.0	63.6	
Construction	68.2	49.8	53.1	51.8	
Trade	65.7	47.3	54.8	54.8	
Hotels, catering	56.0	40.6	41.6	n.a.	
Public administr.	61.9	48.6	63.9	64.9	
Education	41.8	31.9	37.3	n.a.	
Health	51.9	40.3	41.6	n.a.	

Source: INSSE-Statistical Yearbooks.

Investments are a main driving force of the formal economy. It is much harder to take investment decisions in an informal activity, due to restricted access to resources, especially in machinery and equipment. Thus, the investment rate is expected to be an important factor for the development of the informal economy. The higher the machinery and equipment investment share in the GDP, the lower the share of the informal sector is expected.

The investment rate is also dependent on the *savings rate.* When the domestic savings rate is low, the capacity of the economy to grow in a sustainable way diminishes and real income is affected in the long run. There are three main reasons for low savings rates, and therefore for low investment rates.

First, in transition economies, the higher the instability of the financial and banking sector, the more people move into the informal sector. In Romania, as it was pointed out in several interviews and by French et al. (1999), the lack of instruments and infrastructure needed for non-cash transactions increases the probability of engaging in informal cash transactions. A weak financial and banking system impedes the savings process, thus reducing the savings rate.

Second, long periods of recession (two periods of three years in a row from 1990-1992 and 1997-1999) decreased people's real income and increased the poverty rate extremely. Consequently, more and more people were forced to spend their savings. Furthermore, in the period 1998-1999, large companies in Romania experienced a negative profit rate, reducing their reserves as well.

Third, inflation destroys the savings capacity of the country, as every economic agent tends to switch from savings to consumption. Inflation was a main factor leading to the reduction of households' real financial assets during the 90s. Whereas a very few were able to protect their assets by exchanging their reserves to foreign currency, most people experienced a decrease in their purchasing power over the years and tried to get by with in kind (informal) type of incomes.

Inflation is also directly the main disincentive for new investments, because of the increased risk, especially regarding the purchase of machinery and equipment. The blurred context of the formal economy drove many firms to focus their investments in sectors in which they might be able to protect their assets and their businesses (e.g. infrastructure, real estate, trade, hotels, catering). These are traditionally more open to informal activities. This did not allow a fast expansion or recovery of the market economy.

The higher the share of the non-wage-paid labour force in total employment, the higher the incentive to work in the informal sector. The transition reforms in Romania brought another particular problem: Since 1990, the wage-paid labour force has declined in number, while the overall active labour force remained relatively stable, with a slight decrease in numbers. The reason for the growth in the non-wage-paid labour force stems from the increasing number of private businesses, which are often made up of self-employed people or small firms that pay their owners through the profit returns system. This development is fuelled by the taxation (fiscal) system as well, as taxes on corporate profits were lower than on income from wages in recent years.[4] A more flexible working schedule also contributes to this development, which allows people to take on a second job (formal or informal). These are the reasons for introducing the share of non-wage-paid labour force in total employment as a factor in the equation tested.

There is a direct link between informal activity and non-wage-paid labour in the agricultural sector, a link that is connected to general household activity. In Romania, the share of employment in agriculture is extremely high, around 40% of total employment, of which 85% are non-wage-paid persons working their own small farms. Almost all of their activity is informal, as only a part is registered. Most do not have to pay taxes and a large share of their production remains with the household as self-consumption.

The size of the informal economy grows with the increase in the tax burden and in the level of social welfare contributions. The tax burden and the social welfare safety net primarily affect the redistribution of income in society and influence the proportion of labour time to leisure time. 'The bigger the difference between the total labour cost in the official economy and after-tax earnings, the greater the incentive to avoid it and to work in the shadow economy' (Schneider/Enste 2000).

In transition economies, the rise in tax-burdens led to the increased distortions in the distribution of income. During the first years of the past decade, the transition governments:

* switched to different tax systems (from turnover taxes to VAT, from taxes on wages to income taxes),
* introduced new taxes (corporate-profit taxes, taxes on dividends, taxes on financial incomes, etc.),
* introduced a whole system of social welfare contribution (pension, unemployment, health insurance funds, etc.).

All the negative factors that increase the tax burden and distort the level of redistribution and taxation base can be found in Romania during the 90s (for figures, see Table 9.5).

A high number of new taxes were introduced over the years, as the economy declined, unemployment grew, the labour force, and especially the wage-paid force declined, and the number of retired people grew.

Table 9.5   Level of effective tax rates in Romania in percent of the GDP

Tax component\Year	1991	1992	1993	1994	1995
Tax on profit	5.0	5.2	3.8	3.8	3.9
Tax on wages/income	7.6	7.6	6.6	6.5	6.3
Turnover tax, excises and VAT	8.3	6.9	7.3	6.1	6.7
Custom duties	0.7	1.3	1.3	1.1	1.4
Social contribution taxes	7.4	7.8	10.7	9.2	8.2
Memo:					
Direct taxes	12.6	12.8	10.4	10.3	10.2
Indirect taxes	9.0	8.2	8.7	7.2	8.1

Year	1996	1997	1998	1999	2000
Tax on profit	3.3	4.3	3.0	3.2	2.5
Tax on wages/income	6.1	5.5	5.0	5.2	3.4
Turnover tax, excises and VAT	6.3	6.3	8.4	9.2	10.5
Custom duties	1.5	1.3	1.6	1.4	1.2
Social contribution taxes	7.5	7.0	8.1	8.7	10.9
Memo:					
Direct taxes	9.4	9.8	8.1	8.4	5.9
Indirect taxes	7.8	7.6	10.0	10.6	11.7

Source: INS, Ministry of Finance.

• Especially near the election years of 1992, 1996 and 2000, the taxation base was reduced in an attempt to attract the population to the political parties in power. The fiscal system shows a strong pattern of hysteresis: it is easy to reduce a tax rate or to give an exemption to a certain group of population or interest group, but it is far more difficult to return the rate to its previous level or to an even higher one or to cancel the exemption once given. Following the election years, tax rates generally increased as an attempt to compensate for the loss in the real budget revenues. These increases generally took the form of indirect taxes, which contributed to social discontent and upheaval.

• The fiscal system was non-transparent: many exemptions were granted throughout the transition period to interest groups related (unofficially) to the central and local administration staff.

Finally, the mismanagement of the fiscal system led to disincentives within the Romanian formal economy:
- the labour cost to net wage ratio increased to 2.3-2.4 at the end of 1999, based on a progressive wage taxation rate system;
- unemployment benefits were linked to net wages, thus allowing for larger unemployment benefits for those persons formally employed in high-wage sector in comparison to those working for minimum wages in other sectors. In 1997, the average unemployment benefit in the first 9 months of unemployment increased to 135% of the minimum wage, while the long-term unemployment social aid was about half of the minimum wage (Stănculescu/Ilie 2001);
- pensions were unevenly distributed according to the number of years of retirement, as the process of partial adjustment to inflation was not well co-ordinated;
- there were too many exemptions for every type of tax.

The consequence of such a narrow, heavily taxed taxation base was a growth of the informal economy and a decline of the formal economy. The interviews we conducted all point towards the high level of taxes as one major cause for the rise in the size of the informal economy. The representatives of the local authorities and the labour force offices in our inquiry indicated that the private sector did not receive much support in the form of new legislation (especially, the fiscal legislation).

INTERVIEW – The mayor deputy in Ramnicu-Valcea.
The main areas where we witness informal activities are the construction sector,...the small trade activities, and those services in which no more than 2-4 persons are involved. No one knows exactly what amount a radio-TV service person is paid, as an example.
Q: Why are informal activities developing so much lately?
My opinion is that the economic situation before 1999 induced an important increase in the fiscal burden. As state-owned enterprises were very rigid in responding to the new fiscal requirements, the entire burden was oriented towards the private sector, who reacted with self-defence. A second argument is of a subjective reasoning, as very many people working in the small business field consider that paying taxes to the state budget is not a normal thing. There is no culture of fiscal discipline.

Other factors increasing the size of the shadow economy

Several other factors influence the size and share of the informal sector in the total GDP. I will mention those that are difficult to quantify, and therefore, cannot be introduced in a quantitative analysis, but that are mentioned quite often in opinion surveys.

Informal activity increases when the bureaucracy increases. The bureaucracy is related to corruption, rent seeking and the number of special requirements, exemptions and facilities that affect the labour market and the economy at the micro level, with a negative outcome on the business environment. In Romania, regulation was a normal prolongation of the former command economy. The central administration used complicated mechanisms of regulation in various markets, attempting to seek additional rents in order to compensate for the loss of official power and the reduction in their real revenue.

Faced with increasing bureaucratic obstacles and growing corruption, more and more SMEs increased their informal activity. Bureaucracy is perceived as being a major cause of the growth of the informal sector. Dăianu et al. (2001) show that the public is very concerned with corruption, administrative barriers and bureaucracy. On the other hand, empirical evidence (Dăianu et al. 2001) demonstrates that the 'most important barriers to business in Romania are more economic rather than institutional'. These are, by order of ranking: taxes and regulations, inflation, unsafe financial system, policy instability, exchange rate depreciation impact, anti-competition practices, corruption, the judiciary system, economic crime, and poor physical infrastructure.

The deterioration in the quality of public goods and services increases the size of the shadow economy. This is one of the vicious circles of the economy, because a lower availability of public services and goods provokes an ever-increasing informal activity. The decline of the economy, together with the birth of a weakly structured system during transition, induces a chronic (structural) budget deficit, resulting in the reduction in size and quality of the public sector. Public goods providers, such as education and health, decline in quality due to the decrease in their real wages to a far below average level (see Table 9.4). Because of the presence of strong unions and a highly qualified labour force, it was not the number of employees in this sector, but their wages which were reduced. The size of the informal market in these sectors increases, due to an explosion in the number of unofficial teaching hours and in the unofficial fees for healthcare. Households want to maintain the same level of education offered or the same quality of health services.

A quantitative attempt to estimate influencing factors on the proportional size of the informal economy

The data available after 11 years of transition in Romania does not allow for precise quantitative analysis, as the length of the time is not enough to provide reliable statistical (econometric) results. However, the available data does help to test some theoretical assumptions about trends and about the importance of factors influencing changes in the size of the informal economy, in comparison both to the whole economy and to different single sectors.

The relationship that was tested for the Romanian economy is the following:

$$IE_{share} = f(GDP_{level}, U_{rate}, NW_{level}, INV_{rate}, NWPLF_{sh}, TXR_{level})$$

where IEsh stands for the share of the informal economy in the overall GDP. The GDP level is the level of the real formal GDP, considering 1 the level in 1990. U_{rate} is the officially registered unemployed rate (number of registered unemployed in total labour force) while INV_{rate} stands for the investment rate in the GDP (or the rate of investment in machinery and equipment). The $NWPLF_{sh}$ is the share of wage-paid labour in the total labour force and TXR_{level} is an index of the relevant tax rate in the GDP. Finally, the NW_{level} is the level of the (average) real net wage received in the formal economy, again with the 1990 level considered to be 1.

These independent variables are related to the theoretical comments made in the previous section of this paper. The unavailability of data excludes the testing of the other factors named above.

The results of the regression performed on the basis of the equation are presented and commented upon below. All econometric results are given in the Appendix. An explanation may be warranted at this point concerning the choice of the time series describing the share of the informal economy. In the second section of this paper, we see that the Dobrescu model estimation covers the entire time horizon (1990-2000). Moreover, these values are within the range of all the other estimations, which gives them a good degree of confidence. The Dobrescu model series is not strikingly different from the official estimate (except for the year 1998, a case in which the official figure is doubtful). For running the econometric test, I compared the Dobrescu model data with the official data set.[5] The main characteristics of the equation, which include coefficients values, Student-t tests, correlation tests and fitness criteria, are given in the Appendix.

$$IE_{share} = 1.134*SocBdn_{rate} - 0.036*MESGDP + 0.546*NWPLF_{sh} + 2.681*LTU_{rate} + 0.037*NWR_{level} - 0.225*GDP_{level}$$

What conclusions can we draw from this equation and the values of the tests?

First, the results are theoretically reliable, but, statistically, not very strong.[6]

Second, the most credible impact on the informal sector's share in the entire economy comes from three variables with the highest confidence level within the regression: the share of the non-wage-paid labour force in total employment (with a positive sign), the share in the GDP of the social burden[7] (income tax plus the social welfare contribution taxes, also with a positive sign) and the level of the formal GDP (with a negative sign). The long-term unemployment rate also plays an important role (positive sign) and seems to be a better indicator than the overall unemployment rate. The influence of the real wage evolution is unreliable (even though the sign is theoretically correct). Also, the influence of investment on the size of the informal economy in the GDP is uncertain, despite the correct negative sign.[8]

In order to confirm the results,[9] I performed another econometric test (regression in using growth rates instead of levels). The overall results are much more reliable and they suggest that there are four variables that strongly influence the informal economy's growth rates: the growth rate for the formal GDP – GDP_{rate} (a negative sign, as expected), the growth rate for the share of the social burden tax rate in the GDP – SCB_{rate} (with a negative sign), the long-term unemployment rate – LTU_{rate} (with a positive sign, as expected), and the real net wage growth rate – NW_{rate} (with a negative sign). The negative influence of the real wage growth rate, as compared to the positive influence of its level on the size of the informal economy, is very interesting. It suggests that people are interested not in their historical real wage level, but in the momentary variation of this wage when deciding whether or not to enter informal activities. At the same time, the general level of the real wage in one sector is a signal for business opportunities within that particular sector (this may explain the positive sign).

$$IE_{share} = 0.535*LTU_{rate} - 0.408*GDP_{rate} - 0.039*NW_{rate} + 0.559*SCB_{rate}$$

The details of the econometric exercise are given in the Appendix. The second equation seems more reliable in explaining the dynamics of the informal market in Romania.

We may extend this result with a sensitivity analysis for the first equation, since all the variables can be standardised. Normalising the time series (to their average level over the period of time considered), we obtain the share of the impact of each determining factor on the informal economy's size. The computed sensitivities are therefore: the social burden tax rate in the GDP – 0.304 (the social burden tax rate accounts for 30.4% of the total impact on the share of informal economy among all the factors taken into account); the machinery and equipment investment rate – 0.006; non wage-paid labour force share in the total labour force – 0.318; the long-term unemployment rate – 0.062; the real net wage index – 0.035; the GDP index – 0.275.

Three variables have an equally high impact: the *share of the non-wage-paid labour force in the total labour force*, the *social burden tax rate* and the *GDP index* (its level as compared to the initial year of transition). All the other variables show a small influence (less than 7% each), but still we have a significant impact coming from their evolution (except for the investment rate, which seems insignificant).[10]

Other factors of influence were not included in the equation, due to various reasons:

• The increase in income inequality (income gaps) is certainly a factor leading to uncertainty, but it is not clear whether it is a driving force for people to enter the informal market or not. It may also be that more informal activity enhances the income gaps and increases the Gini coefficient. In any case, there are no series of the Gini coefficients in the total system and in each sector for the entire time horizon. I therefore did not include this indicator in the set of explanatory factors.

• The high variability of the fiscal system and the increasing gap between the level of official tax rates and the effective tax revenue shares in the GDP is another factor that may influence the growth of the informal economy. I didn't include the gap in tax rates in the set of indicators because the changes in official tax rates were unevenly distributed over time. Most of the changes happened after 2000, and it is too early to assess their impact on the economy today.

• The institutional structure and the administration inference in the economy are very important as well, but they are difficult to quantify. Nevertheless, future studies should consider this aspect.

• The volatility of the inflation rate, combined with its actual high levels, could be also strong factors of impact for the share of informal economy. The main problem here is the fact that inflation is at the core of the macro-stance of the economy, determining other variables that have been already considered. The results of the regression could then be affected by massive auto-correlation.

A look at the informal economy by sector

The above econometric model was used for estimating the size of the informal sector in various branches of the Romanian economy. We began with the following assumptions:

- Individuals' behaviour regarding informal activities is the same as with the whole economy in each branch. It is thus possible to extend the coefficients, that resulted from the test we did to any of the branches considered if we take into account exactly the same set of factors of influence. We assume that information is not sector-related and the options of the actors are not restricted to one particular sector of the economy.
- We do not need unemployment data desegregated by sector, because the action and mobility of the unemployed is not limited to one sector. In fact, their mobility has increased lately (Oprescu, Păuna & Păuna 1999) Therefore, we may use the unemployment rate in the calibration of each sector's equation.[11]
- It also doesn't makes sense to use tax rates differentiated according to sector. Things could change significantly if we take into account the gap between expected tax revenues (based on official tax rates) and the effective tax revenues. This brings about a margin of error in the estimation.
- The use of the GDP level can be easily replaced by the use of branch value added level, taking into account the very even distribution by sectors of the gap between the GDP and the GVA.
- The impact of investment in machinery and equipment will be dropped, as it appeared to be insignificant in the 'level' equation.

We first calculated the shares of informal activities in various sectors of the Romanian economy in using the sector data for 1996 and 1998 (national accounts).[12] We then calculated the changes as compared to the size of the informal economy in 1990 for the years 1996 and 1998 based on the second equation (in rates of changes). The main results are shown in Table 9.6.

The calculated shares are undervalued due to some model constraints. The main factor inducing errors is the large share of the wage-paid labour force also involved in informal activities. This is particularly important for sectors that appear to have low or no informal activity, such as education, health services, constructions, post and telecommunications, trade, and transportation services (see Table 9.6). The interviewees did not mention informal activities if these were undertaken in the same sector in which he or she had the main official job. The data provided recently by INS for 2000 (Dăianu et al. 2001) points to higher shares in industry (18.5%), the construction

Table 9.6   **The shares and growth rates of informal activity in total sector's value added, by branches, 1996 and 1998, in Romania. The changes in the shares of informal activity in total sector's value added, by branches, in 1996 and 1998, in Romania**

SECTOR	YEAR	1996	1998
Agriculture		52.48%	58.18%
Sylviculture, forestry and hunting		9.74%	14.75%
Industry		8.40%	9.30%
Construction sector		0.63%	6.97%
Trade & hotels and catering		17.68%	20.22%
Transport		13.54%	13.94%
Post and telecommunications		0%	0%
Financial, banking and insurance		1.89%	8.78%
Real estate and other services		5.00%	11.21%
Public administration and defense		0.29%	2.54%
Education		0%	0%
Health; social assistance		0%	3.13%

Note: The distribution of unemployment (in order to calculate the 'total employment' for each sector) was constructed artificially, considering a sector employment-weighted scheme. The data for all variables of impact are reported for each sector in the Statistical Yearbook 1999 – INSSE.

SECTOR	YEAR	Computed Share Variation 1996	1998
Agriculture		5.07%	9.59%
Sylviculture, forestry and hunting		14.05%	15.78%
Industry		4.65%	8.02%
Construction sector		-11.66%	-1.06%
Trade & hotels and catering		7.48%	11.45%
Transport		8.47%	12.84%
Financial, banking and insurance		-12.70%	-1.72%
Public administration and defense		-3.50%	-2.30%
Health; social assistance		-6.74%	-0.73%

Note: The changes for all variables of impact for each sector are computed on the basis of data in the Statistical Yearbook 1999 – INSSE.

sector (25.4%), transportation services (34%), and trade including hotels and catering (38.5%).

The qualitative results linked to the relative share of informal activity among branches within the Romanian economy are interesting, as they confirm the outcome of existing surveys (Neef 2002) and the official estimates of the National Institute for Statistics (see also Ivan-Ungureanu 1998). The economic branches 'more suitable' to encapsulate informal activities appear to be: *agriculture, trade, hotels and catering, constructions, transportation, real estate and other market services (plumbing, mechanical repair).*

Concerning the growth rates, the massive reductions in the share of informal activity in sectors such as constructions, banking, health, and social assistance in 1996 are obviously influenced by the economic growth registered that year and by the measures taken to reduce unemployment. The qualitative results are nevertheless interesting. Compared to 1990, the simulation based on the model shows massive increases in the size of the informal sector in sylviculture, trade, hotels and catering, transport, and an important growth in agriculture and industry. Concerning construction activity, there was an incorrect registration of the labour force due to the large seasonal variations within this sector. Thus, the estimation for constructions seems unreliable.

The survey conducted in 1998 came up with the same branches that are characterised by high informal activity as above (Neef 2002). Officials working in the mayors' offices, in the labour department or chambers of commerce in various regions (Brasov, Valcea, Neamt, Ilfov) were unanimous in referring to agriculture, trade, the construction sector, and small services (mechanical repair, transportation, private lessons) as being the main branches for informal activities. They also named high taxes, unemployment, and low performance of the formal economy as influencing factors.

Conclusions

In poor or developing countries, the informal economy is a substitute for the formal one. Its growth has a certain positive impact on the effective standard of living of the population. In the Romanian case, representing one of the poorest European countries, the large size of the informal economy is the reason why many households living officially below the poverty line can avoid physical deprivation. This is reflected in income surveys in Romania (see especially Ilie in this volume). As we see from our interviews, it is in particular the very large share of the informal activity in agriculture in Romania that produces a means for survival. In Romania, rural areas were 'reservoirs' for the labour force and last resort solutions for both the unemployed and poor social security recipients (see also Golibrzuch in this volume).

The specific features in the Romanian case, related to the proportional size of the informal economy to both the entire economic system and each branch are:

- The agricultural sector makes up a very large portion of the Romanian GDP during the decade of the 90s – around 20%. In 2000, it decreased to 12%, which still is extremely high according to the European standards. Almost 40% of the labour force is employed in this sector, which is again very high. Traditionally, agriculture provides the most room for informal activities. The informal economy in Romania seems still to be increasing. If there is a shrink in the informal economy, it is expected to happen at a slower pace than in other transition countries, because of the high share of agriculture in the economy. On the other hand, informal markets, especially in agriculture, have a positive effect on the formal economy, due to the wide presence of peasant markets in Romania and due to the fact that agriculture provides most basic subsistence.

- Inflation is still high and the financial system is still uncertain (low degree of privatization), inducing a permanent incentive to evade the official economy.

- The distorted tax and transfers system, together with high inflation, may be considered to be the main factors in keeping foreign investment at distance and not revitalising the domestic investment.

- As we see from most of the interviews we conducted, tax avoidance is one of the most important forms of informal activity in Romania, as in other countries.

- The poverty rate has reached a high level, according to European standards. This explains the large size of the informal economy, which helps in increasing the overall (effective) living standard. Therefore, one should be cautious in attacking the informal economy as a whole.

Notes

1　Dobrescu's estimation was confirmed by Dăianu et al. 2001. For the year 2000, the share of underground labour force was 12.8% of the revealed wage-paid labour force supply, but within their methodology the large portion of the labour force working in the agricultural sector is not considered. The fiscal approach estimates the share of the underground economy in the total official GDP (excluding informal activities, such as self-consumption, which is not taxed) at 39.8%, based on the valuation of tax evasion (non-collected tax revenues).

2   The difference to the other calculations may result from the way in which the questionnaire was designed: no direct question was used in the questionnaire in the case of non-accounted activities performed in the same branch in which households report their main official (formal) job. (This is particularly important for health and education services.) Instead, it was left open to the subjects to indicate a higher number of informal activities.

3   There are two years in which a break possibly occured in the series of data on the size of the informal economy: 1995, due to the change in sources of data, and 1998, when the methodology was slightly changed within the INSSE. Therefore, one should consider these two years carefully when analysing the issue dynamically.

4   At present, the income tax for wage earnings reaches the maximum level (40%) quite rapidly. These taxes are joined by the social welfare contributions (which equal another 40% of the gross wage). On the other hand, paying people from dividends would imply tax payments of 25% on the gross profit and an addition of 5% tax on dividends.

5   Because of the potential break within the series for the year 1995, the results were non-conclusive.

6   The set of variables we considered as influential factors seems to relate the dynamics of the informal sector's size. Statistical fitness is good, but is slightly affected by auto-correlation among variables. Even if the reliability is reduced by the shortness of the time series (as the t-statistics are very poor), we still get theoretically normal signs for the coefficients. The series were all tested for stationarity, even though no one would expect any of these series to be non-stationary.

7   I switched from the consolidated tax rate to the social burden tax rate in order to get higher credibility in the estimates.

8   The investment in machinery and equipment was used instead of total investment, as this type of investment is considered to have the strongest relationship with the formal economic sector. When the total investment rate was introduced into the equation tested, the results were completely unreliable.

9   For the equation in shares-levels, the econometric results were poor, as despite an R square of 0.89, DW was uncertain and Student t-tests were quite low.

10 If data on exits and entries on the labour markets existed, the influence of unemployment or long-term unemployment would prove better statistical results and a more credible behavioural equation.

11 In reality, there is no perfect labour mobility. But since the impact of the long-term unemployment rate stands for only 6.2% of the total impact of all the factors of influence, the margin of error seems acceptable.

12 We used both sectoral data for gross value added in real terms compared to 1990 for the real net wages deflated with the CPI deflator and the data provided for the wage-paid and non wage-paid labour force.

References

Albu, L., Dăianu, D., Păuna, B., Pavelescu, F.-M. (1998), *Endogenous Cycles and Underground Economy in Europe*, CEEES, Univesity of Leicester Discussion Paper, Leicester, UK, 20-21 June 1998.

Cagan, P. (1958), *The Demand for Currency Relative to the Total Money Supply*, J. Polit. Econ., 66:3, pp. 302-328.

Dăianu, D., Albu, L., Croitoru, L., Tarhoacă, C., Ivan-Ungureanu, C. (2001), *The Underground Economy in Romania*, Study CEROPE, Bucharest.

Dobrescu, E. (1998), *Macromodels of the Romanian Transition Economy (second ed.)*, EXPERT Publishing House, Bucuresti, July.

Earle, J.S., Păuna, C. (1998), *Long-term unemployment, social assistance and labor market policies in Romania*, Empirical Economics, London, Springer-Verlag.

Feige, E.L., Ott, K. (1999), Several chapters in *Underground economies in transition: unrecorded activity, tax evasion, corruption and organized crime*, E.L. Feige and K. Ott (ed.), Ashgate, Aldershot.

French, R.E., Balaita, M., Ticsa, M. (1999), *Estimating the Size and Policy Implications of the Underground Economy in Romania*, Study released by the Ministry of Finance in Romania, Bucuresti, August.

***National Commission for Statistics in Romania, Periodical Publications.

Neef, R. (2002), *Forms of the informal economy in a transforming country*, International Journal of Urban and Regional Research, vol 18, No. 1.

Neef, R., with cooperation of Ilie, S., Motzenbäcker, S. and Stănculescu, M. (1998), *Working situations, incomes and social situations of households performing informal activities*, in Duchêne (Coord.), The informal economy in Romania. Final Report, Paris, R.O.S.E.S./ Brussels, E.U.

Oprescu, G. (1999), The labour market in Romania, in *The transition Economy in Romania, Volume of Conference*, Bucuresti 21-22 October 1999.

Păuna, C., Păuna, B. (1999), Output decline and Labour reallocation in transitional economies; where does Romania stand?, in *The Transition Economy in Romania*, Volume of Conference, Bucuresti, 21-22 October.

Schneider, F., Enste, D.H. (2000), *Shadow Economies: Size, Causes, and Consequences*, Journal of Economic Literature, vol XXXVIII (March 2000), pp. 77-114.

Stănculescu, M., Ilie, S. (2001), *Informal Economy in Romania*, UNDP/ICCV, Bucuresti.

Weck, H. (1983), *Schattenwirtschaft: Eine Möglichkeit zur Einschränkung der öffentlichen Verwaltung? Eine ökonomische Analyse*, Frankfurt/Main, Lang.

***Interviews conducted in various counties of Romania in 1998 and 1999/2000 in the project 'The development potential of the shadow economy in Romania', coord. R. Neef, financed by the Volkswagen-Stiftung.

APPENDIX

The econometric results for the equation estimating the level of informal economy's share in GDP (IE_{share})
Sample: 1990 2000   Included observations: 11

$$IESH=C(2)*SOCB+C(3)*MESGDP+C(6)*NWPLF+C(1)*LTRATE+C(4)*NWRL+C(5)*GDPL$$

	Coefficient	Std. Error	T-Statistic	Prob.
C(2)	1.133630	1.097194	1.033208	0.3489
C(3)	-0.035611	0.832007	-0.042801	0.9675
C(6)	0.546364	0.405649	1.346888	0.2358
C(1)	2.681287	5.148964	0.520743	0.6248
C(4)	0.037235	0.183791	0.202593	0.8474
C(5)	-0.225016	0.324768	-0.692852	0.5193

R-squared	0.890707	Mean dependent var	30.77273
Adjusted R-squared	0.781415	S.D. dependent var	5.107072
S.E. of regression	2.387714	Akaike info criterion	2.043124
Sum squared resid	28.50589	Schwartz criterion	2.260158
Log likelihood	-20.84551	F-statistic	8.149753
Durbin-Watson stat	1.399218	Prob (F-statistic)	0.018995

The econometric results for the equation estimating the growth rate of informal economy's share in GDP ($IE_{share}\%$)
Sample: 1990 2000   Included observations: 11

$$SHV=C(1)*LTRATE+C(3)*GDPR+C(4)*NWR+C(5)*SCBR$$

	Coefficient	Std. Error	T-Statistic	Prob.
C(1)	0.535449	0.161105	3.323605	0.0127
C(3)	-0.407968	0.060294	-6.766289	0.0003
C(4)	-0.039136	0.031266	-1.251717	0.2509
C(5)	0.559629	0.224460	2.493225	0.0414

R-squared	0.922052	Mean dependent var	1.636364
Adjusted R-squared	0.888646	S.D. dependent var	2.772462
S.E. of regression	0.925165	Akaike info criterion	0.119721
Sum squared resid	5.991509	Schwartz criterion	0.264410
Log likelihood	-12.26679	F-statistic	27.60115
Durbin-Watson stat	1.497846	Prob (F-statistic)	0.000298

PART III
HUNGARY

Chapter 10

Hungary[1]

Endre Sik* and János István Tóth**

Hungary currently has a population of 10,106,017. The number of inhabitants reached its peak at 10.7 million in 1980 and has been diminishing steadily since then. The population decrease in Hungary over the past two decades was accompanied by an ageing of the population. The share of the population older than 60 increased to 19.7%. The mortality rate has been high in European comparison, with higher mortality rates and lower life expectancies only to be found in countries to the East.

In the early years of transition, between 1991 and 1996, Hungary experienced a deep transformational recession. The open Hungarian economy (with a high export/production ratio) was deeply shaken by the collapse of the Comecon, which until then had been considered its main export market. Industrial production fell dramatically to 74% of the 1989 level in 1991, 67% in 1992 and 70% in 1993. The economy managed to outperform this initial (1989) level only in 1998, and then only by a mere 3%. Increasing unemployment, galloping inflation and a dramatic decline in real incomes accompanied the transformational recession.

The decline in the balance of payments and the increase in the state budget deficit compelled the socialist government to take recourse to strict economic measures (curtailing expenditures, curbing salary increases) and to a strict exchange rate adjustment (e.g. a large scale devaluation of the Forint by 9%) in March, 1994. As a result of the so-called Bokros-package, economic growth halted for a short time and households' real incomes declined to a great extent (by over 12%) in 1995. However, in the long run, the austerity provided the basis for Hungary's later economic growth.

Beginning in the last quarter of 1996, the increase in industrial production (11% in 1997) and, through sales, of exports (close to 30%) was of an

* Senior advisor, Hungarian Central Statistical Office. E-mail: sik@tarki.hu.
** Senior research fellow, Institute of Economics, Hungarian Academy of Sciences, 1112 Budapest, Budaorsi ut 45. E-mail: tothij@econ.core.hu, internet: http://www.econ.core.hu/~tothij.

extent that had been unprecedented since the beginning of the transformation period.

The transformational crisis was overcome relatively quickly and the economy regained its foothold in a relatively short time, due to several factors. First, there was a relatively smooth and fast privatization. On the one hand, the specific institutions[2] and certain elements of legal regulation of the market economy had been set up since the wake of the economic reforms of 1968 and were continued in the 80s. On the other hand, after 1990, no decisive player in the Hungarian political arena doubted the importance of a relatively fast-paced privatization[3] based on selling companies and asset items. The selling of state assets was practically completed between 1990 and 1997, with the exception of some strategic companies. Thus, Hungarian companies had practically completed the shift in their market orientation and restored their competitiveness by 1997. Second, foreign capital has played a major role in both privatization and transformation of the Hungarian economy. By purchasing state companies or their assets as well as through green-field projects, foreign capital contributed to the growth of FDI from 569 million USD in 1990 to 19.86 billion USD in 2000. As a result, the FDI stock/GDP ratio has been extremely high, amounting to close to 40% at the end of the nineties. By 1999, the share of firms with a majority foreign ownership had grown to more than 50% in the GDP generation of the manufacturing industry.

The economy displayed a relatively high GDP growth, with an average of 4.8% between 1997 and 2000. Companies were able to respond quickly and flexibly to the shock caused by the Russian crisis in 1998 and were able to change their market orientation relatively quickly as well. Thus, the Hungarian economy had become a remarkably open economy by the late nineties, the main market of exports being the EU. In 2000, over 50% of industrial output was exported, whereby the EU's share was 58% of the total imports and 75% of the total exports. This is the reason why the economic situation and expectations of the developed world and, more specifically, of the EU's leading economic power, Germany, have such a direct and sensitive impact on Hungary's growth perspectives.

In the meantime, a major restructuring occurred in the Hungarian economy: the share of agriculture in the GDP declined to actually 5% from 14% in 1989. At the same time, the share of industry and construction also declined, although to a lesser extent (to 32% from 37%), whereas the share of services increased to some extent (see data in the Appendix). After a large-scale disappearance of jobs, industrial employment has stabilised since the mid-nineties.

By the mid-nineties, the structure of the Hungarian economy had become largely similar to the sectoral distribution of employment characteristic of most EU Member States. The pace of structural transformation slowed down in the second half of the decade. In 1999, 58.9% of the employed worked in the service sector, while 34% worked in industry and a remaining 7.1% were employed in agriculture.

There were two important trends in the Hungarian labour market during the 90s. First, during the transformation-related crisis, there was a rapid rise in unemployment, reaching its peak in 1993 with a 13.6% unemployment rate. Second, the Hungarian labour market experienced high outflows: a huge number of people resigned from the labour market into inactivity during the 90s. Although the unemployment rate declined steadily after 1993 to 6,4% in 2000, employment also continued to drop until 1997. Between 1989 and 1997 about one million jobs (i.e. one-fifth of overall employment) had been lost and more than half a million people had left the (formal) labour market. As to incomes, net real earnings dropped by 26% between 1989 and 1996, and afterwards started to grow again, by a total of 11% by 1999 (see data in the Appendix).

Unemployment insurance was established as early as 1988/89. Entitlements are limited to one year and the level of payments, eroded by inflation in the early nineties, make up about one-third of the average wage. Whereas the pool of the long-term unemployed grew continuously, the coverage by benefits decreased to about only one-quarter of all unemployed persons in the second half of the nineties. In 1991, an independent *pension insurance* was introduced. With payments of 50-60% of one's former wages, it makes possible a relatively acceptable lifestyle for most pensioners. In contrast to most CEECs, where more than half the pensioners receive low payments and suffer poverty, less than one-third do so in Hungary. Faced with growing costs, the government established a second private tier, which has been heavily debated as the beginning of 'Latin-americanization'. Its implementation has been increasingly slowed down.

Starting in 1989, economic liberalization was framed by a liberal system of social security. This offers comparably acceptable standards for the regularly employed, at the disadvantage of some minority groups, especially the Gypsies. On the whole, the new system[4] of social security has been efficient in compensating for the main risks for the labouring majority and it reduced the risks of poverty – especially for pensioners, but also for single parents and for all groups with moderate to median incomes. However, its redistributive efficiency is low: many households in median positions profit more from welfare programs than poor households. As long as the dual-earner model prevails among Hungarian households, they can offset the detriments of liberalization. Only some groups, like the poorly-educated unemployed and families with many children, are faced with poverty, while minorities like the Gypsies fall through the holes in the security net. Since there is no universal system of minimum social welfare, they depend on the mercy of local authorities, who very often lack the means to assist them.

As a result of macroeconomic trends, labour market changes, and shifts in the welfare system, the level of inequality increased during the nineties. In 1992, the average per capita household income in highest decile was 7.1 times higher than that of in the lowest income. In 2000, it had risen to 7.5.[5] The poverty level[6] reached its peak in the mid-nineties, with 16-18% of all households living in poverty (earning less than half of the average income) at the subsistence level (see data in the Appendix).

The increasing level of impoverishment in the mid-nineties and the mild increase in the standard of living in contemporary Hungary can be seen in consumption patterns as well.

Table 10.1   The proportion of some selected consumption goods in the total household budget, 1989–1999 (%)

	1989	1991	1993	1995	1997	1999
Food	31.7	33.4	33.7	34.5	33.3	29.9
Construction	10.1	7.0	7.0	6.8	5.3	4.0
Clothing	8.4	8.5	7.5	6.1	5.9	6.1
House maintenance	10.3	13.5	14.1	16.3	18.6	18.6
Culture, leisure	7.8	6.9	6.1	6.2	5.8	6.6

Source: Statistical Yearbook, 2000, HCSO, Budapest.

The proportion of food consumption to total household budget shows a continuous increase until 1995 and a rather sharp drop since then. According to the Engel-law, this is a clear indication of increasing impoverishment between 1990 and 1995 and an opposite trend after that. The decrease in house-building and the increase in house-maintenance in relation to the total household budget shows, however, that Hungarian households still lack the resources to build new houses. Instead, they satisfy the desire to improve their homes by maintenance. The slightly decreasing level of clothing and cultural and leisure consumption in relation to the total household budget (taking into consideration the sharply increasing level of prices of these goods) is the sign of lasting problems of maintaining the previously higher standard of living.

Nevertheless, there is a significant increase in the distribution of durable goods like washing machines, freezers or video recorders, especially since the mid-nineties. Every second household is now the owner of these goods and, by 1999, 11% of the households own personal computers. The increase in the spread of cars – the most expensive of all durables – is the slowest: between 1989 and 1999 the percentage of car owners vacillated between 35% and 40%, illustrating the temporary impoverishment of the population. Only in the last two years has this figure increased significantly.

Overall, in the second half of the nineties, the Hungarian economy experienced a recovering trend – GDP growth was associated with increasing net real earnings, decreasing unemployment and *slightly* diminishing poverty – while the already existent inequality (long-term unemployment, income inequality) was preserved or deepened. Low employment rates and high poverty characterise the Roma (Gypsy) population, which is in a disadvantage situation compared to the rest of the population. They represent about 6% of Hungary's total population (the largest ethnic minority group), and nearly 53% of Roma households are in long-term poverty, compared with 7.5% for the total population.

Hungary is a border country to the EU. In the last ten years, a large number of migrants entered the country – either seeking better-paid jobs than available in their home-countries (see Sik's contribution in this volume) or attempting to get over the 'Schengen Wall', an endeavor that very often fails. This finds some reflection in the level of xenophobia – measured by the strict exclusion of all asylum seekers – which has increased since 1992. The level of xenophobia reached its first peak in 1995, exceeded again only in 2001, when 43% of Hungarian adults survey favoured closing the Hungarian borders to asylum seekers. According to comparative data from 1995 and 1998, Hungary has the second highest (after Bulgaria) xenophobia value among post-socialist countries.[7]

Whereas economic policies seem quite sustaining since the mid-nineties, the question of whether the social security system and social policies in Hungary can meet the challenges of integration into the European Union remains open.

Notes

1 The article is based on two papers: Kopasz, Mariann: *Hungary. Context report for the Household, Work, and Flexibility Project*, Manuscript, TÁRKI, Budapest, 2001 and István Harcsa and Endre Sik, Social Development in Hungary. Central Europe in Transition: Towards EU Membership, eds.: Gorzelak, Grzegorz, Éva Ehrlich, et al., Scholar, Warsaw. 2001, pp.124-144. Rainer Neef gave some additions, based in the main on: Ulrike Götting: *Transformation der Wohlfahrtsstaaten in Mittel- und Osteuropa*, Leske & Budrich, 1998.

2   Regulations included the permission of certain forms of private businesses and their growing economic role, the enactment both of a law regulating the transformation of SOEs and the corporation act, the establishment of the two-layered banking system, and the expansion of decision-making competencies of the management of SOEs.

3   Both the conservative Antall and Boross cabinets in office between 1990 and 1994 and the socialist Horn government in power between 1994 and 1998 pursued the policy of fast privatization, the core element of which was the direct (often through the stock exchange) sale of state companies.

4   The health system suffers a growing malaise, due to increasing costs and deficits on the one hand, low pay of the personnel and inefficiency on the other. Those patients that can afford it try to get around the inefficiency by giving informal 'donations' to the doctors and nurses. There is little innovation until now; generally the contributors bear the costs of inefficiency – informally starting a long time ago, formally since the mid-nineties (introduction of a cost-contribution system).

5   Szívós P., Tóth I.G. (2000), Household incomes, inequality and welfare benefits, in *TÁRKI Monitor Report*. Eds, Szívós, P., G.I. Tóth. TÁRKI, Budapest.

6   Measured by the proportion of the population falling below half of the average and/or median of the per capita total household income. The authors use both proxies since the former is more accepted as a proxy of the rate of poverty while the latter is more reliable, being less distorted by the extremely large per capita incomes (positive outlyers).

7   Sik, E. (1999) 'The level and social basis of xenophobia in contemporary Hungary', in *Authoritarianism and Prejudice – Central European Perspectives*. Eds. Enyedi, Zsolt and Ferenc Erős, Osiris, Budapest, pp. 193-213.

Chapter 11

Hidden economy in Hungary 1992-1999

János István Tóth and Endre Sik

Introduction

Economic research on hidden economy in Hungary revealed an increasing tendency in the 80s, representing about 27% of the official GDP in 1992 (Lackó 1992 and Árvay-Vértes 1995). Subsequent research pointed out that the process continued well into the 90s (Lackó 1997). We consider the outputs of the following economic activities to belong to the hidden (or unregistered, informal) economy: a) the activity of unregistered enterprises that pursue legal activities, but are not registered; and b) registered (state or private owned) enterprises conducting unreported or underreported activities.

In our paper we argue that the proliferation of hidden economy came to a halt in the middle of the 90s, then, as the GDP began to rise after a long recession period (Figure 11.1), it started to shrink.

Several macro economic and company level factors contributed to this trend, e.g. a new phase of the structural transformation followed the transformational recession, profound changes occurred in the organisational structure and adaptability of the Hungarian firms. The privatization of state-owned enterprises is finished till 1996-97, except some strategic firms. The share of private sector in the GDP rose between 1992-1999 from 46% to 70%. Beginning from the mid-90s, the consolidation of market economy institutions has been accompanied by an improvement in the business perspectives of companies. Such tendencies could not but leave a mark on the attitudes of business actors (firms and households), including their attitude to taxation – though the financial discipline of the still state-owned firms remained weaker than among private (especially foreign owned) ones. The consolidation consequently influenced the size of hidden economy

With the apparent upturn of the economy after 1996, the long-term benefits available through the formal economy became increasingly certain, whereas the short-term ones available through the hidden economy devalued

**Figure 11.1   The growth rate of GDP in Hungary 1989-1999 (%) and
relative share of hidden economy (1989=100%)**

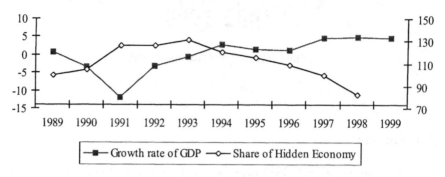

Sources
    – of GDP figures : CSO Statistical Pocketbook 1992, 1994, 1996, 1998 and 1999;
    – of hidden economy figures: Lackó, 2000.
Notes:
    Left-hand scale: Growth rate of GDP (%);
    Right-hand scale: Relative share of hidden economy (1989=100%).

and became more uncertain. Tax burdens of the legal economy started to decline apparently as early as from 1993 (e.g. company tax rate dropped from the earlier 36% to 18%) and, with the tax authority becoming increasingly professional and its technical infrastructure more sophisticated, and the tax laws becoming increasingly transparent and costs tied, the hidden economy started to diminish.

The trends of the 90s

The most general analysis of the shift in the volume of hidden economy since the outset of the economic transformation has been done by Lackó (2000). She used an econometric model examining the components of the electricity consumption of households to assess the weight of hidden economy between 1989 and 1998 based on data of 17 post-communist countries.[1]

As her results suggest, in the period surveyed high tax burdens, relatively low state expenses, major drop in output and high inflation induced an extraordinarily high level of domestic electricity consumption relative to the level that would have been justified by the size of consumption, the proportion of agricultural output, climatic weather conditions and the proportion of other types of energy. The key factor in explaining this extra electricity consumption is imputed to be the prevalence of hidden economy (see also Adair/Neef, in this volume).

The results of the predictions with regard to the tendencies of hidden economy seem to indicate that hidden economy follows an inverse U curve in more advanced former socialist countries (Czech Republic, Hungary, Poland, Slovakia, Slovenia) in the period between 1989-98 (Lackó 2000). Her calculations demonstrate that in the first phase of the transition hidden economy can be assumed to have grown quickly and to a great extent, followed by a gradual decline of the hidden economy as the institutions of market economy started to consolidate and the economy started to grow subsequently (Figure 11.2). Hidden economy declines in each country to the extent as the above process is moving ahead.

Figure 11.2   Assessed trends in the proportion of hidden economy in Hungary (1989= 100%)

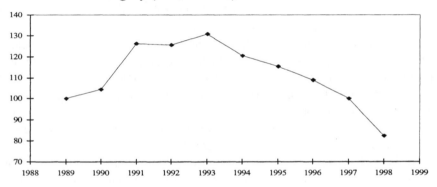

Source of data: Lackó, 2000.

According to Lackó's computation, the weight of Hungarian hidden economy changed relative to the official GDP from 25.2% of 1989 to 20.8% by 1998, whereas it reached its peak in 1993 (33.1%).

Several studies substantiated the validity of the previous observation with regard to the declining tendency of the weight of hidden economy in Hungary since 1996. Tóth (1997-98), Sik-Tóth, (1999) and KSH (2000) proved it by analysing the household consumption patterns, Tóth – Semjén (1998) and Semjén (2000) on the field of the contractual and taxation behaviour of firms, Sik (1999) regarding 'open-air' and informal labour market-places (Czakó – Sik 1999, Sik – Wallace 1999) found similar trends.

The consumption behaviour of households

Hidden economy – as defined in the beginning – had a decisive weight in Hungary in certain fields of consumption of households in the middle of the 90s. Indicative of this have been the surveys that analyzed, on the basis of three empirical surveys of households, the affinity of households to hidden economy and the weight of hidden economy in commerce and services. The first and the second survey covered 1000 households each, in 1995 and 1996 respectively (Tóth 1997-98 and Sik – Tóth 1999); the third one was carried out by the Central Statistical Office (KSH) in 1998 covering over 2600 households (KSH 1998).

Both surveys in 1995 and 1996 pointed out that significant variations could be discerned among the various groups of goods and services in the consumption of the households, in terms of the manifestations of hidden economy (Table 11.1). Households purchased 10% of alcoholic drinks, 15% of coffee and cigarettes, close to 40% of lingerie, 27% of shoes and 12% of washing powder and liquid, without the transaction ever having been registered by the seller (Sik – Tóth 1998). The same proportions were considerably higher in the area of services. In some cases, like the hairdresser and beauty parlors, the weight of the hidden economy amounted to as much as 80%. In the case of masonry, 70% of all payments can be assigned to hidden economy. In medical services, mainly due to the accepted practice of gratuity moneys, 80% of the money paid to physicians and close to 97% of moneys paid in hospitals can be tied to hidden economy.

If taking the total consumption of households into consideration, the ratio of unregistered expenses was around 10-13% in 1995 and 11-14% in 1996, which indicates a stagnation of weight of unregistered expenses. This ratio did not change in 1997 either (KSH 1998).

The social determinants of the hidden economy

As we saw before, during the 90s the hidden economy represented a decisive weight in the consumption of the households (Table 11.1). This, however, did not mean that hidden economy was an experience equally present and of an equal weight in all Hungarian households.

Namely, in the expenses of the respective households the procurement of goods and services represented and continues to represent a considerably varying weight. Close to 30% of the households have not or have hardly spent at all in an unregistered form, whereas in as many as 10% of all the households the value of unregistered purchases amounts to over half of the total expenses surveyed.

Table 11.1 **The proportion of unregistered expenses* within the different groups of expenses in Hungary in 1995-96**

Groups of expenses	Average ratio of unregistered expenses	Ratio of unregistered expenses in the surveyed household expenses (%)			Total (N)
		Zero	Not more than average	Above average	
	(%)	(0)	(1)	(2)	
1. Consumer goods	11.2	85.5	14.5	-	100.0 (1361)
2. Clothes	36.4	52.2	9.5	38.4	100.0 (1170)
3. Other goods	14.0	71.4	6.6	21.9	100.0 (1893)
4. Services	53.8	14.8	32.4	52.8	100.0 (1702)
5. All expenses (1+2+3+4)	27.0	16.2	45.6	38.2	100.0 (1980)

Notes:
* Unregistered expenses = household expenses when the sellers do not report the transaction to the Tax Authority.
The case numbers are in the brackets.
Source: Tóth, 1997-98.

To be involved in the hidden economy is strongly related to the level of household income. We assumed that less affluent households reveal a higher proportion of hidden economy related costs than more affluent ones, since forced consumer adaptation is more likely to occur in less affluent households, a manifestation of which is the increasing weight of unregistered expenses facilitating cheaper bargains within the overall expenses of households. Less affluent households are rather more price- than quality sensitive (Galasi-Kertesi 1985).

It can also be assumed that the affinity to unregistered expenses is related to the perceived, instead of the real income situation and to the dynamics, instead of the actual level of income. Those who perceive their financial situation poor or declining are more likely to spend in unregistered forms, i.e. the proportion of unregistered expenses is higher in the expenses of those who are able to increase their incomes to a lesser extent than the average. The reason for this behaviour is that those more frustrated due to their income situation tend to be more impatient and are more willing to purchase cheaper products and services in the hidden economy to improve their consumption level.

The other assumption is related to the social status of the households. Where the head of the family is more qualified and has a higher social status, the household will spend less on goods and services in unregistered forms, than households at lower rungs of the society. The underlying assumption is that in consumer decisions of households composed of more qualified members, factors unrelated to the price level (guarantee safeguards or customer satisfaction through brand loyalty) play a significant role.

According to an econometric analysis of household surveys (Tóth 1997-98), however, the above mentioned factors have little to do with hidden economy related consumer decisions of households. First of all, it is an illusion that the involvement in hidden economy would only have been the 'privilege' of less affluent households. Just on the contrary, the income level of households in the middle of the 90s had nothing to do with their decisions related to hidden economy. Neither the income- nor the social status of the head of the family revealed any significant correlation with the affinity to unregistered expenses. Nor is it possible to confirm the assumption according to which purchases in the 'open-air markets' or without guarantees would have been characteristic only of the less affluent layers of the society. In the mid-90s, the rich were as likely to shop around on the open-air markets as the members of less affluent households.

These results directed our attention to the fact that the affinity of households to unregistered expenditures is closely related to the type of the settlement where the household resides. One can assume – *ceteris paribus* – a higher proportion of unregistered expenses among inhabitants of larger settlements than among those of settlements with fewer inhabitants. This can be ascribed to two factors: on the one hand, the distribution of the possibilities for unregistered purchases in accordance with the size of the settlement. On the other hand, 'open-air markets' of larger settlements are larger and their opening hours are longer than of the smaller ones (Sik 1999). Another important factor is how *easily* actors involved in unregistered transactions *can reach each other*, namely e.g. what is the chance of the members of the households to get to the closest 'comecom market'.

The role of hidden economy in household consumption and all the indicators related to the size of the settlement reveal a strong positive correlation, if considering either the number of the inhabitants and the commercial outlets at the settlement or the type of the settlement (village, cities, Budapest). Similar is the influence of the public transport means: the easier is the accessibility for the household by public transport means at a certain distance (by bus or train), the more important the role of hidden economy is in the consumption.

Finally, the size of the hidden economy is affected by the purchasing customs of households, as well as the changes of these customs. The proliferation of large shopping malls among commercial businesses and the growth of their share in total turnover considerably reduce the purchases of households in hidden economy markets. In this context, it could be noticed from 1995 that households increased the weight of their 'large-scale' purchases in large shopping malls within their total purchases.

Figure 11.3 **Share of shopping malls and supermarkets in the total purchases of consumer goods of Hungarian households, %**

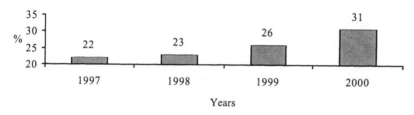

Source: GfK Market Research Institute.

The behaviour of firms

In the period of early transition, in a situation where firms lost their markets to a dramatic degree, the survival of the firm depended on the temporary relief provided by delaying the payments to suppliers or to the tax authority (Laki 1994). Tax arrears became more prevalent in the first years of transformation. Payroll tax arrears nearly doubled in Hungary during 12 months starting from 1990 December (see Laki 1994: 361). An increased reliance on tax avoidance and evasion can provide another survival strategy: the management's efforts to minimize tax liabilities in a legal or illegal way (i. e. by taking advantage of loopholes or by shifting part of the enterprise's output from the visible to the hidden economy) may be of crucial importance, temporarily.

The analysis of empirical surveys of medium sized and large (that time very largely private) businesses carried out in 1996 and 1998 indicated that while medium sized and large businesses perceived their business perspectives as being more favorable, the time horizon of their planning grew, their profitability improved and their output accelerated, their financial discipline improved considerably (both their tax compliance and contractual discipline) (Figure 11.4) and they perceived to a lesser extent that their business partners or their competitors would be involved in hidden economy (Tóth – Semjén 1998).

The results of the research among top managers concerning tax compliance and tax evasion suggested that a perceivable change was starting to take shape in the period between 1996 and 1998, pointing towards the decline of hidden economy (Table 11.2).

The analyses also pointed to the fact that while the probability of unreported sales was significantly higher among suppliers of companies with majority Hungarian ownership in 1996, in 1998 tax compliance had signifi-

cantly improved among them. All managers assess the prevalence of unreported sales to be of a smaller volume than before, and they are affected to
a lesser extent than two years before by the involvement of their competitors
in the hidden economy.

The authors assessed the proportion of tax evading firms to be not more
than 23% in 1997 (Tóth – Semjén 1998). This result points to the fact that
the phenomenon of tax evasion was rather widespread among Hungarian
firms in the latter half of the 90s, yet it can also be stated that such behavior
was not typical of the majority of medium sized and large Hungarian firms.

**Table 11.2   Change of business condition, financial discipline of
medium sized and large firms and estimated involvement
in the hidden economy in Hungarian enterprise sector
between 1996 and 1998, %**

		1996	1998
Firm increases investment			
	Yes	19.5	44.7
	Total	100.0	100.0
	N	277	296
Surplus in operating balance			
	Yes	65.4	82.1
	Total	100.0	100.0
	N	289	295
Firm has payroll tax arrears			
	Yes	17.7	6.8
	Total	100.0	100.0
	N	293	299
Firm has tax arrears in the last two years			
	Yes	38.7	27.1
	Total	100.0	100.0
	N	293	296
Unreported sales in the Hungarian economy....			
	Insignificant		1,2
	Rare	10,6	18,4
	Frequent	89,4	81,4
	Total	100,0	100,0
	N	274	272
Do your competitors' connections with the hidden economy have an adverse effect on your competitiveness			
	Not at all	28,8	38,5
	To a small degree	31,0	27,9
	To a great degree	40,2	33,6
	Total	100,0	100,0
	N	271	276

Source: Tóth-Semjén, 1998.

The final factor we have not mentioned yet, but which is closely related to the diminish of hidden economy is the increasing efficiency of tax administration. Semjén et al., 2000, arrived at the conclusion that the proficiency of tax administration improved between 1992-99. However, even if considering this tendency of professionalization it can also be demonstrated that the size of unreported taxes failed to follow the increased frequency of tax control towards the end of the 90s (Figure 11.4). This fact cannot but be explained as an indirect sign of the improved tax compliance and the decline of tax evasion by the economic actors, though after 1997 we can also see a slight rise.

Figure 11.4   Rate of revealed unreported taxes in GDP and in total revenue of Hungarian Tax Administration (APEH)

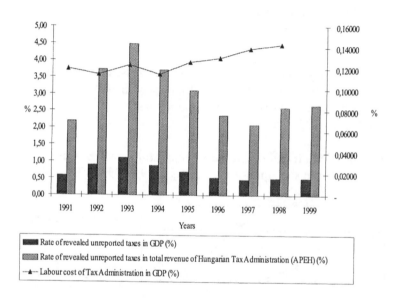

Source: Semjén - Szántó - Tóth, 2001.
Note:

Left scale: revealed unreported tax in GDP and in total revenue of Tax Administration.
Right scale: Labor cost of Tax Administration in GDP.

'Open-air' and informal labour market-places

While the slightly decreasing trend of the spread of open-air markets fits into the general trend of the shrinking hidden economy, the spread of informal labour markets show a sharp increase (Figure 11.5).[2]

Figure 11.5   The spread of open-air market-places and informal labour markets (1995-1999, % of all settlements; indications of mayors)

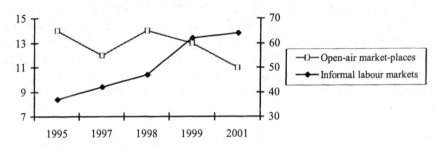

Note:
    Left scale: open-air market-places.
    Right scale: informal labour markets.
Source: Sik 1999, Simonovits (2001).

Behind the slight decrease of open-air markets, one can see a slower decrease of the number of stalls (i.e. of traders) with 30% between 1997 and 1999, and a faster decrease of the opening hours starting quickly in 1995 and reaching 29% in 1999.

Figure 11.6   The trend of the number of stalls and of annual opening hours of open-air markets (1995-1999, 1995=100%)

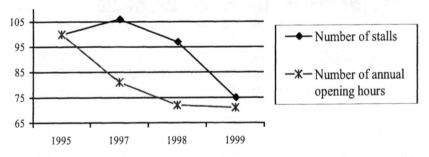

Source: Sik-Tóth (1999).

This implies that while the spread of the open-air markets is rather stable (Figure 11.5), the volume of this informal commercial institution is shrinking (Figure 11.6). The process is that at first, more traders tried to reduce the opening hours; later on, more and more traders left the field.

Conclusions

In the period of transformation, numerous factors drive the increase in the weight of hidden economy. The majority of these factors cannot be avoided, their impact cannot be eliminated, only reduced at the most, or rather, more likely, the length of the period during which they can have impact can be reduced (through actions promoting the development of the institutions of the market and of private economy).

One of the necessary consequences and accompanying factors of economic transformation is the increase of the weight of the hidden economy, manifest at the start of the transformation. We estimate that this tendency reversed with the strengthening of private economy, consolidation of the system of market institutions and the unfolding of economic growth: the attitude of economic actors to hidden economy changes and, as a result, the weight of hidden economy starts to decline. Naturally, this hypothesis needs longer time series to be tested.

In the meantime, however, some factors typical of countries in transformation have to be taken into account, due to which, in the long run, hidden economy will probably be present at a higher level than it is assumed to be at, in more advanced countries. Among such factors is the fact that, during the transition, masses of the active population have been dislocated from the labor market and became inactive[3] (whereas the upturn of the economy results in a slightly perceivable increase in the activity rate), but also such factor is the widespread acceptance of non-compliant behavior, low taxation morale, in which regard only slow improvement can be expected: there is always high inertia in economic behaviour.

The weight of hidden economy, however, cannot merely be traced back to the impact of spontaneous processes. The government, even if only with limited means, is capable of influencing it and of motivating, through co-ordinated steps, actors of the economy to refrain from involvement in hidden economy.

Notes

1 She has used the broader definition of 'hidden economy' than we use in this paper. Her household electricity approach involves that her concept of hidden economy takes into consideration work done at home and do-it-yourself activities as well.

2 The data on open-air markets and informal labour marketplaces is based on five waves of self-administered questionnaires. These questionnaires were sent to all Hungarian municipalities (except Budapest, N=3130). About one third of the majors or experts of the local governments answered the questionnaires. To make the sample representative, the data was weighted by region and settlement size.

3   The employment ratio (number employees in per cent of the working age population) fell radically from 75.9% in 1990 to 58.4% in 1997 in Hungary. See Fazekas. 2000, page 244.

References

Árvay, J. és Vértes, A. (1995), Impact of the Hidden Economy on Growth Rates in Hungary, *Statistical-Journal*, vol. 12, no. 1, pp. 27-39.

Czakó, Á. and Sik, E. (1999), Characteristics and Origins of the Comecon Open-air Market, in Hungary, *International Journal of Urban and Regional Research*, 23, pp. 715-737.

Fazekas K. (2000), *Munkaeröpiaci tükör – 2000*, Budapest, MTA Közgazdaságtudományi Kutatóközpont.

Galasi, P., Kertesi, G. (1985), 'Második gazdaság, verseny, infláció', *Közgazdasági Szemle*, XXXII, Évf. 12, sz. 1424-1444. o.

KSH (1998), *Hidden economy in Hungary,* Központi Statisztikai Hivatal (Hungarian Central Statistical Office), Budapest.

Lackó, M. (1992), 'Az illegális gazdaság aránya Magyarországon 1970-1989 között. Egy monetáris modell'. (The Extent of Illegal Economy in Hungary Between 1970-1989. A Monetary Model), *Közgazdasági Szemle*, vol. XXXIX., No. 9, pp. 861-882.

Lackó, M. (1997), The Hidden Economies of Visegrád Countries in International Comparison: A Household Electricity Approach, IEHAS, Budapest, p. 39.

Lackó, M. (2000), *Egy rázós szektor: a rejtett gazdaság és hatásai a poszt-szocialistaorszá-gokban háztartási áramfelhasználásra épülö becslések alapján*, MTA KTK, Elemzések a rejtett gazdaságról, 1. sz.

Laki, M. (1994), Firm behaviour during a long transitional recession, *Acta Oeconomica*, Vol. 46. (3–4), pp. 347–370.

Särndal, C.E., Swensson, B., Wretman, J. (1992), *Model Assisted Survey Sampling*, New York: Springer Verlag.

Semjén, A., Szántó, Z., Tóth, I.J. (2001), *Adócsalás és adóigazgatás (Tax evasion and tax administration)*, Elemzések a rejtett gazdaság magyarországi szerepéröl, 3. Tanulmány MTA KTK, február, p. 120.

Sik, E. (1999), The Spatial Distribution of Informal Marketplaces and Informal Foreign Traders in Contemporary Hungary, in *Unregistered Economy in Transforming Economies* eds.: Ed Feige and Ott, Katarina, Ashgate, Aldershot, pp. 275-306.

Sik, E. and Wallace, C. (1999), The Development of Open-air Markets in East-Central Europe *International Journal of Urban and Regional Research,* 23:697-714.

Sik, E., Tóth, I.J. (1999), Some Elements of Hidden Economy in Hungary Today, in T. Kolosi, I.Gy. Tóth,Gy. Vukovich (eds.), *Social Report – 1998*, TÁRKI, Budapest, pp. 100-122.

Simonovits, B. (2001), Jelentés – TÁRKI Önkormányzati project 2001 tavasz (Report of the TÁRKI local government project, Spring 2001), Manuscript, TÁRKI, Budapest.

Tóth, I.J. (1997-98), 'The importance of the hidden economy in Hungary, in 1995-96. An estimation on the basis of the empirical analysis of household expenses', *Acta Oeconomica*, vol. 49, nos. (1-2), pp. 105-134.

Tóth, I.J., Semjén, A. (1998), Tax behaviour and financial discipline of Hungarian Enterprises, in L. Csaba, (ed.), The Hungarian SME Sector Development in Comparative Perspective, CIPE/USAID and Kopint-Datorg Foundation for Economic Research, pp. 103-134.

Chapter 12

Informal labour market-place on the Moscow Square[1]

Endre Sik

As we saw in the chapter from Tóth and Sik, the informal labor market is a widespread institution in the hidden economy of contemporary Hungary. Often, such informal markets are located in a market-place setting, helping to match the potential customers with the casual labourer. People hang around on a street corner, at the fringe of an open-air market, close to a major urban center, such as a train station, or at a park-and-ride site and wait to be hired for a day or at best for a week. The typical jobs are low-paid unskilled or semiskilled work on construction sites or in agriculture. As in 1995 and in 1997, in 1998 there was an informal labour market-place in about every fifth Hungarian settlement.[2]

In the Hungarian language, the traditional term for the informal labour market-place is the 'köpködö' (Katona 1956, 1961). The literal translation of this term is 'spitting place'. This refers to the basic activity while hanging around for hours waiting for a job, i.e. smoking a pipe and as a by-product, spitting. The closest corrollary (much smaller and 'local', though) I found to this market-place form of informal labor allocation is 'Tally's corner' (Liebow 1967), an open place in Washington D.C. (USA) where casual labourers find work.

The Moscow Square

We should begin the analysis with a brief introduction of the Moscow Square in Budapest. In this introduction I rely on an excellent historical-architectural-anthropological opus published recently (Bodnár 1998). The author summarizes the major characteristics of the site of the informal labour market-place in the following:

Always a meeting point for different regions of the city, this area developed at the end of the seventeenth century a clay pit that later became the site of a brick-

making factory... During World War II the square evolved into one of the busiest traffic centers on the Buda side of the Duna. In 1946 it was renamed Moscow Square ... In 1972 Moscow Square found a new significance as a traffic center when a major subway station opened there. This addition reinforced its role as the important last inner-city stop for the steadily growing number of suburbanites residing in the Buda hills and valleys. (p 491).

To give the reader an opportunity to become familiar with the everyday life on the Moscow Square, I selected two recent non-participant observations on the Moscow square informal labour market-place. The first is again from Bodnár (1998) who used to live close to the square and therefore despite that – as she put it – 'the bulk of the research was carried out in the summer of 1995 ... the essay operates in an extended time frame, in 'post-socialist' time' (p 492).

The square rises early. Around 5 a.m. newspaper booths open, as the first subway trains, trams, and buses begin running, and the main post office on the Buda side on the northwest perimeter of Moscow Square unlocks its doors. .. By 6.30 there are about a hundred men smoking and talking, waiting to be hired for a day or, if lucky, for more. Luck comes in pickup trucks, transporting the freshly hired to small jobs at construction and renovation sites, mainly villas for the new elite in the Buda hills. .. Employers mostly offer jobs that do not require skills, but skilled laborers are in demand too.

Most of the 'supply' at this brutally simple labor market comes from abroad. M. is a good representative: a citizen of Romania and an ethnic Magyar (Hungarian from abroad), he came to Hungary from Transylvania with his neighbor. The two of them define themselves as jack-of-all-trades... When they first came to Hungary four years ago, they were hired at Moscow Square for a construction job in the Buda suburbs. They were passed on from one employer to the other through the broad interpersonal networks of the family that first employed them. They came in the spring, stayed until cold set in, then exchanged the money they have saved for Romanian currency and returned to their village. By the following spring, direct correspondence brought results, and they came back to Budapest on the basis of a quasi-contract. Employers like them: they are affordable, reliable, and quick...

Hungarians in the square call them 'smokey-faced' evoking the imagery of the racial slurs usually reserved for 'Gypsy', the only widely used, vigorous ethnic derogation in contemporary Hungarian... Among the men gathering in search of work in Moscow Square recently appeared some ethnic Romanians from Romania, as well as Magyars and Roma (Gypsy) with varying citizenship, but Transylvanian Magyars still predominate. Common to all of them is that they walk on a tightrope with the law. Hungarian citizens violate tax regulations and the rules concerning unemployment compensation. The others are undocumented, mostly seasonal, migrants... (pp. 492-494).

The second snapshot is from 1998 and with the help of this brief overview we have a look at the Moscow Square through the eye of an American economic journalist (Reed 1998).

It's another day on Moscow Square, Budapest's version of the illegal urban labor markets in most big German cities. Hungary's surging economy has become a magnet for illegal workers from down-at-heels countries farther east – and for many of those seeking work, Moscow Square is the first stop.

Dániel, from the Romanian port city of Constanta, has been in Budapest seven months, packed with four of his countrymen in a rented room since the shipyard where he worked went belly up. József, a bricklayer from Satu Mare, just across Hungary's eastern border, has been working the square for three weeks without success. If money gets short, he says, he'll bed down in Budapest's Keleti railway station. Living rough here is better than returning to a country and hometown where the prospects for work are far bleaker. 'I love Romania, but it's impossible to live there,' he says. 'We have a rich country, but the adminis-tration is bad.

(The Moscow Square is) a largely unpoliced market where just about anything goes – and where few will supply a surname. János, a 40-year-old ethnic Hungarian from the Transylvanian city of Sighisoara, has nabbed just one piece of work since coming here in March: tearing down a suburban garage. The contractor, a private construction company, promised him 13,500 forints ($64.28) for three days' work; in the end, the company paid János just 1,000 forints. The former bricklayer owes 17,000 forints in back rent for his room; until he finds enough cash to pay the tab, he says, he can't return home to his wife and daughter.

If the living on Moscow Square is anything but easy, it isn't hard to see why people like János keep coming. Hungary's economy grew 4.4% in 1997, and is expected to grow by at least that much again this year. Romania's economy contracted 6.5% last year, and it continues to shrink. A worker in industry in Romania can expect to take home about one million lei ($119) a month; in Budapest, he can earn the same amount in about half the time, even at the cut-rate wages offered on Moscow Square.

Also keeping this market and others like it alive are employers in construction, restaurants and other service industries, who turn to it to avoid paying Hungary's West European-level social-security and other taxes, which can add as much as 60% to wage costs. 'If you get a Hungarian painter, he will ask for a lot of money to paint a flat,' says József, the bricklayer. 'We will do it for cheaper.' (In fact, some of the job-seekers on Moscow Square are native Hungarians who have fallen out of the labor market.)

Romanians, along with Ukrainians and other inhabitants of the former Soviet Union, can stay in Hungary visa-free for 30 days; when the visa runs out, the men of Moscow Square say, they just hop a train to the border for a new stamp. Short of slamming shut Hungary's eastern borders, there isn't much Budapest can do about illegal labor. Two police officers on Moscow Square checking for permits among a group of Hungarian women selling flowers ignore the Romanians and Ukrainians seeking work just a few paces away. Standing around isn't illegal, one of the officers says; you have to catch them on the job.

By 4 p.m., the Moscow Square men have thinned out to perhaps two dozen, lost in a surging rush-hour crowd. One of them is János, the bricklayer looking to pay off his back rent. He didn't pass muster with a construction-firm tout, who passed him over for younger men. Nor was he offered anything by two Chinese men in the market for help painting a house. Still, he figures he'll keep waiting around until day is done. 'Where else am I going to go?' he asks with an eloquent shrug. 'I'll stay as long as I need to get work'.

The non-participant observations we did while preparing to do the research (Hideg – Grajczar, 1994) had very much the same results as the two observations above. These observations were used to develop the hypotheses of the research and fine-tune our special observation technique (see next chapter). The hypotheses we wanted to test by our research were as follows:

1 – the 'open hours' of the informal labour market-place are short, it is 'open' only in the morning, with the peak hours between 5 and 7 a.m.
2 – it is a seasonal market place with the peak of the demand during the spring and summer,
3 – the typical employer is either the owner of a villa from the neighboring elite suburbs (or their emissary) or someone from the agglomeration of Budapest organizing a work group mostly to do agricultural or construction work;
4 – the typical job is unskilled or semiskilled;
5a – the typical employee is ethnic Hungarian (and neither ethnic Romanian nor Gypsy);
5b – most workers come from Romania (more precisely from Transylvania);
5c – towards whom the local employees are hostile since their presence decreases the average wage;
5d – the typical employee is also male and poor (often homeless);
6 – the hourly wage is low and does not keep up with the inflation rate.

Based on the almost constant flood of newspaper articles, we assume that (7) the informal labour market-place on the Moscow Square is the major institution of the allocation of unskilled labor in Budapest (if not all over Central Hungary).

The method

The method of the research was a version of non-participant observation. The two young scholars who did the pre-research observations (Gergely Hideg and István Grajczjar) were the observers all year long. In the beginning, there was some suspicion concerning their presence (and that they made notes). This changed, however, partly because they explained the reasons of being there, partly because by the end of the first month the employees realized that no harm came from their presence, and last but not least since there is a constant flow of all sort of observers (including not only the rather tolerant police, but several researchers and journalists) the actors of the informal labour market-place are accustomed to be in the open.

During the research period (between April, 1995 and March, 1996) there were 84 observation periods allocated in a way that they represented season, day and the three periods of a working day: dawn (around 6 a.m.), morning (around 8 a.m.), and late morning (around 10 a.m.) proportionally.

An observation period lasted for two hours and covered the following tasks:

- At the beginning and end of the period, the observer made an estimate concerning the number of potential employees on the square and gave a general description of the context of the market, i.e. the weather conditions and the presence of the police.
- Every time the observer selected 20 workers (randomly, having a preselected part of the square as starting point and going clockwise) and described their visible (or audible) characteristics (clothing, ethnic origin, group to which they belong, age, gender).
- Finally, they observed as many bargaining situations as they could follow. They registered the first offer, the final wage agreed upon, the in-between offers, the non-pecuniary wage elements, the length and place of the job, and the visible (and audible) features of the employer.

The basic characteristics of the informal labour market-place

A market-place by definition should be *public*. As the two case studies showed, the Moscow Square is open to the public. However, in case of a market institution, openness has a different meaning, i.e. the offers are made public for several potentially interested actors. The informal labour market-place meets with this requirement as well, since 92% of the offers were made in a way that several workers (and groups of them) heard them and entered into negotiation simultaneously. On average, 13.3 employees listened to the offers.

Beyond being public spatially and as a market, the informal labour market-place is a market institution with a high degree of *freedom* as well. This is true again, in two senses. On the one hand, being part of the informal economy, there are no state regulations or trade union, chamber or guild restrictions whatsoever to curtail the freedom of the bargain (whether the issue is the level of wage, the working conditions, the travel or non-pecuniary subsidies, the length of the job, or the sanction of failing with the mutually accepted terms of the non-written contract). On the other hand, the informal labour market-place is free from any close and continuous police surveillance. Police presence was observed in about half of the observation periods, but was characterized by the two observers as active (walking around and asking for documents, sending or taking away the undocumented migrants, etc.) only in every fifth period.

Finally, regarding the typical *type and regional distribution of work*, the informal labour market-place allocates mostly short-term informal jobs. 34% of the observed offers (N=158) were daily jobs and 13% of them consisted only of work for less than a full day.[3] Two-third of the jobs offered were unskilled ones – the rest being semi-skilled or skilled jobs (mostly masonry) – and 63% of the jobs concentrated in Budapest, (the rest, in the vicinity of Budapest).

The demand

The crudest estimate of the volume of demand on the informal labour market-place is the total number of offers, i.e. the number of all offers observed. On average, it was 3,6 (N=84) per observation period. Both the median and the mode were significantly below the level of the average (2 and 0, respectively), which shows that there was a big deviation in the number of offers per observation periods.[4]

The more proper estimate of the volume of demand is the effective demand, which covers only those offers when there was at least one employee listening to the offer (i.e. a bargaining process has begun). Its average in the sample (N=84) was 2.9.

The demand for informal labor is the highest in the summer (total 5.6 and effective 4.5) and at dawn (total 6.9 and effective 5.8) and the lowest in winter (1.2 and in the late morning). There is not much difference between the total and effective demand, which implies that the unsuccessful offers are not concentrated in any particular time period.

As to the joint effect of the three time periods on the volume of total and effective demand, we find that the period of the day and the season play a significant role. The data of our regression calculations are given in the appendix.

Both the total and the effective demand is higher at dawn (this is the strongest factor and is only slightly decreased by controlling with the level of supply), in the morning and in the summer. To hire a casual laborer (and to be hired) at dawn gives the maximum utility for both actors (a full day work on the site for the employer and a full day wage for the employee).

From the regression data (see appendix at the end) we see also the role of the two major contextual factors of the informal labour market-place transactions. We assumed that the better the weather is (the more work can be done both on construction sites and in agriculture) and the less strong the police presence is (less danger to be caught in an illegal action) the higher is the demand.

In case of total demand, both hypotheses were confirmed. However, in case of effective demand, the influence of the weather and policing conditions disappear. This might indicate that when there is strong demand and the negotiation is already on, it does not matter whether the weather is good or bad and if there is police around. The show must go on.

The supply

There are two measures to estimate the volume of supply. The term *total supply* refers to the total number of potential employees (i.e. those hanging around on the square during an observation period, i.e. two hours) while the *effective supply* is equal to the number of potential employees who listened to the offers observed.

The average volume of total supply per hour is 58 persons.[5] It is significantly higher in the spring, at dawn and in the morning (73, 78, 78 persons, respectively), and significantly lower in winter, and in the late morning (36 and 18 persons, respectively). There is no significant difference between the level of demand on working days and in the weekend.

Our calculations also show the joint effect of time periods on the level of supply. As it was the case with the level of demand, it is the period of the day and the season that have the strongest influence on the volume of both the total and the effective supply.

The volume of total supply strongly increases at dawn, in the morning and in the spring and summer. The volume of effective supply is also higher at dawn and in the summer, but the weekend and the presence of ethnic Romanians also increase slightly its size.

As to the demographic composition of the supply, 95% of the observed casual laborers (N=1290) were male, and two third of them were in their twenties or thirties.

Concerning ethnicity and citizenship, the two major groups (36% each) were the ethnic Hungarians from Hungary and the ethnic Romanians from Romania. The proportion of ethnic Hungarians from Romania was only about 10%, and of Gypsies, about 16% (the rest being unknown).

As to the economic conditions of the casual laborers, more than half of them wore 'normal' clothing (fitting to the everyday composition of urban male population), and only about 8% of them wore 'poor clothing', i.e. rags.

The informal labour market-place is composed of several small groups. 27% of the casual workers were standing in pairs, 38% of them, in groups consisting of three or four persons, and only 21% stood alone.

As to the characteristics of the market, both the total demand and the number of hired employees is higher among the unskilled than among the skilled workers, but the latter group is more likely to enter negotiations. These associations might mean that, while the informal labour market-place is dominated by unskilled offers and workers, the smaller, skilled segment is the more competitive. This evaluation is reinforced by the slightly higher value of the relation between the wage first asked to the wage first offered (WAGEWAR) and the more individualistic nature of the bargain (the proportion of professional recruiters is lower).

The wage level is significantly higher in the skilled segment compared to the unskilled one. This is obvious if we take into consideration the different human capital and productivity of the two groups. However, this difference might also be connected to the differences in the regional distribution of the jobs (Budapest has higher wages in every labor market segment and the unskilled labor is more concentrated in this local labor market) and social composition of the employees. As to this latter association, there is a significant difference between the ethnic composition of the two groups. Gypsies and the ethnic Romanians are over-represented among unskilled workers, while ethnic Hungarians from abroad are over-represented among skilled workers.

Equilibrium and wage on the informal labour market-place

There are various ways to estimate the level of success of the informal labour market-place. One option is to estimate the level of success of the market by the number of employees who were hired compared to the volume of the total supply.[6] In average, there were 2.5 employees hired in a successful contract. Multiplying this figure with the daily number of successful contracts, we arrive to the estimate of 45 employees hired on an average day. This is about 10% of the total average daily supply (there were about 120 potential employees observed per observation period). One in ten workers hired does not seem to us to be a very successful market, although we have no comparative data of the 'real' labor market or any other informal labour market-place.

Finally, the level of success of the bargains themselves was definitely high, 86% of the bargains finished with an agreement. This clearly shows that on an informal labour market-place, the main aim of both parties involved in the negotiations is to get to establish an agreement.

However, there must be the proper amount of demand and supply to have favorable circumstances for a successful negotiation. In other words, a market place should have a quasi-equilibrium between the volume of demand and supply. Figure 12.1 contains a crude proxy[7] to estimate the equilibrium of demand and supply.

Figure 12.1   The equilibrium of supply and demand by time periods

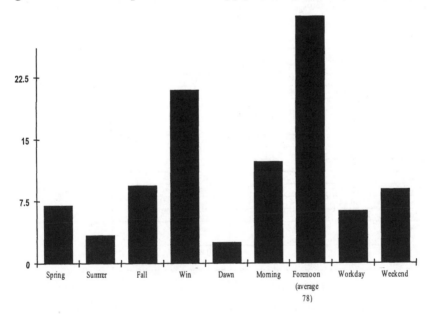

In the total sample (N=84), the average of the proxy was 7.46. This shows that the normal situation in the informal labour market-place is the oversupply of labor. Because we do not have comparable data on the unskilled labor supply in Budapest, we do not know whether this figure is similar to the supply/demand relation in the 'real' labor market or on other informal labor market-places. As to time periods, the labor oversupply is much lower at dawn and in the summer and much higher in the forenoon and in winter than in general.

Besides the level of success and equilibrium between demand and supply, the most crucial characteristic of a labor market is the level of wage. It is not by chance that in three-fourths of the cases in which there was any bargaining at all (53% of all offers), wage was the only issue of the bargain.[8]

To set the scene, we see from table 12.1 that the wage first asked was about 30% higher then the wage first offered.[9] The ultimate question of the bargain was what the finally accepted level of wage would be. To analyze the process of bargaining, we should exclude those cases in which there were no negotiations. However, if we compare the average wage first offered and first

Table 12.1   The basic characteristics and the determinants of wages bargain on the informal labour market-place

	Wage first offered	Wage first asked	Wage agreed	WAGEWIN	WAGEWAR	Wage first offered (in case bargaining)	Wage first asked (in case bargaining)
N	185	78	70	70	76	78	70
Average	1486	1873	1571	1.12	1.3	1447	1882
Median	1300	1600	1500	1.07	1.3	1300	1600
Mode	1200	1500	1500	1.00	1.3	1200	1500
OLS-Regression:							
Unskilled labor	- 0.36 [xxx]	- 0.34 [xxx]	- 0.44 [xxx]				
Length of job		- 0.27 [x]	- 0.26 [x]			- 0.29 [x]	
Fall	- 0.24 [x]					- 0.30 [x]	
Summer	-0.23 [x]						
Spring					- 0.36 [x]		
Morning	- 0.36 [x]						
Dawn	- 0.44 [x]						
Gypsy						0.30 [x]	
Ethnic Romanian			- 0.39 [xx]	- 0.42 [xx]			
Job in Budapest				0.29 [x]			

[xxx] = T-value significant on 0.0001 or below.
[xx] = T-value significant between 0.001 and 0.0002.
[x] = T-value significant between 0.05 and 0.002.
WAGEWIN = Wage accepted/Wage first offered.
WAGEWAR= Wage first asked/Wage first offered.

asked in general to those cases in which there was bargaining (last two columns, respectively) we see no significant difference. In other words, in the beginning phase of the bargaining process, the starting offers and expectations do not deviate from the general wage level. This shows that both bargainers and those who do not bargain have similar knowledge and attitudes.

As a result of negotiations, the agreed upon wage is a sum between the first offered and first asked wage, but much closer to that which was first offered. This shows, on the one hand, that it makes sense from the labour point of view to enter into bargaining. On the other hand, the result clearly in the favor of the employer shows the power relations and the role of over-supply on the informal labour market-place.

A large proportion of employees are able to strike a good bargain while a smaller subset of them are real losers.

Restricting our analysis to those cases in which negotiation took place (N=76), the WAGEWAR variable shows that the average wage asked is about one-third higher than the average wage first offered. Since the median and modal WAGEWAR values are similar to that of the average, we assume that in this respect, there are no major differences among the employees.

The fact that the value of WAGEWIN is lower than that of the WAGE-WAR, we can conclude that, while in average there is a 10% increase of the average wage due to the successful bargaining (N=70), the agreed upon wage remains below the original expectations of the workers. The median and mode being close to one shows again that for large groups there is even less gain in the course of bargaining, and, in consequence, a small group has larger gain from it.

Beginning with the three elements of the bargaining process (first three columns in the regression data from Table 12.1), one can see that the wage offered, asked and accepted for unskilled work is smaller. This clearly shows that the labour market value of the job is negatively associated with the level of education of the worker and that this fact is known to both actors of the labor market.

The length of the job has no influence on the wage first offered, but does have a low negative impact on the wage asked and accepted. This is a sign that temporary workers are willing to earn less per hour if they can get a longer job and vice versa.

Time periods influence only the level of wage first offered. In winter and in the late afternoon, the wage first offered is higher than any other time. This is partly due to the fact that these are the periods with the lowest amount of offers, but paradoxically also the periods in which the oversupply is the highest. Very likely these offers are 'deviant cases', i.e. a small sample of skilled workers who do urgent (indoor) jobs.

Finally, to be ethnic Romanian does not influence the level of wage first offered (i.e. no discrimination on behalf of the employer), but significantly decreases the accepted wage level. This might be a sign of the bad bargaining resources of ethnic Romanians (lack of proper Hungarian, different bargaining strategy.

As to the two summarizing bargaining proxies (last two columns in Table 12.1), three factors decrease WAGEWIN: to be ethnic Romanian, to have the job in Budapest and, for the season, to be spring. The first influence was already mentioned, the latter two show that the more offers there are, the more difficult it is to strike a good bargain.

The boldness at the beginning of the bargaining process (WAGEWAR) decreases according to the length of the job and when it is fall. The first point is again related to the rationality of the workers. A risky wage fight is not worth, it if there is a chance to get a longer job. The latter point might be a sign that the workers are more cautious about making a high first bid in the fall.

A Gypsy origin increases the boldness at the beginning of the bargaining process. This can be a culture-specific bargaining practice (to begin the bargain with a high bid) and/or can be the result of discrimination (the first offer is extremely low to discourage the potential employee to continue to bargain). However, neither of the previous alternative but non-exclusive explanations can be true, since neither the wage first asked nor the one first offered was decreased by the Gypsy origin.

Summary

Most of the hypotheses we developed as a result of the pre-research field-work and of the case studies were proven by the yearlong non-participant observation research. Most of the transactions of the informal labour market-place take place before 10 a.m. and the peak hours are before 7 a.m. (hypothesis 1). The informal labour market-place is seasonal, with the peak months in the spring and summer (hypothesis 2). The jobs are concentrated in Budapest and its vicinity (hypothesis 3). The typical work offered is made up of informal, unskilled jobs in construction (hypothesis 4) and the typical employee is a male (hypothesis 5d) who earns a low wage (hypothesis 6).

However, there are some features of the Moscow Square informal labour market-place that differ from what the pre-case studies suggested. First, even if there is a substantial number of ethnic Hungarians from Transylvania among those looking for work, the dominant groups are 'Hungarian Hungarians' and ethnic Romanians from Romania (see hypothesis 5a). One possible reason for misjudging the ethnic composition of the employees is rooted in the history of the Moscow Square. Ethnic Hungarians from Transylvania were likely the dominant group of employees in the beginning. However, their share has decreased, partly since they have become familiar with the Hungarian labor market in general and proved to be good workers. Thus, by 1995, they could afford to avoid the informal labour market-place. Another explanation may be that, by 1995, the Romanian temporary migration was dominated by ethnic Romanians following the tracks of their Hungarian predecessors. Finally, impoverishment and lasting unemployment in Hungary have pushed Hungarians onto the informal labour market-place.

Secondly, unlike what hypothesis 5c suggests, not every ethnic group of migrant labor has lower wages than those of locals. Only those of Romanian ethnicity (and in a special form, the Gypsies), have a wage disadvantage on the informal labour market-place.

Last but not least, despite what the media and common sense suggest, the Moscow Square informal labour market-place is far from being the major institution of allocation on the Budapest (let alone the Central Hungarian) labor market (hypothesis 7). Even labor market specialists were surprised when they learned that on an average day there are no more than about 20 successful transactions on the Moscow Square, and the total number of those seeking work, present between 6.00 and noon, is less than 300 persons. Nevertheless, the Moscow Square informal labour market-place is definitely very important, in that it offers informal jobs to a certain type of native and migrant, poorly educated and unemployed workers. Further, it serves as a convenient market for building contractors from North Buda and from the vicinity of Budapest. Nonetheless, its visibility (due to its spatial situation and media coverage) is far greater than its real importance.

Notes

1   The research was commissioned by the ILO/Japan Project and ICCR-Budapest. The first Hungarian version of the paper was written while I was a Visiting Mellon Fellow at the Institute for Human Sciences (Wien).

2   As to the source of data, in 1995, in 1997 and in 1998 we interviewed all the mayors (or a representative of the municipality) of the ca. 3100 Hungarian settlements, asking whether there were informal market(s) on their settlement. We supposed that local authorities must have fresh and reliable information concerning the existence and (if there is any) the activity of informal markets within the boundaries of their settlements. The self-administered questionnaire sought only the basic information on the number and composition of the informal labour market-places. We got approximately 800, 1200 and 1100 answers in 1995, 1997 and 1998, respectively. The data was weighted by location (six territorial units of Hungary, Budapest excluded), size and status (county capital, city or village) using the HCSO settlement data from 1995.

3   The longest job offered was a harvesting job for two weeks, and 10% of all offers covered jobs for at least fourteen days.

4   While in 38% of all observation periods there was no offer at all, the maximum number of offers was 16.

5   Both the mode and the median are significantly lower than the average (10 and 38, respectively).

6   Another option is to estimate the number of successful contracts, i.e. the number of bargains which were finished by an agreement. In average, three successful contracts were made per hours (six per observation periods). This means that on an average market day (between 6 a.m. and noon) there were 18 contracts sealed. The problem with this figure is that we cannot compare it to any other result since the 'real' labor market (controlled for region, type of job and branch) has no identical measures and there is no similar research of informal labour market-places in the literature.

7   The proxy was computed as follows: we divided the total supply (number of potential employees observed) with the number of potential jobs (number of effective offers multiplied with the number of hired employees). If the proxy is close to 1.0, than there is equilibrium on the informal labour market-place, if it is larger than 1.0, there is surplus labor, if lower than 1.0, there is a labor shortage on the informal labour market-place.

8   As to the rest of the bargains, the issues included meals, length of the job, and working conditions.

9   The difference between skilled and unskilled labor can give us a hint to what extent the wages we observed on the Moscow Square informal labour market-place fit to the wage level in general. We saw that the wage first offered of skilled labor is about one third higher than to that of unskilled labor. Figures of the National Labor Market Service shows that in 1998 the wage level of masons was about double of unskilled construction workers and two and half times higher that that of agricultural unskilled laborers (Sik 1998).

References

Bodnár, J. (1998), Assembling the Square: Social Transformation in Public Space and the Broken Mirage of the Second Economy in Postsocialist Budapest, *Slavic Review*, 57, no. 3 (Fall), pp. 399-415.

Hideg G., Grajczar, I. (1994), *A Moszkva téri emberpiac*, Kézirat, Budapest.

Katona, I. (1956), A baráber, *Ethnográfia* 1-2 sz., 13-26 o.

Katona, I. (1961), Munkaszervezeti formák és ideiglenes életközösségek idénymunkákon a kapitalizmus korában Agrártörténeti Szemle, 3-4 sz., 534-563 o.

Liebow, E. (1967), *Tally's Corner* Little, Brown and Company, Boston.

Reed, J. (1998), Hungary's Economy Lures Illegal Labor From the East, The *Wall Street Journal* Europe, April 27, 1998.

Sik, E. (1986/7), A casual labour market, *Angewandte Sozialforschung*, Jg. 14, No. 1, pp. 63-71.

Sik, E. (1998), Bérek a feketemunka piacán, in *50 éves a BKE*, BKE, Budapest, 133-149 old.

Appendix

	Total demand ($R^2 = 0.52$)	Effective demand ($R^2 = 0.48$)	Total supply ($R^2 = 0.47$)	Effective supply ($R^2 = 0.10$)
Dawn	0.70 [xxx]	0.71 [xxx]	0.65 [xxx]	0.37 [x]
Summer	0.36 [xxx]	0.33 [xx]	0.65 [xxx]	Non sign.
Morning	0.26 [xx]	0.25 [xx]	0.32 [x]	0.24 [x]
POLICE	- 0.19 [x]	Non sign.	0.26 [x]	
GOODWEA	0.19 [x]	Non sign.	Non sign.	0.18 [x]
			Non sign.	0.18 [x]

xxxx = T-value significant on 0.0001 or below.
xx = T-value significant between 0.001 and 0.0002.
x = T-value significant between 0.05 and 0.002.

PART IV
RUSSIA

Chapter 13

Russia

Alexander Nikulin[*]

The collapse of soviet economy

At the end of the 80s, simultaneously, the economic base of production enterprises of all economic forms in the USSR was weakened. The average annual increment of the GNP dropped from 3.7% in 1981-1985 to 2% in 1986-1990, of the production national income – from 3.2 to 1.3%, of industrial output – from 3.6 to 2.5%, of labour productivity – from 2.7 to 1.5%. At the same time, the growth of the monetary incomes of the population reached 9.2% as compared to former 4.2%. Especially sharp drop was witnessed in 1990, when the GNP decreased by 2.3%, as compared, 1989 figure, the national income – by 4%, while the monetary incomes of the population grew by 16.9%. The ratio between the state budget deficit and the GNP, which was 1.8% in 1985 and reached 8.6% in 1989, dropped to 4.1% in 1990. However, this reduction was mostly achieved due to the excessive tax pressure on enterprises and the population, and was definetely of a temporary character.

By 1991, the situation in the Soviet Union was characterized by the undermined confidence in the authorities, which rapidly aggravated, as their inability to cope with the economic, social and national problems became increasingly apparent. For the first time after the Civil War (1917-1921), the authorities were faced with either passive or quite active disobedience of a great part of the population and of the national, administrative-territorial, economic, and other structures. This disobedience, so far, did not bear an openly destructive character for the existing state structure, and was mainly expressed in an increase of all kinds of movements and of these demands changed becoming more radical demands, aimed at the extension of national, regional, social, political and economic rights and freedoms.

[*] Dr. coordinator of Peasant Studies and Agrarian Reforms Center, Moscow School of Social and Economic Sciences, Academy of National Economy, Moscow. E-mail: nik@msses.co.ru.

As is known, ten years ago (in August 1991) a part of the Union top leadership, torn apart by internal contradictions, made an attempt to preserve the old system with the help of extraordinary measures and military force. However, people's attitude to them was extremely negative, so their putsch failed. The old political system collapsed, followed by the disintegration of the Soviet Union. A new stage in the development of Russia as an independent state began. It had to solve basic problems of social and economic choice and state structure.

The shock therapy and the big privatization – 1992-1994

The leadership of Russia had chosen the way of overcoming economic devastation, which was earlier considered unacceptable – the shock therapy.

It was declared the only possible and short, although painful, way towards, stabilization of the economy and establishment of market relations. It was substantiated by the necessity to restore the commodity market, to consolidate the monetary and financial system, to achieve the market balance and carry out structural changes. It was expected to solve all these tasks on the basis of the financial stabilization achieved by rigid methods in the conditions of rapid liberalization of the economy.

The corner stone of the new policy was the immediate liberalization of prices for most of goods with few restrictions to the trade margins, so as to avoid a large gap between wholesale and retail prices. The new mechanism of price formation was to be accompanied by rigid financial policy, the reduction of state allocations, abolition of subsidies, limitation of credits, a brake on the growth of wages, the introduction of the added value tax, etc.

Such was a general scheme of the assumed course and results of the shock therapy. Moreover, it was expected to achieve economic equilibrium within several months, which meant that the shock from a sharp rise in prices and the lowering of living standards should have been short-lived. It was supposed that already in the second half of 1992 the living standards would begin to improve. However, in the course of shock reforms corrections, sometimes radical ones, had to be introduced into their scheme tasks and dates. It primarily referred to the liberalization of prices. The expectations that the growth of prices would be not greater than five-fold did not materialize. The leap of prices exceeded all forecasts. Within one year, the prices grew by 100, 200 and more and continued to grow.

In this case the mistake of the strategists of the shock reforms is evident. It stems from various factors and circumstances. First of all, the liberalization of prices took place in the conditions of a high level of monopolization of the economy. So the prices were not free, but exclusively high. Such prices cannot serve as a basis for market equilibrium.

In contrast the general rise of the nominal monetary incomes of the population in 1992 by approximately 10 times, the average wage in some sectors grew by 15-30 times. The growth of wages in non-budget spheres became practically uncontrolled. Within 1992, the gap between the wages of highly paid and underpaid groups of workers and employees grew by more than three times, and according to official data, their ratio was 1:16 and actually even greater (1:25). Instead of promised stabilization in the second half of 1992 and improvement of the wellbeing of the population, its mass impoverishment began with the simultaneous sharp social differentiation. This inevitably resulted in the growth of social dissatisfaction and tension, which began to permeate different strata of society, to differentiate them and, bring forth social economic and political instability.

Privatization process began in 1992, after the liberalization of prices, i.e. in the conditions of inflation and price leaps, with the so-called small privatization, that is, the privatization of trade and services establishments and enterprises producing cooperative goods. The auctions and similar forms of sale limited the particular of this privatization to the circle of large representatives of the speculative Mafia capital, or at best – work collectives of these enterprises. Speculative capital began to use privatized enterprises for the purposes of speculation. The transfer of enterprises into the hands of work collectives in the conditions of the production recession changed little in the results of their activity. Many of such enterprises found themselves on the brink of bankruptcy. Small privatization was followed by the second wave – the actual privatization in these economic spheres, i.e. the purchase of these enterprises by private owners.

Big privatization (of large enterprises) actually began in the second half of 1992, and, at first, assumed the character of a quick campaign of turning 5.615 enterprises selected for this purpose into joint-stock companies. The number and the branch affiliation of these enterprises rapidly expanded. So this process was followed by a stage of buying up of shares and their concentration in the hands of a relatively small group of people. Big privatization furnished grounds for the beginning of the process of forming future oligarchies.

On the whole, the privatization of all types did not led to the freedom of choice and the provision of equal opportunities for the existence of various forms of ownership and economic ventures. Probably that was why the 1992-1995 privatization failed to positively affect the general economic situation in Russia, although, in the course of it, the share of the state economy rapidly diminished. In 1994, the number of employees at non-state enterprises exceeded the number of employees at state ones, and in 1995 reached 60% of the gainfully employed population. Moreover, privatization became a means for drawing resources away from production, for money received from it was not used for production promotion. The absence of the friendly atmosphere of entrepreneurship can be largely explained by the existing tax policy and the striving to take as much as possible from the economic subjects, thus undermining not only the stimuli, but the direct possibilities for investments into production. At the same time, this fiscal policy and economic situation again stimulated the development of shadow economy.

With the legalization of private entrepreneurship, the scale of the shadow economy grew significantly. Situation when there was no normally functioning market and the state mostly lost its economic control functions brought forth a wide spectre of new informal ties and mechanisms. These existed alongside old ones, formed in Soviet times, which received new stimuli to the development, during perestroika. According to statistical data, the shadow economy supplied 25% of the GDP, while in trade, its turnover reached 40%, in individual services to the population – 60%, in housing services – 18% of the cost of registered services. Latent wages in 1993 amounted to 5%, in 1994 – to 9%, in 1995 – to 10% of the gross domestic product. The correlation of the revenues and expenditures of the population showed that in 1993 the expenditures exceeded the revenues by one trillion rubles, in 1994 – by 22.2 trillion rubles, in 1995 – by 53.6 trillion rubles. According to the data of the Central Bank of Russia, the annual outflow of capital from the country was $10-15 billion, and according to the Interior Ministry – $24 billion.

The 1995-1997 stagnation period and the 1998 financial crisis

From 1996 on, the Russian government was mainly concerned with the task of ensuring the stability of the ruble rate at any cost, that is by outside borrowing and through monetary policy towards the country's industry. These measures were expected to bring about economic growth. However, three years passed, accompanied by a further economic slump, non-payment of salaries and social benefits, introduction of barter into economic relations on a wide scale – with no signs of a future revival.

The political situation also looked gloomy. Although president Yeltsin had to stop the Chechen war (1995-1996) in order to win the coming presidential elections, he himself had already turned into a weak person hardly able to run the country. Oligarchic clans – groups of the most powerful Russian bureaucrats and bankers – tried to share in his authority pursuing their egoistic interests. Meanwhile, in the second half of 1998, Russia was shaken by a severe financial crisis. That crisis was a part of the world financial crisis that, at the turn of 1998, spread over Indonesia, South Korea and Japan. In August 1998, the crisis reached Russia, then moved on to Brazil and Argentina. In Russia, the financial crisis manifested itself in a sharp devaluation of the national currency (the real rate of the Russian ruble fell by almost 60%); the crash of the banking system; considerable reduction of production volumes; the negative balance. The crisis took on a very severe form, for lack of any structural reforms in the major economic sectors. Among other reasons, there were the extreme dependence on short-term foreign investments, the sharp reduction of prices of crude oil, the main item of Russian export, and the low level of tax collection. To a great extent, the depth of the crisis was caused by the mistakes of the Russian government that underestimated the potential consequences of the Asian crisis for the Russian economy. The economic crisis in Russia worsened at the turn of 1998, and a noticeable fall of production started already in May. The financial crash mirrored the weakness of the real economy sector, as well as the lack of co-ordination in the budget, monetary and banking policy. The default on the inner debt and temporary suspension of payments on several types of Russia's external debt led to a government crisis, Sergei Kirienko's cabinet of ministers resigned, and a new government with E. Primakov at the head was formed.

The economic growth in 1999-2000

The ruble devaluation after August 1998, and shortly after, the sharp increase of oil prices in the world markets were used to advantage by the new Russian government to revive and boost the Russian economy. As a result, the post-crisis economic indices in Russia were mostly positive. The GDP grew by 7.6%. However, this only helped to return economic production volumes to the level of 1994. At the same time, Russia's external economic indices appeared quite solid: the gold reserves more than doubled in one year and reached a record level for the past decade – 28 billion dollars. The federal budget finally entailed no deficit, inflation was relatively mild and manageable. In 1999-2000, economic growth was accompanied by a real increase of the people's incomes. However, neither in wages or savings the Russian population reached the level of the pre-crisis 1997. Thus, the average per capita income amounted to 86% of the 1997 level, wages and salaries – 91%, pensions – 80%.

At the same time, by the end of the year 2000 there arose the first concerns about Russia's further economic development. Oil prices seemed to be going down. Russia had not seriously started any drastic structural reforms in economy. Neither had it found any new niches for external economic activities in the world markets, even after the considerable devaluation of the ruble after 1998. Besides, the so-called 'unfavorable investment climate' still persisted in Russia.

On the eve of the new millenium, many social issues remained unsolved too. These include, first of all, the problem of inequality in income distribution and, as a result, mass poverty.

Beginning from 1992, there was a sharp polarization of wealth and poverty in Russian society. In 1999, 20% of wealthy Russian citizens received 47% of all revenues, including 38% of the total volume of paid salaries, 27% of social transfers, 70% of property revenues and 62% of business revenues.

Officially, in Russia, people with incomes below the 'poverty level' are considered to be poor, i.e. the survival minimum corresponds to the price of the 'consumer basket'.

In the 90s, the years 1992 and 1993 were the most unfavorable in terms of poverty. At that time, the number of poor people increased because of the liberalization of prices, when the population's real incomes decreased on average by 40%. In 1999, the number of poor people increased following the 1998 crisis.

In 1992, the minimal salary amounted to 33% of the survival minimum. In 1995, this level dropped further to 14%. In 1999, the minimal salary equaled 8% of the survival minimum. In such spheres as agriculture, healthcare, education and culture, about 60% of workers' pay was below the survival level.

The minimal pension also remained below the level of the pensioner's survival minimum. In 1992, the minimal pension amounted to 85% of the survival minimum. In 1999, it was only 45%.

The low pay level is the main reason for the working population's poverty. In 1999, the average pay in Russia was 158% of the survival minimum.

It is also noteworthy that the official statistics of salaries and wages do not reflect the reality of the population's income. In post-Soviet Russia the practice of informal payment for work done on the basis of oral agreement between the employer and worker became quite widespread. Thus, the problem of raising work pay and bringing it out into the open also remains one of the most important tasks of the Russian economy under reform.

Chapter 14

Informal economy of rural households: restructuring of family networks and strategies

Olga Fadeeva[*], Alexander Nikulin and Valerij Vinogradsky[**]

This chapter is based on the materials of the budget analysis of 34 village families in two settlements – stanitsa Privolnaya (Krasnodar region) and Povolgie village Danilovka (the Saratov region). In each selected family the budgets were drawn regularly in the course of one year – from September 1, 1999 till August 31, 2000. Considering the small volume of sampling, the composition of the families for analysis in each village was selected according to the existing age parameters and the level of their material well being. In addition, we attempted to represent the main professional groups, reflecting the specific structure of jobs in each village.

The specific nature of our sampling does not allow to make full-fledged (statistically valid) inter-regional comparisons, to determine the impact of climatic conditions, of the existing markets, of the settlement structure, cultural peculiarities and employment traditions on the level of life of Kuban and Saratov families. Actually, we did not set such goals, especially because we believe that the differences in communities are caused not so much by the regional factors, but rather by the situation in the local labor market. Our research[1] shows that today the economic and social life of a village community to a great extent depends on the level of production and the economic situation in the reorganized collective farm (the former kolkhoz or sovkhoz).

The wide range of factors affecting the economic behavior of village families and, correspondingly, the evident variety of adaptation ways in

---

[*] Dr., researcher, Institute of Economy and Organisation of Industrial Production, Russian Academy of Science, Novosibirsk.
[**] Professor, Leading Research Fellow, Institute of Social and Economic Problems of Rural Development, Russian Academy of Sciences, Saratov.

families to the influence of these factors, given the limited volume of sampling, predetermine the approach where each family is considered as a separate 'artifact', studied both with qualitative (deep interviews) and quantitative methods (budget analysis).

The Kuban stanitsa

Stanitsa Privolnaya is, by Russian standards, quite a big settlement. As of March 1, 2000 it had over 2100 houses with 7705 inhabitants.

The chief employer in the stanitsa is a big agricultural enterprise – a shareholding company (AO), which in 1997 got the status of a Breeding Factory.

The relative variety of jobs and potential accessibility of natural resources (a broad range of Azov estuary salt lakes, rich in fish and wild-fowl) create a reasonable space of economic opportunities, and the degree of using them characterizes the families' 'income' strategies. According to the prevailing source of income, the majority of families can be classified into the following three groups:

- families with predominant employment in agricultural production and processing;
- families not employed in agricultural production that can be divided into those employed on the territory of the stanitsa and shuttle migrants (in our sample, they work in the gas industry on the expedition-shift basis);
- families living on the natural resources of the area (professional poaching and 'amateur' fishing).

Intermediate, combined variants are possible, too, when family members are employed in different spheres of income earning. The family homestead can be considered as an important income source (not necessarily in the form of money) for the majority of the Kuban families. The volumes and specialization of family farms are to a great extent linked to the place of the main (formal) employment.

Our research shows that efficient family farming is impossible without a stable link with big farming.

Contradictions of the symbiosis[2]

At the beginning of 2000, the total number of people employed by the pro-duction and non-production units of the said enterprise amounted to 812 people. The assets of the Breeding Factory, in addition to those which are indispensable for big production (machine-and-tractor station, garage, electric workshop, forage shop), include a brickyard, 3 mills, a cannery, a bakery, a sanatorium, a House of culture (with a picture gallery), a hospice, kindergarten, cafeteria and a summer camp.

During almost 30 years, the BF (first under the name of 'kolkhoz', and later, since 1992 – as a new legal person, AOZT, a limited shareholding company) has been among the best farms of the region. It has high results in the production of grain, milk and meat and in the processing of agricultural products. As of March 1, 2000 the farm had 12250 ha of cultivated land. Besides grain and corn, they also grow sugar beet, sunflower, fruits and vegetables (potatoes, onions, carrots and tomatoes).

By the year 2000 the enterprise had mostly managed to overcome the crisis of the mid-90s. Their work had become highly efficient, the farm preserved a good dairy herd of 1600 milk cows, restored the size of the pig herd (over 4000 pigs). According to the report data of the AO, in 1999 the grain crop was 50.1 c/ha, the yield of milk per cow – 5222 kg, profits amounted to 2883 rubles per 1 ha of arable land, the overall cost effectiveness of production was 66%.

At the same time, the restoration of the pre-reform volumes of production was accompanied by a gradual reduction of employment in the main branches, which was caused by higher productivity rates. In the recent 8 years, the number of workers in crop-growing teams has dropped almost two times; on the cattle farms, the number of workers has dropped by a quarter.

Redundancies at the enterprise have led to the appearance of unemployed people in the stanitsa.[3] The ensuing tension in the labor market to a certain extent strengthened the positions of the farm leaders in their relations with the subordinates, allowed them to hold in check the growth of salaries and dictate their terms to the workers under the threat of redundancy.

> *The people sacked from the kolkhoz stay at home, without work! Look at our neighbor – he spent 3 years at home. And later, with great effort, became a cattle-yard worker. For a bribe... And beware, don't make a mistake, don't steal, don't get caught – or, who knows, they may sack you. That's how they speak with you in the kolkhoz: 'You don't like it, you aren't happy with the salary – leave this place!'.*

On average, the workers of the AO make about 900 rubles per month. This modest figure is in sharp contrast with the high economic indices of the enterprise. Thus, one can say that one of the factors of effective economic activity at this enterprise is economizing on payment for the production workers' labor and their actual discrimination.

However, as we will show later, the actual pay is far from being the main stimulus for working on the farm or in the field. The people are 'retained' by closeness to the resources and opportunities of the farming enterprise, which indirectly, through work on the individual farms, bring additional incomes to these workers and their family members.

The enterprise leadership's financial policy in the recent years has been aimed to gradually reduce the share of various forms of payment in kind and to introduce full money settlements. The company stopped using the coupon system, which was widely practiced in the mid-90s to supply the workers with bread, milk and butter at a cut price; barter settlements between the farm and the workers are being reduced in every possible way.

In the old times, they used to give us milk, butter, grain. And the price was reasonable, so we could afford it. Now – it's over! Now we cannot afford even grain. Some girls stopped buying sugar – there's no money. Earlier, they used to pay our dividends on the shares either with piglets, or sugar or other. And now, they've stopped everything.

Besides food products, the shareholders received about 200 rubles as dividends. The size of a land share is 4.56 ha. If we sum up the profit from selling the cut-price products at market prices and the paid-up dividends, we see that the land leased to the AO brought its owners, on average, about 2000 rubles, which amounts only to 15% of the claimed land profitability. The owner can sell his/her share only at the inside exchange at a hugely undervalued rate (as of the time of this study, the share was valued just at 3500 rubles).

In recent years, the management of the enterprise has shown some new trends, which considerably affect the relationship between the employees and the managers (owners).

First: There has been an establishment of real owners of the AO, interested in raising production efficiency and toughening control over the safety of property and products. The director and several chief experts, running the departments, have become real masters of the enterprise. Concentration of power resulted in their attempt to impose upon the workers standard terms of employment, under which they would get a certain remuneration and some resources for individual farming (to keep poultry, a couple of pigs for the family, not for sale) to prevent stealing. In reality, there is a peculiar 'vicious circle': low pay forces the people to seek other forms of material support, the legally allotted fodder is not enough for productive individual farming, they cannot produce fodder themselves for lack of land and special machinery. Thus, the people are doomed to illegal 'borrowing' of resources from the enterprise, which allows them to provide their families and themselves with the habitual (high, by rural Russian standards) life level.

*Earlier, it was possible to steal, and now the fields are guarded by militia. But
we try to take little, not to get caught... Earlier, we could take two or three sacks
of fodder, now – barely one. Sometimes I say to the team-leader: 'For God's
sake, give me something, I have no food for the pigs at home!' And he says:
'Take it, but if we catch you, you will be fired immediately.' So, it's getting worse
and worse with fodder...*

Second: The possibility of half-legal redistribution of the 'common (earlier – kolkhoz, now – shareholding company's) pie' in favor of family budgets has turned from the general standard into the privilege of the few 'close
to the feeding-trough', having scarce resources at their disposal. It became
dangerous for the average worker to steal on the same scale – the risk of losing one's job became too great. This complicated the position of those who
had no direct access to the 'resource opportunities' of the big farm.

*It has become difficult to get fodder. Impossible to steal... Can't exchange for
vodka, as before. Now you are served only for money. Formerly, you could get
even petrol for vodka; not any more.*

Tactics of stealing have changed, too: it is not very productive to make a
deal with an 'ordinary' farm-yard worker or combine driver – drink with
him to load into the car a couple of sacks of fodder or seeds. To make one's
position safe and regularly use the shadow channel, one needs the support of
close 'bosses' (for example, the head of the farm or vet doctor, who do not
belong to the group of proprietors and are themselves interested in guiding
the resource rivulet towards their homestead). The ways to approach the
'bosses and important persons' are quite varied: providing small and big
services (giving a lift, fixing something, organizing 'on one's own initiative'
the delivery and unloading of fodder, sharing something of one's own), joint
feasts, trips and business, etc. This helps to construct – as one of the respondents put it – 'a business atmosphere', conducive to mutually advantageous
contacts, materializing in fodder and money from selling what was stolen.

We will show how this mechanism works on the example of one of the
most well off families in the Kuban sample. The husband works as a tractor
driver on a farm in the AO, the wife keeps house. For the whole year of work
the husband earned in the 'kolkhoz' only 11000 rubles, while the stock of
fodder and hay made with the help of various 'business' ties allowed the
family to raise and sell 2 calves and 17 pigs for over 62000 rubles. A sum of
5600 rubles was earned by selling 2 tons of grain and 4 containers of sunflower seeds. With all this money they bought a car and finished the construction of a house. To a certain degree, such behavior of the employee,

whose work is systematically underpaid, may be understood as an attempt to restore the 'suppressed' justice. In addition, such actions are fully justified by those around him: the 'kolkhoz property' was not wasted, the family managed to put it to good use and earn 'fairly'.

It is worth pointing out once again that this 'symbiotic' coexistence of the Share-holding Company and individual farm in the past few years has been widely attacked by the top managers (at the same time – chief proprietors) of the enterprise.

The only accessible to all way of acquiring part of the kolkhoz crop is the 'voluntary-compulsory' work: weeding and harvesting vegetables (potatoes, tomatoes, carrots, beet, onions and cabbage). People do this work, substituting their manual labor for expensive special machinery with the purpose not so much to earn a symbolical sum, but rather to get a maximum natural compensation, considerably higher than the set standards.

Here are some arguments in favor of such 'vegetable work off' that a woman from the mud-baths, who never refuses to help the Company in the 'struggle for crops', gave us:

> *The kolkhoz resources help me out in a big way. Last year, my vegetable crop was very poor, because there was no watering. So, everything that I stored in the basement I procured from the kolkhoz, when I worked there in the vegetable field. I brought all of it from there – tomatoes, cucumbers, cabbages, potatoes, beet and carrots. The kolkhoz has no cash to pay us for this work, and we are not interested to these 'peanuts'. So I'd rather steal from the kolkhoz as many products as I need. Enough even to spare. Many people do it in the stanitsa...*

The analyzed budgets show how 'heavy' the baskets and sacks secretly carried and removed from the kolkhoz vegetable field are. Six families, that were actively involved in this business, brought home in total 1 ton of cabbage, carrots and beet, 250 kilos of tomatoes, 100 kilos of potatoes, 100 kg of cucumbers and 100 kg – onions. To note, the standard volumes of preserves for the winter in an ordinary Kuban family are quite impressive: during one year the average housewife made about 200 liters of jam and fruit compote, 300 liters of vegetable preserves.

Reduction of the possibility to provide for the individual farm, a sharp growth of prices on forage, younger poultry and cattle, petrol and gas led to consolidated social inequality. This inequality was fixed between those whose position and status in the 'symbiotic' structure allowed them to build up their homestead, and those who had to give up breeding pigs and poultry even for home consumption. First of all, in this situation the biggest loss was suffered by the low-paid workers of the budget sphere and other organizations, not connected with agriculture. For them, the homestead could no longer serve as an additional source of income, their families had to cut expenses. And their consumption pattern was getting closer and closer to urban families, considerably limiting the consumption of quality products (in the first place, meat and meat products).

Here are the opinions of the housewives from families whose members were not employed by the AO or had absolutely nothing to do with it.

The Director of a picture gallery:

> *Our homestead is small – 20 hens. My husband does not steal, this is why we cannot expand, and it is pointless to buy fodder (50-70 rubles per sack), breeding pigs will not pay off. And it is not so easy to buy fodder, in the old days one could do it in exchange for home-brew... The homestead is profitable only for those who can get some fodder. For example, our neighbors work on the farm, so their homestead is big.*

Traditionally, the chief product of the homestead in the stanitsa has been pork. The post-reform crisis of the 90s taught the villagers to separate the produced foodstuffs into those for themselves and for sale. They began breeding pigs mostly for the market (leaving just a little for themselves), while at home they ate mostly poultry meat, for which they bred 200 or 300 hens, ducks and geese. At the end of the decade, this proportion changed. The old model was preserved only in the families employed in agriculture (7 families in our sample). On average, each of these families took on 8-10 piglets for fattening and bred up to 200-250 younger poultry. The money income from the homestead in 5 families amounted to 8-10 thousand rubles a year (or about a third of the family's overall money income), and in two cases this level reached 20 and 60 thousand rubles. Contrary to this, in the group of 10 families not engaged in agricultural production, pigs were kept only in two of them and the number of poultry was, as a rule, limited to 50 or 70. They sold in the market mostly the surplus of eggs, berries or fruit, this is why their money income from the homestead was rather low (500-700 rubles a year, or just 1-3% of their budget income.)

The effectiveness and versatility of network resources

At the same time, as our findings show, the formal alienation from the resources of the enterprise does not always present an absolute barrier for the development of the family mini-farm and raising the family's well being. A developed system of inter-family exchanges comes to their rescue. These exchanges, in the form of compensation, provide for some 'remote' (non-agrarian) families an indirect access to cheap resources and illegally received products.

This is how a respondent from Kuban defines the social effectiveness of this practice:

> *Although we do not visit each other as often as before, we help one another. We share what we have, otherwise we will not survive. It's necessary, especially now. In the old times – we used to live on what we stole ourselves, and now – we only ask those who have access: 'hey, brother, give me some of this, can I have some of that!.. I will pay you back when I can'. And you keep begging like this! My Godmother works somewhere in a good place. So I would say: 'Let's exchange something, it'll be good for you and for me!..' And so we go around and beg. And help one another. This happens because of our need. Do you think I would go to my Godmother to beg for corn flour?! My chickens have hatched, I have nothing to feed them with – so I go and bow!..*

Such exchanges can be based on kindred relations, purely business ties involving an exchange of various services, and sometimes – 'amorous ties', accompanied by regular deliveries of foodstuffs, as a rule, by men working in the kolkhoz or other 'privileged' places, to their beloved.

Exchanges between relatives, as a rule, lead to the formation of family co-operatives of a kind, that bring together various resources and opportunities (money, material, time) of several families. Often, co-operatives are formed by parents (pre-pension age) and their children, busy at work from morning till night. Having a lot of time at their disposal, pensioners go to their daughters' or sons' poultry yards to prepare feed for the birds and pigs, or keep the cattle bought by their children at their place. The children, in their turn, provide the family farm with fodder and younger animals and birds, make arrangements about veterinary services, using for this the opportunities of their working place or the numerous useful ties.

Sometimes, the home farms of the parents and the children are separate, however, the exchange flows of money, fodder, labor efforts from one farm to another optimize the 'partners' actions. For example, the son, working on the cattle farm of the Company, 'hired' his mother and grandmother to feed and look after a dozen piglets during the day. He regularly brought his mother combined fodder for her hens and ducks, so that she had surplus produce and every month she was able to sell 20-30 dozen eggs (which gave her in the course of the year 2000 rubles of additional income).

One family shared with a shop assistant they knew sunflower seeds and vegetables, which they brought from the AO, to express their gratitude for having sold them goods on credit (payment was postponed till the end of the month). Our analysis of budget notes shows that such practice of giving informal credit has recently become quite popular. They buy goods on credit (recorded debt) from a private seller they know in the market and the 'kolkhoz' stall, at the chemist's and department store. To a great extent, people are compelled to do this, especially those with scanty means, living 'from payday to payday'. Sometimes, on great festive occasions (birthdays, weddings, etc) even well off families resort to this measure. Clearly, these services are not accessible to every stanitsa inhabitant. In the first place, one must be acquainted with the shop assistants, have their trust, and the better they know each other, the bigger the amount of the opened 'credit line'.

If they know me, trust me – I will get goods at the shop on record. I used to constantly buy razor blades for my son. Others do the same – we help each other. When I was working at the 'kolkhoz' stall, I used to write down in the book the names of AO workers who did not pay for the buys, later their debts were deducted from their pay. At the market I often buy on credit. They give me things, because they know that I will certainly return the money. I've been living here for 16 years, people know me.

Often, an exchange of niceties takes place, when people 'pleasant' to each other (neighbors, colleagues, relatives and God parents) supply each other with extras of food products, seedlings and saplings, things that they no longer need and other goods. On average, the volume of such food supplies in one year per family is estimated at 2500-3000 rubles (which amounts to one third of the family's expenses on buying food).

In the stanitsa, people carefully observe marking birthdays, christenings, seeing-off to the Army, weddings and others. This unshakable cultural norm supports the very network of relations and its spirit. Each of these events has its own etiquette, including, among other things, the price and type of presents, and there may be up to 30 people celebrating at table. Although many respondents noted a considerable decrease of the scope of festivities in the past years, expenses on buying presents and organizing celebrations were quite considerable in half of the studied families (from 4000 to 8000 rubles a year, or 7-10% of expenses in the family budget). In this place it is customary to give lavish presents and make feasts in honor of children, even very small, thus indirectly expressing respect for their parents.

Being part of a social network not only secures possibilities of mutually advantageous exchanges of material goods and services. Personal ties and useful acquaintances turn out to be indispensable in matters of provision of favorable employment, all kinds of mediation, in particular – finding and creating clientele for a home-based worker. Thus, one of our respondents was able to support herself by sewing and restoring clothes, repairing shoes and sewing machines at home only due to a stable circle of clients among her neighbors and acquaintances, who, in their turn, referred to her new clients, providing their own advertising. Payment for her work also bore a mark of 'non-formality'. The seamstress fulfilled many orders on credit, and in many cases she did not specify the time of payment. Many times, people paid her by 'barter settlements'. For regular service to her neighbors and her family members, every month the seamstress had 9 l of milk, 1.5 l of sour cream and 2 kg of cottage cheese. According to the 'service for service' policy, her clients-artisans (the carpenter, the stove-maker) made new window frames and repaired the stove for her.

In our estimation, the material effect from using the 'network resource' (help given, presents and credits) amounted on average to 14% of the total income in the family budget. Against this background it is necessary to mention two families, for whom network exchanges and support became literally the basis of survival in difficult, practically deadlock life situations. In the first case, it is the family of a widow with three children, one third of whose money-natural income was of 'network' nature.

In the second case, the housewife was unemployed for 8 months. At the same time, her husband left her and she had to support three children by herself and pay for her son's tuition in the Sports Academy in Krasnodar. Her need forced the woman to 'turn over' her land share to the AO. The 'beheaded' family survived at the expense of the homestead, odd jobs and the assistance provided by acquaintances and close people to this housewife with a special gift of communication.

Sometimes friends, sometimes God parents would stand a treat. Well, they gave us some fish, we fried it. Sometimes I exchange something to have food on the table. A neighbor would give us a jar of milk. Here – I would beg, there – exchange, I try to avoid expenses, try not to buy much in the market. Friends, acquaintances, God parents – they are still around. In the time I've been living here so many ties have been established. There's no getting away from that! Here, there – somebody would give us something.

Special support was given to this family by the 'amorous' ties. A close friend of the housewife brought her, all in all, more than 6 tons of combined fodder, she sold one fourth of that, and the rest was used to feed piglets. He helped his friend several times with money. Others also rendered assistance: to organize her son's seeing off to the Army, friends collected almost two thousand rubles. They also raised money to buy clothes for her younger daughters. Besides, the housewife managed to borrow a total of five thousand rubles to cover the expenses, connected with her son's final exams and call to military service. As a result, the outside help provided the family with a third of all kinds of revenues and she survived the hard times. The son finished his education (the budget shows that 40% of all the family means was spent on the three children's education), the housewife found a new job, the father returned to the family.

Far from everybody can boast of such a 'talent' for survival. It takes the person a lot of energy to constantly keep up the existing network of relations, alternating the 'pleading' and 'giving' roles. One must keep and develop the image of a 'useful friend', by one's appearance and way of life demonstrating to those around that one is coping with difficulties, that one is reliable. The following words of our respondent can be considered to be the life credo of a 'network person': *'Every day I clutch to life, and every day I must survive – there is no other way out.'*

The significance of network resources is most obviously demonstrated by the situation of those people to whom they are barely accessible. Among them there are, first of all, migrants, immigrants from a different culture. Even after living for decades in a new place, they sometimes find it hard to settle down in the local community and are left out from many network relations. The local community is particularly solid and has inner solidarity. To become part of it one needs to prove and present oneself. For example, to occupy a high post in the AO or get a promising job, to receive recognition by one's skills and craftsmanship, to attract people by personality traits, credibility and empathy.

The Povolgie village

Danilovka village is situated 100 km away from Saratov and 14 km away from the region center. It has the population of 1000 people (380 homesteads), about half of them (478 people) are able-bodied persons. Out of that number, only 56% of villagers at least have a permanent job. Danilovka is a typical example of a depressed rural labor market with a chronic deficit of jobs.

Historically, the chief employer in the village was the kolkhoz. The reforms that started at the end of 1991 split the collective farm into two parts. The then head of the farm suggested to his team a strategy of drastic market reforms, which was not supported by the majority of workers. Then, in protest, the head of the farm resigned from his post, left the kolkhoz and organized his own farm. Three dozen most qualified workers and experts followed suit, taking along the best machinery as their property shares. Later, these people established an association of peasant homesteads and farms, which has been successful all these years. The process of apportionment of small farms from the former kolkhoz continued until the mid-90s and, as a result, 90 people left it. Today, 59 farms are registered on the territory of the village, only 40 of which are actually working. These farms work 2538 ha of land, while the collective farm owns 4700 ha.

The agricultural enterprise, weakened after the re-division of property (the kolkhoz was transformed into a limited partnership, and later – into an agricultural production co-operative – APC) for a few years, by inertia, continued to stay afloat, spending the remaining funds on food and enjoying financial support of the local authorities. But the previously accumulated potential did not last long, and during the last 5 years, the volume of production could no longer secure stable pay for the farm workers. The monetary payment system was gradually replaced by natural allotments of grain, flour, meat, butter, sour cream and other products.

Employment in the kolkhoz was beginning to be considered as the right of access to the kolkhoz resources. In expert estimation, about a third of the crop started pouring from the kolkhoz fields, legally or illegally, into private 'corn-bins', thus bringing closer the time of the final bankruptcy of the enterprise. Cash payments to ordinary workers were made only in extreme cases, which were preceded by special agreements with the leadership.

All this time, cattle slaughter was one of the few ways to keep up the liquidity of the enterprise and to finance sowing and harvesting. It also helped prolong the period of 'sluggish agony'. Now, the enterprise has no more pig-breeding and sheep-breeding. The dairy herd has dropped four times (from 600 to 150 cattle). To compare, the 'private' herd is three times bigger than the 'collective' one.

By the end of the 90s, another enterprise on the territory of the village had gone bankrupt: the affiliate region poultry farm. This even more complicated the situation in the local labor market.

Actually, 'normal' (in the traditional sense of the word) jobs in Danilovka could be found only in the non-productive sphere (education and culture, medical care, trade, post and communications). These jobs, as a rule, guarantee their holders stable employment and payment in cash, which raised them to the level of highly sought for. The rural school had most of the deficit jobs. On the staff of the school there are 35 people (mostly, women), and, in our estimation, there are even more people on the waiting list to get a job there.

As the influence of the former kolkhoz continued weakening, there began a resurrection of elements of rural self-organization and self-management. In the mid-90s, when the kolkhoz had practically ceased to participate in keeping up the infrastructure, the problem of water supply in the village had become quite critical. Money was needed to repair the water-supply system and, eventually, it was repaired with individual donations of the village inhabitants. They went even farther: at the general meeting it was decided to establish a special reserve fund to maintain the water-supply system in the village. In certain cases, concerning problems of general interest (roads, schools, etc), money was allotted under the powerful pressure of public opinion or by initiative from the most successful farmers.

The obvious slump in the village economy brought about the degradation of traditional behavioral standards and the emergence of a new marginal-criminal group. Thirty-five people in the village have previous convictions. The stealing of cattle and poultry, grain and non-ferrous metals has acquired a mass scope, but is very rarely taken to court. The villagers prefer to restore justice themselves, without the participation of the authorities.

Peculiarities of the Saratov sample: woman as the head of the family

Most of the sample (10 families out of 17) consisted of families working in the budget sphere. In the majority of such families, constant pay was earned only by the women, working in schools. Whereas their husbands, in most cases, were reckoned to be working at the collective enterprise (the former kolkhoz), in real fact, during the whole period of budget analysis they were their wives' dependants. Although the received 'budget' pay (the only one in the family) in such families was rather low (from 500 to 1000 rubles per month) and definitely insufficient to meet all the family needs, these families with a guaranteed monthly cash income undoubtedly had advantages over those employed purely in agriculture.

This is clearly seen on the example of the other group of respondents. In 3 families, the husbands worked as machine-operators or drivers in the old or new agricultural co-operative, and their wives kept house. In these cases, and in another similar one, when none of the spouses had a permanent job, their family budgets had no regular income from the production sphere. In 2 out of 4 such families, the main sources of income were disability pensions and children allowances.

A relatively satisfactory situation was found in the families of pensioners, whose stable income provided them with the 3rd-5th positions in the rating of families per personal income.

On the example of the Saratov village, one can easily see how the devaluation of labor in agriculture broke the habitual tenor of life. The working man, against his will, was deprived of his traditional role of the main family bread-winner. His pay in the 'kolkhoz' became virtual, invisible. *'It's not that my husband gets no pay. But his pay is just on paper. The pay is good, but we don't see it.'*

According to our data, in 10 cases the wife earned more than her husband, and in 5 families this difference was 5-8-fold. Having acquired this unnatural financial independence, the woman shouldered the responsibility for the support and survival of the family, pushing the man away from solving financial problems. The latter ceased to manage money, making his wife the principal manager of the family budget.

> *In our family it's mostly me who makes money. My husband knows how much I make. If he finds an odd job, he tells me, gives me all the money. Because I pay for everything, I buy all the food. Oftentimes he doesn't even know the prices. When he makes some money by chance, he asks me: 'Buy me a can of beer, some coffee, cigarettes'. I have to buy it. Sometimes I say there is no money, he'll have to wait. My husband waits until there's some cash. He has no pocket money. I say to him: 'If you earned something, then you could ask'. He stopped asking me.*

The woman's employment in a budget organization is highly valued. Sometimes her more or less stable position stops the family from cardinal changes.

Unemployment among women in its seriousness is quite comparable with the problem of men's job placement. There is practically no work left for women in the former kolkhoz. All the jobs at the school, club and nurse's post are already taken, so novices have no chance. In addition, the situation is made worse by the absence of kindergartens, closed six years ago. If the family with small children has no parents or grandparents ready to take upon themselves looking after grandchildren, the young mother, despite her education and qualification, is doomed to become a housewife (probably for good).

The agony of the symbiosis

We can say that our respondents managed to overcome the negative consequences of canceling cash pay at the kolkhoz quite quickly. There was a quick, though painful, reorientation of family efforts towards increasing the volumes and capacity of homesteads mainly due to 'pumping over' the resources of the collective farm.

The ensuing breakage in the 'symbiotic' mechanism of family-farm coexistence because of the weakened potential of the latter marked the beginning of a new stage in the adaptation of Danilovka families. This stage began when people stopped receiving grain and grain by-products as natural pay and the people consequently had to sharply reduce pork production based on grain fodder and poultry farming on their farms. Thus, in 2000 each Danilovka yard had, on average, just 0.5 piglet, 5 hens and 1 goose.

In 1992 we did not worry about fodder for the cattle. We were sure that we could go to the kolkhoz and earn this money and fodder. In the kolkhoz every earned ruble went a long way. We even sold wheat, bought with that ruble. Now that they stopped giving us grain, we reduced the number of pigs, stopped keeping sheep – in 1992 we had 16 of them. We used to keep a lot of poultry, now – very few. They need grain, but there's no grain.

Because of fodder defecit and the urgent need for money the optimal pattern of cattle breeding was broken. More and more often families are forced to slaughter calves, without waiting until they grow bigger. Six-month-old underweight piglets are slaughtered too.

The stock of pigs remained on the same level only in those families who resorted to special (often – illegal) ways of replenishing their fodder reserves. Because of the general production drop on the collective farm, the number of such privileged families became considerably smaller, and our respondents were not among them. Our calculations show that if one buys fodder at the market price, with the prices of purchasing pork from peasants, current at the moment of our studies (20-25 rubles per 1 kg), its production at the family homestead is obviously unprofitable.

In essence, in the past year there has been a restructuring of the homestead, which was brought about by the forced change of the criterion of 'production profitability'. The concept of 'profitability' has become an equivalent of impossibility of getting resources. Now the family has to rely on its own efforts in storing fodder, this is why hay has become the main type of fodder, the chief element of the farmstead is cattle, while sheep and goats, competing for this fodder, had to be sacrificed. Abundance of pasture and haying lands in the region helped preserve the family farmstead, so that money expenses on the family farm remained practically the same at the average level of 600 rubles per family per year (with an estimated volume of production of 23.5 thousand rubles).

For lack of money the efficiency of the homestead is going down. The peasant family cannot pay for the selection of younger cattle and seed stocks, or provide balanced rations to feed the herd. Hence – big losses of younger cattle, low milk yields and other unfavorable long term consequences.

The condition of households: genteel poverty, survival, autonomy

In the whole sample in the Saratov village, only one family exceeded the level of subsistence minimum (within 1000 rubles around Russia and about 800 rubles – for rural inhabitants) per 1 family member. In all the other cases, the average monthly income did not exceed 1000 rubles, and in 10 out of 17 families it was from 250 to 500 rubles per person. This allows us to say that, in accordance with the accepted methods of determining material wellbeing, more than a half of the families in our data sample live far below the poverty level. However, given the volumes of natural consumption, this sad picture is somewhat assuaged – the group with the total income of 1000 rubles per person numbers already 10 families. This is a sign of high naturalization of the family farmstead. Thus, in one half of the studied families the share of natural income amounted to 50% in the overall family revenues.

Strategically, orientation at self-provision with food products and, tough money economizing, mark the behavior of Danilovka families. This is reflected in what we found when analyzing the family budgets: there was a different evaluation of the prices of bought and produced food products. During the year, the 'average' family bought food-stuffs worth about 6.5 thousand rubles, while on the family farm it produced and processed for itself and the closest relatives meat, milk, eggs and vegetables worth a sum 2.1 times bigger. The assortment of purchased food is very scanty. They buy in the shop only those things that cannot be produced at home: salt, sugar, cheap pasta, cereals and tea, vegetable oil, sometimes caramels, biscuits, fish and tinned food. On average, families spend 400-500 rubles a month to buy food, which amounts to one third – one half of all their expenses. Last year's default in the cooperative farm forced many housewives to give up baking homemade bread (as there was no more cheap flour) and start buying bread. The families with a little more means were able to give themselves a treat of sausage, fruit, chocolate sweets and coffee. Their food expenses amounted to 1000 rubles per month.

Under the conditions of extreme money deficit, the families rationalized their consumption as much as possible, singling out as a separate item their 'first order' expenses. According to the housewives, many families established a peculiar system of budgeting. First of all, they buy bread and the minimum of food products. Then, if possible, they pay gas and electricity bills, buy fuel for the winter. Many parents, by limiting their needs, try and save money to buy school supplies and clothes for the children. Only after these priority expenses, the remaining money is spent on something less important: they replenish the stock of household goods, buy clothes for the adults.

However, no matter how hard our respondents' life is, in their evaluation of their material situation almost everybody interviewed defined their level of wellbeing as average, arguing that the majority of the people in the village lived the same way. To substantiate their point, they gave another argument: *'We aren't dying of hunger, we'll always find something to eat and we aren't dressed in rags, like the poorest in the village.'* Poverty was admitted only by those who did not have stable sources of income and earned money from time to time, or received so little that they could hardly make both ends meet.

In their definition of the desirable level of family incomes, the house-wives were quite modest. The better-off people thought the sum of 5000 rubles a month sufficient, for the majority – the sum of 2000-3000 rubles would be acceptable. To note, in both cases we are speaking about personal income on the verge or even below the level of subsistence minimum. As a rule, the people are more concerned about the regularity of getting paid, rather than the amount of money they receive.

If we received salaries, at least fifteen hundred a month, it would be more than enough. We could then provide ourselves with normal food and save for bigger buys. Could even help others. Now we get money only occasionally, so financial planning is practically impossible. If we get a big sum of money (about 500 rubles), it goes almost at once, we can't save any money.

At the interviews, our interlocutors repeatedly recalled the times of 'replete', secure life, the model of which in the kolkhoz village was the 80s. A standard kolkhoz family, where the wife worked as a milkmaid and the husband was a machine operator, could earn in the kolkhoz, between the two of them, up to 1000 rubles a month. Only 1/5 of that money was spent on the family's current needs. In those times they also kept cattle, the money made by selling it was put in the savings bank. Many respondents had considerable bank accounts – from 5 to 30 thousand rubles (enough to buy several cars). But this money disappeared without a trace in the 'inflation furnace' in the early 90s. Nostalgically, the people look back at the time when they did not limit their diet, bought boxes of sweets and sacks of sugar and vermicelli in the village shop. And now they cannot afford to buy enough macaroni and cereals, so they have to eat more potatoes and home-made preserves.

Recollections of the past were also brightened up by the fact that many people noted that now, 10 years later, many stocks made in those years had run out. The 'deposits' of bed linen and clothes, 'heaps' of plates and dishes and other household goods put away in the 'Soviet' times now need to be replaced. So does the house furniture. Many families do not have money to replenish or renew all this, so the birthday ritual has acquired a new meaning:

I feel ashamed, but we are wearing our last good clothes. As a birthday present we get from friends the most essential things: a shirt, a pair of trousers, a dressing-gown, a dress – because we have no money to buy all these things.

Working on the home farm, autonomous to a great extent, became part and parcel of the life style in Danilovka families. In the village, not counting the disabled pensioners, only 5 families do not breed cattle (the rural 'lumpen'). Not a single able-bodied family in the sample could do without the farmstead and selling their products. In every third family the private farm provided more than half of their money income, and the highest index of self-provision was 84%. We can say that the material wellbeing of the examined families directly depended on the size, composition and efficiency of the family farm. Its level was determined by a number of factors: availability of sufficient turnover capital, the time and physical health necessary to work on the individual farm and to sell in the market, availability of stable and inexpensive sources to replenish fodder stocks, inclination to do traditional peasant work. Interest in individual farming grew as the situation on the collective farm deteriorated. Cattle herds and the number of feeding calves and piglets were growing, and the horse, the chief draught force of the turn of the century, appeared more and more often on the family farm. A slow but unmistakable return to the times of individual peasant farmsteads of the beginning of last century was taking place.

We can single out several types of family farms differing in production specialization. The biggest revenues (within 22-24 thousand rubles a year) are characteristic for multi-profile (low degree of specialization) family farms (meat and dairy production), aimed at continuous deliveries of their products to the market. They have practically no seasonal breaks in sales, neither in winter, when milk yields drop and the production of the most popular dairy products naturally stops. This is immediately compensated: a calf or a young pig is slaughtered for sale, etc. In the hardest times, depending on the amount of fodder stocked, they usually keep 2-3 cows and the accompanying 'train' of 4-6 growing calves, up to a dozen of pigs. These families have already decided how to live in the future. They have no more bright hopes concerning the prospects of the cooperative-farm. There is no intention to return to the permanent job on the collective farm. The family is planning to increase their own cattle on the family farm, physical labor does not frighten them away. Their chief concern is to 'get' or earn some grain, to store a lot of hay. This is why in the outside employment there prevails temporary hiring by the kolkhoz for the period of harvesting in exchange for fodder.

> *Everything depends on the fodder. If there were more of it, I would keep more cattle. But in my situation – how can I feed them? My husband is working for fodder, he went to transport grain from under the combine. We have no money to buy fodder.*

In families like this one, breeding cattle is often viewed as the most lucrative and reliable way to save money. '*Now I'm afraid of putting money aside, it's better to keep cattle. You feed them, sell them and get the money when you need it.'*

The number of cows can be considered to be the chief differentiating factor of the farm's profitability. Two cows in the yard (with the corresponding number of calves) ensure, according to our data, an additional income of 10-15 thousand rubles. If a family has only one cow (10 such families in our sample), there is practically no surplus milk. But this does not stop the family in need of money, and in this case, they sell part of the product needed by the family. *'Now we sell almost everything, leaving just a little for ourselves.'* The 'milk' receipts in such cases are not high, about 900 rubles a year.

The weak families find themselves in a vicious circle: in order to 'expand', buy one more cow, raise and feed pigs, it is necessary to have the 'starting' capital of about 10 thousand rubles. The family has no cash on hand for this and loans are impossible to get. If this money could be found, many would 'scramble out' of their need, return their investments. The housewife from the poorest family in our sample says:

We are good workers. If we had the money, we would buy a cow. We would buy fodder and pigs – and our life would be normal. I don't want anybody to help me with food or labor.

Most respondents consider that selling milk or made from it sour cream, cottage cheese or butter to be the most profitable business for their families. All in all, the examined families produced in one year over 46 thousand litres of milk. Sixty per cent of that volume was processed into 1700 kg of sour cream, a little over 1000 kg of cottage cheese and almost 300 kg of butter. seventy per cent of these products were sold.

Production of dairy products ensures a relatively constant inflow of money, mostly covering the current needs of the family. That is why with the onset of winter, when the yields of milk drop sharply, the family finds itself on hunger rations and lives on the stocks laid in autumn. Feeding cattle and pigs allows to make a big lump sum of money, which is 'assigned' beforehand to cover specific expenses. Counting on these revenues the family plans to send the children to school or save money for their tuition in town, to buy clothes, shoes, a long-ago-planned expensive thing, to settle their debts. The problem just is that cattle slaughter does not happen often, investments into feeding calves pay off only in a year or 18 months. So, with few cattle, it is rather difficult to provide long-term financial reserves for the family budget. On average, income fluctuations in winter and summer months can be as big as 5-7-fold.

Networks of inter-family mutual assistance: from support to development

For lack of sufficient jobs in the village, work on the private farm becomes a necessary prerequisite of existence. Most of all this situation affects young and economically weak families. In contrast to the more mature families, young farmers do not, as a rule, have a strong farmstead. As a result, they usually 'become a burden' to their parents. Thus, marriage of grown-up children does not only alleviate the burden of dependency from the parents' shoulders, but on the contrary – with the birth of grandchildren it makes it worse.

In this respect, the example of a young 'working' family with a 6-year-old child tells a tale. The husband is a tractor driver in the former kolkhoz, the wife is a librarian, who got this job due to 'backstairs influence'. For the whole year, the husband received just 1000 rubles (and at the end of our examination at that) and a cow that became the starting point (the 7th year of married life) of their private farm.

The family would not be able to survive on the salary of a village librarian (300 rubles), so their parents came to the rescue. Their money relief made up 55% of the family revenues (9000 rubles a year, or 750 rubles every month). In essence, it compensated for the husband's lack of salary. The parents even divided among themselves the items of the children's budget.

> *We get good help from our parents. My husband's parents are pensioners, they give us 200 rubles from their pension every month to pay for electricity and gas. Although my parents do not get a salary in the kolkhoz, but they sell cattle pretty often and give us 200-300 rubles every month to buy things… We don't help anybody. We keep 'drawing' money from our parents. They must be worn out.*

In other cases, when parents cannot afford to pamper their grown-up children, their help can be less noticeable, but with the same regularity. For example, a young family, where neither the husband, nor the wife work, keep receiving food products from the parents' farm. And every month the wife's mother buys for her daughter's family a month ration of macaroni, cereals and sugar. Sometimes, cigarettes are bought for the son-in-law. It is possible to say that most Danilovka pensioners by all means regularly give loans to their children or other close relatives.

Sometimes, help comes from afar, from other regions and even countries (in Danilovka there are many migrants from Kazakhstan, whose relatives moved to Germany to stay). Here, neither the age of the receivers, or the distance separating the people play an important role.

In Danilovka, the inter-family assistance network is characterized by the fact that money assistance is limited to a small group of families, having the closest of ties, and, in comparison with the Kuban stanitsa, it is more significant. If in Kuban barter exchange is more widespread, money is rarely given to anybody without compensation, in Danilovka, on the other hand, aid is urgent and therefore is given free of charge. Very often, family-donors have to literally make sacrifices, giving to relatives or very close friends in a very difficult situation not only excess products, but also what they need themselves. Credit relations are not as frequently found as in Kuban: it is customary to lend small sums of money only to reliable and trustworthy people.

Almost all the young mothers put their children in temporary or permanent care of grandmothers and grandfathers. They turn to their parents every time they need help in decorating the house, washing and other household work. The young people's help to their parents is less noticeable and is usually manifested at the time of pooling the efforts of the whole family clan to plant and raise potatoes or to store hay.

In the past few years, a considerable disassociation of values between generations has become obvious in the village. Young people feel oppressed by the necessity of physically hard peasant labor, taking health and energy, limiting their freedom of movement. This is why the young couples put off as long as possible the beginning of independent farming. They make a kind of deal with the parents, under which the parents' farm becomes common, and the young 'go shares' with them by procuring or laying in fodder, 'on schedule' they come to look after the cattle, and as full 'founders' have a claim on part of the produce.

Grown up children have to 'pay off their debts' in full measure only when the parents become disabled and can no longer keep the farm. From this moment, the product flow changes its direction. And from this time on, the elderly people depend on their children: milk, sour cream, cottage cheese, meat are delivered to them when necessary. And the parents are unwilling, even when in bad need, to accept money from the children. Paternal feelings come to the fore: '*the young need money more, we'll get by, we'll survive.*'

Neighborly mutual assistance manifests itself in joint farm work – gathering potato crops, hay cutting, construction. The return to the practice of 'aid and pooling' is objectively predetermined by weaker positions of the big farm, the former patron of homesteads. Quite invaluable are the services of neighbors, when they agree to look after the farm for one or several days, while the owners go on a short visit to town. Actually, only due to such mutual favors, housewives occasionally manage to leave home, visit friends, go shopping, and if they get into hospital, they do not worry about the safety and order at home. In winter, when cows stop milking, relatives or good friends in turn provide milk for each other.

The 'young' families often have to play the role of social workers: help their disabled neighbors around the house, bring food to them, visit if they get sick, make injections.

*

Despite some regional and social differences, both the Kuban and the Saratov cases have demonstrated an equally significant role of non-formal economy in the rural communities of modern Russia. Both in the well-off Privolnaya and the poor Danilovka villages we find the decisive importance of the symbiosis between the big industrial structure of the enterprise and the combination of small family enterprises, as well as the highly significant networks of inter-family support.

Both cases have also demonstrated a surprising flexibility of network resources, capable of evolving and developing both in conditions of the relative well-being of a big agrarian enterprise (Privolnaya), and in conditions of actual bankruptcy of a big industrial structure (Danilovka). The Saratov case also shows that in an economic crisis the role of the woman, as the actual head of the household, becomes considerably more important.

On the whole, the flexible restructuring of family networks and strategies proves to be the most significant factor for rural families' and communities' survival and development during the economic recession in Russia.

Notes

1   Fadeyeva, O. Mezhsemeinaya: Mekhanizmy vzaimopodderzhki v rossiiskom sele (The Interfamily Networks: Mutual Aid in the Russian Villages), in: Shanin, T. (ed.): *Neformalnaya ekonomika: Rossiya i mir* (Informal Economy: Russia and the World). Moscow: Logos, 1999, 183-218. Fadeyeva, O., Khozyastvennye strategii selskikh semei (Economic Strategies of Rural Families), in: *Sotsialnaya traektoriareformiruemoi Rossii* (Social Trajectory of Reforming Russia). Novosibirsk: 1999. Vinogradsky V., Logika i formj povsednevnogo vijivania (Logic and Forms of everyday surviving) *Chelovecheskie Resursj*, 2000, No. 2.

2   The Symbiosis: The former collective farm already represented a symbiotic complex of the large ('modern') and small ('traditional') units. Now the post-soviet collective farms have formally become joint-stock companies, but in reality are based on natural economy of a symbiotic type. In this symbiosis, rural inhabitants continue to work in an industrial postkolkhoz complex for a symbolic salary (or without any), but receive (legally or illegally) natural resources, such as grain, fodder, fuel and so on. They use also common collective farm's support welfare (school, hospital, social protection, etc.). About symbiosis see Nikulin, A., Konglomeraty i Simbiozy v Rossii: Selo i Gorod, Semyi i Predpriyatia (Conglomerates and Symbiosis in Russia: Village and City, Family and Enterprise), in: Shanin, T. (ed.): *Neformalnaya ekonomika: Rossiya i mir* (Informal Economy: Russia and the World). Moscow: Logos, 1999, p. 240-269.

3   Although the state employment agency has 17 people on the list of unemployed, our estimation is that about 200 people have lost their jobs and been unable to find a new one.

4   Field research of Danilovka was made by Saratov's sociologists I. Steinberg and M. Morechanova.

PART V
METHODS OF RESEARCH

Chapter 15

Of methods and findings on the informal economy[1]

Philippe Adair* and Rainer Neef

The term 'informal economy' (coined by ILO) encapsulates activities whose common character lies in the fact that they escape social and tax regulations, as well as statistical recording, in developed, less developed and transition countries.

The informal economy is a controversial issue in regard to three aspects: estimates (regarding its scope), explanations, and remedies.

First, the actors and the branches of industry involved in the informal economy are well identified, but scholars disagree about the magnitude and trend of the informal economy. Thus, according to the variety of definitions and methods of estimates which are adopted, the informal economy in Eastern Europe is assumed to have grown only during the very first years of transition and to have remained stable since then or, on the contrary, is assumed to be expanding – although going through cycles – and to reach a fairly large part of GDP (see Ciupagea in this volume).

Second, beyond their agreement on the conditions required to perform informal activities (availability, incentives and opportunities), scholars do not agree on the relevant explanatory factors: Is the informal economy caused by the fluctuations of economic activity and the changes affecting the labour market,[2] or is it a largely structural phenomenon induced by the various regulations (i.e. social, labour and tax constraints) which affect incomes and work?

Third, despite the fact that scholars may agree on the consequences of informal activities (regarding competition, employment, and incomes), they advocate different remedies depending on the extent and the expansion of the informal economy within the institutional context of the various coun-

* Associate Professor of Economics, Faculty of Economics and Management, University Paris XII, Val de Marne 61, avenue du Général de Gaulle 94010 Créteil, France. E-mail: adair@univ-paris12.fr.

tries. The informal economy may be considered as a 'social buffer' by liberals, which legitimates an accommodating policy of tolerance, whereas for mere interventionists it is a threat which calls for a policy of enforcement.

Definitions and modes of evaluation of informal activities

By and large, informal activities encompass both traded and non-traded goods and services, which take part in three different modes of production and exchange: non-declared market activities, household production, and in kind transfers which are non-market activities (Adair 1985; Neef, in this volume).

Although these modes may combine, a sharp distinction should be drawn between market and non-market activities. Traded goods and services should again be split into two sub-categories: non-declared labour or so-called 'moonlighting' and tax evasion on the one hand, and criminal activities on the other hand. The first category encompasses activities of production and exchange which escape social and tax regulations but are not illegal as such. The second category encompasses strictly prohibited activities (narcotics trade, clandestine gambling, money laundering, corruption, smuggling, fraud ...) (Thomas 1992; Gilmore 1995), which prove very difficult to measure (see endnote 10) and therefore cannot be part of our analysis, although they are, of course, an important issue in various EECs (e.g. Russia).

Non-market activities can be analysed through qualitative enquiries and time-budget investigations and one would agree not to separate them from market activities, since their interactions are underlined at a micro-level: households do combine or substitute social transfers, declared work and non-declared work as well as do-it-yourself and household production (Pahl and Wallace 1985). Household production depends on assets the household can fully dispose of (land or housing, available workforce within the household, qualifications). In kind transfers are related to modes of functioning of social networks – such as ethic principles, reciprocity, social nearness (Portes 1994). However, research on household production and exchange within social networks mostly includes regionally or sectorally restricted enquiries which are difficult to generalize. In addition, estimates of their monetary value display huge variations according to the methods employed (replacement cost, opportunity cost) (Thomas 1992; Adair 2000). Therefore, these non-market activities are only briefly dealt with in the following ways:

Indirect methods of enquiry

The measurement of the informal economy is built on two types of approaches: indirect and direct. Each kind of approach deals with several methods which, unfortunately, will prove to be non-comparable, and consequently, produce very different outcomes depending on the more or less extensive coverage of activities which are selected. Indirect approaches rely on five distinct methods: national accounts, physical output and electricity consumption, monetary aggregates and currency demand, soft modelling, and implicit labour supply. Direct investigations may be used in order to provide the raw data or to check the various estimates computed through indirect approaches.

1. National Accounts. There are three different methods by which the informal economy represents neither a very significant part of GNP (or GDP) nor seems to display clear-cut trends.

The 'discrepancy method' consists in measuring the gap between National Income and the Expenditure, or between adjusted National Income (through tax investigations) and National Income, ascribed to the informal economy. Results are contradictory: an increasing discrepancy was detected in the United Kingdom in the 70s and in Croatia in the early 90s, whereas a decreasing discrepancy was detected in the USA and in Canada in the 70s, or in Croatia in the later 90s. The improvement which occurred in the accounting treatment can be used to explain decreasing discrepancies. Therefore, one cannot reach the conclusion that the informal economy has declined (Barthélémy 1988).

The second method which is more restrictive, the logarithmic model, attacks the underestimation of National Income in terms of growth rate. It takes into account three ratios relating to the wage bill, total employment and National Income and identifies the branches of activity in which the presence of the informal economy is suspected (building and construction, retail trade, commercial services). It seems that the informal economy in the USA, defined in terms of non-declared wage incomes, could possibly have increased from 1949 to 1982 and reached less than 5% of GNP. However, underestimation which approximately represents 0.14% for each 1% of growth in National Income more likely results from uncertain statistical measurement than from the presence of the informal economy (De Leeuw 1985; 1986).

A third, more extensive method consists in measuring the informal economy in the broad sense, i.e. non-declared legal traded goods and services (tax evasion and moonlighting) to which the misappropriated in kind incomes are added (diversion of the equipment of the firms and pilferage committed by salaried workers) and production of illegal goods and services (criminal activities). This measurement relies on disparate statistical sources in order to reach a plausible weighting of GDP. Thus defined, the informal economy in the OECD countries would account for 2 to 5% of GNP in the 70s and would not have evolved significantly since then (Blades 1982, Willard 1989).

These methods suffer from several drawbacks. First of all, the reliability of the figures may be disputed. Most of the time, statistical offices are not independent from political authorities, at least because the figures computed by the former depend in last resort on the approval of the latter. Therefore, there are incentives for higher estimates, especially when the tax burden is a political controversial issue; incentives for lower estimates occur when the country is entitled to financial assistance or must bear financial costs (Tanzi, 1999). Second, measurement is lacunar and inadequate because Income and Expenditure are not estimated according to independent sources (Barthelemy 1988; Feige 1989; Thomas 1992). On the other hand, missing income and non-reported revenue may not be linked: for instance, the agricultural sector is not biased by National Accounts, although it presumably evades taxes (Tanzi 1999). In addition, tax evaded income may be overestimated due to the fact that the level of earnings of the informal workers could be too low to pay taxes (Bhattacharyya 1999), but given the lack of coverage, National Accounts underestimate the size of the informal economy according to Giles (1999).

2. Physical output and electricity consumption. Insofar as electricity consumption is supposed to stand for the best indicator of both official and informal economic activities, the physical output approach is advocated by Schneider and Enste (2000). Unfortunately, it is not necessarily relevant.

The first method used by Kaufmann and Kaliberda derives an estimate of unrecorded GDP from the difference between the growth of official GDP and the growth of the overall use of electricity. This method can be criticised on two counts: electricity is not the only source of energy; variations in the elasticity of electricity/GDP occur and are due to factors that may not be related to informal activities of both the households and the firms.

Lackó's (2000) method is based on those households activities which include DIY and home production (i.e. non-monetary activities), thus defining the informal economy in a much broader sense. Computations are made for the price of electricity, its various uses (heating...), the taxes/GDP ratio and the public expenditure/GDP ratio (including social transfers). Unfortunately, the size of the informal economy is not derived from these computations (i.e. derived from exogeneous factors) and remains unexplained. One should also be aware that the public expenditure/GDP ratio is not well suited to transition and developing countries.

Regarding the EEC in the mid 90s, estimates from Lackó's method are unsurprisingly higher (31.6%) than the estimates provided by the Kaufmann-Kaliberda method (20.9%) and display an increasing growth rate of the informal economy (see table 5 in Schneider and Enste 2000).

3. Monetary approaches. The monetary approaches can be subdivided into two categories: monetary aggregates, which are based on the money supply, and the currency demand.

The method pioneered by Gutmann (1985) assumes that non-declared transactions are paid in cash and takes into account the variation of the cash /deposits (C/D) ratio according to the basic period (or year) considered as an indicator of the 'underground' economy. The method used by Feige (1989), which takes Fisher's quantity theory as a starting point to compute transactions (T) with regard to money supply (M), assumes that non-declared transactions are paid in cash as well as in cheques. Although such an assumption seems realistic, non-declared transactions being not exclusively paid in cash, it overestimates the extent of these transactions, since cheques are also used to carry out transfers having no connection with non-declared transactions.

The second category, the currency demand approach pioneered by Cagan, is advocated by Tanzi (1982). This approach incorporates explanatory variables, tax load ratio or marginal rate of taxation, with which their robustness can be tested.[3]

All monetary approaches provide, in absolute value, estimates of variable range: Feige's ratio displays an increasing difference from Gutmann's ratio which in turn is higher than Tanzi's ratio. In terms of logarithms, they seem to show either a growing trend (currency demand) or cycles which converge or diverge according to the country under review (cash ratio, transactions)[4] (Schneider and Enste 2000).

The approach of monetary aggregates faces several criticisms. First of all, the choice of the basic period (or year) is debatable, as this assumes that no 'underground economy' did exist in a given period of time; in other words, the implicit but heroic (i.e. naive) assumption is that no regulations occurred in the past. Second, the velocity of circulation is not directly observable and the crucial assumption that velocities are identical within both the 'underground economy' and the official economy is debatable. Third, theoretical explanations are lacking: no economic theory is provided in order to explain preferences relating to the various ways in which currency is used and kept (species, current accounts ...), which can vary depending on the institutional framework and periods considered. Finally, no explanatory variable appears in the equations (Thomas 1992; 1999).

Savings or currency hoarding are not taken into account (Thomas 1999), possibly causing an overestimation or, with previous hoarding, an underestimation of the hidden economy; Bhattacharyya (1999) assumes that these two opposite forces cancel each other out but provides no evidence.

According to Giles (1999), monetary approaches overestimate the size of the informal economy; although they point out several restrictions, Schneider and Enste (2000) make an extensive and amazingly uncritical use of the currency demand approach. One reason why such an approach is widely used, despite its drawbacks, is probably the availability of monetary data.

4. *'Soft modelling'* or MIMIC (Multiple Indicators, Multiple Causes) is based on latent (i.e. non-observed) variables (Frey, Weck-Hannemann 1984). This method retains quantitative variables – relating to tax and legal constraints (tax burden, public employment) as well as to the labour market (rate of activity, rate of unemployment, duration of work) – and qualitative variables (perception of the tax burden, attitude towards fraud) (see Ciupagea in this volume).

This method, which was used in a repeated cross-section analysis of 17 OECD countries (conducted in 1960, 1965, 1970, 1975, 1978) simultaneously, makes it possible to classify the countries with regard to the importance of the informal economy and to account for the evolution of the phenomenon which has expanded since the 1960s, although its speed varies from country to country.

However, without calling into question that this method is of interest, Helberger and Knepel (1988) point out that the estimators are very unstable with regard to the periods considered, so that the same explanatory variables can account for upturns as well as slowdowns. Giles (1999) advocates this method which he applied to the case of New Zealand and according to which the informal economy follows the peaks and throughs of the business cycle. There is also evidence of some causality (in Granger's sense) between measured activity and informal activity, but the reverse does not occur.

This method faces a double criticism: the estimation of the parameters by means of the maximum likelihood is not very robust, there is a bias due to the fact that all the variables bear the same weight (i.e. absence of weighting) (Helberger and Knepel 1988).

5. *The implicit labour supply.* Given the fact that high levels of unemployment seem to develop at the same pace as the underground economy, the

deficiency of employment estimates or the so-called implicit labour supply fills the gap between the official labour force participation and the effective labour force participation measured through various investigations, surveys and computations. The official labour force is thus raised by a coefficient resulting from the conversion of the multiple job holding and non-declared activity into full-time employment. After that, it is multiplied by the value added per unit of employment (VAPUE) in order to compute the missing output.

Italy carried out the calculation of the implicit labour supply which made up 17.7% of GDP in 1987 and was officially added to National Accounts.[5]

This approach was also adopted by Portugal and has been considered examined with interest in France, although it is not applied (Wagner 1993). It remains quite popular within less developed and transition countries, but faces several drawbacks.

On the one hand, the official definition of the labour force (according to ILO) takes neither children nor retired people into account, although such categories may well represent an increasing part of the underground work force which would then be underestimated.

On the other hand, the basic assumption, which in turn leads to an over-estimation, is that the VAPUE in the underground economy is the same as in the official economy, while there are reasons to believe that the VAPUE of the former is weaker than the latter, since those who work within the underground economy have less capital (e.g. human capital, such as skills and education, or equipment) and therefore yield a lower productivity (Tanzi, 1999). According to Giles (1999) or Schneider and Enste (2000), labour force participation rate data are biased and underestimate the size of the informal economy.

Direct enquiries

Direct enquiries are directed at subjects informally active, households or experts. They cover various fields such as tax non-compliance, informal labour supply, consumption of informal goods and services, working conditions in different informal branches, household strategies including self-production, exchange of informal goods and informal monetary gain. Depending on the research topic, large scale representative samples with standardized procedure are carried out in order to produce estimates of the informal economy, while qualitative methods are used in order to explain the interrelation and workings of the various segments of the informal economy.

In view of the heterogeneity of these various segments and their mostly piecemeal character, *representative surveys* require large numbers of subjects in order to produce sufficiently detailed classifications and to enable a multi-factorial analysis. But since essential parts of the informal economy are hidden and irregular in character, the subjects are, at least in costumary interview situations, unlikely to admit these (see Wallace/Haerpfer, in this volume). Therefore, even at high response rates, subgroups can fall short of statistical acceptable limits. Closed questions include pre-determined categories, usually taken from expert's knowledge (see Ungureanu 1998). This precludes all unforeseen kinds of informal activities, of consumption items and of interrelations. Open questions help to detect these, but the subjects often use vague terms which diminish the precision of the analysis, and highly visible or much debated activities might be over-represented. Thus, in standardized enquiries illegitimate and non-legal activities will be largely under-represented and items concerning illegitimate transactions[6] will mix formal and informal activities which are difficult to disentangle.

Qualitative interviews intend to create an atmosphere of confidence, and thus, produce more valid information as they facilitate openness between interviewer and subjects (Kvale 1996, 147 ff.). Thus, one might discover unknown and hidden activities within the rapidly transforming EEC.

Each form of field access presents inconveniences.[7] Qualitative research adopts the perspective of the enquired subjects, and in analyzing the data, a general perspective may be derived from a general theory – but when theories are deficient or contradictory there is no possibility of attaining an empirically based general level.

Explorative interviewing is most suitable for discovering hidden activities and interrelations, but difficulties arise in understanding and structuring the material. Structured (i.e.guided) qualitative interviewing requires general knowledge of the topic in order to produce precise information (e.g. knowledge of informal working, market conditions, branch features, social networks implied). Qualitative samples are limited to small numbers of subjects and can never cover the whole field so that many black boxes remain. They may establish types of informal activities and behaviour but cannot assess the importance or the distribution of informal activities.

Sociological enquiries on informal activities call for a combination of methods. Explorative enquiries may form a first step for producing the dimensions and categories useful for systematic qualitative or quantitative surveys. In-depth-interviewing following standardized procedure elucidates complex and hidden informal activities. In-site open interviewing or observation can produce the reliable data on sensitive or illicit aspects which escape standardized interviewing. Interrelating both procedures may also be helpful for verifying data, though many questions remain unsolved.[8]

1. Social surveys concerning informal economies have been realized in different EECs (see Sik e.a., Stănculescu, Ilie, and Wallace and Haerpfer in this volume). They often refer to the concept of a portfolio of different economies disposable for households (Haerpfer/Wallace, and Stănculescu in this volume). Findings are blurred by the difficulties indicated above: participation ratios of about 95% in the 'household economy' are not conclusive, since routine housework and self-production cannot be disentangled. The value of agrarian self-production, forming part of the household economy, has been estimated much more precisely by using methods of Income and Expenditure surveys; in Romania, for example, this made up between 30 and 40% of the household consumption. The black 'cash economy' on the other hand will be underestimated, especially in terms of its monetary outcome, making up about 6-8% of gross national household income in Romania (see Ilie in this volume, and Adair 1998). Participation rates in the 'informal cash economy' of about one third in different EECs – representing the most important source of livelihood ranging from 1% (Czech Republic) to 12% (Yugoslavia) of the households – will also be underestimated (Wallace and Haerpfer in this volume). The rate of participation in the informal economy (cash economy and agrarian self-production) in Romania amounted to 36.3% in 1996 (Adair 1998) and 45.8% in 1998 (see Ilie), the difference being either due to the severe crisis since 1996, or to different phrasings in the enquiry.

Surveys regarding the households expenditure devoted to informal goods and services have taken place in different western countries (Belgium, Norway, U.K., Canada), as well as in Hungary and Romania. They are carried out on the relevant assumption that it is easier to collect data from the customers of the informal economy (i.e. the demand side) than from those who provide their provisioning (the supply side). In Hungary, 11-12% of the household expenditure – ranging from 9% (kitchenware) and 14% (clothes) to 30% (food) – was estimated to be informal (Sik and Tóth in this volume). In Romania, Duchêne (1998) estimated the rate of informal consumption to account for between 3% (clothes) and 32% (food) of the households expenditure, amounting to 6-8% of National Income. As quite a number of informal items are excluded (Neef 1999), this figure is an underestimation. Purchasers are not necessarily aware that the goods and services they bought are informal, unless purchasers and vendors are surveyed simultaneously (Fortin et al. 2000). However, it is far more difficult to estimate the incomes on the supply side than to draw conclusions from the purchases on the demand side.

Studies regarding the informal employment of the households have been conducted in various countries, many of them on a qualitative basis (some of them in this volume). Large samples and longitudinal surveys are very rare, recent Canadian studies being a noticeable exception (Fortin *et alii* 1996; 2000).[9]

2. *Fiscal audits* investigating tax evasion focus on sub samples which are not representative of the entire population. Such is the case of the Tax Compliance Measurement Program (TCMP) which was carried out on a sample of some 50.000 households in the USA for the first time in 1976 (Carson 1984). TCMP which took place in 1988 shows that while 40% of the households are underpaid (by a percentage of 25% , equalling on average 1.500$), 7% are overpaid (equalling on average 150$) (Feinstein 1999). In addition, fiscal audits are expensive and may furthermore not be conducted either because confidentiality laws prevent their use as is the case in the United Kingdom or because of the complexity of tax laws as in the case of Italy (Tanzi 1999).

On the other hand, indirect detection-controlled estimations are based on characteristics of potential offenders, providing both the estimates of the probability of compliance vs violation (by means of maximum likelihood) and the proportion of violations remaining undetected (applying Bayes' law). However, violation and detection cannot be properly separated (Feinstein 1999). Surveys of tax compliance generally underestimate the size of the informal economy (Giles 1999; Schneider and Enste 2000).

Actors and branches of the informal economy

Non-declared activities or 'moonlighting'

The majority of studies emphasize that two categories are mainly concerned: on the one hand, the labour-intensive branches employing many unprotected salaried workers (building and construction, clothing industry, agriculture) whose activity can be either seasonal or regular; on the other hand, the branches employing much non-salaried labour (agriculture, household services, repair, retail trade).

The employment and the professional status of the actors (depending on whether they are employers or employees, wage earners or self-employed workers, performing a regular or an occasional activity) is quite well identified (Klatzmann 1982; Neef 1999, for Romania). 'Moonlighting' (or black labour) covers two categories: clandestine precarious labour of salaried workers and multiple-job holding which concerns formally employed persons.

Clandestine workers are employed mainly in labour-intensive branches; given their illegal status, they are generally forced by employers to carry out a full-time salaried activity, without being able to influence their working schedule and their income. They have low-paid precarious jobs, mostly a single activity, and tend to live in a dependent situation (see Neef in this volume).

Multiple-job holding generally implies that the workers concerned already have a first and rather stable employment. The socio-professional groups most represented are the professions, office employees and craftsmen. The developing branches such as business services or IT industries, which lag behind in EECs, offer rewarding opportunities for qualified non-declared labour. Multiple-job holding thus relates to salaried as well as self-employed work. In the European Union, second salaried jobs on a regular basis within the service sector prevail. The magnitude of moonlighting seems to increase during the period of recovery and to decrease during the period of recession (Eurostat 1995). In EEC, irregular secondary employment of formal jobholders seems to prevail.

Fraud on taxes and social contributions

Fraud on welfare transfers is often ascribed to the unemployed and/or to the recipients of the Welfare state benefits who are supposed to cumulate transfer incomes and non-declared activities. However, investigations show that non-declared activities of these categories are rather carried out on a purely occasional basis and limited to fields requiring only little professional skills and equipment (Adair 1985; Lacroix and Fortin 1992).

Tax evasion covers three categories, affluent taxpayers (the professions), small entrepreneurs and self-employed workers, both groups acting as craftsmen and tradesmen and service workers. It is appropriate to make a distinction between two categories: the first consists of households endowed with a personal or professional inheritance, who are at the same time induced to escape tax compliance and have the opportunity to successfully intermingle legal tax avoidance and tax evasion itself. In EEC these are mostly qualified middle or top former managers of State firms. The second category consists of households of small entrepreneurs and of self-employed workers evading taxes on a reduced scale because their income only covers basic necessities. They tend to be unemployed specialists and service and manual workers. Small informal businesses often include the cheap labour force of family members; self-employed workers more often have poor qualifications (Neef 1999).

Misappropriated or concealed in kind incomes

The concealed in kind incomes represent the various misappropriated perks the employees of the firms and the administration gain from small larcenies or the diversion of the professional equipment: pilferage of goods and parts, use of the equipment (telephone, tools, vehicles...) on a purely private basis, private informal activities during the formal working time. The tolerance of the employers towards these practices can be explained in two ways. Either employers consider such perks as an almost normal fraction of the wages (i.e. a perquisite) paid in kind, if it does not exceed a reasonable limit. Or employers do not consider it as normal, but the marginal costs of control and prevention would exceed the amount of misappropriation. This form of fraud used to be common in a 'command' or 'shortage economy' before the 90s; it remains especially prevalent within state owned entreprises which have not been privatized in various ECCs. However, it should not be confused with other forms taking place outside the firm (or administration) which belong to the criminal economy itself.[10]

Subsistence agriculture

In many EECs the economic downturn and mass impoverishment have sped up the extension of or the retreat into agrarian self-production taking place on restituted or simply squatted land. Contrary to most other informal activities, subsistence farming is a backward form of producing ('re-traditionalization' – see Benovska in this volume) which is generally tolerated by State authorities and, moreover, is also largely exempted from taxing in some countries. It is the most common way of complementing those wages and pensions that have fallen below subsistence level. For certain groups of the unemployed who have lost most of their social entitlements, farming is the pillar of an informal 'survival economy' in which they remain trapped for lack of resources preventing them from extending their economy or from changing their occupation. For the regularly employed and pensioners, subsistence farming, though tiresome and mostly unproductive, has the advantage of offering regular income.

Explanatory factors and remedies

The growth of informal economies in EECs is related to factors such as the weakness of the institutional environment and the slow and lacunary economic modernization on the one hand, and to consequences such as the transformational recession and mass impoverishment on the other hand. The debate among economists has mainly revolved around the factors up to now: they raise the question whether tax and social burdens as well as labour regulations stimulate informal activities.

The first answer implies that the elasticity of the labour supply regarding the tax rate is positive. The microeconomic foundations of the tax load curve, the so-called Laffer curve[11], postulates that an increasing tax load induces an arbitration in favour of non-declared work which replaces official work or comes to supplement it.

The second answer stresses the subjective evaluation of the risks and the profits associated with tax evasion. The tax avoidance model (Sandmo 1981) is based on a maximization of an expected utility function by the defrauder encapsulating the income (consumption) and the labour supply as variables, the rate of return, the tax rate, the penalties and the probability of detection as parameters.

A third answer assumes that labour regulations are entry barriers, according to the segmented labour market theory.

These explanations have been tested by the Canadian studies previously referred to (see above for direct approaches of labour supply surveys).

Lacroix and Fortin (1992), assuming an imperfect substitutability of declared and non-declared working hours, introduced the risk of detection and penalties into the labour supply function. This reveals that if the rise of the marginal rate of taxation generates an increase of non-declared working hours, this effect is ambiguous; indeed, the increase in controls and penalties involves a decrease in non-declared working hours. Four modes characterize the behavior of the labour supply of individuals: those who work in both the official and the informal labour markets[12] (mode 1), those who work only in the official labour market (mode 2), those who work only in the informal labour market (mode 3), and those who do not take part in any of the two labour markets (mode 4). The result is that taking part in the informal labour market is inversely proportional to the available income and is particularly significant for students, the unemployed and the recipients of welfare transfers. However, the elasticity of the informal labour supply in comparison with the tax rate is greater for individuals in mode 1 than for those in modes 2 and 3.

This perspective suits best with the answers of social scientists. As can be seen from the contributions in this book, scholars stress the heterogenity of informal activities. They do not deny the dynamics of high taxing pressure and they insist on the consequences of a weak institutional framework and of non-compliant behaviour, especially in South Eastern Europe and in the former Soviet Union. But they focus on the social functions and on the behavioural dynamics of consumption and subsistence-oriented informal activities as well as working out the background of social polarization.

Before turning to the issue of remedies, three theoretical conclusions may be drawn: the relevance of the segmented labour market theory should be

questioned; the robustness of the explanation connecting tax load and informal activities is far from being proven; the aspects of impoverishment and
social polarization should be worked on.

Either the informal economy results from the inefficiency generated by
regulations and the tax load, thus emphasizing the entrepreneurs' capacity to
take the initiative as well as the pressure of survival necessities; or it consti-
tutes a premium for fraud and deprives the State of necessary resources (Frey
1989). However, information gaps generate perverse effects regarding both
fairness and efficiency which affect the social situation and the behaviour of
the actors as well as the relevance of the decisions of economic policy.

Fraud distorts the taxation schedule and the social security schemes and
is detrimental to average incomes, thus threatening the fairness of the con-
tributive burden-sharing. Tax evasion affects fiscal policy: missing tax
receipts impede the financing of public expenditure and/or the balancing of
the budget; the ignorance of the incomes of the agents can cause public
authorities to take inappropriate decisions regarding taxation and/or social
security contributions (Houston 1987).

With regard to 'moonlighting', the breaching of labour regulations by the
employers worsens both the working conditions and the living standards of
the employees, overexploitation of clandestine migrants, increasing precari-
ousness of income and of the social coverage of salaried workers and
self-employed harnessed by subcontracting). On the other hand, in most
EECs moonlighting buffers the decrease of real income and improves the
lives of people that are often in danger of falling below minimum subsistence level. Subsistence agriculture plays precisely this role, or even makes
up/compensates for deficient basic social security systems, although it is
mostly without any perspective of development and often encloses the actors
in a dependent situation.

On the one hand, some economists maintain that informal activities form
a necessary part of the market economy: contending it would therefore be
useless or even harmful to enforce regulations, their advice is 'to tolerate'
and even to stimulate such activities by advocating deregulations of tax and
labour standards. On the other hand, other economists point out that on the
commodity market as well as on the labour market, informal activities create an unfair competition as regards price and cost and weaken the fiscal
potential of the State.

Social scientist do not propose 'strong' theses but differentiate between
those informal activities which secure or improve a minimum livelihood,
those that contribute to modernizing the economy and those activities which
are economically and/or socially destructive (see Stănculescu and Ilie 2001).
Therefore, the option is either to repress informal activities by reinforcing

the penalties and/or by calling upon moral persuasion, or to implement differential policies by furthering or tolerating informal activities.

Notes

1   This short synthesis of various works dealing with the informal economy in industrialized countries since the 70s is a largely revised draft of a paper first presented in Bucharest (Adair 1995), later revised in Adair (1998). Rainer Neef provided the pieces regarding sociological approaches and information on Eastern Europe.
2   Of course, the collapse of the so-called 'command' or 'shortage' economy which the transition period entailed was a major disruption. But the pace towards a market economy varies greatly among the Eastern and Central European Countries (EEC) and the main institutions of a modern market economy are not yet fully operating or may still be lacking after a decade.
3   According to his own calculations carried out on the data of Tanzi, Thomas (1992) concludes that the tax variables are not significant.
4   The average size of the informal economy in percent of GDP in the early 90s varies between 9-16% in the Czech Republic, Slovakia and Romania, 20-28% in Poland, Bulgaria and Hungary as well as in the Baltic countries, and up to 28-43% in the former Soviet Union countries (Schneider and Enste 2000, table 2). The authors' calculations are based on physical output (electricity) and currency demand approaches. Unfortunately, both indicators overestimate the size of the informal economy and are strictly non-compatible. Moreover, sources are not provided and the method regarding physical output is not mentioned. See also *in this volume* Ciupagea which computes data on the growth of the informal economy in the EEC (especially Romania).
5   The analysis of employment splits the labour market into five segments: regular employment, irregular employment, occasional work, work done by clandestine immigrants, second jobs (multiple job handling). The measurement of employment is based on three sources of statistical data: the census of the population (CP), the quarterly labour force survey (EFT), the census of firms – industry, trade, services (CIC). The first two sources refer to households, the third refers to firms (which are splitted according to their size). No tax source (file or investigation) is used. The gaps between the sources of statistical data are ascribed to the existence of particular forms of employment: when household sources exceed firm sources, the gap is ascribed to the existence of moonlighting; when the firm sources exceed household sources, the gap is ascribed to the existence of multiple job holding.
6   For example questions concerning 'non registered secondary employment' or 'activities that help to live better' (see Stănculescu in this volume).
7   Snowball access produces the most reliable information, but runs the risk of being caugth up in specific social networks or milieux; random interviews in public *areas* (streets, pubs, etc.) are cheap and quick, but produce only limited data from a sample whose composition cannot be controlled; structured samples, if drawn from representative surveys, provide more systematic insights, but cannot be related conclusively to representative data.

8 How to tackle discrepancies in data on informal incomes, which are significantly higher in qualitative enquiries compared to standardized procedure (see Ilie in this volume)? The propositions of Huberman and Miles (1994) are remarkably vague in this respect.

9 Several convergent analyses were conducted on the same representative sample of some 2.000 adults from the town of Quebec first interviewed in 1986 and then again in 1993. *It was* found out that 8% of the labour force engaged in non-declared activities and that this proportion remained stable. However, whether Quebec is representative of the overall situation in Canada is still an open question.

10 However, the boundary between the so-called 'tolerable misappropriation' and robbery is blurred. Criminal activities encompass *illegal production* as well as robbery which are both prohibited. On the one hand, narcotics trade, prostitution (or procuring, depending on the country) and possibly counterfeit produce value added and do not concern robbery; on the other hand, data-processing hacking, smuggling, embezzlements, corruption, fraud on credit cards (or on invoices, cheque books...) are illegal transfers on property which do not add value to GDP. Classification and thus measurement are made even more difficult by the fact that these activities may be overlapping (e.g. smuggling counterfeited commodities involves production and exchange which are both illegal) or because separating smuggling (or clandestine gambling) from fraud on taxes proves to be difficult.

11 On the macro-economic level, this curve assumes the existence of a limiting threshold of the tax load which induces a decrease in the tax return. The argument favours a reduction in the tax rate in order to maintain rising optimal receipts tax without discouraging the activity (Canto *et alii* 1978). If such a limit exists, it varies according to countries and periods, casting serious doubts on the relevance of the explanation initially provided by Laffer. In this respect, it is not so much the average (or the marginal) rate of taxation but the tax structure which matters (basis and thresholds).

12 It is necessary to distinguish individuals who *are not* subjected to constraints on their working schedules from those who *are constrained*.

References

Adair, P. (1985), *L'économie informelle – Figures et discours*, Anthropos, Paris.

Adair, P. (1995), 'L'économie souterraine dans les pays industrialisés', Congrès de l'Association Internationale des Economistes de Langue Français (AIELF), *Contraintes et limites de l'économie de marché*, 29 juin-1er juillet, Bucarest, Roumanie.

Adair, P. (1998), 'The informal economy in industrialized countries', in Duchêne G. (ed.), 1998, *The Informal Economy in Romania*, PHARE ACE Programme, European Union, Brussels, September, pp. 296-310.

Adair, P. (2000), 'Déclin, renouveau ou permanence de l'économie domestique?' in A. Alcouffe, B. Fourcade, J.M. Plassard, G. Tahar (eds.), 2000, *Efficacité versus équité en économie sociale*, L'Harmattan, vol. 2, pp. 221-232.

Barthélémy, P. (1988), 'The macroeconomic estimates of the hidden economy: a critical analysis', *Review of Income and Wealth*, vol. 34 (2), pp. 183-208.

Bhattacharyya, D.K. (1999), 'On the Economic Rationale of Estimating the Hidden Economy', *The Economic Journal*, 109, June, pp. F 348-F 359.

Blades, D. (1982), 'The Hidden Economy and the National Accounts', *OECD Economic Outlook*, June, pp. 28-45.

Canto, V.A., Joines, D.H., Laffer, A.B. (1978), *Foundations of Supply Side Economics – Theory and Evidence*, Academic Press.

Carson, C.S. (1984a), 'The Underground Economy: an Introduction', *Survey of Current Business*, vol. 64, 5, May, pp. 21-37.

Carson, C.S. (1984b), 'The Underground Economy: an Introduction', *Survey of Current Business*, vol. 64, 7, July, pp. 106-117.

Cebula, R.J. (1997), 'An empirical analysis of the impact of government tax and auditing policies on the size of the underground economy: the case of United States, 1973-94', *American Journal of Economics and Sociology*, vol. 56, 2, April, pp. 173-185.

De Leeuw, F. (1985), 'An indirect technique for measuring the underground economy', *Survey of Current Business*, vol. 65, April, pp. 64-72.

De Leeuw, F. (1986), 'An indirect technique for measuring the underground economy – A note on revised data', *Survey of Current Business*, vol. 66, September, pp. 21-22.

Duchêne, G. (ed.) (1998), *The Informal Economy in Romania*, PHARE ACE Programme, European Union, Brussels, September.

Eurostat (1995), 'Personnes ayant plus d'un emploi dans l'Union Européenne en 1992', *Statistiques en bref – populations et conditions sociales*, no 2.

Feige, E.L. (ed.) (1989), *The Underground Economies – Tax Evasion and Information Distorsion*, Cambridge University Press.

Feinstein, J.S. (1999), 'Approaches for estimating non-compliance: examples from federal taxation in the United States', *The Economic Journal*, 109, June, pp. F 360-F 369.

Fortin, B., Garneau, G., Lacroix, G., Lemieux, T., Montmarquette, C. (1996), *L'économie souterraine au Québec: mythes et réalités*, Presses de l'Université de Laval, Québec, Canada.

Fortin, B., Lacroix, G., Montmarquette, C. (2000), 'Are underground workers more likely to be underground consumers ?', *The Economic Journal*, 110, October, pp. 838-860.

Frey, B.S. (1989), 'How large (or small) should the underground economy be?', in Feige (ed.), 1989, chap. 4, pp. 111-126.

Frey, B.S., Weck-Hannemann, H. (1984), 'The hidden economy as an 'unobserved variable', *European Economic Review*, 26, pp. 33-53.

Giles, D.E.A. (1999), 'Measuring the Hidden Economy: Implications for Econometric Modelling', *The Economic Journal*, 109, June, pp. F 370-F 380.

Gilmore, W.C. (1995), *Dirty Money*, Council of Europe Press, Strasbourg.

Grazia (de), R. (1983), *Le travail clandestin*, BIT.

Gutmann, P. (1985), 'The subterranean economy, redux' in: W. Gaertner and A. Wenig (eds.) (1985) *The Economics of the Shadow Economy*, Springer Verlag, Berlin.

Helberger, C. & Knepel, H. (1988), 'How big is the shadow economy? A re-analysis of the unobserved-variable approach of Frey and Weck-Hannemann', *European Economic Review*, 32, pp. 965-976.

Houston, J.F. (1987), 'The Underground Economy: a Troubling Issue for Policymakers', *Business Review*, Federal Reserve Bank of Philadelphia, September/October, pp. 3-12.

Hubermann, A.M., Miles, M.B. (1994), Data Management and Analysis Methods, in: N.K. Denzin and Y.S. Lincoln (eds.), *Handbook of Qualitative Research*. Sage, Thousand Oaks.

Klatzmann, R. (1982), *Le travail noir*, PUF, 2nd edition, 1990.

Kvale, S. (1996), *Interviews: an introduction to qualitative research interviewing*, Sage, Thousand Oaks e.a.

Lackó, M. (2000), Do Power Consumption Data Tell the Story? Electricity Intensity and Hidden Economy in Postsocialist Countries, in E. Maskin and A. Simonovits, *Planning, Shortage, and Transformation*, MIT Press, Cambridge (Mass.) & London.

Lacroix, G. and Fortin, B. (1992), 'Utility-based Estimation of Labour Supply Functions in the Regular and Irregular Sectors', *The Economic Journal*, vol. 102, November, pp. 1407-1422.

Lemieux, T., Fortin, B., Frechette, P. (1994), 'The Effects of Taxes on Labour Supply in the Underground Economy', *American Economic Review*, vol. 84 (1) March, pp. 231-254.

Neef, R. (1999), 'Formen und soziale Lagen der Schattenwirtschaft in einem Transformationsland: Rumänien' in *Berliner Journal für Soziologie* vol 9 (3) pp. 397-414.

Pahl, R.E., Wallace, C. (1985), 'Household work strategies in economic recession', in Redclift N. and Mingione E. (eds.), 1985, *Beyond employment*, Blackwell, Oxford (ed.), 1985, pp. 189-227.

Portes, A. (1994), 'The Underground Economy and Its Paradoxes' in N. Smelser and R. Swedberg (eds.) *The Handbook of Economic Sociology*, Princeton University Press, Princeton.

Sandmo, A. (1981), 'Income Tax Evasion, Labour Supply and the Equity-Efficiency Tradeoff', *Journal of Public Economics*, vol. 16, pp. 265-288.

Schneider, F and Enste, D.H. (2000), 'Shadow Economies: Size, Causes and Consequences', *Journal of Economic Literature*, vol. 38, March, pp. 77-114.

Stănculescu, M. and Ilie, S. (2001), *Informal Economy in Romania*, UNDP/RIQL, Bucharest.

Tanzi, V. (ed.) (1982), *The Underground Economy in the USA and Abroad*, Lexington Books

Tanzi, V. (1999), 'Uses and Abuses of Estimates of the Underground Economy', *The Economic Journal*, 109, June, pp. F 338-F 347.

Thomas, J.J. (1992), *Informal Economic Activity*, LSE Handbooks in Economics, Harvester Wheatsheaf.

Thomas, J.J. (1999), 'Quantifying the Black Economy: 'Measurement without Theory' yet again?', *The Economic Journal*, 109, June, pp. F 381-F 389.

Ungureanu, C. (1998), 'Non-observed economy in Romania' in Duchêne (ed.), *The informal economy in Romania*, ibid.

Wagner, C. (1993), 'La prise en compte de l'économie au noir: l'exemple de la méthode italienne', *Economie et statistique*, 285-286, pp. 81-87, INSEE.

Willard, J.C. (1989), 'L'économie souterraine dans les comptes nationaux', *Economie et statistique*, 227, novembre, pp. 25-51.

APPENDIX:

Country tables of socio-economic data

TABLE OF ECONOMIC INDICATORS FOR BULGARIA

INDICATOR/YEAR	1989	1990	1992	1996	1999	2000
Real GDP Index (1989 =100)	100	90.9	77.2	71.5	70.6	74.7
Nominal GDP per capita (in USD)	5307.9	2377.3	1007.6	1175.5	1510.7	1467.2
GDP per capita at PPP (US$)	n.a.	4487	4098	4990	5610	n.a.
Agriculture Value Added (share in GVA -%)	10.9	18.3	12.1	15.4	17.3	14.5
Share of private sector in GDP (except agriculture - %)	n.a.	n.a.	19.6	41.2	48.5	42.8
Inflation rate (annual -%)	n.a.	n.a.	91.3	123.1	0.4	10.1
Investments (share in GDP - %)	26.3	21.6	21.7	15.3	20.2	18.6
Share (estimated) of informal economy in total GDP (formal+informal) (%) Nenovsky&Hristov; NSI	n.a.	n.a.	n.a.	n.a.	24.1 23.0	n.a.
Active population (thousand people)	4365	4162	3851	3576	3388	3272
Share of agricultural employment in total employment (%)	18.1	17.9	20.7	23.4	25.8	26.2
Share of people working in services to firms (market services) (%)	19.1	21.0	21.8	43.1	45.4	46.1
Share of people working in public services (and services to households)(%)	15.9	16.8	19.0	18.3	18.4	18.0
Retirement including early retirement as share of total population (%)	25.7	27.2	25.1	29.0	29.6	30.7
Registered unemployment (% of working population + unemployed)	n.a.	n.a.	15.3	12.5	15.7	17.9
Share of unemployed receiving benefits in total unemployed (%)	n.a.	n.a.	34.4	35.1	30.2	n.a.
Average real wages Index (1991 = 100)		116.8	40.4	81.1	86.4	
Average nominal wage in US$ equivalent (Average annual wage divided by annual average exchange rate)	3919	1977	1053	894	1313	1345
Share of social transfers including distribution items like unemployment benefits, social aid, special pensions) in GDP (%)	11.8	12.6	14.5	8.9	11.5	13.2

Sources of data: Bulgarian National Statistical Institute (ed. Statistical Yearbooks for the period 1989-2001), Bulgarian National Bank Reports, WIIW Vienna Institute Statistics for Transition Countries; For the share of informal economy: Study by Nenovsky, N.; K. Hristov (2000) 'Currency Circulation after Currency Board Introduction in Bulgaria (Transaction Demand, Hoarding, Shadow Economy)', Bulgarian National Bank Discussion Papers no. 13.

TABLE OF ECONOMIC INDICATORS FOR HUNGARY

INDICATOR\YEAR	1989	1990	1992	1996	1999
Real GDP Index (1989 = 100)	100	96.5	82.4	86.7	99.2
Nominal GDP per capita (equivalent in US$, using exchange rate)	n.a.	3189	3608	4433	4787
GDP per capita at PPP (US$)	n.a.	n.a	7759	9322	11275
Agriculture Value Added (share in GDP -%)	n.a.	n.a.	6.7	6.1	n.a.
Share of private sector in GDP (except agriculture - %)	29	41 (in 1991)	48	70	80
Inflation rate (annual -%)	17.0	28.9	23.0	23.6	10.0
Investment rate (share in GDP - %)	21.6	20.2	20.4	22.3	21.2
Share (estimated) of informal economy in total GDP (formal+informal) (%) (Sources: Kaufmann-Kaliberda method)	27	28	30.6	29 (in 1995)	21 (in 1998)
Active population (thousand people, mid-year)	5278	5251	4940	4240	4203
Share of agricultural employment in total employment (%)	n.a.	17.5	11.3	8.3	7.1
Share of people working in market services sector in total empl. (%)	n.a.	n.a.	28.2	31	32.1
Share of people working in public services (and services to households)(%)	n.a.	n.a.	25.5	28.1	26.4
Retirement including early retirement as share of total population (%)	n.a.	21.5	24.2	26.5	27.0
Registered unemployement rate (% of active population, mid-year)	0.6	0.7	10.3	11.0	9.7
Share of unemployed receiving benefits in total unemployed (%)	n.a.	69.6	61.5	22.6	24.9
Average Real Wage Index in manufacturing (PPI based) (1989 = 100)	100	95.3	90.8	93.1	112.3
Average nominal gross wage in US$ equivalent (source: Homepage of OECD)	178.9	212.8	282.3	306.9	325.7

Sources of data: CSO (Central Statistic Office, Labour Force Accounting Census); 1992-98: KSH MEF (CSO Labour Force Survey); CSO Yearbooks; Balance of current account: MNB (Hungarian National Bank); For the share of informal economy, different sources (1989-1996: Johnson-Kaufmann-Shleifer 1997, 1998: EBRD Transition Report, 1997, 1998, 1999, 2001 (also for real wages). In M. Lackó: A Risky Sector: The Informal Economy and its Influences in the Post-Socialist Countries Based on the Estimation of the Electric Current Consumption of the Households, Budapest, MTA KTK 2000). Data were compiled by Bori Simonovits.

TABLE OF ECONOMIC INDICATORS FOR ROMANIA

INDICATOR/YEAR	1989	1990	1992	1996	1999	2000
GDP annual growth rate (%)	-5.8	-5.6	-8.8	3.9	-2.3	1.6
Nominal GDP per capita (equivalent in US$, using exchange rate)	1674	1680	861	1563	1514	1636
GDP per capita at PPP (US$)	n.a.	n.a	n.a.	6595	6000	6102
Agriculture Value Added (share in GDP -%)	13.8	21.2	18.6	18.8	12.9	11.4
Share of private sector in GDP (except agriculture - %)	10.6	11.4	18.6	46.6	58.5	60.7
Household (private) consumption (share in GDP - %)	57.9	65	62.2	69.1	72.1	69.9
Inflation rate (annual - %)	1.1	5.1	210.4	38.8	45.8	45.7
Investment rate (share in GDP - %)	22	19.8	19.2	22.9	18	18.4
Share (estimated) of informal economy in total GDP (formal+informal) (%) (Sources: Dobrescu / INS)	n.a.	21.3	31.0	27.1 / 33.7	37.8 / 40.2	37.2 / 38.3
Active population (thousand people, mid-year)	10946	10893	11256	10264	9695	9911
Share of agricultural employment in total employment (%)	27.5	28.2	32.1	34.6	40.6	40.8
Share of people working in market services sector in total empl. (%)	27.0	25.4	27.0	25.9	24.7	n.a.
Share of people working in public services (and services to households)(%)	14.2	9.9	10.1	11.5	11.8	n.a.
Retirement including early retirement as share of total population (%)	14.8	15.9	18.8	24.1	26.5	27.4
Registered unemployment rate (% of active population, mid-year)	0	0	5.6	8.1	11.1	10.8
Share of unemployed receiving benefits in total unemployed (%)	0	0	90.7	70.2	77.1	74.7
Average real net wages growth rates (%)	2.8	4.5	-12.7	9.4	-3.8	2.8
Average nominal net wage in US$ equivalent (Average annual wage divided by annual average exchange rate)	n.a.	1808	785	1250	1192	1203
Share of social transfers (including distribution items like unemployment benefits, social aid, special pensions) in GDP (%)	n.a.	10.4	9.1	9.3	11.9	11.2

Sources of data: Romanian Statistical Yearbook INS (National Statistical Institute); For the share of informal economy, two different sources (see text on Romania: the Dobrescu Model and the official INS estimates); Some of the figures are authors' calculations on the basis of INS data.

TABLE OF ECONOMIC INDICATORS FOR RUSSIA

INDICATOR/YEAR	1991	1992	1995	1998	1999
Real GDP Index (1990 = 100)	95.0	81.2			
Nominal GDP per capita (in new rubles)	6	48	6.365	11.682	12.014
Agriculture Value Added (share in GDP -%)	14.0	7.2	7.2	6.0	6.1
Share of private sector in GDP (except agriculture - %)	8,9	17,2	57	67	68
Inflation rate (annual -%)	50.4	2508.8	131.3	84.5	36.2
Investments (share in GDP - %)	*	*	23.1	20.3	17.5
Share (estimated) of informal economy in total GDP (formal+informal) (%)	18	24	36	35	35
Active population (million people)	74.5	74.9	70.8	66.7	69.7
Participation rate according to ILO standard (%)	100	97.6	90.0	86.2	87.7
Share of agricultural employment in total employment (%)	13.5	14.0	14.7	13.7	13.4
Share of people working in services to firms (market services) (%)	7.6	7.9	10.1	14.5	14.9
Share of people working in industry (%)	n.a.	29.6	25.9	18.7	n.a.
Retirement including early retirement as share of total population (%)		35.2	37.1	38.4	38.3
Registered unemployement (% of working population + unemployed)	*	0.8	3.8	3.6	1.8
Share of unemployed receiving benefits in total unemployed (%)	*	71	89	71	70
Average Real Wage Index in manufacturing (1989 = 100)	63.8	44.5	24.8	25.2	22.9

Sources of data: For share of employment in industry, and average nominal wage: EBRD Reports 1997, 1999, 2001.

Index